Religious Higher Education in the United States
A Source Book

Edited by
Thomas C. Hunt
James C. Carper

Garland Publishing, Inc.
New York and London
1996

Library of Congress Cataloging-in-Publication Data

Religious higher education in the United States : a source book / edited by
    Thomas C. Hunt and James C. Carper.
          p.   cm. — (Garland reference library of social science ; vol. 950.
Source books on education ; vol. 46)
    Includes indexes.
    ISBN 0-8153-1636-4 (alk. paper)
    1. Church colleges—United States—Bibliography. 2. Church and
college—United States—Bibliography.   I. Hunt, Thomas C., 1930–   .
II. Carper, James C.   III. Series: Garland reference library of social
science ; v. 950.   IV. Series: Garland reference library of social science.
Source books on education ; vol. 46.
Z5814.R34R45   1996
[LC383]
016.377'8—dc20   95-36782
                                                                           CIP

Printed on acid-free, 250-year-life paper
Manufactured in the United States of America

Dedication and Acknowledgements

We dedicate this book in thanksgiving to Almighty God who has blessed the editors in countless ways. In particular, we wish to note our wives and children, our parents, our siblings, our teachers, colleagues, friends, and students.

We acknowledge with thanks the assistance of Staci Hunt, Dr. Hunt's daughter, for her work in completing the indexes, and of David Starkey, of the Word Processing Center in the College of Education at Virginia Tech, for his labors in typing and printing the text. Finally, the editors wish to express their gratitude to the Division of Curriculum and Instruction of Virginia Tech for its support of this project.

Thomas C. Hunt
Blacksburg, Virginia
James C. Carper
Columbia, South Carolina

IN MEMORIAM

The editors wish to note with sadness the unexpected death of Mary Grant. Ms. Grant died suddenly on June 21, 1994. She had worked with us on several edited books, and, in 1992, had co-authored *Catholic School Education in the United States* with Thomas Hunt, which was also published by Garland Publishing. To her family, friends, and colleagues, we say: *REQUIESCAT IN PACE!*

CONTENTS

INTRODUCTION

In 1985, following favorable reviews of the editors' *Religious Schooling in America: Historical Insights and Contemporary Concerns*, Garland Publishing contacted the writers regarding the possibility of producing a reference volume on schools with a religious affiliation in the United States. That phone call has led to five reference works, published on the topics of religious schools, religious colleges and universities, religious seminaries, and Catholic schools in 1986 and 1993, 1988, 1989, and 1992 respectively. Charles Kniker joined the editors in assembling the first work; the writers were solely responsible for the second, third, and fourth works; and Mary Grant joined Thomas Hunt in the publication of the book on Catholic schools.

This volume, titled *Religious Higher Education in the United States*, is an extension and revision of the 1988 book entitled *Religious Colleges and Universities in America: A Selected Bibliography*, and, to some extent, of *Religious Seminaries in America: A Selected Bibliography*, published in 1989. It is an extension of the 1988 and 1989 editions because it contains annotated bibliographies of the various denominational colleges, universities, and some seminaries, and of the relationship of government to these institutions from 1987 through 1993. It qualifies as a revision because each of the chapters begins with a historical essay that serves as an overview.

The reader will note that several of the authors included seminaries in their chapters. The editors left this decision to the authors of the chapters, because the place of the seminary in the higher educational offerings of the denominations varied considerably. Thus, there was no "one best way" of dealing with this question throughout the volume.

Putting together this volume was not without its tragedy. Mary A. Grant, with whom Thomas Hunt co-authored the 1992 volume on Catholic schools, died suddenly on June 21, 1994. The editors are grateful to Anna M. Donnelly, who finished the annotations on Catholic colleges which Ms. Grant had begun. We are also appreciative of the help provided by Brother Emmett Corry, of St. John's University, for enlisting Ms. Donnelly's aid in this effort. To Mary Grant, her family and friends, we utter a solemn *"Requiescat in pace!"*

Thomas C. Hunt
Blacksburg, Virginia
James C. Carper
Columbia, South Carolina

CHAPTER 1
Government Aid to and Regulation of Religious Colleges and Universities

Ralph D. Mawdsley

Introduction

Religious colleges and universities have been an integral part of the American higher education scene for over three hundred years. The earliest colleges, such as Harvard and Yale, were private-controlled but considered by many "public," and were started to train persons for the ministry.[1] But in subsequent years all of the pre-revolutionary war colleges, as well as those founded after that war, became increasingly secularized, so that by 1901 only 6.5% of the college students were studying for the ministry, down from 50% in the first half of the eighteenth century.[2] Part of the secularization was reflected in a change in universities from following the Harvard curriculum based on the medieval trivium and quadrivium which required Latin and Greek, courses which were necessary for one entering the ministry. In the mid-eighteenth century, colleges such as Yale, the College of New Jersey (Rutgers), and Kings (Columbia) began broadening the curriculum by offering other courses such as math, history, geography, and English.[3]

With the decline of private colleges founded in the seventeenth and eighteenth centuries as primary teaching sites for the ministry, preparation for the ministry became the responsibility of the various denominations, each of which founded seminaries for that purpose.[4] The oldest college founded by a religious order that has retained its religious ties seems to be Georgetown University, established in 1791 by the Jesuits.[5] Along with seminaries came a proliferation of liberal arts colleges founded by religious denominations, in part reflecting cultural as well as religious distinctions.[6] Many of these religious colleges and universities have continued to the present time, and, indeed, a cursory review of one of the many descriptive catalogs on colleges and universities will reveal that approximately one-third of the higher education institutions in the United States still claim to have some religious affiliation.

The legal history of these religious colleges and universities (hereafter referred to simply as universities) in their relationships with government is very much identified with the latter half of the twentieth century. The early and famous Dartmouth College case in 1819,[7] where the state legislature sought unsuccessfully to alter the board of trustees established by a royal charter, is an interesting historical artifact, but had nothing to do with the religious nature of Dartmouth College. Litigation regarding religious universities and government aid and regulation is the product of the past 25 years and reflects interpretation of the Establishment and Free Exercise Clauses of the First Amendment. Under the aegis of what has become popularly known as the "doctrine of separation of church and state," religious universities have been scrutinized both as to their eligibility for government aid and their exemption from government regulation. The operative judicial interpretations in determining eligibility or exemption have been the *Lemon*[8] test for the Establishment Clause and the *Yoder/Smith*[9] tests for the Free Exercise Clause.

Lemon and Yoder/Smith Tests

Since these tests are the templates for determining eligibility for government aid or exemption from government regulation, an understanding of their requirements is necessary. The *Lemon* test, which was developed in the context of eligibility for government aid, has three components. A court must decide whether: (1) the statute, regulation or government action at issue has a secular purpose; (2) the statute, regulation, or action has the primary effect of advancing or inhibiting religion; and (3) the statute, regulation, or action results in an excessive entanglement between the state and the religious university.[10] Failure of any one of these three components will result in ineligibility for government aid. Although the *Lemon* test was formed in the context of determining eligibility for government aid, the test has been raised in non-aid settings by proponents of separation of church and state to challenge religious practices at secular universities,[11] as well as by authorities at religious universities to challenge government entanglement with religious practices at those universities.[12]

The *Yoder/Smith* tests are the product of two United States Supreme Court decisions 18 years apart. In *Yoder*, the Court established a threefold test to determine whether a government statute, regulation, or action violated the Free Exercise rights of religious claimants: (1) whether the claimant's activity interfered with by the government is motivated by and rooted in a legitimate and sincerely held religious belief[13]; (2) whether the claimant's free exercise of religion has been burdened by the government activity[14]; and (3) whether the government has a compelling interest in its action that justifies the burden on free exercise of religion.[15] Although the compelling interest test frequently did not prevent imposition of government statutes or regulations on religious universities, the test did seem to have the salutary effect of requiring courts to weigh the effect of government action on religious practices.[16] In 1990, the Supreme Court revisited the Free Exercise Clause and the *Yoder* test in the context of a non-education case, *Employment Division* v. *Smith*.[17] This case, which involved the application of Oregon's criminal statutes to Native Americans who used the hallucinatory drug peyote as part of religious services, determined that free exercise of religion is not a defense when the religious claimant is affected by a "neutral, generally applicable law." On its face, *Smith* would seem to have effectively eviscerated the compelling interest test of *Yoder* since most laws that might affect religious organizations are neutral and uniform in application.[18]

On November 19, 1993, however, President Clinton signed the "Religious Freedom Restoration Act of 1993"[19] which had as one of its purposes "to restore the compelling interest test as set forth in ... *Wisconsin* v. *Yoder* ... and to guarantee its application in all cases where free exercise of religion is substantially burdened." The statute provides that:

> Government shall not substantially burden a person's exercise of religion even if the burden results from a rule of general applicability, [except that] ... Government may substantially burden a person's exercise of religion only if it demonstrates that application of the burden to the person -- (1) is in furtherance of a compelling governmental interest; and (2) is the least restrictive means of furthering that compelling governmental interest.[20]

Whether this Act does, in fact, restore the *Yoder* analysis remains to be seen. The act seems to imply that a person's (or university's) religious beliefs can be intruded upon as long as those beliefs are not "substantially burdened." One line of analysis of the Act might suggest that the "substantially burdened" requirement places a higher standard on the religious university than existed prior to *Smith*.[21] A second line of analysis might suggest that the "substantially burdened" test is not significantly different from the "substantial risk" test in an earlier Supreme Court case, *National Labor Relations Board (NLRB)* v. *Catholic Bishop*,[22] where the Court determined that protection under either the Free Exercise or Establishment Clauses requires evidence that infringement of religious beliefs is real and not speculative.[23]

Religious Colleges and Universities and Church Control

The legal standard to be applied to religious universities in terms of either eligibility for government aid or exemption from government regulation varies with the amount of control over the universities by churches (or other comparable religious organizations such as synagogues or temples). The extent of church control varies among various universities. Some are owned and controlled by churches or associations of churches; others that once were so owned and controlled have ceased their relationship with the churches. Even those universities that continue to maintain some form of church control may have diminished the extent of that control.[24] Extensive church control that may have included at one time such measures as membership in the church for all faculty and students, written agreement by faculty and students with the church's doctrinal statement, and required attendance by students and faculty at on-campus chapel services may have become so relaxed that participation has become voluntary rather than compulsory.[25] Religious universities may have also undergone change in response to statutory or judicial pressure. A religious belief subscribed to at one time with sincere devotion may have been eliminated when significant penalties against the institution were threatened.[26] Even in the absence of penalties, universities may have diluted church control or religious elements in order to qualify for a benefit not available to religious or pervasively religious universities.[27]

Even if religious universities are not interested in imposing requirements on employees/students, the institutions may have other reasons for advancing a claim that they are religious or church-controlled. For example, religious universities are generally exempt from state unemployment compensation statutes,[28] and church-controlled universities can be exempt from Social Security[29] and ERISA[30] requirements.

Church control carries with it certain benefits for a higher education institution, including exemption from some legislative requirements. For example, religious universities may be exempt from statutes prohibiting discrimination on the basis of religion.[31] Colleges and universities are finding it more difficult, however, to maintain the same level of contacts with churches or church organizations that once had a significant role in establishing their higher education institutions. At stake may be issues of state approval or licensure or eligibility for government financial assistance. Pervasively religious higher education institutions may be ineligible for government aid under either the federal constitution or the constitution of the state in which the university is located.

The difficulty religious universities are having walking the tightrope between church control and eligibility for government benefits was recently addressed by the Virginia Supreme Court.[32] In that case, Liberty University, a religious university that from 1971 to 1989 had advertised itself as an integral part of Thomas Road Church, an independent Baptist congregation in Lynchburg, Virginia, sought $60,000,000 worth of tax-exempt municipal bonds to refinance indebtedness. Until 1989 the university had required faculty members to be members of the church and to subscribe annually to a doctrinal statement; required students to attend church and chapel six times a week; and punctuated university publications with references to the university's religious mission.[33] Subsequent to the city's decision to issue the bonds, the university began a comprehensive review of its policies in preparation for a court challenge to the issuance of tax-exempt bonds to the university as violative of the

Establishment Clause of the U.S. Constitution and a comparable provision in the Virginia Constitution prohibiting the General Assembly from conferring "any peculiar privileges or advantages on any sect or denomination."[34] Church/chapel attendance and membership requirements for employees were eliminated and many of the university's references to its religious mission were diluted or excised from publications. In addition, some of the courses with a religious focus were no longer required for students, and students could be admitted without necessarily having to claim a "born-again" religious experience.[35] Nonetheless, the Virginia Supreme Court ruled that at the time the tax-exempt bonds had been approved by the city, the university was a pervasively religious institution and therefore was not eligible under either federal or state constitutions for the tax-exempt bonds.

Following this state supreme court decision, a challenge was made to the state council of higher education that, if the university was pervasively religious as the state supreme court had ruled, students attending the university should not be eligible for state tuition grants. After a lengthy investigation by the state council, the university agreed to eliminate the doctrinal statement requirement for faculty (which had been interpreted by the state as restrictive of the faculty's academic freedom) and to eliminate virtually all church/chapel requirements for students and faculty.[36]

The role that church affiliation/control plays in eligibility for government benefits or exemption from government regulation has become a significant question in light of a recent non-higher education case, *E.E.O.C.* v. *Kamehameha Schools/Estate*.[37] In that case, a religious school that required all faculty to be Protestants was held by the Ninth Circuit Court of Appeals to not be entitled to one of the religious exemptions under Title VII because the school was not church-controlled. The effect of this decision could be that non-church-controlled higher education institutions might be discriminating against job applicants or employees if they seek to enforce religious requirements. On its face, *Kamehameha* does not require that an educational institution be church-controlled in order to qualify for a Title VII exemption. A broad reading of *Kamehameha* suggests, however, that a Title VII exemption is not available where there is no church control. This interpretation seems justified at least as to the exemption for religious educational institutions; the court observed that it had found "no case holding the exemption to be applicable where the institution was not wholly or partially owned by a church."[38] The court found support for its position in the statement of a member of Congress that the exemption was "limited to church-affiliated colleges and universities, part of whose mission ... is to propagate the belief of the denomination that is supporting that educational institution."[39]

Religious Colleges and Universities and Government Aid

The First Amendment to the federal constitution provides that "Congress shall make no law respecting an establishment of religion...." Government aid to nonpublic schools has generated considerable litigation in elementary and secondary religious schools. This litigation has prohibited a wide range of direct financial aid to religious schools.[40] Under what came to be known as the child benefit doctrine, the Supreme Court carved out exceptions to the general prohibition of aid to religious schools.[41] Recent permutations of this doctrine have recognized exceptions for parents.[42] While none of these cases are directly applicable to higher educational institutions, they have established the constitutional parameters for measuring government aid in relationship to establishment of religion.

Although courts have generally been quite restrictive as to direct or indirect government aid permitted to religious elementary and secondary schools, they have been much more supportive of aid to religious universities. Except in rare cases where a court has found a university to be pervasively religious,[43] a wide variety of federal and state aid to religious universities has been upheld. In *Tilton* v. *Richardson*,[44] a companion case to *Lemon*, the Supreme Court had occasion to interpret the Higher Education Facilities Act of 1963 which provided federal construction grants for colleges and university facilities, excluding "any facility used or to be used for sectarian instruction or as a place for religious worship, or ... any facility which ... is used or to be used primarily in connection with any part of the program of a school or department of divinity." Under the Act, the United States also retained a twenty-year interest in any facility constructed with Title I funds. Four church-related colleges and universities in Connecticut had received federal construction grants under Title I for a variety of campus buildings, including libraries, a science building, a music, drama, and arts building, and a language lab. In a close 5-4 decision, the Court upheld the grants to these colleges and universities, but struck down the twenty-year provision. Under the second *Lemon* "primary effects" test, the Court declared that "[t]he crucial question is not whether some benefit accrues to a religious institution as a consequence of the legislative program, but whether its principal or primary effect advances religion."[45] Evidence that this "primary effect" was not present was that: no religious services or worship were held in the buildings; no religious symbols or plaques were in or on the buildings; the buildings were used solely for nonreligious purposes; and the institutions subscribed to the 1940 Statement of Academic Freedom and Tenure. Under the third *Lemon* "excessive entanglement" test, the Court found that the institutions did not have religious indoctrination as "substantial purpose or activity"[46] because they admitted non-Catholic students and hired non-Catholic faculty and taught religion courses that were other than the Catholic religion.

In the shadow of *Lemon* the South Carolina Supreme Court had occasion to consider the constitutionality under both the state and federal constitutions of the State Education Assistance Act which made, insured or guaranteed loans to residents attending institutions of higher education.[47] In addition to the

Establishment Clause addressed in *Lemon*, the South Carolina Constitution prohibited "the use of the 'property or credit' of the State, 'directly or indirectly' in aid of any church controlled college or school."[48] In finding the Act constitutional under the state constitution, the court held that the Act did not give loan money to colleges and universities because "the emphasis is on aid to the student rather than to any institution or class of institutions.... This is aid, direct or indirect to higher education, but not to any institution or group of institutions."[49] The Act did not violate the Establishment Clause of the U.S. Constitution because "[i]t simply aids and encourages South Carolina residents in the pursuit of higher education, and leaves all eligible institutions free to compete for their attendance and dollars...."[50]

In 1973, the United States Supreme Court addressed the constitutionality of the South Carolina Educational Facilities Authority Act that assisted higher education institutions to construct, finance and refinance projects.[51] Excluded from the Act was "any facility used or to be used for sectarian instruction or as a place of religious worship nor any facility which is used or to be used primarily in connection with any part of the program of a school or department of divinity of any religious denomination." The Act which authorized tax-exempt revenue bonds to be issued to finance projects at higher education institutions required the college to convey to the funding authority title to the project, which in turn would be reconveyed to the college after payment of the bonds. But even after reconveyance, the project could not be used for sectarian purposes. Baptist College at Charleston submitted an application requesting $1,050,000 to refund short-term financing of capital improvements and $200,000 to complete dining hall facilities. Even though the members of the Board of Trustees were elected by the South Carolina Convention, approval of the Convention was required for certain financial transactions, and the charter of the College could be amended only by the Convention, the College was not pervasively religious because there were no religious qualifications for faculty membership or student admission, and the 60% Baptist representation among the students was the same as the percentage of Baptists in the area where the college was located. The conveyance and reconveyance process did not create an excessive entanglement because the financing authority could not take action against the college as long as rental payments were made.

A fourth case challenged a Maryland statute which provided for state aid in the form of an annual fiscal-year subsidy for private institutions offering associate and baccalaureate degrees.[52] Excluded from the aid were institutions offering seminarian or theological degrees. At the time of the lawsuit, the subsidy amounted to 15% of the state's per-full-time-pupil appropriation for a student in the state college system and approximately 30% of the funds distributed went to church-related institutions. In a lengthy analysis of the distinction between religious elementary/secondary schools and religious colleges, the Court observed that "College students are less susceptible to religious indoctrination; college courses tend to entail an internal discipline that inherently limits the opportunities for sectarian influence; and a high degree of academic freedom tends to prevail at the college level."[53] Factors that the Court identified in finding that four Catholic colleges at issue were not pervasively sectarian were: none of the colleges received funds from, nor reported to, the Catholic Church; Catholic Church representation on the College boards did not influence college decisions; attendance at religious exercises on campus was not required for students; mandatory religion courses were taught within the 1940 Statement of Principles on Academic Freedom of AAUP; before-class prayer in a minuscule number of classes was not pursuant to college policy; and the faculty were hired without having to be Roman Catholic. The Court found no excessive entanglement in the annual funding process because the colleges' secular and sectarian activities were separated and occasional audits would be quick and non-judgmental.

In the year following the Maryland case, the U.S. Supreme Court affirmed a district court decision declaring the Tennessee Student Assistance Act not to have violated the Establishment Clause.[54] The Act made state funds available to students attending "in Tennessee a public college or university, a public vocational or technical institute, or a nonpublic college or university accredited by the Southern Association of Colleges and Schools."[55] The Court quite frankly observed that "some, but not all, of the private schools whose students benefited from this program are operated for religious purposes, with religious requirements for students and faculty and are admittedly permeated with the dogma of the sponsoring organization."[56] The Tuition Grant Program, however, did not have the primary effect of advancing or inhibiting religion under the *Lemon* test because:

(1) Students were not limited to using the funds only for tuition and fees and could not use funds for personal needs such as room and board, bus fare, clothing and health care expenses.[57]

(2) Child benefit doctrine applied in that assistance was available to students attending both public and nonpublic institutions and there was "no proof showing the predominance of benefits to one religious group."[58]

(3) "[T]he emphasis of the aid program is on the student rather than the institution, and the institutions are free to compete for the students who have the money provided by the program."[59]

In a more recent case, the Supreme Court ruled that the First Amendment did not prohibit the State of Washington from extending assistance under a state vocational rehabilitation assistance program to a blind person studying at Inland Empire School of the Bible, a Christian college in Spokane, and who was seeking to become a pastor, missionary, or youth director.[60] In upholding this aid, the Court observed that "[a]ny aid provided under Washington's program that ultimately flows to religious institutions does so only as a result of the genuinely independent and private choices of individuals."[61] Because "the decision to support religious education is made by the individual, not by the State ... [none of the aid flowing to the school results] from a *state* action sponsoring or subsidizing religion."[62] On remand to the Washington Supreme Court, however, the state court found that even though the aid did not violate the U.S. Constitution, it did violate a provision of the Washington Constitution which provided that "[n]o public money ... shall be appropriated for or applied to any religious ... instruction."[63] In interpreting its own state constitution, the Washington Supreme Court ruled that "the State [paying] for a religious course of study at a religious school, with a religious career as his goal ... falls precisely within the clear language of the constitutional prohibition against applying moneys to any religious instruction."[64] In rejecting the student's free exercise of religion claim, the court found that he "is not being asked to violate any tenet of his religious beliefs, nor is he being denied benefits because of conduct mandated by religious belief.'"[65]

A significant recent state aid benefit to religious universities is reimbursement by the state to the higher education institution for work taken by high school students. Two recent Minnesota cases of the same name (*Mammenga I* and *Mammenga II*) challenged the constitutionality of that state's Post-Secondary Enrollment Options Act.[66] Under the Act, high school students could take courses at higher education institutions for either secondary or post-secondary credit. If the courses were taken for high school credit, the student did not have to pay tuition, fees, or the cost of books, and instead the state would reimburse the colleges and universities at a cost that was generally considerably less than the actual instructional charges. Evidence at the trial indicated that reimbursement for all colleges was only about 53% of actual costs.[67] Since, in addition to public higher education institutions, high school students could enroll at "a private, residential, two-year or four-year, liberal arts, degree-granting college or university located in Minnesota," some of the students elected to enroll at church-related institutions. The constitutionality of the act was challenged under the state constitution which provides as follows concerning establishment of religion:

> [N]or shall any money be drawn from the treasury for the benefit of any religious societies or religious or theological seminaries.[68]

> In no case shall any public money or property be appropriated or used for the support of schools wherein the distinctive creeds or tenets of any particular ... religious sect are promulgated or taught.[69]

With the exception of Bethel College which was the subject of the second case (*Mammenga II*), the court in *Mammenga I* found for the following reasons that high school student enrollment in church-related colleges and universities did not violate state constitutional criteria comparable to the *Lemon* secular purpose and primary effects tests:

> (1) neither course structure nor course content is controlled by the church or denomination with which the ... colleges are affiliated;
>
> (2) the ... colleges admit both [high school students and high school graduates] without regard to creed and they select students only if they demonstrate academic excellence and personal maturity through their high school record, activities and personal references;
>
> (3) the ... colleges do not require attendance at religious services, do not enforce adherence to religious dogma, and do not attempt to indoctrinate or proselytize students;
>
> (4) the ... colleges all follow the 1940 Statement of Principles on Academic Freedom of the American Association of University Professors such that 'all courses are taught

according to the academic requirements
which are intrinsic to the subject matter, and
the individual teacher's concept of
professional standards';
(5) [high school] students may not take religion
or theology courses.[70]

In *Mammenga II*, the court determined that Bethel College, a presumptively sectarian school,[71] could receive reimbursement under the Act without violating the state constitution. Once the court decided that benefits to the college were "indirect and incidental as a matter of law,"[72] the court refused to examine whether the college was pervasively sectarian; under Minnesota judicial interpretation of its constitution, "even if a college is pervasively sectarian, state funds may be accorded it, if the benefit to the college is indirect and incidental."[73] The benefit to the college was indirect and incidental because the college had no control over the number of students who selected it, the state's reimbursement amounted to only 42% of the actual costs for tuition, textbooks, materials for fees, and the college separated reimbursement funds from its other funds to ensure state benefits were used only for nonsectarian purposes.[74]

As reflected in the discussion above, what constitutes an establishment of religion has generated considerable litigation, but not nearly the amount of litigation as in religious elementary/secondary schools. The standard for determining establishment of religion has been, for over twenty years, the tripartite test formulated in *Lemon* v. *Kurtzman*, and, despite some deviations by the Supreme Court,[75] the *Lemon* tripartite test has demonstrated a remarkable resiliency. Generally, educational institutions that have pervasive religious characteristics are ineligible for financial aid under the federal constitution. Eligibility for government aid, however, may depend on whether the direct recipient of the aid is considered to be the individual student or the institution. This distinction is reflective of the child benefit doctrine developed by the United States Supreme

Court forty years ago to justify government provision of textbooks and bus transportation to religious schools.

Government Regulation of Religious Colleges and Universities

Although formulated in the context of evaluating financial assistance to religious educational institutions, the *Lemon* test has been expanded to test government regulation of religious institutions. The *Lemon* test has also become an important vehicle to challenge government regulation of religious higher education. Basically, the argument states that such regulation inhibits religious practice or promotes excessive government intrusion into the operation of the religious organization. An intriguing constitutional issue is how protection under the Establishment Clause of the First Amendment interfaces with protection in the same clause providing that "Congress shall make no law ... prohibiting the free exercise [of religion]." Although the two provisions can be viewed as advancing quite different legal theories, reliance on the Establishment Clause has become prominent because of judicial constraints on religious practices protected by the Free Exercise Clause.

The religious practices of colleges and universities may also raise as an issue whether federal or state governments must attempt to accommodate those practices even if government polices might be subverted. At stake may be revocation of a benefit as significant as tax exemption or a requirement that universities conform to local, state, or federal statutes, any of which may present a conflict between belief and practice that is difficult for the religious institution to resolve. Of concern to the government in local ordinances or state or federal statutes may be the necessity to maintain a consistent national policy on a matter of fundamental social importance. From the government's perspective, religious practices opposing that social policy, however well-meaning, may not be possible to accommodate without fragmenting the important social policy at issue.[76] From the religious university's perspective, however, conformity to the social policy, however important that policy may seem to be, represents a declaration that the religious belief at issue is of lesser importance than national social policy. While enforcement of the government's social policy in overriding religious practice does not necessarily mean that the religious belief is wrong, a religious university may have difficulty distinguishing between a religious belief that is not wrong but will be penalized if practiced[77] and a religious belief that will be punished because it is wrong.[78]

NLRB v. Catholic Bishop: Testing the Regulatory Flavor of Government

In *National Labor Relations Board (NLRB)* v. *Catholic Bishop,*[79] the United States Supreme Court determined that the National Labor Relations Act (NLRA) did not apply to lay teachers in Chicago area Catholic elementary and secondary schools for purposes of collective bargaining. The Court avoided the constitutional issues under the Free Exercise and Establishment Clauses by resolving the case on the basis of statutory construction.

In ruling that lay teachers were not subject to collective bargaining under the NLRA, the Court announced a three-step level of analysis for resolving the conflict between statutory language suggesting application to religious institutions and alleged constitutional infringement if the statute were to be applied to those institutions. The first step in the analysis is to determine whether government action presents a "substantial risk" of constitutional infringement.[80] A court need not decide that an infringement has occurred, only that an infringement might occur.[81] If a "substantial risk" of infringement exists, the second step is to determine whether the statute at issue applies to the religious institution.

The second step gives emphasis to a basic principle of the United States Supreme Court that constitutional issues will not be addressed if a case can be resolved on statutory grounds.[82] Statutory construction primarily concerns a review of legislative history to determine whether the legislative body responsible for the statute intended the statute to apply to the kind of religious institution before the court. A court can take two approaches to determining legislative intent. One approach would find no statutory application unless the legislature affirmatively expressed an intent to include the religious institution.[83] The second approach would find statutory application unless the legislature expressly excluded the kind of religious institution before the court.[84] If the court determines that the legislative intent was to exclude the religious institution before the court, the *Catholic Bishop* analysis is at an end and the court will find in favor of the religious institution. If the religious institution cannot be excluded by examining legislative intent, however, the court must move to the third step and address the merits of the constitutional objections under the Religion Clauses.

The constitutional standard applied in the *Catholic Bishop* third step has depended on whether an objection is raised under the Free Exercise or Establishment Clauses. In the past, courts applied the *Yoder* compelling interest test where the objection was grounded in free exercise[85] and the excessive entanglement part of the *Lemon* test[86] where the objection was grounded in establishment of religion.[87] The difficulty with the third step of the *Catholic Bishop* analysis is that the standards for reviewing the merits of a constitutional objection themselves are under attack. The tripartite *Lemon* test has increasingly been attacked as an inappropriate standard for resolving religious issues, especially those that are outside the financial aid matrix in which the *Lemon* test was formulated.[88] Although the Supreme Court has yet to overrule or alter the *Lemon* test, considerable difference of opinion concerning the viability of the current *Lemon* test can be found on the Court.[89]

Free exercise can also be a defense to government regulation under the third part of the *Catholic Bishop* test. Under the *Smith* analysis, a free exercise claim would have been nullified since regulatory statutes generally are "neutral, generally applicable laws."[90] Ostensibly, the Religious Freedom Restoration Act of 1993 will place the free exercise defense back into the first and third steps of the *Catholic Bishop* test. The Act's defense that a person's (or university's) religious beliefs have been "substantially burdened" is similar to the "substantial risk" requirement in the first step. Even assuming the first step of the Act has been met, however, there is no assurance that courts will be any more reluctant to find a compelling interest in applying government regulations than existed under *Yoder* prior to *Smith.*

Government Regulations and Religious Colleges and Universities

Religious universities can be subjected to a wide range of municipal, state, or federal statutes and regulations. Objections to application of these statutes or regulations do not have to involve issues of religious freedom.[91] Discussion of religious universities and government regulation will be limited in this section, however, to those institutions where religion clause issues are raised under either the U.S. or state constitutions.

"Regulatory" can refer to a broad range of statutes, including comprehensive guidelines that could affect management of an institution as well as remedial guidelines that are impacted only when a person files a specific complaint. Application of collective bargaining statutes to religious universities has been cited as an example of the former while nondiscrimination statutes have been cited as examples of the latter. From the standpoint of the religious university, however, both kinds of statutes that call into question the distinctively religious mission of the university can be equally intrusive.

In *Universidad Central de Bayamon* v. *National Labor Relations Board (NLRB)*[92] the First Circuit Board of Appeals, in a close decision, refused to enforce an order of the NLRB directing a Catholic university to bargain collectively with a faculty union. Writing for an evenly divided court sitting *en banc*, Circuit Judge

Breyer found the following factors were adequate to establish Catholic control over the university: the university was part of a larger educational complex that included a seminary and elementary/secondary schools, the latter of which were used by university education for student teaching; the Dominican Order provided gifts of land, scholarships, and administrative salaries; the president of the university was required by the by-laws to be a Dominican priest; a majority of the five-member executive committee of the Board of Trustees was required to be Dominican priests; and the Board of Directors must include the Regional Vicar of the Dominican Order, the Prior of the Convent of Our Lady of the Rosary, and the university president, all of whom were Dominican priests.[93] In finding that *Catholic Bishop* was controlling in prohibiting application of collective bargaining under NLRA to the university, the court identified four reasons to support its conclusion:

1. *Catholic Bishop* did "not distinguish colleges from elementary and secondary schools."[94]

2. The entanglement issue under the third *Catholic Bishop* step of analysis might be implicated because not only did "moral and religious principles" underlie the curriculum and counseling of students, but the University might have to impose sanctions upon faculty that "relate to counseling in the sensitive area of abortion ... [and NLRB] review of such sanctions would place the Board squarely in the position of determining what is 'good faith' Dominican practice in respect to such counseling."[95]

3. The Court in *Catholic Bishop* refused to accept the NLRB's distinction between "completely religious schools" and "merely religiously affiliated schools"; "to promise that courts in the future will control the [NLRB's] efforts to examine religious matters [University's control over priests, seminary, curriculum and religious philosophy] is to tread the path *Catholic Bishop* forecloses."[96]

4. NLRB's reliance on the financial aid cases of *Titlton* v. *Richardson, Hunt* v. *McNair,* and *Roemer* v. *Board of Public*

Works to support government regulation of religious higher education institutions is not appropriate; "in the context of Labor Board jurisdiction, the constitutional concern is one, not of state promotion, but of state interference through regulation."[97]

The power of governmental regulation can have a devastating impact on educational institutions. Nowhere was the impact of this power more evident than in *Bob Jones University* v. *United States*.[98] In *Bob Jones University*, the Supreme Court upheld IRS's enforcement of its regulation revoking tax-exempt status for educational institutions with racially discriminatory policies. Despite the fact that the university's policies prohibiting interracial dating and marriage among students were grounded in religious beliefs and had been practiced by the university since its establishment, the Court upheld imposition of a federal regulation enacted approximately forty-five years after the founding of the university.[99] The Court held that a "fundamental national public policy"[100] could override the sincerely held religious beliefs of the university despite the "substantial impact"[101] denial of tax exemption would have on the operation of a private school. This case highlights the considerable effect of government regulation on religious universities; it does little good to say that revocation of tax exemption will not prevent the university from "observing [its] religious tenets"[102] if an effect of revocation could be closure of the university. The right to hold religious beliefs may not seem so inviolable if the practice of those beliefs will face some regulatory penalty.

The relationship between religious belief and fundamental public policy was more recently raised in *Gay Rights Coalition* v. *Georgetown University*.[103] In this case, student homosexual groups brought suit against the university under a District of Columbia ordinance prohibiting discrimination in the use of or access to facilities and services based wholly or partially on sexual orientation.[104] Despite the university's religious belief opposing homosexuality, the federal appeals court for the District of Columbia determined that providing facilities and services to homosexual students would not require the university to change its beliefs[105] and in addition would meet the District's interest in "the eradication of sexual orientation discrimination."[106] Citing the decision in *Bob Jones University* as support for the principle that "government has a compelling interest in the eradication of other forms of discrimination,"[107] the appeals court concluded that "discrimination based on sexual orientation is a grave evil that damages society as well as its immediate victims."[108]

Probably, the most important interest that a higher education institution has is the right to confer degrees. Any limitation on that right can affect the institution's ability to attract and retain students. The broad authority of states to regulate education within the state extends to higher education. Apart from issues of reasonableness of regulatory authority and criteria which can apply to all nonpublic universities,[109] attempts to regulate religious universities can raise questions of infringement of religious liberty. The legal issues relevant to state regulation of higher education institutions were thoroughly debated and resolved in the important case of *New Jersey State Board of Higher Education* v. *Board of Directors of Shelton College*.[110]

Shelton College was a higher education institution operated by the Bible Presbyterian Church as part of the church's religious mission. Even though only 30 students were enrolled at the college at the time of the lawsuit, religion pervaded the college with every academic subject "taught from a Christian fundamentalist perspective and students [required to] conform their behavior to religiously derived codes of conduct."[111] Actually, the *Shelton College* case had already had a long history of confrontation between the college and the State of New Jersey. As far back as 1967, the college had lost on free speech, equal protection, and state constitution challenges to the state's authority to set criteria for the conferring of baccalaureate degrees.[112] Following the *Catholic Bishop* analysis, the New Jersey Supreme Court in *Shelton College* found that the state statute prohibiting the conferring of baccalaureate degrees without securing a license from the state department of education applied to all higher education institutions with no exemptions for sectarian colleges. Thus, the history of the higher education licensing provisions in New Jersey demonstrated "a legislative intent to regulate the conferring of baccalaureate degrees by religious as well as secular institutions."[113] The court assumed that the state legislature in passing the licensing statute "was aware of the existence of religiously oriented colleges."[114] In addressing the merits of the college's free exercise claims, the court rejected the State Board's argument that the licensing statute posed "no direct interference with religious practice ... because [the College's] religion [did] not require attendance at Shelton College."[115] In language that may have some significance under the Religious Freedom Restoration Act, the *Shelton* court concluded that "the New Jersey licensing statutes, as applied to Shelton College, impose[d] *some burden* on the exercise of religion."[116] The licensing requirements were upheld as the least restrictive means to carry out the state's interests in "maintaining minimum academic standards and preserving the basic integrity of the baccalaureate degree."[117] Whatever excessive entanglement arguments might have been viable in *Shelton College* were dismissed by the court as speculative since the college had declined to participate in the licensing process.

Shelton College stands for the important principles that states have the authority to regulate religious colleges and universities and that the Religion Clauses will not exempt higher education institutions from regulation unless there is evidence of legislative intent to exempt the institutions or unless a substantial burden to the institution's religious mission can be proved. Religious universities have claimed exemptions on both grounds.

Some statutes contain provisions exempting religious universities from some or all of the statutory requirements. One such prominent example is Title VII, the federal workhorse prohibiting discrimination on the basis of race, color, religion, sex or national origin.[118] Title VII has several exemptions that specifically apply to religious organizations:

(1) The act exempts hiring, discharge or classification based on religion ... where "religion ... is a bona fide occupational qualification (BFOQ) reasonably necessary to the operations of that particular business."[119]

(2) The act exempts employment of persons of a particular religion if the institution is "in whole or in substantial part, owned, supported, controlled or managed by a particular religious corporation, association, or society, or if the curriculum of such school, college, university, or other educational institution or institutions of learning is directed toward the propagation of a particular religion."[120]

(3) The act does not apply to "a religious corporation, association, educational institution, or society with respect to the employment of individuals of a particular religion to perform work connected with the carrying on by such corporation, association, educational institution, or society or its activities."[121]

Because the statutory exemptions are so clear, religious universities have generally been successful in litigating restrictive employment practices. In *EEOC* v. *Mississippi College*,[122] a white Presbyterian female part-time instructor who had not been hired for a full-time teaching position in the psychology department, a position subsequently filled by a white Baptist male, was entitled to an evidentiary hearing for the college to present evidence regarding its preference for hiring Baptists. Once the college, which was controlled by the Mississippi Convention, presented convincing evidence of its preference for hiring Baptists, however, EEOC could inquire no further to determine whether the religious discrimination was a pretext for some other kind of discrimination. In *EEOC* v. *Southwestern Baptist Theological Seminary*,[123] an EEOC request for record-keeping information did not have to be honored as to all employees "at the Seminary [that] fit the definition of 'ministers'": all faculty, "[t]he President and Executive Vice President of the Seminary, the Chaplain, the deans of men and women, the academic deans, and those other personnel who equate to or supervise faculty."[124] Nevertheless, the request had to be honored as to the several hundred full- and part-time support personnel and "those administrators whose functions relate exclusively to the Seminary's finance, maintenance, and other non-academic departments."[125]

Mississippi College and *Southwestern Seminary* are unusual in reported case law in that both dealt with religious employment restrictions for large numbers of employees. A more typical pattern among less pervasively sectarian higher education institutions is a more limited religious restriction. In *Prime* v. *Loyola University*,[126] the Philosophy Department's decision to maintain "an adequate Jesuit presence in the Department"[127] of seven Jesuits out of a total 31 faculty was found to be "reasonably necessary to the normal operation of the enterprise."[128] In *Prime*, a Jewish part-time instructor at the university had applied unsuccessfully for one of three full-time positions in the Philosophy Department that the department had determined would be filled by Jesuits in order to maintain the seven-faculty-member "Jesuit presence." In *Maguire* v. *Marquette University*,[129] an unsuccessful female applicant for an associate professor position in the university's theology department alleged sex discrimination because of her position on abortion. Relying on the "Jesuits' influence and control ... in the school's theology department," the court categorically ruled that "definitions of what it is to be a Catholic [is a] question ... the First Amendment leaves to theology departments and church officials, not to federal judges."[130] The court was careful to point out that "[t]here is probably no teaching position at Marquette University which is more closely tied to the University's religious character than that of theology professor. Plaintiff has not applied for a position in one of the more secular departments, such as the plaintiff in *E.E.O.C.* v. *Mississippi College*...."[131] Thus, *Mississippi College*, which actually dealt with a college-wide preference for Baptist faculty, was interpreted by the *Maguire* court to apply to a department rather than the entire college.

More problematic in terms of exemptions for religious universities are statutes that contain no exemption language. The Age Discrimination in Employment Act (ADEA)[132] prohibits discrimination on the basis of age (40 and older). Unlike Title VII, ADEA contains no exemptions for religious organizations and the legislative history is silent regarding the application of the statute to religious organizations.[133] In *Soriano* v. *Xavier University*,[134] the university attempted to claim that ADEA did not apply to it in relation to a claim filed by a discharged employee. In following the *Catholic Bishop* analysis, the court observed that in the absence of a finding of a "substantial risk" to the free exercise and establishment rights of the university, "courts have not rendered large groups of employers immune from liability, as such exemption would substantially frustrate the intent and purpose of the federal laws."[135] The court found "the relatively narrow focus of the ADEA" did "not entangle nor endanger the religion clauses of the first amendment."[136] Further, the court found unwarranted and speculative the university's claims that "constitutional implications may arise in a future case."[137] The *Soriano* court was influenced in its conclusion by an earlier unreported case, *Ritter* v. *Mount St. Mary's College*,[138] where the Fourth Circuit Court of Appeals had held that application of ADEA did not present a significant risk of infringement upon the First Amendment rights of the college.

In addition to the regulatory statutes discussed above, many more are applicable to religious higher education institutions, not the least of which are the Rehabilitation Act of 1973[139] and the Equal Pay Act.[140] Likewise, the new Americans with Disabilities Act (ADA) applies to both religious and secular universities; however, since ADA seems to have made no substantive changes in the Rehabilitation Act of 1973, as amended, religious higher education institutions which participate in Title IV (and other Department of Education) aid programs have already been required to comply with regulations pertaining to disabilities for both students and employees.[141] Most regulatory statutes have generated no litigation challenging application to religious universities on the basis of an infringement of the religion clauses.[142] Even if such objections were to be made, the outcome can probably be fairly easily predicted from the first and third steps of *Catholic Bishop*: the alleged infringement will be dismissed as speculative; or the infringement will be justified as furthering a substantial government interest.

Conclusion

Religious colleges and universities are in a time of difficult transition. Many have departed from the religious fervor that brought them into being and have minimized their religious identity. As much as these institutions would like to have minimal church control, however, most would also desire minimal government regulation. Reduction in church control has had the salutary effect of permitting religious higher education institutions to participate in state and federal aid programs, but such reduction has had the less desirable effect of decreasing the likelihood that government efforts at regulating religious institutions will negatively affect religious tenets. Short-term financial survival may drive religious colleges and universities to dilute religious control in order to eliminate the risk of being labeled as "pervasively sectarian," but the long-term cost may be loss of religious distinctiveness and protection under state or federal religion clauses.

Endnotes

1. John S. Brubacher and Willis Rudy, *Higher Education in Transition*, New York: Harper and Row, 1976, p. 7.
2. *Id.* at 8.
3. *Id.* at 12.
4. *See generally*, Thomas C. Hunt and James C. Carper (eds.), *Religious Seminaries in America* (Garland 1989).

5.   Zygano, "Sectarian Universities, Federal Funding, and the Question of Academic Freedom," 85 *Religious Freedom* 136, 137 (1990).

6.   *E.g.*, compare Bergendoff, *Augustana: A Profession of Faith* (Augustana College Library, 1969) (Augustana College in Rock Island, Illinois founded by Swedish Lutheran immigrants) with Chrislock, *From Fjord to Freeway* (Augsburg Library, 1969) (Augsburg College founded by Norwegian Lutheran immigrants) and Hansen, *We Laid the Foundation Here: The Early History of Grand View College* (Grand View College, 1972) (Grand View College founded by Danish Lutheran immigrants).

7.   *Trustees of Dartmouth* v. *Woodward*, 17 U.S. 518 (1819).

8.   *Lemon* v. *Kurtzman*, 403 U.S. 602 (1971).

9.   *Wisconsin* v. *Yoder*, 406 U.S. 205 (1972); *Employment Division* v. *Smith*, 494 U.S. 872 (1990).

10.   *Lemon*, 403 U.S. at 612-13.

11.   *E.g.*, see *Widmar* v. *Vincent*, 454 U.S. 263 (1981) (meetings of students at University of Missouri-Kansas City for religious purposes upheld over *Lemon* test challenge because University had created a public forum under First Amendment free speech clause).

12.   *E.g.*, see *Maguire* v. *Marquette University*, 627 F.Supp. 1499, 1503 (E.D.Wis. 1986) (court could not intrude into hiring practices of theology department of Jesuit university as to whether a female applicant's views on abortion were consistent with the university because "such an inquiry would require the Court to immerse itself not only into the procedures and hiring practices of the theology department of a Catholic University but, further, into definitions of what it is to be a Catholic").

13.   *Yoder*, 406 U.S. at 215-16.

14.   *Id.* at 217-19.

15.   *Id.* at 219-34.

16.   See *Bob Jones University* v. *United States*, 103 S.Ct. 2017 (1983) (tax revocation upheld for religious university even though university's rules opposing interracial dating and marriage were based on long-held religious beliefs because

government had compelling interest in eradicating discrimination); *New Jersey State Bd. of Higher Education* v. *Board of Directors of Shelton College*, 448 A.2d 988 (N.J. 1982) (state statutes prohibiting any college in state from conferring baccalaureate degree without securing license from State Board of Education were enforceable against religious college whose religious doctrine opposed state licensure because state had a compelling interest in uniform application of higher education laws).

17.   494 U.S. 872 (1990).

18.   Situations where government statutes or regulations are directed at a particular religious group would still permit that group to invoke free exercise protection. See *Church of the Lukumi Babalu Aye, Inc.* v. *City of Hialeah*, 114 S.St. 2217 (1993) (city ordinances directed at prohibiting Santeria religion practice of animal sacrifice held unanimously by Supreme Court to violate Free Exercise Clause).

19.   103 P.L. 141 (1993).

20.   *Id.* at §3 (a) and (b). The "least restrictive means" requirement of the Act derives from *Thomas* v. *Review Board of Indiana*, 450 U.S. 707 (1981). In *Thomas*, the United States Supreme Court, in upholding the payment of unemployment compensation benefits to a Jehovah's Witness who had been discharged for refusing to work on military equipment because of religious belief, ruled that "[t]he state may justify an inroad on religious liberty by showing that it is the least restrictive means of achieving some compelling interest." *Id.* at 718.

21.   Although the Supreme Court in *Yoder* expressed concern about "a very real threat of undermining the Amish community and religious practice as they exist today ... [representing] almost 300 years of consistent practice with strong evidence of a sustained faith pervading and regulating respondents' entire mode of life," [*Yoder*, 406 U.S. at 218, 219] there is no indication that courts subsequent to *Yoder* gave serious consideration to the substantiality of the burden; rather, they assumed a burden existed and focused on the state's

compelling interests and their effect on religious beliefs. By providing that religious beliefs must be "substantially burdened" before a religious party is entitled to a defense under the Act, interpretation of the Act may have two unanticipated effects: (1) a religious party may have an additional burden of proof to produce evidence of "substantiality," a burden which seemed to be important under the *Yoder* test prior to the Act only as related to the government's compelling interests; and (2) the government may be entitled to a directed verdict and may not have to produce evidence of compelling interest at all where "substantiality" has not been demonstrated to the satisfaction of a trial court. See *Bob Jones University*, 103 S.Ct. at 2035 where the relationship between burden to religion and governmental compelling interests were stated in a confusing manner; on one hand, the Court stated that "[d]enial of tax benefits will inevitably have a *substantial impact* on the operate of private religious schools ...," but then shortly thereafter stated "that governmental interest substantially outweighs *whatever burden* denial of tax benefits places on [the University's] exercise of religious rights" (emphasis added). *Bob Jones University* suggests that, while a court under the *Yoder* test was interested in examining the burden to religion in terms of a compelling interest, it was not necessarily concerned about examining the "substantiality" of the burden in isolation.

22. 440 U.S. 490, 506 (1979). In *Catholic Bishop*, the Supreme Court decided that the NLRB did not have jurisdiction under the National Labor Relations Act over teachers in religious schools.

23. See *N.L.R.B.* v. *St. Louis Christian Home*, 663 F.2d 60, 65 (8th Cir. 1981) (in response to allegation by *Home* that it might have to disclose source and destination of contributions from an affiliated Christian Church if collective bargaining required for its employees, the court observed that "[t]he Home has not demonstrated that such impairment will likely occur."); *Volunteers of America-Minnesota-Bar None Boys Ranch* v. *N.L.R.B.*, 752 F.2d 345, 349 (8th Cir. 1985) (*Ranch*'s claim that NLRB might

intervene if staff were to be disciplined for not carrying out duties related to *Ranch*'s religious tenets held to be insufficient to deprive NLRB of jurisdiction over maintenance, laundry, housekeeping, and child care workers).

24.   *E.g.*, see "Georgia Baptists Reject Fundamentalist Plan to Control Mercer University," *Chronicle of Higher Education*, Nov. 18, 1987, at A1; "Trustees Limit Baptist Control Over University," *New York Times*, Oct. 21, 1990, at 47; "Baptists Board OKs New Governing Plan for Baylor University," *Houston Post*, Sept. 11, 1991, at A1; "Fundamentalists Lose Bid to Control Baylor," *Washington Post*, Nov. 12, 1991, at A3.

25.   See "Falwell's College Alters Mission to Keep It Alive," *New York Times*, Aug. 19, 1992, at B7.

26.   See *Bob Jones University* (although Bob Jones University, which had its tax-exempt status revoked because of racially discriminatory rules of conduct, has not changed its rules as a result of the revocation, the companion institution in the litigation, the Goldsboro Christian Schools, did abolish its discriminatory policy and had its tax-exempt status restored).

27.   See Mawdsley, "Access to Tax Exempt Bonds by Higher Education Institutions," 65 *Ed. Law Rep.* 669 (1992).

28.   *E.g.*, Ohio Rev. code §4140.01 (B) (h) (i) (Page's 1991) (exempt from unemployment compensation are employees "in the employ of a church or convention or association of churches, or in an organization which is operated primarily for religious purposes and which is operated, supervised, controlled, or principally supported by a church or convention of churches." In *St. Martin Evangelical Lutheran Church* v. *South Dakota*, 451 U.S. 772 (1981) the Supreme Court determined that a state unemployment compensation statute did not apply to religious elementary/secondary schools because Congress had never evidenced an intent to include such schools. See *Czigler* v. *Bureau of Employment Services*, 501 N.E.2d 56 (Ohio Ct. App. 1985) (teacher of Hebrew and Jewish religious subjects at Hillel Academy denied unemployment compensation benefits because following elements made school "pervasively sectarian" even

though not controlled by a specific Jewish congregation: reception of funds from Jewish community fund; recognition of traditional holidays and Jewish holy days; student body exclusively Jewish; included among board of directors were rabbis from each Jewish congregation serving in *ex officio* capacity). See also *Murray* v. *Kobayashi*, 431 P.2d 940 (Hawaii 1967) (Kamehameha Schools determined by Hawaii Supreme Court to be exempt from unemployment compensation as a result of connection and affiliation with Bishop Memorial Church, even though the Church was actually controlled by the Schools).

     29.   42 U.S.C. §410 (a) (8) (B) ("Service performed in the employ of a church or qualified church-controlled organization," provided an exemption has been filed by the organization with IRS, is exempt from coverage under Social Security).

     30.   29 U.S.C. §§ 1002 (A) (33); 1321 (b) (3); 26 U.S.C. § 414 (e) (3) (B) (church benefit plans exempted from reporting and disclosure requirements of Employment Retirement Income Security Act for "a church or ... a convention or association of churches [and] an employee of an organization ... which is controlled by or associated with a church or a convention or association of churches." Under § 414 (e) a church or convention or association of churches is one "which is exempt from tax under section 501," which would distinguish organizations claiming tax exemption only as educational institutions).

     31.   See *E.E.O.C.* v. *Mississippi College*, 626 F.2d 477 (5th Cir. 1980) (college controlled by Mississippi Baptist Convention could have hiring preference for Baptists over other religions without violating Title VII).

     32.   *Industrial Development Authority of the City of Lynchburg, Va.* v. *All Taxpayers, Property Owners and Citizens of the City of Lynchburg, Va. and Others*, 400 S.E.2d 516 (Va. 1991) (unpublished opinion).

     33.   *Id*. at 7-13.

     34.   Virginia Constitution, Art. I, § 16.

35. See Mawdsley, "Access to Tax Exempt Bonds by Religious Higher Education Institutions," 65 *Ed. Law Rep.* 289, 290 (1991). Cf. "Falwell Tells Employees to Join His Church or Lose Job," *Atlanta Journal Constitution*, March 11, 1989, at A4 with "Falwell's College Alters Mission to Keep Alive," *New York Times*, Aug. 19, 1992, at B7.

36. *Lynchburg Daily Advance*, June 2, 1993, p. 1.

37. 780 F.Supp. 1317, rev'd 990 F.2d 458 (9th Cir. 1993).

38. 990 F.2d at 461, n. 1.

39. *Id.* at 464, quoting from Representative Purcell, 110 Cong. Rec. 2585-86 (Feb. 8, 1964).

40. *E.g.*, see *Committee for Public Educ.* v. *Nyquist*, 43 U.S. 756 (1973) (Court voided New York statute providing limited reimbursement to private school parents in low-income brackets and state tax-relief to middle-income parents); *Meek* v. *Pittenger*, 421 U.S. 349 (1975) (Court struck down Pennsylvania statute authorizing public educators to provide students at nonpublic schools with diagnostic, counseling, psychological, speech, and hearing therapy services); *Grand Rapids School District* v. *Ball*, 105 S.Ct. 3216 (1985) (Court struck down shared time and community education programs that exposed publicly employed teachers to potential influence of the sectarian environment of church-sponsored schools); *Aguilar* v. *Felton*, 105 S.Ct. 3232 (1985) (Court struck down New York's use of Title I funds for the benefit of minorities by paying salaries of public school teachers, psychologists, and specialists who visited parochial schools to teach and serve educationally deprived children from low-income families).

41. See *Board of Education* v. *Allen*, 392 U.S. 236 (1968) (state statute authorizing loan of textbooks to religious school upheld as providing direct benefit to children and not school); *Everson* v. *Board of Educ.*, 330 U.S.1 (1947) (upheld state program reimbursing student bus fares to parents of children attending public or nonpublic schools).

42. See *Mueller* v. *Allen*, 463 U.S. 388 (1983) (Minnesota statute permitting parents to deduct education-related expenses

for both public and private schools upheld as providing direct benefits and not to school, even though over 90% of nonpublic students were in religious schools); *Zobrest* v. *Catalina Foothills School Dist.*, 113 S.Ct. 2462 (1993) (provision of sign-language interpreter in parochial school upheld under IDEA as providing direct benefit to parents and child and not school).

43. See *supra* note 31 where Liberty University was denied tax-exempt bonds as a pervasively religious university.

44. 403 U.S. 672 (1971).

45. *Id.* at 679.

46. *Id.* at 687.

47. *Durham* v. *McLeod*, 192 S.E.2d 202 (S.C. 1972).

48. *Id.* at 203.

49. *Id.*

50. *Id.* at 204.

51. *Hunt* v. *McNair*, 413 U.S. 734 (1973).

52. *Roemer* v. *Board of Pub. Works of Md.*, 426 U.S. 736 (1976).

53. *Id.* at 750.

54. *Americans United for Separation of Church and State* v. *Blanton*, 434 U.S. 803 (1977), affirming 443 F.Supp. 97 (M.D.Tenn. 1977).

55. *Blanton*, 433 F.Supp. at 99.

56. *Id.* at 100.

57. *Id.* at 100, 101.

58. *Id.* at 103.

59. *Id.* at 104.

60. *Witters* v. *Washington Department of Services for the Blind*, 106 S.Ct. 748 (1986).

61. *Id.* at 752.

62. *Id.* at 752-53 (emphasis in original).

63. RCWA Const. Art. I, §11.

64. *Id.* at 1121.

65. *Id.* at 1123, quoting from *Thomas*, 450 U.S. at 718.

66. *Minnesota Federation of Teachers* v. *Mammenga* (Mammenga I), 485 N.W.2d 305 (Minn. Ct. App. 1992); *Minnesota*

Federation of Teachers v. *Mammenga* (Mammenga II), 500 N.W.2d
136 (Minn. Ct. App. 1993).
   67.   *Mammenga* I, 485 N.W.2d at 307.
   68.   Minn. Const. art I, § 16.
   69.   Minn. Const. art. 13, § 2.
   70.   *Mammenga* I, 485 N.W.2d at 307.
   71.   Bethel College permitted the presumption that it was
presumptively sectarian for purposes of summary judgment
because the college had permitted discovery regarding its use of
state funds received under the Act, but would not comply with
discovery requests regarding its sectarian nature. *Mammenga* II,
500 N.W.2d at 138.
   72.   *Id.*
   73.   *Id.* at 139.
   74.   *Id.*
   75.   See *Lee* v. *Weisman*, 112 S.Ct. 2649 (1992) (in striking
down graduation prayers, the Court relied on psychological
coercion test rather than *Lemon*); *Marsh* v. *Chambers*, 463 U.S. 783
(1983) (in upholding legislative practice of prayer before each
session, Court relied on history of practice that antedated the
Constitution and ignored the *Lemon* test).
   76.   *E.g.*, see *United States* v. *Lee*, 455 U.S. 252 (1982)
(Amish employer's free exercise opposition to payment of Social
Security tax for work done by Amish employees on the ground
that the Amish religion prohibited acceptance of government
social payments offset by government interest in soundness of
social security system); *Hernandez* v. *Commissioner*, 490 U.S. 680
(1989) (disallowance of contribution as charitable deduction for
auditing and training services to Church of Scientology not
violative of free exercise because even substantial burden to
religious beliefs justified by broad public interest in maintaining
a sound tax system).
   77.   See *Bob Jones University*, 103 S.Ct. at 2035 (despite
upholding revocation of the University's tax-exempt status
because of its racially discriminatory policies, the Court
nonetheless observed that such "[d]enial of tax benefits ... will

not prevent [the University] from observing [its] religious tenets").

78.   This distinction between belief and practice is referred to as the belief/action dichotomy which owes its origin to *United States* v. *Reynolds*, 98 U.S. 145 (1879) where the criminalizing of the practice of polygamy was upheld against a free exercise claim that the practice of polygamy was necessary for religious salvation according to a particular religious belief system. See also *Employment Division* v. *Smith* where the Court upheld application of the state's criminal statutes prohibiting the use of peyote to Native Americans who used the drug under controlled conditions in religious ceremonies.

79.   440 U.S. 490 (1979).

80.   *Id*. at 506.

81.   A "significant risk" of constitutional infringement requires a likelihood of harm, not merely speculation about the possibility of harm. See *supra* note 22 and cases cited.

82.   *Catholic Bishop*, 440 U.S. at 500 ("An Act of Congress ought not to be construed to violate the Constitution if any other possible construction remains," citing *Murray* v. *the Charming Betsy*, 2 Cranch 118 (1804). But see *Zobrest*, 113 S.Ct. at 2469-70 (four dissenters, in this decision where the majority had held that permitting publicly paid deaf interpreter in parochial school did not violate establishment clause, argued that the case should have been remanded to a lower court for consideration of statutory and regulatory issues: "[i]f there is one doctrine more deeply rooted than any other in the process of constitutional adjudication, it is that we ought to pass on questions of constitutionality ... unless such adjudication is unavoidable").

83.   See *Cochran* v. *St. Louis Preparatory Seminary*, 717 F.Supp. 1413 (E.D.Mo. 1989) (Age Discrimination in Employment Act [ADEA] did not apply to Seminary where there was no language statute or in legislative history suggesting that Congress intended to include church-operated schools under the ADEA). See also *St. Martin Evangelical Church* v. *South Dakota*, 451 U.S. 772 (1981) where the Supreme Court decided that South

Dakota could not impose unemployment compensation on church-controlled schools because Congress had not expressed an intent to include them.

84. See *Soriano* v. *Xavier University*, 687 F.Supp. 1188 (S.D.Ohio 1988) (in refusing to exclude the University operated by the Society of Jesus from ADEA, the court observed that the "ADEA, on its face as well as in its legislative history, gives no indication that religious institutions are exempt from its provisions"). See also *Lukaszewski* v. *Nazareth Hospital*, 764 F.Supp.57, 61 (E.D.Pa. 1991) (in finding that the ADEA applied to the hospital, the court declared "[t]he fact that Congress subjected religious organizations to most of Title VII strongly suggests that Congress also intended to extend ADEA coverage to the institution. The statutory provisions defining the scope of coverage are virtually identical in the two statutes...").

85. See *Catholic High School Ass'n of Archdiocese of New York* v. *Culvert*, 753 F.2d 1161 (2d Cir. 1985) (under *Yoder* analysis, state had compelling interest in applying labor laws to Catholic high school lay teachers because "[s]tate labor laws are essential to the preservation of industrial peace and a sound economic order"); *E.E.O.C.* v. *Southwestern Baptist Theological Seminary*, 651 F.2d 277, 285 (5th Cir. 1981) (providing data to EEOC for non-ministers not so great a burden so as to violate free exercise under *Yoder* test); *E.E.O.C.* v. *Pacific Press Publishing Ass'n*, 676 F.2d 1272 (9th Cir. 1982) (religiously affiliated defendant not exempted under Title VII from sex discrimination claim being filed by discharged female employee because government has compelling interest in "assuring equal employment opportunities"); *E.E.O.C.* v. *Mississippi College*, 626 F.2d at 488 (EEOC's authority to inquire under Title VII into nonhiring of non-Baptist faculty member upheld for religiously-controlled college because the government's "compelling interest in eradicating discrimination is sufficient to justify the minimal burden upon the College's free exercise of religious beliefs...").

86. See *supra* note 9 and accompanying text.

87.   See *Lukaszewski*, 764 F.Supp. at 60 (less risk of excessive entanglement where ADEA applied to discharge of custodial employee at religiously affiliated hospital than where NLRA applied to teachers at religiously-controlled Catholic schools in *Catholic Bishop* because "[r]eligious doctrine is a much less important factor in most hospital decisions than it was in religious school decisions to hire and fire teachers"); *DeMarco* v. *Holy Cross High School*, 4 F.3d 166 (2d Cir. 1993), reversing 797 F.Supp. 1142 (E.D.N.Y. 1992) (application of ADEA to former lay teacher who had religious duties, including leading his students in prayer and taking them to Mass, did not pose serious risk of violating nonentanglement part of *Lemon* and therefore, ADEA applied to teacher's age-discrimination claims against school); *Scharon* v. *St. Luke's Episcopal Presbyterian Hospitals*, 929 F.2d 360, 363 (8th Cir. 1991) (discharge of hospital chaplain not subject to ADEA and Title VII scrutiny because "to review such decisions would require the courts to determine the meaning of religious doctrine and canonical law and to impose a secular court's view of whether in the context of the particular case religious doctrine and canonical law support the decision the church authorities have made").

88.   See, for example, Esbeck, "The *Lemon* Test: Should It Be Retained, Reformulated, or Rejected?" 4 *Notre Dame J.L. Ethics and Pub. Policy* 513 (1990); Redlich, "Separation of Church and State: The Burger Court's Torturous Journey," 60 *Notre Dame L.Rev.* 1094 (1985).

89.   For an analysis of the views of the Justices on the Court prior to *Lee* v. *Weisman*, see Mawdsley and Russo, "High School Prayers at Graduation: Will the Supreme Court Pronounce the Benediction?" 69 *Ed. Law Rep.* 189, 195-202 (1991).

90.   *Smith*, 110 S.Ct. at 1601.

91.   *E.g.*, see *Corporation of Mercer University* v. *Smith*, 371 S.E.2d 858 (Ga. 1988) (merger of two higher education institutions, both affiliated with the Georgia Baptist Convention, raised issues of application of Georgia statutes concerning standard of care for trustees, but no Religion Clause issues were

raised); *A.H. Belo Corporation* v. *Southern Methodist University*, 734 S.W.2d 720 (Tex. Ct. App. 1987) (determination as to whether Texas Open Records Act applied to private universities, most of which were church-affiliated, raised question of statutory construction but no Religion Clause issues); *Johnson* v. *Lincoln Christian College*, 501 N.E.2d 1380 (Ill. ASpp. Ct. 1986) (application of Mental Health and Developmental Disabilities Confidentiality Act to religious college after college counselor's divulgence of student's homosexuality resulting in college's refusal to confer degree on student raised statutory issue but no Religion Clause issues).

92.   793 F.2d 383 (1st Cir. 1985).

93.   *Id*. at 399-400.

94.   *Id*. at 401, citing to *Catholic Bishop*, 440 U.S. at 506-07.

95.   *Id*. at 401, 402.

96.   *Id*. at 402.

97.   *Id*. at 403.

98.   103 S.Ct. 2017 (1983).

99.   *Id*. at 2022 (the university was founded in 1927 and the racially nondiscriminatory IRS Revenue Ruling was adopted in 1971). *Id*. notes 3 and 4.

100.   *Id*. at 2029.

101.   *Id*. at 2035.

102.   *Id*.

103.   536 A.2d 1 (D.C. 1987).

104.   For wording of Ordinance, see 536 A.2d at 4 n.1.

105.   *Id*. at 25.

106.   *Id*. at 33.

107.   *Id*. at 38.

108.   *Id*.

109.   For a discussion of the authority of states to regulate nonsectarian nonpublic education institutions, compare *Nova University* v. *Educational Institution Licensure Commission*, 483 A.2d 1172 (D.C. 1984) (denial of license for nonresident university to offer a doctoral program in the District of Columbia was upheld on the basis of the reasonableness of the criteria pertaining to

library resources and number of full-time faculty) with *Nova University* v. *Board of Governors*, 287 S.E.2d 872 (N.C. 1982) (North Carolina Supreme Court rejected by the Board of Governors of University of North Carolina that it could establish minimum criteria for out-of-state private universities).

110.   448 A.2d 988 (N.J. 1982).

111.   *Id*. at 990.

112.   *Shelton College* v. *State Bd. of Educ.*, 226 612 (N.J. 1967).

113.   *Shelton*, 448 A.2d at 992.

114.   *Id*. at 993.

115.   *Id*. at 994.

116.   *Id*. (emphasis added).

117.   *Id*. at 996.

118.   42 U.S.C. § 2000e-2(a).

119.   42 U.S.C. § 2000e-2(e) (1).

120.   42 U.S.C. § 2000e-2(e) (1).

121.   42 U.S.C. § 2000e-1.

122.   626 F.2d 477 (5th Cir. 1980).

123.   651 F.2d 277 (5th Cir. 1981), reversing in part 485 F.Supp. 255 (N.D.Tex. 1981).

124.   651 F.2d at 284-85.

125.   *Id*. at 285.

126.   803 F.2d 351 (7th Cir. 1986).

127.   *Id*. at 352.

128.   *Id*. at 354.

129.   627 F.Supp. 1499 (E.D.Wis. 1986).

130.   *Id*. at 1503.

131.   *Id*. at 1504.

132.   29 U.S.C. § 623.

133.   See H.R. Rep. No. 805, 90th Cong., 1st Sess., reprinted in (1967) *U.S. Code Cong. & Admin. News*, pp. 2213, *et seq.*; *S. Rep.* No. 723, 90th Cong., 1st Sess. (1967); 113 *Cong. Rec.* 35,228-35,229 (1967); 113 *Cong. Rec.* 31,248-31,257 (1967).

134.   687 F. Supp. 1188 (S.D.Ohio 1988).

135.   *Id*.

136.   *Id*. at 1189.

137. *Id.*

138. 814 F.2d 986 (4th Cir. 1984).

139. See *Barnes* v. *Converse College*, 436 F.Supp. 635 (D.S.C. 1977) (college required to furnish interpreter at its expense after hearing-impaired teacher admitted as student in its summer program).

140. See *Ritter* v. *Mount St. Mary's College*, 824 F.2d 986 (4th Cir. 1987) (EPA applied to religious university but difference between plaintiff and competitor was sufficient to justify pay differential).

141. See Wenkart, "The Americans with Disabilities Act and its Impact on Public Education," 82 *Ed. Law Rep.* 291 (1993).

142. See Daugherty, "Uniform Management of Institutional Funds Act: The Implications for Private College Board of Regents," 57 *Ed. Law Rep.* 319 (1990) which discusses standard of care for university boards of trustees in mismanagement of funds; Steinbach, "Regulatory Issues on Campus: The Handwriting on the Wall," 53 *Ed. Law Rep.* 1 (1989) where higher education responsibility is discussed under a number of acts, such as the Resource Conservation and Recovery Act, the Clean Water Act, and the Safe Drinking Water Act.

Bibliographic Entries

1. Cobb, Calvin. "Tax-exempt Status of Racially Discriminatory Religious Schools." 37 *Tax Lawyer* 467 (1984).

   Reflects upon the implications of the *Bob Jones University* case both in terms of tax law and religious practice.

2. Cook, Ann Marie, William Cowden, Eric Heichel, and Elizabeth Saunders. "*Universidad Central de Bayamon* v. *National Labor Relations Board*: Jurisdiction Over Religious Colleges and Universities -- the Need for Substantive

Constitutional Analysis." 62 *Notre Dame Law Review* 255 (1987).

Reviews *Universidad Central de Bayamon* case where the First Circuit Court of Appeals refused to enforce an NLRB order requiring Catholic University to bargain with a faculty union. Presents the argument that the First Circuit was incorrect in its application of *Catholic Bishop* and the *Lemon* excessive entanglement test.

3. Daugherty, Mary. "Uniform Management of Institutional Funds Act -- The Implications for Private College Board of Regents." 57 *Education Law Reporter* 319 (1990).

Analyzes the responsibility of Boards of Regents at private universities under the Uniform Management of Institutional Funds Act in terms of standard of care, responsibility for restitution, acceptable types of investments, and acceptability of the use of the total return method.

4. Gibney, Mark. "State Aid to Religious Affiliated Schools: A Political Analysis." 28 *William and Mary Law Review* 119 (1986).

Surveys Supreme Court decisions involving aid to religious schools and criticizes the inconsistent leadership offered by the Court. Indicates that the *Lemon* test needs to be changed and proposes a solution based on proportional religious population representation.

5. Gray, John and Andrew Ciafola. "Student Press Protected by Faculty Academic Freedom Under Contract Law at Private Colleges." 52 *Education Law Reporter* 443 (1989).

Examines validity of the premise that where an institution contractually acknowledges its faculty right to academic freedom, that right in turn protects students from administrative interference with student newspaper publications that are a result of classroom assignments.

6. Lee, Barbara. "The Qualified Academic Freedom Privilege: A Closer Look at *EEOC* v. *Notre Dame.*" 41 *Education Law Reporter* 1209 (1988).

    Discusses *EEOC* v. *Notre Dame* and its importance as the first case in which a federal court applied an academic freedom privilege to deny disclosure of otherwise discoverable information in a Title VII case where a black faculty member had been denied tenure.

7. Mawdsley, Ralph. "Access to Tax Exempt Bonds by Religious Higher Education Institutions." 65 *Education Law Reporter* 289 (1991).

    Discusses the unsuccessful efforts by Liberty University to secure $60,000,000 of tax-exempt bonds in order to consolidate indebtedness. Analyzes the Virginia Supreme Court's decision in light of existing U.S. Supreme Court decisions and implications of the Liberty University decision on other religious universities.

8. Mawdsley, Ralph. "Comparison of Employment Issues in Public and Private Higher Education Institutions." 65 *Education Law Reporter* 669 (1991).

    Discusses the difference between public and private universities in terms of constitutional issues, but also discusses similarities in terms of statutory and contractual limitations.

9. Mawdsley, Ralph. "God and the State: Freedom of Religious Universities to Hire and Fire." 36 *Education Law Reporter* 1093 (1987).

Reviews several important federal cases addressing the right of religious universities to use religious requirements in employment decisions and the impact that statutory, constitutional, and public policy concerns have on the exercise of that right.

10. Mawdsley, Ralph. "Immigration Reform and Control Act: New Problems for Educational Employers." 38 *Education Law Reporter* 1143 (1987).

Reviews the Immigration Reform and Control Act (IRCA) in light of its philosophy to include employers as part of the enforcement process, its requirements for compliance, its penalties for failure to comply, and problems of implementation.

11. Mawdsley, Ralph. "Judicial Deference: A Doctrine Misapplied to Degree Revocation." 70 *Education Law Reporter* 1043 (1992).

Examines the few reported cases where universities have revoked degrees. Questions whether universities should use internal review procedures to revoke degrees and suggests that universities should instead have to seek a judicial order to revoke a degree.

12. Mawdsley, Ralph. "Religious Universities and Title VII: The Right to Discriminate on Religious Grounds." 43 *Education Law Reporter* 491 (1988).

Examines *Amos* v. *Corporation of Presiding Bishop* as it interpreted Title VII and the implication of that case for religious organizations which seek to impose religious requirements on employees, even those employees who are not directly involved in the religious mission of the institution.

13. McConnell, Al. "Abolishing Separate But (Un)Equal Status for Religious Universities." 77 *Virginia Law Review* 1231 (1991).

Discusses the Liberty University case where the university was denied tax-exempt bonds by the Virginia Supreme Court because of the university's pervasively sectarian program. Argues that denial of such assistance places religious schools in the same disfavored class as racially discriminatory schools and places a formidable barrier to religious practice.

14. McConnell, Michael. "Academic Freedom in Religious Colleges and Universities." 53 *Law and Contemporary Problems* 303 (1990).

Compares academic freedom in secular and religious colleges and universities especially with regard to the 1940 AAUP Statement of Academic Freedom.

15. McConnell, Michael. "The Selective Funding Problem: Abortions and Religious Schools." 104 *Harvard Law Review* 989 (1991).

Compares and contrasts the constitutional implications of government funding policies regarding abortions and religious schools. Concludes by offering a theory of selective governmental funding that could promote dispassionate decision making and more predictable results.

16. Morrison, Richard. "Price Fixing among Elite Colleges and Universities." 59 *University of Chicago Law Review* 807 (1992).

Reviews the consent decree signed between the eight Ivy League schools and the Department of Justice preventing the schools from jointly fixing tuition or financial aid and from exchanging financial aid information on admitted applicants. Discusses generally application of the Sherman Anti-trust Act to colleges and universities.

17. Noonan, John. "A Catholic Law School." 67 *Notre Dame Law Review* 1037 (1992).

Presents three intellectual aspects of a Catholic law school's origins and activity that make it different from a non-Catholic law school in light of secular accreditation standards of AALS.

18. Nordin, Virginia, and William Turner. "Tax Exempt Status of Private Schools: Wright, Green and Bob Jones." 35 *Education Law Reporter* 329 (1987).

Examines three separate standards that seem to exist for granting tax-exempt status to private schools depending on the nature of the racial discrimination and the location of the school.

19. Parsons, Mark. "Post-Secondary Options Act Triggers Constitutional Challenge." 68 *Education Law Reporter* 201 (1991).

Discusses comprehensively the provisions of Minnesota's Post-Secondary Enrollment Options Act (PSEOA) and the several unsuccessful challenges to its constitutionality. Includes a very helpful chart identifying factors examined by the court as to whether the religious colleges participating in PSEOA were pervasively sectarian.

20. Russo, Charles. "Academic Freedom and Theology at the Catholic University of America: An Oxymoron?" 55 *Education Law Reporter* (1990).

    Discusses briefly the protracted and successful effort by Catholic University to remove Charles Curran as a professor of theology over objections grounded in breach of contract.

21. Smith, Margaret. "Must Higher Education Be a Hands on Experience? Sexual Harassment by Professors." 28 *Education Law Reporter* 693 (1986).

    Examines remedies available to student victims of sexual harassment, directing special attention to sexual harassment by a teacher or professor as a form of professional malpractice.

22. Steinback, Sheldon. "Photocopying Copyrighted Materials: Doesn't Anyone Remember the NYU Case?" 50 *Education Law Reporter* 317 (1989).

    Discusses the New York University case settling a copyright lawsuit involving the use of professor-prepared anthologies that were to be sold to students but had not received permission from copyright owners, and the apparent lack of awareness of the implications for violating the Copyright Act.

23. Steinback, Sheldon. "Regulatory Issues on Campus: The Handwriting on the Wall." 53 *Education Law Reporter* 1 (1989).

Identifies several prominent existing federal regulations that should be reviewed by officials in higher education institutions to ascertain the current state of compliance. Includes discussion of such Acts as Resource Conservation and Recovery Act; the Comprehensive Environmental Response, Compensation and Liability Act; and the OSHA "Hazard Communication Standard."

24. Thomas, Stephen. "Freedom of Choice in Higher Education: *Witters* v. *Washington Department of Services for the Blind*." 31 *Education Law Reporter* 373 (1986).

Discusses the *Witters* case, providing state aid to a blind student at a religious college, in light of its facts and consistency with other United States Supreme Court decisions.

25. Thomas, Stephen and Deborah Barber. "The Right to Rescind a Degree." 33 *Education Law Reporter* 1 (1986).

Reviews in cursory fashion the important case *Waliga* v. *Board of Trustees of Kent State University* that upheld the right of the University to rescind the baccalaureate degrees because of dishonesty.

CHAPTER 2
The Educational System of The Church of Jesus Christ of Latter-day Saints

Robert L. Millet

An axiom of religious faith among the Mormons was given by Joseph Smith, founder of The Church of Jesus Christ of Latter-day Saints, or LDS, in 1833: "The glory of God is intelligence, or, in other words, light and truth."[1] "In knowledge there is power," Smith explained on another occasion. "God has more power than all other beings, because he has greater knowledge."[2] Thus it was that education assumed a prominent position among Mormon priorities from the very beginning.

Early Educational Efforts

In the first issue of *The Evening and the Morning Star*, the official Church periodical in Independence, Missouri, is found the following:

> The disciplines should loose [sic] no time in
> preparing schools for their children that they
> may be taught as is pleasing unto the Lord, and
> brought up in the way of holiness. Those
> appointed to select and prepare books for the
> use of schools, will attend to that subject, as soon
> as more weighty matters are finished. But the
> parents and guardians, in the Church of Christ
> need not wait -- it is all important that children,
> to become good should be taught so. Moses,
> while delivering the words of the Lord to the
> congregation of Israel, ... says [quotes
> Deuteronomy 6:6-8] ... If it were necessary to
> teach their children diligently, how much more
> necessary is it now, when the Church of Christ
> is to be an ensign, yea, even a sample to the
> world for good?[3]

Schools were established for adults as well as children. For several years Joseph Smith directed a number of men in what came to be known as the "School of the Elders" or the "School of the Prophets." Although theology was at the core of all that was studied, instructions were given to the effect that this body of men should immerse itself in a varied curriculum. They were instructed to study "things both in heaven and in the earth, and under the earth; things which have been, things which are, things which must shortly come to pass; things which are at home, things which are abroad; the wars and the perplexities of the nations, and the judgments which are on the land; and a knowledge also of countries and of kingdoms."[4] In addition, Joseph Smith and a number of others taught and studied English grammar and Biblical Hebrew.[5]

The philosophy of education in early Mormon society placed theology at the hub of the wheel, with the secular disciplines serving as spokes. In the mind of Joseph Smith, the other disciplines had meaning only as they drew the same from the religion of the people. From the writings of Parley P. Pratt, an

early Mormon church leader, comes the explication of the place
of "the science of theology":

> It is *the science of all other sciences and useful arts,*
> being in fact *the very fountain from which they
> emanate.* It includes philosophy, astronomy,
> history, mathematics, geography, language, the
> science of letters; and blends the knowledge of
> all matters of fact, in every branch of art, or of
> research ... all that is useful, great, and good; all
> that is calculated to sustain, comfort, instruct,
> edify, purify, refine, or exalt intelligences;
> originated by this science, and this science alone,
> *all other sciences being but branches growing out of
> this* -- the root (emphasis added).[6]

Sidney Rigdon, former Campbellite minister and later counselor
to Joseph Smith, asked the question: "What is religion without
intelligence? An empty soul." Rigdon then continued:
"Intelligence is the root, from which all time enjoyments flow.
Intelligence is religion and religion is intelligence, if it is anything"
(emphasis added).[7]

Joseph Smith and the Mormons established school systems in
Ohio, Missouri, and Illinois. It was in Illinois that interest in
formal education reached a peak in the formative period of
Church history, for it was in the city of Nauvoo that the Saints
were able to live in relative peace (freedom from persecution) for
seven years. Having been granted an extremely liberal and broad
charter (act of incorporation) by the State of Illinois, the Latter-
day Saints set about to establish common schools and a local
university. The University of the City of Nauvoo, organized
February 3, 1841, "was a strange combination of the traditional
church college and the French inspired 'university of the state'
under which were combined all educational functions within the
state.[8] The University of the State of New York (1784) and the
University of Michigan (1817) may have furnished the pattern for
the university at Nauvoo, although in Nauvoo both the universal

direction of education in the city and the parent university were established in fact under one authority."[9]

John C. Bennett, who later became disaffected from the Church, was appointed Chancellor, with Joseph Smith, Sidney Rigdon, and twenty-one additional persons acknowledged as regents of the university.[10] Orson Pratt, another early Church leader, was asked to give direction for the departments of Mathematics and English Literature. In addition, courses were taught by Pratt in Algebra, Geometry, Conic Sections, Plane Trigonometry, Surveying, Navigation, Differential and Integral Calculus, Philosophy, Astronomy, and Chemistry.[11] Orson Spencer, a graduate of Union College and the Baptist Literacy and Theological Seminary in New York, was given supervisory responsibility for the Department of Languages. Sidney Rigdon was appointed as head of the Department of History. Gustavus Hill was given the position of head of the Department of Music.[12] Besides the supervision of higher education, the regents of the Nauvoo school system were expected to "take the general supervision of all matters appertaining to education, from common schools up to the highest branches of a most liberal collegiate course. They will establish a regular system of education, and hand over the pupil from teacher to professor, until the regular graduation is consummated and the education finished."[13]

A continued push for education was evident in the administration of Brigham Young, even as the Saints had been driven from Illinois following the murder of Joseph Smith. On the banks of the Missouri River near Council Bluffs, Iowa (en route to the Great Basin), President Young stressed that "all the Saints should improve every opportunity of securing at least a copy of every valuable treatise on education -- every book, map, chart, or diagram that may contain interesting, useful and attractive matter, to gain the attention of children, and cause them to love to learn to read."[14] Regular school classes were held at the more permanent sites along the way. The establishment of school buildings was one of the primary considerations of the

Mormons upon reaching the Salt Lake Valley, and the early growth of "private" educational facilities (no public funding was available until some years later) followed the pattern that had been set in Illinois. One of the first acts of the legislative assembly of the State of Deseret (what was later to be known as Utah) was the institution of the University of Deseret (later known as the University of Utah). Like the university in Nauvoo, this university was intended to provide supervision and control for all educational endeavors within the state.[15]

Religious instruction was, from the beginning, an essential part of the curriculum of the school system in Utah. This came to be a problem as more and more non-Mormons found their way into the valley. A separation of Church and State in educational matters seemed inevitable, although ecclesiastical leaders resisted such a move on the part of the schools. As late as 1867, Daniel H. Wells, a counselor to Brigham Young, expressed the feelings of a number of citizens:

> Let us provide schools, competent teachers, and good books for our children, and let us pay our teachers. I would have no objection to seeing the standard works of the Church [the scriptures -- Bible, Book of Mormon, and Doctrine of Covenants] introduced into our schools, that our children may be taught more pertaining to the principles of the gospel in the future than they are in the present, and let one test of the fitness on the part of those who teach be a thorough acquaintance with and love for the principles which we have received, that our children may be taught the principles of truth and righteousness, and be trained from their youth in the nurture and admonition of the Lord. Let this course be taken in our schools, and let us pay our teachers.[16]

A similar sentiment was expressed by Wilford Woodruff on another occasion. Note how in 1888 the man who became the fourth president of the LDS Church sensed that moral and religious principles must be a part of the overall educational experience. He wrote:

> Religious training is practically excluded from the district schools. The perusal of books that we value as divine records is forbidden. Our children, if left to the training they receive in these schools, will grow up entirely ignorant of those principles of salvation from which the Latter-day Saints have made so many sacrifices. To permit this condition of things to exist among us would be criminal. The desire is universally expressed by all thinking people in the Church that we should have schools where the Bible, The Book of Mormon, and the Book of Doctrine and Covenants can be used as text books, and where the principles of our religion may form part of the teaching of the schools.[17]

The Mormon Church soon began to establish academies and colleges. From 1875 to 1911, twenty-two such institutions were organized, in which all students were required to enroll in a course of religious instruction. The expenses associated with the construction and maintenance of the academies, plus the cost for parents of sending children (from the home community) to other areas where the Church schools were located, eventually led to a close evaluation of the entire philosophy of education. By 1920, a Church commission on education recommended that a number of the academies be sold to the state or converted to Church-related buildings.[18] Over the years since that time, The Church of Jesus Christ of Latter-day Saints has involved itself in the development of educational facilities (in foreign countries) only when the government has not made provisions to provide the same for the community. Schools have been built over the years in such places as Mexico, Chile, Paraguay, Bolivia, Peru, Indonesia, Hawaii, Samoa, Tonga, Tahiti, New Zealand, Kiriabas, and Fiji. Most have been closed as public education has become available. By 1934, all but four academies had been closed or turned over to the state.

Universities, Colleges, and Weekday Religious Education

Brigham Young University. Brigham Young University traces its roots to Utah's rich pioneer heritage. The school was established as the Brigham Young Academy on October 16, 1875, on a little over one acre of land in what is today Provo, Utah. In spite of steady growth during the early years, the new institution was almost dissolved through a series of setbacks -- constant financial problems, as well as a fire in 1884 that destroyed the first campus building. As the school's high school and college curriculum improved and expanded, the academy officially became Brigham Young University on October 23, 1903. The greatest era of growth in regard to the physical plant took place during the period of the 1950s and 1960s under President Ernest L. Wilkinson. Beginning in 1971, under President Dallin H. Oaks, there was a deepening and refining of the scholastic mission of BYU, which by then had climbed in enrollment to 26,000. The university maintains its quest to provide excellent instruction in a moral and religious environment. Today there are approximately 27,000 students from all fifty states and more than one hundred foreign countries. BYU offers courses in 73 departments in ten colleges, two areas of general undergraduate education, two professional schools, and graduate studies. Bachelors' degrees are offered in 130 areas, masters' degrees in 115 areas, and doctoral degrees in 56. As a part of maintaining a balanced education, all students are required to enroll in fourteen hours of religious instruction in order to graduate.

In 1875, Brigham Young appointed Karl G. Maeser as President of the Brigham Young Academy. President Young's instructions to Maeser were brief: "You should teach not even the alphabet or multiplication tables without the inspiration of the Lord. That is all. God bless you, good-bye."[19] Brigham Young University continues to face the challenge of expanding its horizons in its effort to become a first-rate academic institution while maintaining its religious heritage and a Christian LDS identity. Every President of the LDS Church (who also serves as the head of the Board of Trustees for the university) and every president of the university since Maeser has labored to make of BYU a university that provides an education that is as stimulating to the mind as it is soothing and faith-building to the soul. Spencer W. Kimball, twelfth president of the Mormon Church, said:

> We must do more than ask the Lord for excellence. Perspiration must precede inspiration; there must be effort before there is excellence. We must do more than pray for these outcomes at BYU, though we must surely pray. We must take thought. We must make effort. We must be patient. We must be professional. We must be spiritual. Then, in the process of time, this will become the fully anointed university of the Lord, about which so much has been spoken in the past.[20]

He further instructed the faculty to speak the language of faith, as well as the language of the academy. "Your double heritage and dual concerns," he pointed out, "with the secular and the spiritual require you to be 'bilingual.' As LDS scholars you must speak with authority and excellence to your professional colleagues in the language of scholarship, and you must also be literate in the language of spiritual things. We must be more bilingual, in that sense, to fulfill our promise to the second century of BYU."[21]

BYU-Hawaii. On September 26, 1955, classes began at what was then known as the Church College of Hawaii in Laie. The

153 students who sat in a chapel that day were greeted by twenty new faculty members and administrators. The kickoff meeting was held in a local chapel because the school buildings were still in the planning stage. The first classes were offered in army surplus buildings, containing government-issue desks, chairs, and equipment, all brought from a nearby Air Force base. From that humble beginning has developed one of the great cultural-educational enterprises in the world, what is now known as Brigham Young University-Hawaii. Changes in focus, as well as development of new programs, have led to an enrollment of over 2,000 students from all over the world, including many of the Polynesian islands.

Ricks College. In November 1888, the LDS Church created Bannock Stake Academy in Rexburg, Idaho. Three teachers were appointed to meet the needs of 59 students in the basics of elementary education and spiritual growth. By 1915 the academy was growing and college-level courses were added to the curriculum. Within two years the school was authorized by the state of Idaho to train elementary school teachers and was given the new name of Ricks Normal College, after Thomas E. Ricks who had founded the school. Later the institution became known simply as Ricks College.

After struggling though its formative years (including the Depression), Ricks became a four-year school in 1949 but by 1953 settled into its role as a two-year institution. A large era of growth in the physical plant began in 1961, and today approximately 8,000 students from all fifty states and more than forty foreign countries take part in what is one of the finest two-year college experiences in the nation. Like BYU, Ricks is founded on religious principles, and religious education is a vital part of the Ricks College life. In addition, 335 full-time faculty members oversee a comprehensive liberal arts, vocational, and scientific curriculum consisting of approximately 1,000 courses, 150 majors, and 40 career programs. The college offers 86 associate degree programs in arts and science, 40 associate degrees in specialized disciplines, 7 one- or two-year certificate programs, a three-year interior design program, a bachelors' degree in nursing, an Honors program, and an Army ROTC program.

LDS Business College. The Church has also established the LDS Business College in Salt Lake City, which provides specialized training in business and technical fields and also a limited number of general education courses (transferrable to four-year institutions).

Continuing Education. Through a large Continuing Education program (centered at BYU in Provo), a major outreach in terms of credit and non-credit programs takes place. Both LDS and non-LDS persons may take advantage, through independent study or through distance learning, of what is available through church schools and colleges.

Weekday Religious Education. In 1912 a "released-time" seminary program was established adjacent to the Granite High School in Salt Lake City, in which high school youth would be permitted to leave the public school to receive one hour of religious training. This idea spread throughout the Western states. Later this particular program was adapted to a "home study" and then an "early morning" format, in which LDS youth living in remote areas might also participate in weekday religious instruction. Today hundreds of thousands of young people take part. In 1926, a "college seminary" program was established at the University of Idaho to provide religious instruction for university students. The Church has since organized such programs (known now as Institutes of Religion) adjacent to most colleges and universities in the U.S. and in a number of foreign countries.

Education and Religiosity

For some time now, studies have indicated that higher education tends to have a strong negative influence on religiosity. Various explanations have been offered, but perhaps the most popular is the secularizing effect of post-high-school study on one's commitment to the faith. The British physicist Paul Davies observed: "If the church is largely ignored today it is not because science has finally won its age-old battle with religion, but because it has so radically reoriented our society that the biblical perspective of the world now seems largely irrelevant."[22] A related explanation posits that "higher education tends to both expand one's horizons and increase exposure to countercultural values. Such exposure works to erode the traditional plausibility structures which maintain the poorly understood religious convictions so typical of American religion. In other words, poorly grounded religious beliefs have simply been unable to stand in the face of challenges generated by modern science and higher education."[23]

Since their beginnings, the Latter-day Saints have placed tremendous stress on the value of education; it is a religious principle that men and women should strive to gain all of the education and training possible to better themselves and their circumstances in life. Thus for both males and females, the percentage of Latter-day Saints who have completed post-high-school education or training is significantly higher than the nation as a whole. Research demonstrates that 53.5% of LDS males have some type of post-high-school education, compared to 36.5 for the U.S. population. For females, 44.3% have received some post-high-school education, compared to 27.7% for the U.S. population. In addition, the Mormons defy the long-held thesis regarding higher education and religiosity. Weekly attendance at church for males works as follows: those with only a grade-school education attended 34% of the time, while Mormon males with post-high-school education attended 80% of the meetings. The same results followed in such other areas of religiosity as financial contributions, frequency of personal prayer, and the frequency of personal scripture only. In short, the secularizing influence of higher education does not seem to hold for the Mormons.[24]

Conclusion

The Latter-day Saints often speak of "education for eternity." They believe that learning and growth and development are central to their religious way of life inasmuch as the Almighty expects them to magnify and expand upon their mental and spiritual capacities. One of the cardinal principles of their faith is stated as follows: "Whatever principle of intelligence we attain unto in this life, it will rise with us in the resurrection. And if a person gains more knowledge and intelligence in this life through his diligence and obedience than another, he will have so much advantage in the world to come."[25] Education for eternity is more than the collection of facts, more than the acquisition of skills. For the Mormons it entails the development of morality and goodness, the enhancement of character. As a former president of BYU observed in 1977, "One of the most distinctive characteristics of Brigham Young University in this day is our proud affirmation that character is more important than learning. We are preoccupied with behavior and consider personal worthiness an essential ingredient of our educational enterprise."[26]

In an address to BYU students in 1985, Dr. Winfried Bohm observed: "History, religion, art, literature and the theater offer an almost inexhaustible fund of actual and possible examples of the choices and life projects of others. The most important decisions of our lives are not well served by an over-emphasis on the quantitated conclusions of empirical inquiry or the objectified selections of a programmed textbook, but in the qualitative review of the lives of others who have previously struggled with similar human concerns." Summing up, Professor Bohm stated that "what our world needs the most is not an education for only further making, but an education for doing what is right and good; not a secular and pseudo-academic, but an authentic and profound Christian education."[27] To that enterprise and that rather lofty idea The Church of Jesus Christ of Latter-day Saints has dedicated itself.

Endnotes

1. Doctrine and Covenants of The Church of Jesus Christ of Latter-day Saints, Salt Lake City, 1981, section 93, verse 36; cited hereafter as D&C 93:36.

2. B.H. Roberts, ed., *History of the Church of Jesus Christ of Latter-day Saints*, 7 vols. Salt Lake City: Deseret Book Co., 1957, 5, p. 340.

3. *The Evening and the Morning Star*. Vol. 1, No. 1. Independence, Missouri: The Church of Jesus Christ of Latter-day Saints, June 1832, p. 6.

4. D&C 88:79.

5. See *History of the Church*, 2, pp. 301, 363, 376-77; 3, p. 26.

6. Parley P. Pratt, *Key to the Science of Theology*, 9th edition. Salt Like City: Deseret Book Co., 1965, p. 12.

7. Speech delivered by Sidney Rigdon at the laying of the cornerstone of the temple to be built in Far West, Missouri, 4 July 1838; in files of the Chicago Historical Library.

8. *History of the Church*, 4, p. 293.

9. Wendell O. Rich, *Distinctive Teachings of the Restoration*. Salt Lake City: Deseret News Press, 1962, p. 10.

10. *History of the Church*, 4, p. 293.

11. *Times and Seasons*, 6 vols. Nauvoo, Illinois: The Church of Jesus Christ of Latter-day Saints, 1839-46, 2, p. 517; 3, pp. 630-31.

12. *Ibid.*, 3, pp. 630-31, 646.

13. *History of the Church*, 4, pp. 269-70.

14. *The Latter-day Saints Millennial Star*, Liverpool, England: The Church of Jesus Christ of Latter-day Saints, 1840-1970, 10, p. 85.

15. See Rich, *Distinctive Teachings of the Restoration*, pp. 12-18.

16. *Journal of Discourses*, 26 vols. Liverpool, England: F.D. Richards and Sons, 1851-86, 12, pp. 376-77.

17.   Orson F. Whitney, *History of Utah*, 4 vols. Salt Lake City: George Q. Cannon & Sons, 1892, 3, p. 685.

18.   Rich, *Distinctive Teachings of the Restoration*, pp. 30-31.

19.   See Ernest L. Wilkinson and W. Cleon Skousen, "Karl G. Maeser: Spiritual Architect of BYA," *Brigham Young University: A School of Destiny*. Provo, Utah: Brigham Young University Press, 1976.

20.   "Second Century Address," delivered at the Founder's Day Convocation on 10 October 1976; in *Brigham Young University Studies*, 16 (Summer 1976): 452, 453.

21.   *Ibid.*, p. 446.

22.   Paul Davies, *God and the New Physics*. New York: Simon & Schuster, 1983, p. 2.

23.   Stan L. Albrecht, "The Consequential Dimension to Mormon Religiosity," *Brigham Young University Studies* 29 (Spring 1989): 100.

24.   See Stan L. Albrecht and Tim B. Heaton, "Secularization, Higher Education, and Religiosity," *Review of Religious Research* 26 (1984): 49-54.

25.   D&C 130:18-19.

26.   Dallin H. Oaks, "A House of Faith," Annual University Conference, Brigham Young University, Provo, Utah, August 1977.

27.   "Is Christian Education Possible in a Secular World?" Forum address delivered at Brigham Young University, Provo, Utah, 8 January 1985.

Bibliographic Entries

26.   Backman, Robert L. "Education, Molding Character." In *1990-91 Brigham Young University Speeches of the Year*. Provo, UT: BYU Publications. 1991, pp. 153-61.

Stresses the importance of morality in education and of the development of godlike characteristics and attributes. After a discussion of the overarching purposes of life, it focuses on the challenge of developing character in harmony with those purposes and the joy to be had in learning.

27. Eyring, Henry B. "Teaching Is a Moral Act." Address delivered at the Annual University Conference, Brigham Young University, Provo, UT, August 1991.

States that old-fashioned virtues like kindness and generosity are the hallmark of morality. Suggests that among the most important things students may learn at college is who they are and what they can become.

28. Flinders, Neil J. "Our Celestial Agenda and Language Barriers in the Academy." In *Proceedings of the First Annual Laying the Foundations Symposium.* Brigham Young University: Provo, UT, 22-23 March 1991, pp. 5-12.

Discusses the difficulties scholars face in seeking to work in an environment of faith but maintain the vocabulary and worldview of traditional academia. Points to the importance of revealed truth and of the need to think and research and write from that foundational perspective.

29. Flinders, Neil J. *Teach the Children: An Agency Approach to Education.* Provo, UT: Book of Mormon Research Foundation, 1990.

Offers a solution to many of the problems of modern school systems and educational dilemmas -- a system based on timeless truths found in scripture, individual agency and commitment, and moral principles. It discusses a theistic approach to educating the youth.

30. Green, Jon D. "Can a Humanist Get to Heaven? Issues of the Sacred and the Secular in the Humanities." In *Proceedings of the First Annual Laying the Foundations Symposium*. Brigham Young University: Provo, UT, 22-23 March 1991, pp. 55-62.

Instructs religious educators to assist the youth in their study of scripture that thereby they might gain confidence in scripture as a lasting spiritual resource in their lives. Stresses the need to strike the delicate balance between feeling and fact, between a genuine spiritual experience and an intellectually stimulating one.

31. Lee, Rex E. "Mount Everest Found: What BYU and Undergraduate Education Can Do For Each Other." Address delivered at the Annual University Conference, Brigham Young University, Provo, UT, 27-28 August 1990.

Seeks to address the question as to why the LDS Church should maintain a large university and what can take place at BYU that cannot take place elsewhere. Further, proposes that academic freedom carries with it the responsibility to think, to write, as well as to teach and write about matters of study and faith.

32. Lockhart, Barbara Day. "Observations of a Newcomer: Are We Laying the Foundations of Gospel Truth, or Are We Laying Gospel Truth Aside?" In *Proceedings of the First Annual Laying the Foundations Symposium*. Brigham Young University: Provo, UT, 22-23 March 1991, pp. 107-10.

Points out the kinds of academic freedoms to express one's faith and commitment at a religious university that are not available at a secular institution. Challenges faculty at Brigham Young University to be excellent academicians and at the same time serious students of scripture and builders of faith in students.

33. Millet, Robert L. "BYU as a Covenant Community: Implications for Excellence, Distinctiveness, and Academic Freedom." Religious Education Faculty Lecture, Brigham Young University, Provo, UT, 29 October 1992.

   Focuses on the meaning of being "under covenant" as individuals and an institution, as well as the challenge of maintaining excellence as an academic institution while at the same time striving to remain true to a religious heritage. Suggests what academic freedom at a religious school does and does not entail.

34. Millet, Robert L. "Knowledge by Faith: A Concept of Higher Education in Zion." In *Proceedings of the Second Annual Laying the Foundations Symposium*. Brigham Young University: Provo, UT, 20-21 March 1992, pp. 33-40.

   Outlines briefly Joseph Smith's educational philosophy with theology at the center or hub of the educational wheel. Discusses how faith provides an interpretive lens through which the strengths and limitations of academic disciplines may be assessed.

35. Millet, Robert L. "The Leap of Faith at BYU." Address to Brigham Young University Honors and General Education students, Brigham Young University, Provo, UT, 30 March 1994.

Emphasizes the need for simple or childlike faith in the divine at a time of growing disbelief and cynicism on college campuses throughout the world. Calls upon students at Brigham Young University to stretch themselves in the pursuit of academic excellence and to expand their spiritual horizons through the development of an informed and dynamic faith.

36. Oaks, Dallin H. *The Lord's Way*. Salt Lake City: Deseret Book Co., 1991.

   Compares and contrasts the world's way of knowing and understanding truth with the way men and women come to know the things of God. Offers counsel and warning in regard to learning, reason and revelation, and the limitations of the human intellect and perspective.

37. Oaks, Dallin H. "Meeting the Challenges of the Nineties." Address delivered at the Annual University Conference, Brigham Young University, Provo, UT, August 1990.

   Reviews major developments and changes at Brigham Young University during the 1980s and focuses on those matters that must not change: the mission of the university, relationship with the board of trustees, and the preeminence of teaching but the supportive role of research. Calls upon faculty to teach faithfully as well as competently, essentially to move against the natural academic tide that runs in universities.

38. Packer, Boyd K. "I Say Unto You, Be One." In *1990-91 Brigham Young University Speeches of the Year*. Provo, UT: BYU Publications, 1991, pp. 81-91.

Summarizes some of the more significant periods and events of the Church Educational System in the LDS Church, including the establishment of Brigham Young University. Notes the unusual nature of a board of trustees made up almost exclusively of members of the Mormon Church's First Presidency and Quorum of the Twelve Apostles and comments on the unique strengths of such a governing body. States that strenuous effort must be expended in order to maintain a spiritual and moral climate on a university campus.

39. Winder, Barbara W. "Education: Unlocking Opportunity." In *1988-89 Brigham Young University Speeches of the Year*. Provo, UT: BYU Publications, 1989, pp. 1-9.

Proposes that education begins to unlock opportunities when students have a thirst for knowledge, learn to convert knowledge into wisdom, and offer themselves to the world through dedicated service.

40. Woodworth, Warner P. "The Redesign of Education: New Paradigms and Practices for Building a School in Zion." In *Proceedings of the Second Annual Laying the Foundations Symposium*. Brigham Young University: Provo, UT, 20-21 March 1992, pp. 89-95.

Details some of the challenges in universities across the nation and suggests that Brigham Young University is suffering from some of the same problems. Offers the following solutions in meeting student needs: reinforce scholarship through higher quality academic work; combine the secular with the sacred by moving from a defensive stance to an offensive one; take on the theories and philosophies of the world through analyzing rather than canonizing the thought of the central intellectual figures.

41. Wright, H. Curtis. "The Mantic and Sophic Traditions." In *Proceedings of the First Annual Laying the Foundations Symposium.* Brigham Young University: Provo, UT, 22-23 March 1991, pp. 125-49.

   Distinguishes between the competing and contradictory worldviews of the sophic (naturalistic) and mantic (supernaturalistic) traditions. Provides historical context for the alternative perspectives of a sophic or horizontal religion, with its secular theology of immanence and its insistence that all things are present in nature, and the mantic worldview of vertical religion, with its theology of redemptive truths which transcend the natural order because they are revealed by God, the creator and determiner of nature.

42. Wright, H. Curtis. "The Sophic-Mantic Problem at BYU: A Case Study." *Scholar and Educator* 14 (Spring 1991): 57-82.

   Suggests that revealed knowledge that comes through the gospel and humanly originated knowledge that is transmitted by the universities come together at Brigham Young University. Poses the question: Which is to control which?

CHAPTER 3
Quakers and Higher Education

William C. Kashatus

In 1668, when Quaker founder George Fox urged the establishment of schools to teach children whatever things were "civil and useful in the creation," his vision did not extend beyond the fundamentals, namely, the three Rs and the rudiments of a religiously based education.[1] Nor did his follower, William Penn, anticipate much more than an elementary education for the children of his new-world colony, Pennsylvania, when he established it in 1682. In fact, Penn, who had been educated at Oxford University, had soured on higher education, believing it to be "an oppression of the mind."[2] Their reservations were common among the early members of the Religious Society of Friends which regarded higher education as impractical for the spiritual and vocational needs of its members.

Three hundred years later, the fourteen Quaker colleges, seminaries, and adult study centers that exist across the United States are perhaps the most visible contributions of a religious society that numbers no more than 100,000 members. Known for their intellectual rigor as well as their emphasis on social responsibility, at least four of the colleges -- Bryn Mawr,

Earlham, Haverford, and Swarthmore -- have been rated among the top twenty-five liberal arts institutions in the country. Nevertheless, these communities of higher education continue to struggle to find a proper balance between academic excellence and Quaker mission.

Theological Origins of Quaker Education

Quakerism was born out of the Puritan struggle for world transformation that occurred in seventeenth-century England. Many of the early Friends were originally Puritans, concerned with vital faith, total dedication to worship, and a Christian remaking of the social order.[3] In 1652, disillusioned by the unsuccessful efforts to reshape the English nation into Christ's kingdom through civil war, they left the Puritan ranks and began a new movement that placed a greater emphasis upon inner transformation, the belief that seeking Christ personally was the only sure method of transforming the larger society.

Under the leadership of George Fox, a tradesman from the northern part of England, Friends (alternatively called "Quakers" for their tendency to "quake" and "tremble" in their evangelizing) preached the necessity of turning inward for divine guidance. Their inspiration came from the New Testament, particularly the Gospel of John which emphasizes the universal nature of the Eternal Light of Christ or that of God in each person. This Inner Light doctrine made Friends aware of their common relation to the one God through the Light of Christ. Their silent meditative worship was based on waiting upon the Light for spiritual inspiration so that they could go out into the larger society and act on their peculiar set of beliefs: the non-violent resolution of conflict; the equal treatment of all human beings regardless of race, sex, or creed; and the practice of a lifestyle grounded in Christian simplicity.[4]

Essentially religious in inspiration, the Quakers were inevitably political in effect. Their vocal support for the radical doctrines of equality, democracy, and individuality were interpreted as subversive of the social order, and Quakers were roundly persecuted for them. Their philosophy of education was just as controversial. Friends tended toward simplicity of doctrine and a strong contempt for learned theologizing which often deteriorated into outright anti-intellectualism.

At a time when other religious groups emphasized the necessity of a university education to prepare for the ministry, Friends discouraged learning anything more than the rudiments of literacy and the ability to "wait upon the Lord for divine inspiration."[5] To this end, they established elementary schools that would allow future generations to contribute to the agrarian economy in which they lived and to worship God without the intermediary of a priest. Their children would learn that their "church" was the gathered fellowship of Friends and that their only "intermediary" was the Inner Light of Jesus Christ that was present in all persons.

These educational ideas were refined and implemented in America by William Penn who believed that universal education combined with vocational training and exposure to a broadly defined religion would cultivate the virtuous citizens he desired to people his religiously tolerant, democratic society. Such a "Holy Experiment," as he called it, would only be as successful as the quality of education that directed it -- and the success of that experiment did not require university training.[6]

The Need for Quaker Colleges, 1800-1833

By the early nineteenth century, American Friends were separated by great geographic distances as well as by different social and theological perspectives. Instead of searching for common ground, they resorted to schism; much of their energy was spent in arguments over discipline and theology. Considerable tension existed over the new spirit of independence and personal freedom inspired by the American Revolution. Younger Friends, in particular, strayed from the discipline of the Society, marrying out of the faith, or worse, neglecting to educate their children in Quaker faith and practice. But more dangerous to the survival of Quakerism was an emerging evangelical that challenged the fundamental conviction in the Inner Light and the mystical implications of that doctrine. At issue were the final authority of scripture; the deity of Christ; His substitutionary death on the cross; the depravity of human nature through Adam's fall; and the necessity of a personal religious experience through the Inner Light.[7]

Many Friends were attracted to evangelicalism, believing that it would combat the spiritual lethargy that had come to characterize the Meeting for Worship. They advocated a more scripturally-based education for their young, as well as more education in general. Other Friends who emphasized the mystical element in Quakerism believed that personal religious experience would be compromised by their evangelical counterparts; they refused to entertain the idea of any kind of education -- religious or academic -- above the secondary level. The tensions between these two groups culminated in 1826 in a schism known as the Orthodox-Hicksite Separation.

While several interpretations of this tragic event exist, most Quaker historians agree that the split emerged largely as a result of a revolt of rural Friends against urban Friends -- or the "rank-and-file" against the "elders." In general, the wealthy urban Friends, who became the Orthodox, embraced the evangelical position and advocated the greater use of scripture as well as the establishment of institutions for higher learning. The rural Friends, on the other hand, comprised the Hicksite group that was greatly disturbed by the worldliness of their Orthodox brethren as well as by their scriptural emphasis and desire for higher education.[8]

Almost every Yearly Meeting in the United States, except for New England, Virginia, and North Carolina, experienced this division. Fifteen years later, a second schism occurred within the Orthodox branch. Having the same evangelical roots as the earlier Hicksite Separation, this Wilburite split divided New England and North Carolina Friends among others and heightened the need for higher education as a means to propagate the beliefs of the different Quaker groups that were emerging across the country.

The Establishment of Quaker Colleges, 1833-1900

While individual Friends played a major role in establishing institutions of higher education such as Brown University and John Hopkins University, the first endeavor to establish an exclusively Quaker college was undertaken by the members of Philadelphia and New York Yearly Meetings. In 1833, these Orthodox Friends established Haverford College near Philadelphia in response to the ultra-conservative view of some Friends that even classical literature was un-Christian. Funds were raised by subscription and a charter obtained that proposed to establish "an institution in which the children of Friends shall receive a liberal education in ancient and modern literature, mathematics, and natural sciences under the care of competent instructors of our own religious Society, so as not to endanger the religious principles or alienate them from their early attachment." This was an all-male institution that aimed to prepare young men for the role of teaching in the smaller Friends schools that dotted southeastern Pennsylvania.[9]

By the 1860s, Hicksite Friends recognized the need for their own institution for higher education. Since they were not comfortable with sending their sons to Haverford, the Friends of three Yearly Meetings -- Baltimore, New York, and Philadelphia -- established their own college in 1864. The college was named Swarthmore, for Swarthmoor Hall in England where George Fox conducted some of the earliest Quaker meetings. Swarthmore was located on a farm at Westdale in Delaware County, Pennsylvania. Unlike Haverford, Swarthmore was a co-educational institution. When it opened its doors in 1869, the college had an enrollment of 82 female students and 88 males, and the faculty consisted of both men and women. Like Haverford, Swarthmore remained essentially a Quaker institution until after World War II, guaranteeing admission to any qualified graduate of a Friends school.[10]

Bryn Mawr College came into existence not under the care of any organized Friends Meeting, but as the quest of Dr. Joseph Taylor, a Quaker physician from Burlington, New Jersey. Having twenty years experience on the Board of Haverford College, Taylor decided to devote his wealth to the creation of a women's college with the highest academic standards. To this end, he purchased a hilltop site of thirty-nine acres in Bryn Mawr, Pennsylvania, and paid for construction of the first college building. Although Taylor did not live to see the opening of the college, his will provided for its organization, and he left his entire estate for its endowment.[11]

When Bryn Mawr opened its doors in 1885, it offered the bachelors, masters, and doctoral degrees to its students and was thus the first women's college in the nation to develop graduate training for women. It was also considered a Quaker institution until 1893 when the Board of Trustees broadened its mission by deciding that the college would be non-denominational. M. Carey Thomas, the first dean and second president of the college, gave Bryn Mawr its special identity as an institution determined to prove that women could successfully complete a curriculum as rigorous as any offered to men in the best universities. She also used the college as a vehicle to express her Quaker concern for outreach. In 1910 she launched an experimental high school in which Bryn Mawr students could be trained to teach and, ten years later, she established a summer school for female industrial workers.[12]

Because of their illustrious traditions and academic reputations, these three colleges are perhaps more widely known outside of Quaker circles than any of the other Friends colleges. Yet Quaker involvement in higher education was certainly not limited to the Philadelphia area.

While many of the Quaker secondary academies that were established in the South and in the Midwest throughout the early nineteenth century were replaced by public high schools, a few of them became colleges under the care of Friends. In 1837, for example, Guilford College in Greensboro, North Carolina, opened its doors as the New Garden Boarding School. By 1889 the academic program was expanded to that of a liberal arts and sciences institution.[13] Similarly, in 1847, Earlham College was established by Indiana Yearly Meeting as the Friends Boarding School at Richmond, and, twelve years later, in 1859, attained collegiate status.[14]

The establishment of these two colleges coincided with larger changes in American culture itself, many of which profoundly affected the ways Quakers viewed their role in the larger secular society. Advances in transportation and communication had not only removed many of the physical barriers that had separated Friends from the rest of American society, but they also made re-settlement a more viable alternative for Friends who no longer wished to live in the Antebellum South where chattel slavery had become firmly entrenched in the culture.

Between 1800 and 1860, approximately 6,000 Southern Friends moved west, establishing yearly meetings at Ohio, Indiana, and Iowa.[15] This great migration continued throughout the nineteenth century as yearly meetings were eventually established in Kansas, Nebraska, Oregon, and California. During this period, Friends turned increasingly to colleges as a main focus for education, resulting in the establishment of seven more institutions: Washington (1871) and Malone (1892) in Ohio; William Penn (1873) in Iowa; Barclay (1893?) and Friends University (1899) in Kansas; George Fox (1891) in Oregon; and Whittier (1887) in California. Generally, the further west these colleges were located, the more evangelical they were in tradition. Despite their theological differences, the founding of all these colleges fulfilled three major objectives: (1) to train both young men and women as teachers for the Quaker elementary schools that existed throughout the nation; (2) to ensure that a particular Quaker theology -- whether evangelical, rational, or mystical in nature -- be propagated among the next generation; and (3) to prevent young Friends from seeking admission to non-

Quaker colleges, something that was becoming commonplace by the mid-nineteenth century.[16]

Most of the Friends colleges were insular, parochial institutions until World War I. Events outside the colleges had little effect on the cloistered Quaker world they hoped to create. This isolation was partly by design. Primary attention was necessarily given to financial security as well as to building a strong faculty and academic program. Additionally, the isolationist attitude stemmed from the Quaker philosophy of their founders who aimed to provide students with a "guarded" education that would nurture their spiritual development and insulate them from the material society. In short, the twelve Quaker colleges that existed at the end of the nineteenth century represented a divided legacy in terms of theology and humanitarian outreach, a legacy that had been a hallmark of Quakerism from its establishment in the seventeenth century.

The Search for Common Identity, 1900-1960

Quakers did not escape the conflicts of modern thinking that challenged Christianity in the twentieth century, especially those discussions involving evolution and a modern interpretation of scripture. While conservatives and modernists within the Society of Friends wrestled with these ideas, there was a strong effort on both sides to work towards a common understanding of the Quaker tradition and its implications for the future. Much of this effort focused on healing the wounds cased by past separations between evangelicals and quietists. The eventual reconciliation was, in large measure, the result of efforts by Quaker communities of higher education.

Where at the beginning of the nineteenth century large numbers of American Friends adopted evangelicalism, a similar transformation occurred at the end of the century where evangelicalism was dropped in favor of liberalism. Like evangelicalism, liberalism originated outside the Society of Friends but was easily adopted because its principles were quite compatible with existing Quaker tenets: that the source of authority in religion came from personal and group experience, that creeds were secondary, and that religious commitment should ultimately express itself in service to others.[17]

The major figure in this process of reconciliation was Rufus Jones, a professor of philosophy at Haverford College. Jones pointed out that both evangelicals and quietists had distorted the vital testimony of the early Friends. While quietists divided existence into discrete physical and spiritual realms and required passive waiting in order to achieve an imaginary purity, evangelicals had embraced a set of static dogmas that violated the essence of the Bible and the religious impulses of early Friends. By using Quaker history, Jones demonstrated to contemporary Friends that the religious vision of the early Quakers had a moral dimension to it that went beyond scripture or silent worship.

A prolific writer who served as editor of the *American Friend*, Jones became a major figure among Protestant liberals and the most influential Quaker leader of the early twentieth century. As a chairman of the American Friends Service Committee, he served as a mediator for peace during World War II and was an active leader in the relief missions afterward. As a representative from New England Yearly Meeting, he lectured widely among Friends and served to break down the barriers between Philadelphia's Orthodox (evangelical) and Hicksite (quietist) Friends, beginning a process that eventually resulted in their reunification. His success was due, in large measure, to the fact that the public saw him as a man touched by God -- a quality that allowed him to disarm quickly whatever differences existed between conflicting groups.[18]

Jones was also instrumental in recruiting the active involvement of Friends' colleges in the spiritual rejuvenation of Quakerism. In 1937, for example, the Quaker professor served as presiding clerk of the Friends World Conference held at Swarthmore and Haverford colleges. This conference resulted in the creation of the Friends World Committee for Consultation which exists to foster intervisitation among Quakers throughout the world.[19] Subsequent conferences were held at Guilford College in 1967 and Friends University in 1977. The true value of this on-going dialogue has been the common search among Friends for their spiritual roots as well as a growing understanding and respect for persons and groups within the different branches of Quakerism. It is also a fitting legacy to the life's work of Rufus Jones, who restored the creative and dynamic impulses of Quakerism in our modern society.

Another issue that has served to unify the colleges has been their common witness of the Quakers' historic peace testimony. During World War I, the American Friends Service Committee (AFSC) was founded at Haverford College to provide constructive service for young men whose conscience forbade participation in war. Although Haverford became the training site for AFSC's first one-hundred volunteers, the students of several other Friends colleges participated in this organization as a form of alternative service.[20] Similarly, when asked to house a military unit during World War II as many colleges were doing, virtually all of the Quaker colleges stipulated that such units, if they were to be permitted on their campuses, must be non-combatant and that the training had to be useful in constructive ways after the war. During the Vietnam War era it was common for the colleges to support those students who applied for conscientious objector status, either by writing to the Selective Service administration or marching alongside them in demonstrations to protest the draft.[21]

Two other institutions of higher education were also founded during this period of reconciliation to ensure the practice of Friends' ideals in the modern world as well as to encourage a continuing discussion among Friends on spiritual, theological, and humanitarian concerns.

Pendle Hill, established in 1930, is a unique combination of an educational community and religious retreat. Named after the location in northwestern England where George Fox had a vision of "a great people to be gathered," Pendle Hill is situated on a twenty-two-acre campus in Wallingford, Pennsylvania. Here, students -- Quaker and non-Quaker, American and foreign, ranging in age from adolescents to senior citizens -- take courses in religious thought, Quakerism, scripture, and social action. At the center of their learning is the daily Meeting for Worship, a period of silent fellowship and personal reflection. This curriculum is tailored for three ten-week terms during the year; however, throughout the year, lectures, weekend seminars, and conferences are held for those who wish to attend for shorter periods of time. Regardless of the length of stay, Pendle Hill seeks to provide its visiting students with a center of religious and moral purpose where they can explore their faith and its application to emerging world problems.[22]

The other institution that has enriched the wider Quaker community is the Earlham School of Religion (ESR). Opened on an experimental basis by Earlham College in the autumn of 1960, ESR's program was expanded two years later to offer both the bachelor and master of divinity degrees. While the school is intended primarily for the training of Quakers interested in becoming pastors, religious directors, and leaders in other religious work, it has attracted many persons from other religious denominations. At ESR, faculty and students worship together daily with the understanding that the spiritual experience of God forms the foundation of their study together.[23]

Theologically, ESR is committed to a historic view of Quakerism grounded in the Free Church tradition of Christian faith and life. The education is informed by the Biblical message illuminated by the Light of Christ and inspired by the Holy Spirit. The Bible is considered to be an authoritative witness of God's living acts in history and in human progress, and as a vehicle through which God speaks to us today. In this sense, ESR operates on the understanding that the Bible serves not only as a history sourcebook of living faith, but as a sourcebook of living faith in response to the leading of God's Holy Spirit.

While ESR is committed to the Biblical revelation of God in Jesus Christ as the source, guide, and object of faith, it is also committed to the historic Quaker concept of continuing revelation. In other words, Christian truth is to be discerned within the context of worship and prayer, listening and dialogue, study and research, and in a spirit of respect, love, and understanding of one another. Such truth has universal meaning and validity because it is grounded in the universal Word (*Logos*) of God. The good news of the Gospel is that we cannot only know this truth but also act on it for the healing and redemption of the world.[24]

This theological perspective informs ESR's broad understanding of the Quaker calling which can be pursued in a variety of settings, including the formal ministry, education, social work, or business. At the same time, the school seeks to encourage in its students the same commitment to spiritual renewal and world transformation embraced by the earliest Friends.

Contemporary Concerns

During the last thirty years, there has been an increasing concern among Friends over the erosion of Quaker values at the Friends colleges. This concern has been triggered by several trends that have occurred: the number of Quaker students has plummeted; fewer Quakers sit on the faculty and board; and there has been a lessening of involvement in the operation of the school by the Yearly Meetings or Quaker trustees who oversee them. Many worry that this dilution of Quaker influence will have severe repercussions for the financial welfare and future governance of the colleges.

Since many of the Quaker alumni have entered the "helping professions" instead of the more lucrative field of business, there is a decrease in the number of Friends with financial resources substantial enough to give generously to their *alma mater*. Therefore, many of the colleges are forced to depend on the financial generosity of non-Friends -- parents, alumni, and local citizens. Because these groups are asked for their financial support, these donors often press for more of a voice in the governing of the college and are rewarded with trusteeships or supervisory status over the institution. Although many of these non-Friends are selected by the Quaker trustees for their sympathy with the goals of a Quaker education, there is still concern over their understanding of Quaker governance and decision-making by consensus.[25]

Additionally, Friends colleges struggle to preserve their intimacy as small learning communities. Often faculty and administration feel compelled to succumb to the "bigger-means-better" syndrome to which many other small liberal arts colleges have fallen victim. Their criteria of value become, like the society in which we live, based on quantity and prestige rather than quality. "Growth" is defined by the number of new facilities built or the number of faculty publications. Friends colleges must remember that the distinctiveness of the Quaker educational tradition depends not upon these "achievements," but upon the values of community, the intimate relationships that form between teachers and students, and the moral and academic integrity of the education that is offered. Thus, Friends colleges have begun to implement the following measures to strengthen Quaker presence in their institutions:

(1) Placing the emphasis on teaching and learning as well as the personal contact between faculty and students rather than research in order to create an environment conducive to learning and to the sense of community that embraces the Friends' values of honesty, justice, equality, and respect.

(2) Developing a sense of Quaker heritage by orienting the new students and faculty to Quaker values and practice, establishing Quaker archives, community service programs, and leadership training that will enable the members of the college community to witness to the institution's Quaker mission.

(3) Recruiting Quaker faculty, students, and board members who will become actively involved in the Quaker mission of the institution.

(4) Stressing general education in order to go beyond the narrowness that comes with specialization. Recognizing that the first two years of an undergraduate education are critical in building the general communication skills needed to become an articulate and constructive member of society. To create a two-year core curriculum that will meet this need.

While Friends enjoy a fine reputation as progressive educators, we cannot rest on the laurels of that reputation if we hope to contribute to the education needs of our contemporary society. Quaker history reveals that it was those Friends who had the ability to adapt to the changing circumstances of their time and still retain the spiritual integrity of their faith that enabled them to become a "people among peoples" and that the true spirit of Quakerism lies not so much in knowing religious or intellectual truth as it lies in the *process* of arriving at truth.

Perhaps James Michener, a Quaker graduate of Swarthmore College, offers the best witness to these principles. Years after he had become a famous author and world traveller, Michener remarked: "Swarthmore nurtured in me a supreme dedication to service and an intellectual approach to the solution of a problem. *What* Swarthmore taught me was not as important as *how* Swarthmore taught me. The tangibles were not worth a thing; the intangibles have been the core of my life. My college degree was the passport into a fuller participation in the problems of civilization." So, too, should it be for *every* graduate of our Quaker colleges.

Endnotes

1.   George Fox, *Journal* (1668) edited by John L. Nickalls. Philadelphia: Philadelphia Yearly Meeting, 1985, p. 520.

2.   William Penn, "Fruits of a Father's Love," in *The Complete Works of William Penn*, edited by J. Sowle. (2 vols. London, 1726), I, p. 898.

3.   Hugh Barbour, *The Quakers in Puritan England*. New Haven, CT: Yale University Press, 1964, pp. 1-72; and Christopher Hill, *The World Turned Upside Down. Radical Ideas During the English Revolution*. London: Maurice Temple Smith, 1972, pp. 231-58.

4.   Howard Brinton, *The Religious Philosophy of Quakerism*. Wallingford, PA: Pendle Hill Publications, 1973, pp. 1-18.

5.   Lawrence Cremin, *American Education: The Colonial Experience, 1607-1783*. New York: Harper and Row, 1970, p. 304; and Richard L. Greaves, *The Puritan Revolution and Educational Thought*. New Brunswick, NJ: Rutgers University Press, 1969, p. 24.

6.   *Ibid.*, pp. 305-08; and William C. Kashatus, "William Penn's Holy Experiment in Education," in *Reflections of William Penn's Life and Legacy*, edited by William C. Kashatus, Philadelphia: William Penn Charter School, 1994, pp. 87-96.

7.   Hugh Barbour and J. William Frost, *The Quakers*. New York: Greenwood Press, 1988, pp. 170-71.

8.   *Ibid.*, pp. 172-73.

9.   Greg Kannerstein, ed., *The Spirit and the Intellect: Haverford College, 1833-1983*. Haverford, PA: Haverford College, 1983, p. 9.

10.   Robert H. Wilson, *Philadelphia Quakers, 1681-1981*. Philadelphia: Philadelphia Yearly Meeting, 1981, p. 99.

11.   *Ibid.*

12.   Patricia H. Labalme, ed., *A Century Recalled: Essays in Honor of Bryn Mawr College*. Bryn Mawr, PA: Bryn Mawr College, 1987, pp. 45, 47.

13.   Guilford College, *College Catalogue, 1993-1995*. Greensboro, NC: Guilford College, 1993, p. 2.

14.   Tom Hamm, "Earlham: Where We Are and How We Got Here, 1832-1992," (Unpublished paper, Earlham College, 1992), p. 3.

15.   Leonard Kenworthy, *Quakerism: A Study Guide on the Religious Society of Friends.* Kennett Square, PA: Quaker Publications, 1981, p. 34.

16.   Leonard Kenworthy, *Quaker Education: A Source Book.* Kennett Square, PA: Quaker Publications, 1987, p. 14.

17.   Barbour and Frost, *Quakers*, pp. 219-23.

18.   *Ibid.*, pp. 225-28; See also Elizabeth Gray Vining, *Friend of Life. A Biography of Rufus M. Jones.* Philadelphia: Philadelphia Yearly Meeting, 1981.

19.   E.R. Orr, *Quakers in Peace and War, 1929-1967.* Sussex, England: n.p., 1974, p. 23.

20.   Kannerstein, *Haverford College*, p. 25.

21.   Orr, *Peace and War*, p. 38.

22.   Eleanore Price Mather, *Pendle Hill. A Quaker Experiment in Education and Community.* Wallingford, PA: Pendle Hill Publications, 1980, pp. 5-9, 111-13; and Kenworthy, *Quaker Education*, pp. 310-14.

23.   Wilmer A. Cooper, *The ESR Story: A Quaker Dream Come True.* Richmond, IN: Earlham School of Religion, 1985, pp. 1-10.

24.   Earlham School of Religion, *Catalogue, 1993-1995.* Richmond, IN: Earlham School of Religion, 1993, pp. 3-4.

25.   Kenworthy, *Quaker Education*, p. 222.

Bibliographic Entries

43.   Barbour, Hugh and J. William Frost. *The Quakers. A History of Friends in America.* New York: Greenwood Press, 1988.

Surveys the American Quaker movement from 1650 to 1987. Written for college students and scholars. Covers all the major branches of American Quakerism and is the first attempt to synthesize their twentieth-century trends and their relation to developments in the wider American culture. Provides biographical vignettes of important Quaker educators as well as accounts of the establishment and development of Quaker higher education in America.

44. Caldwell, Samuel. "New Eyes for the Invisible: Toward a Clearer View of Quaker Education," *Friends Journal.* (April 15, 1987): 8-10.

Examines whether the objectives and values of a Quaker education in the twentieth century are really different from any other enlightened, progressive school. Concludes that the uniqueness of Quaker education at all levels is its ability to teach spiritual courage as a means to testify outwardly what the student has come to know inwardly.

45. Cooper, Wilmer A. *The ESR Story. A Quaker Dream Come True*. Richmond, IN: Earlham School of Religion, 1985.

Interprets the history of the Earlham School of Religion from its founding in 1960 to the 25th anniversary in 1985. Traces the struggle to win the support for a Quaker theological seminary from the many diverse traditions within the Religious Society of Friends as well as the development of the institution. An appendix includes the original feasibility study completed for the school and statistics pertinent to the history and operation of ESR.

46. Hamm, Thomas. "Earlham: Where We Are and How We Got Here, 1932-1992." Unpublished paper, Earlham College, 1992.

Surveys the history of Earlham College, Indiana, and how it was shaped by Quaker migration from the South, the evangelical and interdenominational movements of the 19th century, and the influence of important Quaker personalities such as: the English Quaker minister Joseph John Gurney; Biblical scholar and Quaker historian Elbert Russell; and founder of the Yokefellows movement D. Elton Trueblood.

47. Johns, David, ed. *Hope and a Future. The Malone College Story.* Richmond, IN: Friends United Press, 1993.

Explores the role of evangelical Friends associated with founding Malone College, Ohio. Challenges the misconception often associated with evangelicalism, namely that of anti-intellectualism and social irresponsibility. The personalities addressed in this collection of essays -- Walter Malone, Emma Brown Malone, and Everett Cattell -- were not only concerned with doctrinal purity, but also with an active social agenda and educational sophistication.

48. Kannerstein, Gregory, ed. *The Spirit and the Intellect: Haverford College, 1833-1983.* Haverford, PA: Haverford College, 1983.

Examines the early history of Haverford College, near Philadelphia, its Quaker background, student life, athletics, and faculty. A very entertaining and readable sketch of the oldest Quaker college in the world.

49. Kashatus, William C. "The Inner Light and Popular Enlightenment: Philadelphia Quakers and Charity Schooling, 1770-1820," Ph.D. Dissertation, University of Pennsylvania, 1993.

Explores the reasons behind the Quaker stress on elementary and secondary education rather than university training. Also provides an extensive explanation of the theology and humanitarian impulse directing Friends education.

50. Kenworthy, Leonard S. *Quaker Education: A Source Book.* Kennett Square, PA: Quaker Publications, 1987.

Surveys all Quaker colleges, adult study centers, and seminaries in the United States, emphasizing the distinctive Quaker elements of education given at the various schools. An indispensable reference source.

51. Kenworthy, Leonard S. *Quakerism: A Study Guide on the Religious Society of Friends.* Kennett Square, PA: Quaker Publications, 1981.

Provides a broad-based account of Quakerism that offers a balanced fairness to the various theological traditions within the Society of Friends. Integrates a dependable overview of the origins, development, and contemporary expression of higher education among Friends.

52. Mather, Elinore P. *Pendle Hill. A Quaker Experiment in Education and Community.* Wallingford, PA: Pendle Hill Publications, 1980.

Interprets the story of the Quaker study center's first fifty years, its aims and policies, and the many achievements as well as problems that beset the enterprise. A masterly handling of the way the basic philosophy of Quakerism has continued to inform the life of Pendle Hill through all the shifting moods and interests.

53.   Vining, Elizabeth G. *Friend of Life. A Biography of Rufus M. Jones*. Philadelphia: Philadelphia Yearly Meeting, 1981.

Examines the life of Rufus M. Jones, for many years Professor of Philosophy at Haverford College, Pennsylvania. Jones was also an eminent historian and an authority of mystical religion. His wide influence as an author and speaker was enhanced by a gift for apt and humorous illustration. Jones made a great contribution towards ending divisions among American Friends and enlisted the support of the Quaker colleges in this effort.

54.   Wilmington Yearly Meeting, *Partners in Education: Wilmington College and Wilmington Yearly Meeting of Friends*. Wilmington, OH: Wilmington Yearly Meeting, 1992.

Contains a collection of essays that address the spiritual, financial, and outreach partnership between Wilmington College and Wilmington Yearly Meeting. Examines the historical background, peace education, Quaker decision-making and governance procedures, international aspects of education, and a vision for the future of this association.

CHAPTER 4
Lutheran College Education in the United States

Richard W. Solberg

The Lutheran concern for higher education is rooted in the theological and educational work of Martin Luther and the Reformation of the church in sixteenth-century Germany. As a university professor himself, Luther's emphasis on higher education in general is self-evident. As a reformer of the church, he recognized the importance of training pastors who had the competence to understand and interpret the Holy Scriptures. As a pastor, he was concerned for the teaching of both parents and children.

Together with his friend and colleague, Philip Melanchthon, he reformed the Latin schools in Germany and established the classical secondary school, or gymnasium, that prepared the Latin-school graduate for university entrance. Future pastors were thus assured a thorough grounding in the humanities and in the languages of the Bible.

As the Lutheran Reformation spread throughout northern Germany and Scandinavia, Luther's emphasis upon the thorough preparation of the clergy in the humanities and the classical languages persisted. Successive waves of emigrants from these countries that made their way across the Atlantic to North America, especially during the 18th and 19th centuries, made this concern their primary motive for establishing institutions of higher learning.[1]

Lutheran immigrants from Germany, Norway, Sweden, Denmark, and Finland all have established academies, seminaries, and colleges in North America. Not all of them have survived. As of 1994, 44 colleges and universities within the United States maintain a relationship with one of the Lutheran denominations. Twenty-nine are affiliated with the Evangelical Lutheran Church in America (ELCA), 11 with the Lutheran Church-Missouri Synod (LC-MS), and four with smaller Lutheran synods.

The first college in which Lutherans formally participated was founded jointly in 1787 at Lancaster, Pennsylvania, by Germans of the Reformed and Lutheran traditions. It was named Franklin, in honor of Benjamin Franklin, chief executive of the Supreme Council of Pennsylvania, and celebrated its opening on June 6, 1787, at the very time the Constitutional Convention of the United States was meeting in Philadelphia, just a few miles away.[2] Unfortunately, due to a lack of interest in English language instruction among rural Germans, the joint venture failed. Its endowments were eventually divided between two institutions: Franklin and Marshall College, of the Reformed tradition, and Gettysburg College, the first permanent Lutheran college.

Gettysburg and the American Tradition

Gettysburg Theological Seminary opened in 1826. From the outset it became clear that the more basic classical preparation would be needed for proper study of theology. Consequently, Samuel S. Schmucker, the young president of the seminary, first established a "gymnasium," on the German model. Then, in response to interest expressed by non-theological candidates, he applied to the Pennsylvania State Legislature for a collegiate charter. His petition was granted, and Pennsylvania College (whose name was changed to Gettysburg College in 1921) was opened in 1832. Pennsylvania College was one of several hundred small colleges that emerged between 1830 and 1860 as part of the "American college movement."

In founding the college, Schmucker took as his model the one he knew best, the one that had been in America for 200 years, namely, the New England college. The curriculum was classical in content, the standard preparation for anyone entering law, medicine, or public affairs, but an absolute necessity for pre-theological study. Although the founders, faculty, and trustees of the college were nearly all Lutherans, its public statements strongly affirmed its "non-sectarian" character. In its first 22 years, 165 of 303 Gettysburg graduates became pastors.[3]

The beginnings of Lutheran higher education in America were thus rooted in the colonial influx of German Lutherans of the 18th century and their descendants. By 1830, they were almost entirely English-speaking. As these groups moved south into western Virginia and the Carolinas, and west into Ohio and Illinois, the need for pastors called into being other preparatory schools that ultimately blossomed into seminaries and colleges. The initiative often came from individual pastors, who gathered groups of young men in their homes to "read theology." Such initiatives in South Carolina in 1830 and in Virginia in 1842 led to the creation of "classical academies" that developed into full-fledged colleges: Roanoke in 1853 and Newberry in 1856. Each of these institutions eventually gained recognition from one or more synods, or regional associations of Lutheran congregations; but especially in early years, financial support was limited to tuitions and individual gifts.

The decade of the 1850s, just preceding the Civil War, was a period of optimism and economic growth in the South, and Lutheran enthusiasm for higher education also blossomed. North Carolina College, chartered in 1859, became one of the first colleges directly sponsored by a Lutheran synod. The early entry by Lutherans into college education for women resulted in the founding of four female seminaries, two of which later became pioneer degree-granting institutions. However, of all the Lutheran collegiate ventures in the South before the Civil War, only Roanoke and Newberry survived the disasters of war and subsequent economic reversals. One additional college, Lenoir-Rhyne in Hickory, North Carolina, founded in 1891, completes the present triad of Lutheran collegiate institutions located in the southern states.[4]

The history of the Lutheran church in the United States has been strongly determined by two characteristics: its ethnicity and its preoccupation with questions of doctrine. Both of these factors have had great influence on the number and location of its educational institutions. In contrast to other mainline denominations such as Episcopal, Baptist, Methodist, and Presbyterian, all of which have linguistic roots in England or Scotland, Lutheran immigrants have come from European countries speaking at least five different languages: German, Norwegian, Swedish, Danish, and Finnish. They have also come to this country at different times, and settled in different locations. Each group has established its own church structure and its own institutions, depending, at least for a generation or two, upon its mother tongue.

Colleges of the Later German Migration

As stated earlier, the large German influx of the colonial period had moved south and west from Pennsylvania and New York and by the 1830s was largely English-speaking. But following the War of 1812, new waves of immigrants swarmed into the United States, among them a large German Lutheran contingent, committed both to the use of the German language and to more conservative theology than their earlier, more Americanized counterparts. Large numbers of these newer immigrants moved into western New York, Pennsylvania, and Ohio, and established their synods and their institutions.

The ensuing conflicts between the newer group and the older, "Americanized" Lutherans resulted in the founding of two seminaries and colleges in Ohio, 40 miles apart. Wittenberg College in Springfield, chartered in 1845, was modeled after Gettysburg and the New England colleges, and gave instruction, including theology, in the English language. Capital University in Columbus, chartered in 1850, insisted that orthodox Lutheran theology must be couched in the German language. Its founders also made the first, albeit unsuccessful attempt to transplant the classical structure of the German university, with its four faculties of Letters, Law, Medicine, and Theology, to America.[5]

Three other colleges of German Lutheran origin, reflecting at least in part the cleavage between the older "American" Lutherans and the theologically more conservative newcomers, emerged in Pennsylvania during the 1850s and 1860s. Susquehanna University in Selinsgrove began in 1858 as a training school for missionary pastors for the American frontier. Muhlenberg College in Allentown was chartered in 1867 as part of the conservative reaction by the Ministerium of Pennsylvania against both the theological and linguistic "Americanism" of Gettysburg College and Seminary. Thiel College, in Greenville, founded in 1866 and chartered as a college in 1870, provided the conservative anchor in western Pennsylvania.[6]

The German emigration to America in the 19th century differed in many ways from that of the 17th and 18th. Most of the earlier immigrants were refugees, either economic or religious. Many actually came as indentured servants. They had no organized leadership. The later immigrants were more often prosperous farmers, merchants, and professionals, dissatisfied with economic, political, or religious conditions in Germany.

During the 1830s large groups of German emigrants often organized as companies and migrated *en masse* to America or elsewhere. One such group of particular significance to American Lutheranism left Saxony in 1839 and settled in Perry County, Missouri, south of St. Louis. Their reason for leaving Saxony was to distance themselves both from the structure and the rationalistic theology of the Lutheran state church. This group became the major element in the organization of the Missouri Synod in 1847.

With several ordained clergy in the colony, the Saxons had no immediate need for a seminary, but they lost no time in starting a classical school, patterned after the German gymnasium. Increasing requests for teachers for the colony's parochial schools, however, and a recognition of future pastoral needs for their congregations shifted the focus of the classical gymnasium exclusively to the preparation of church workers.

In 1849, students and faculty left rural Perry County and moved their school, now called Concordia College, into new quarters in St. Louis. This marked the first step in the development of a system of higher education quite different from the American college tradition as followed by Gettysburg, Wittenberg, and most other Lutheran colleges. It transferred the format of the German gymnasium to this country virtually without change. After a six-year course in the "gymnasium," a young man (women were not eligible) might qualify as a parochial school teacher, or he might begin the three-year professional study of theology at Concordia Seminary in St. Louis. Protected from American influence by the exclusive use of the German language, the Missouri educational system was maintained without modification for nearly a century.

As the overwhelming flood of German immigrants poured into the United States, especially into the Midwest, during the late 19th century, the Missouri Synod grew in numbers. More pastors and teachers were needed. One by one, new regional prep schools were established, drawing their recruits from the parochial schools of the congregations.

The first regional prep school was established in Milwaukee in 1855, and moved to Fort Wayne, Indiana, in 1858. With the opening of Concordia Teachers College in Addison, Illinois (later River Forest), in 1864, teacher education was established as a distinct curriculum.

Between 1881 and 1893, congregations in several parts of the country opened local schools called "pro-gymnasia." Pro-gymnasia offered the first two or three years of studies that could then be completed at Fort Wayne or (after 1891) at Milwaukee. Some of the pro-gymnasia developed into full six-year schools; they included schools in New York; St. Paul, Minnesota; Concordia, Missouri; Portland, Oregon; and Oakland, California. A growing need for parochial-school teachers resulted in the opening of an additional teachers college in Seward, Nebraska, in 1894. When the small "English Synod of Missouri" was integrated into the larger Missouri Synod in 1893, it brought with it St. John's College of Winfield, Kansas, a four-year degree-granting coeducational college that had been founded and given to the English Synod by a wealthy Winfield businessman. By the turn of the century, the Missouri System had been firmly established as a closely integrated network of preparatory colleges and seminaries, devoted exclusively to the preparation of pastors and church workers, quite isolated from the rest of Lutheran higher education. Only during the 1920s did the Missouri System yield to the American pattern, replacing the six-year gymnasium with the four-year high school and two-year junior college.[7]

Although not all were as single-minded as the Missouri Synod, some other German Lutheran groups of this later migration also retained a primary emphasis upon the preparation of pastors and parochial-school teachers. One of these groups settled in Iowa in 1853. Drawing its pastors mostly from missionary societies in Germany, the Iowa Synod concentrated primarily on preparing parochial-school teachers. However, classical and scientific courses were gradually added, and Wartburg College emerged in 1885 in Waverly, Iowa. A somewhat similar development occurred in Brenham, Texas, where German Lutherans established a school for pastors and teachers in 1891. Following a move to Seguin and a merger with a Swedish Lutheran academy, it was established in 1932 as Texas

Lutheran College. Both Wartburg College and Texas Lutheran College gradually adopted the American collegiate plan.

Yet another German settlement developed in eastern Wisconsin. Following the lead of the conservative Lutherans in Missouri, the Wisconsin Synod also established a German gymnasium, focusing exclusively upon the preparation of parochial-school teachers and pastors. Northwestern College, founded in 1865 in Watertown, Wisconsin, gave only pre-theological training, although it modified the pattern of the German gymnasium sufficiently to award the bachelor's degree before a graduate entered the seminary. Dr. Martin Luther College was founded in New Ulm, Minnesota, to prepare teachers, but it, too, broadened its curriculum, and eventually awarded bachelor's degrees.[8]

There have thus been two distinct patterns in the development of Lutheran higher education in America: the New England college pattern, an adaptation of the English tradition; and the German gymnasium, directly transplanted from Germany. Lutherans have employed both systems to assure their primary objective, a properly-educated clergy. Eighteenth-century German Lutheran immigrants chose the English college pattern. The nineteenth-century group remained loyal to the German gymnasium -- even limiting its scope to the exclusive preparation of pastors and church workers -- until well into the 20th century. Neither of these patterns is, by definition, Lutheran. But both have been employed for the transmission of the Lutheran tradition in higher education in North America for nearly 200 years.

The Scandinavian Impulse

A third major stage in the development of Lutheran higher education in America was introduced with the advent of the Scandinavians, who began to emigrate to the United States in the late 1830s and 1840s. Although the major motivation of Scandinavian emigration was economic, most of the early

Norwegian immigration came from parts of Norway where the influence of religious revivals had been very strong. These revivals also had a distinctly anti-clerical and democratic flavor and were largely led by lay preachers. During the early years of Norwegian immigration, no ordained pastors of the Lutheran state church accompanied the emigrants. Indeed, the state church in Norway opposed emigration, and labeled those who left the country as "disloyal." Therefore, from 1835 to 1845, Norwegian settlements in Illinois and Wisconsin were served by lay preachers. There was no call for schools of theology.[9]

Significant Swedish emigration to America began a few years later and eventually contributed the largest numbers among the Scandinavians. Revivalism and dissatisfaction with the state church also brought the first groups of Swedes to America. In 1849, a Lutheran pastor, Lars P. Esbjorn, led a company of more than 100 persons, mostly from his own congregation in Sweden, to western Illinois. Within two or three years he was involved in a joint effort with both Norwegians and Germans in Illinois to establish a university that had a theological department for training pastors.

This unique effort, initiated by a synod of English-speaking German-Americans from southern Illinois, in 1852 resulted in the formation of a Lutheran institution in the state capital in Springfield called Illinois State University. Unfortunately, this inter-ethnic experiment foundered on the rocks of theological diversity and a touch of the "nativism" that became acute during the decade of the 1850s in the United States. Led by their Scandinavian professor, both the Norwegian and Swedish students left the university in quest of a more congenial climate.

Its "American" supporters maintained Illinois State University until 1868, and then transferred their educational efforts to the creation of Carthage College, modeled after its older counterparts, Wittenberg and Gettysburg. The Scandinavians returned to Chicago to organize Augustana College and Seminary, the first of an expanding network of Scandinavian Lutheran colleges to be founded between 1860 and 1903.

The alliance of Swedes and Norwegians was short-lived. As part of a Scandinavian colonization plan, they accepted a real-estate proposal from the Illinois Central Railroad and moved the college to Paxton, Illinois, about 100 miles south of Chicago. But neither group was satisfied, either with the colonization plan or the location, and some differences also developed between them over methods of pastoral preparation. An amicable separation was agreed upon, and in 1869 the Norwegians and Danes founded Augsburg Seminary and moved into southern Wisconsin, seeking closer contact with the strong Norwegian immigrant settlements there. The Swedes, too, soon abandoned Paxton, relocating Augustana College and Seminary in 1875 in Rock Island, close to the well-established Swedish settlements in western Illinois.[10]

Norwegian-American Colleges

Among the Scandinavians, the Norwegians were the most prolific in establishing seminaries and colleges. During the period from 1860 to 1903, seven of the still-surviving Lutheran colleges were founded, either by Norwegian Lutheran church bodies or by private groups of lay persons and clergy. This was related partly to the westward movement of Norwegian settlement, and partly to the course of Norwegian Lutheran ecclesiastical and theological history during the 19th century. The story is one of fragmentation. With each new division, a new seminary and a new college was founded to represent the views of the respective church fathers. Ecclesiastical reunification came about only in the 20th century, but most of the colleges outlived the controversies and are vital institutions today.

No sooner had the Norwegian-Danish groups withdrawn from the Swedish Augustana Synod and established their own synod and seminary at Marshall, Wisconsin, than a further division occurred that resulted in moving Augsburg Seminary to a permanent location in Minneapolis, Minnesota. After a brief sojourn in Marshall, the remaining Norwegian-Danish Augustana

Synod moved its school west, following the direction of
Norwegian migration, into Iowa and eventually to Sioux Falls,
South Dakota. The school retained the name, Augustana College,
thereby affirming historical continuity with the Norwegian co-
founders of Augustana College and Seminary in Chicago in
1860.[11]

While one group of Norwegians in northern Illinois was
experimenting with Swedes and Germans in cooperatively
training pastors during the 1850s, other groups in Illinois and
Wisconsin were taking steps to establish their own training
programs. Even the lay-oriented group, called Hauge's Synod,
made several attempts, finally locating a prep school and
seminary in Red Wing, Minnesota, in 1879. In 1853 the
Norwegian Synod was organized in southern Wisconsin under
the leadership of a group of theologically conservative pastors
trained in Norway. Until the synod could raise sufficient funds
to build its own school, it sent its prospective pastors to
Concordia College in St. Louis for preparatory training.

When the Civil War broke out in 1861, military activity in the
St. Louis area caused Concordia to suspend operation
temporarily. Students returning to their homes in Wisconsin and
Iowa brought reports that Concordia faculty members were
sympathetic to slavery. Strong reaction to these reports by lay
delegates to the synod convention led to a decision to terminate
the arrangement with the Missouri Synod, and to establish a
preparatory school immediately. Luther College began its
operation in a vacant rural parsonage in Wisconsin in 1861, and
moved the following year to its permanent location in Decorah,
Iowa. Although it operated at first on the pattern of a German
gymnasium, Luther College granted the bachelor's degree at the
conclusion of the six-year pre-theological course. It thus became
the first Norwegian Lutheran college to grant an academic
degree.[12]

While Augustana, Augsburg, and Luther Colleges were
founded primarily for the purpose of preparing pastors, other
Norwegian Lutheran colleges emerged out of what has been

called the "Academy Movement." This movement flourished in the Scandinavian communities largely in the Midwest from about 1870 to 1920. While the Germans developed a strong parochial school system in their congregations, Scandinavians tended to support the American public, or "common" school. They preferred to concentrate the religious instruction of their children in the Sunday school and in extended summer parochial schools. But they developed a network of secondary schools, sponsored by groups of individuals or congregations. These schools offered subjects of a more practical nature, together with religious subjects, to aid young immigrants in making the adjustment to life in their adopted country, and also to provide some basic teacher training. More than 75 such secondary and normal schools were spread across the country from Illinois and Wisconsin to the Dakotas, and into Canada. These academies thrived until the public high school was added to the common school. As the Scandinavian young people in increasing numbers chose public high schools, the academies declined. The stronger academies were translated into two-year colleges or four-year baccalaureate institutions. Among the Norwegian colleges owing their origin to this practical service to the immigrant community are St. Olaf College in Northfield, Minnesota; Concordia College in Moorhead, Minnesota; Waldorf College in Forest City, Iowa; and Pacific Lutheran University in Tacoma, Washington.

St. Olaf's School was founded in 1874 by a group of farmers, pastors, and one businessman, for the "advancement in education of pupils [both boys and girls], from fifteen years of age and upwards, as a college" and for the preservation of its pupils "in the true Christian faith." In 1886, it opened a college department, and graduated its first baccalaureate class in 1890.

Concordia and Pacific Lutheran, both founded in 1891, reflect the movement of Norwegian settlement north and west into the Red River Valley, North Dakota, and the Pacific Northwest. Concordia was founded by an association of nine laymen and three pastors, and has flourished in an area with a strong concentration of Scandinavian Lutherans. It awarded its first baccalaureate degree in 1917. Pacific Lutheran was the lone survivor among the four colleges established by three competing Norwegian Lutheran bodies in the state of Washington between 1891 and 1909. Although its growth in early years was restricted, by 1940 it awarded its initial baccalaureate degree, and has since developed into a small university. Waldorf College emerged from its academy status as the only junior college of Norwegian Lutheran origin.[13]

Swedish Regional Colleges

The Swedish story bears some similarity to the Norwegian, except that apart from the Norwegian secession in 1870, the Swedish Augustana Synod maintained its ecclesiastical unity until it became a part of the concerted series of Lutheran mergers in 1960 and thereafter. Unlike the Norwegians, it maintained a single theological seminary and a college at Rock Island, Illinois, also called Augustana.

Other colleges of Swedish Lutheran origin are not the result of theological division, but of Swedish migration and regional settlement in Minnesota, Nebraska, Kansas, and the New York area. These colleges were not founded as pre-theological schools, but as elementary schools and academies, out of the same concern for the general education of Swedish immigrants as was evidenced by the Norwegian academies and colleges.

The largest of these, Gustavus Alolphus College, began in 1862 as a Christian day school in the home of a missionary pastor in Red Wing, Minnesota. The school was adopted by the Minnesota Conference of the Swedish Augustana Synod, expanded in size and scope, and finally, in 1876, located permanently in St. Peter, Minnesota. Its first baccalaureate degrees were awarded in 1890.

During the 1880s and 1890s, a so-called "college mania" occurred among the Swedes. Actually, eight academies were founded during these years, two of which ultimately emerged as four-year colleges. Bethany, founded in 1881 in Lindsborg,

Kansas, enjoyed spectacular growth during its first two decades, and became the centerpiece of a unique Swedish cultural community. A counterpart in neighboring Nebraska, Luther Academy, developed into a two-year college, and in 1962 was merged with Midland College, the westernmost collegiate extension of the early German-American tradition that produced Gettysburg and Wittenberg Colleges.

A significant number of Swedish immigrants remained in New York upon their arrival in America, many of them in Brooklyn, where they organized the New York Conference of the Augustana Synod. In 1893, the Conference took the initiative to found Upsala College, naming their school after the prestigious Swedish University of Upsala. In 1898, it was moved to a campus in New Jersey, and in 1929 to its present location in East Orange.[14]

Schools of the Danes and the Finns

Danish and Finnish immigrants to the United States were fewer in number and arrived later than the Norwegians and Swedes. Danes came in large numbers only in the 1870s and after; Finns especially from 1890 to 1918. Educational initiatives among the Danish immigrants were colored by a controversy within the Church of Denmark, centered around the teachings of Bishop Nicolai F.S. Grudtvig. His theology stressed the positive potential of human life, while his opponents in the Inner Mission Movement stressed a more pietistic and subjective view of the Christian life. Both groups sent pastors and theological students to America and both established schools and colleges.

Between 1872 and 1884 the Inner Mission group sent ten young men from Denmark to Augsburg Seminary in Minneapolis for their training, but in 1884 they established Trinity Seminary in Blair, Nebraska. The preparatory department at Blair eventually developed into Dana College. The Grundtvigians initially were served by pastors trained in Denmark, but eventually they, too, established a school in Des

Moines, Iowa, called Grand View College. Although it included a theological department, it combined several features of the Danish "folk school" that had been a hallmark of Grundtvig's educational philosophy. Its "Winter School," a three-month term emphasizing general lectures on a variety of subjects, without examinations or grades, but intended to broaden the cultural horizons of adult students, was its most popular program.[15]

Immigrants from Finland came to America later than other Scandinavians, and settled largely in the Great Lakes area. Reaching significant numbers only in the late 1890s, Finnish immigration peaked in the period from 1900 to 1918, responding in large measure to oppressive policies in czarist Russia. Although all Finns were nominally members of the Lutheran Church, large numbers of the immigrants were estranged from the church, finding a sense of community in political and economic organization instead. Religiously oriented groups were fragmented, but one group of pastors and laymen organized the Suomi Synod in 1890. Six years later the synod established an academy at Hancock, in the upper peninsula of Michigan, to prepare teachers and pastors. By 1906, Suomi College and Seminary graduated its first class of seven theological candidates.[16]

Operational Patterns in the 19th Century

The turn of the century also marked the close of the "founding period" for Lutheran colleges in the United States. Beginning with Gettysburg College in 1832, each of the immigrant groups from the five major Lutheran countries of Europe had established basic collegiate institutions. By 1904, 36 of the 44 presently-operating Lutheran colleges and universities had been founded. During these founding years, there was little question of the Lutheran character of any of them. They were founded by Lutherans, basically to serve the needs of Lutherans, primarily, though not exclusively, to prepare pastors. They reflected the geographical distribution and the ethnic divisions among Lutherans -- and often the theological conflicts that characterized 19th-century American Lutheranism.

Most Lutheran colleges in the 19th century were founded on the initiative of individuals, both clergy and lay. Synods or church bodies might authorize or endorse an institution, but most were not financially able to handle capital projects, or, in many cases, even to support the meager professorial salaries. College locations were often determined by competition between towns or land companies, offering cash, land, and a guaranteed number of students. Augustana, Pacific Lutheran, Upsala, Midland, and others got their start through land speculation and nearly collapsed when the deals fell through.

The formal patterns according to which a college related to a church or a synod varied widely. In some cases, boards of trustees were self-appointed; others were elected by synods, or townspeople, or alumni. Whether ownership was vested in individuals, associations, stock companies, or synods, the Lutheran identity of the schools was taken for granted.

Financial support during most of the 19th century came from private gifts, tuitions, or modest endowments. Beginning in 1874, the Augustana Synod supported its colleges through an annual assessment of 25 cents per member. The Norwegian Synod directly supported Luther College from its beginning in 1861. The Missouri Synod, an exception to the rule, provided virtually total support for its institutions of higher education.

Like most American colleges throughout the 19th century, student enrollments in Lutheran colleges and universities were very small. Preparatory departments often provided the income needed to maintain the collegiate levels. Female students were few in number. In 1866 Thiel College in Greenville, Pennsylvania, became the first Lutheran college to admit women.

During the years following the Civil War, profound changes occurred in the climate of higher education in America. The Morrill Act of 1862 brought the land-grant colleges and state universities into being, and they became the purveyors of a more scientific and utilitarian curriculum that challenged the rigid classical pattern of the traditional American college. Charles Eliot's "elective system" called for more diversified course offerings, one effect of which was to increase the need for faculty who had the advanced graduate training needed to teach specialized courses. Responding to these trends, Lutheran colleges, too, began the quest for Ph.D.s, and encouraged their own younger scholars to enroll in the new graduate schools such as Johns Hopkins or Yale.[17]

Beginnings of Inter-Institutional Cooperation

As Lutheran colleges became increasingly involved in the academic issues that were affecting American higher education in general, a sense of corporate identity began to develop among them. There were common concerns to be faced that reached beyond the local concerns for which individual schools had been established. As early as 1898, a professor at Roanoke College issued an appeal for inter-institutional meetings to explore common attitudes that Lutheran colleges might develop toward the newer issues in higher education. In 1910 a group of college presidents met to organize the Lutheran Educational Conference, a forum for corporate discussion of church-related higher education, which remains today as the oldest of all existing inter-Lutheran associations. Lutheran church bodies began to establish denominational boards of higher education as early as 1885, but more general action followed a series of synodical mergers in 1917 and 1918.

Concerns over accreditation emerged as early as 1870, when the University of Michigan began to require certain units of high school instruction, defined in terms of class hours per week in certain disciplines, for admission. Other universities followed suit. States also adopted similar patterns for teacher preparation. Colleges and universities established regional associations that set their own standards for institutional membership, in areas such as library holdings, faculty size and qualifications, and endowments. Lutheran college presidents at Wittenberg and

Muhlenberg were among the leaders in establishing several of the early associations: Ohio in 1867, and the Middle States Association in 1887. Augustana College at Rock Island, Illinois, appeared on the first accreditation list published by the North Central Association in 1913, and five other midwestern Lutheran colleges were so recognized by 1916.

Not until late in the 19th century was the centrifugal movement of American Lutheranism arrested and replaced by a trend, however halting, toward unity. A merger of three Norwegian bodies in 1890 presaged this trend, and in 1917 more than 90 percent of all Norwegian Lutherans found their way into a single body called the Norwegian Lutheran Church of America (NLCA). A year later, in 1918, three segments of old colonial Lutheranism, split by the Civil War and by doctrinal issues, merged to form the United Lutheran Church in America (ULCA).

One of the results of merging church bodies was the drawing together of institutions related to each of the merging synods. Both the NLCA and the ULCA established boards of education, the ULCA embracing sixteen colleges and the NLCA four. Most of the other independent Lutheran bodies followed suit. The role of boards of education varied according to church policy. In the ULCA the board acted only in an advisory capacity, although it maintained a full-time staff and offered a variety of services to its colleges. Boards of the other Lutheran bodies tended to be supervisory, in some cases even determining college policies.[18]

Effects of World War and Depression

The sudden plunge of the United States into World War I in 1917 and its emergence into the tempestuous decade of the 1920s brought a host of new concerns both to colleges and churches. Enrollments were drastically reduced as the young men entered military service. Several colleges of German background were forced to defend their loyalty, and both churches and colleges that still used European languages felt public pressures to speed the transition to English. But as they emerged from the wartime experiences, Lutherans joined all of American higher education in a decade of unprecedented expansion. Enrollments exploded; facilities and faculties expanded. When the North Central Association announced in 1923 that no college could be accredited if it did not have at least a $500,000 endowment, virtually every Lutheran college was compelled to conduct a financial campaign, most of them for the first time in their history. Agendas of the National Lutheran Educational Conference dealt largely with issues of publicity, finance, student social life, and accreditation standards.

In large measure as a response to the cultural pressures exerted upon it during World War I, the Missouri Synod made sweeping changes in its system of education. In 1920 the old German gymnasium pattern was abandoned in favor of an American system of four-year high schools and two-year junior colleges. Curricular changes de-emphasized German and Latin and strengthened the natural and social sciences. During the 1930s, when enrollment declined, enrollment was opened to women and to general students not preparing for church vocations.

One of the salutary outcomes of this period of developing corporate consciousness among both colleges and church bodies was the beginning of an on-going process of self-examination and assessment of the nature of church-related higher education and, more specifically, Lutheran higher education. The financial collapse of 1929 and the ensuing depression forced the closing of several Lutheran academies and normal schools and severe rigors, but no closures of any of the colleges. Even crises of such magnitude called forth renewed examination of fundamental issues. During these years the Lutheran Educational Conference held joint sessions with the Council of Church Boards of Higher Education and the Liberal Arts College Movement. In 1930, five independent Lutheran synods, associated as the American Lutheran Conference, established a Commission on Higher Education that included presidents and faculty representatives from twelve colleges. In extended meetings over a two-year period, they not only discussed depression economics, but the strategies for maintaining the integrity of the liberal arts in the face of rising academic secularism. One of the outcomes was the establishment of the Lutheran Faculties Conferences, which has continued to supply a forum for such discussion for more than sixty years.

As the 1930s drew to a close, the grip of the Great Depression began to loosen. The community of Lutheran colleges emerged from a period that had capsuled war, prosperity, and economic disaster into two dramatic decades. Through this experience the colleges had reached a new degree of maturity and had become more closely knit as a community of self-consciously Lutheran institutions. As a group they had become identified with a well-defined movement in American higher education to advance the liberal arts.[19]

The Educational Explosion

If the experiences of Lutheran colleges in the decades of the 1920s and 1930s were traumatic, those of the 1940s, 1950s, and 1960s were cataclysmic. World War II itself saw the colleges virtually drained of male students, though many Lutheran campuses were fortunate in hosting military training programs that brought some relief, both in enrollments and finances. The real educational revolution occurred with the passage of the GI Bill of Rights in 1994, offering educational opportunities to all returning veterans. Colleges were swamped with students, and, aided by the government, feverishly sought to provide teachers and classrooms.

The Korean War added further complications as men were again called into service. But the national fright that swept the nation in 1957 when the Russians launched Sputnik had an even more drastic effect on higher education. The President of the United States took to the platform with passion, virtually demanding sweeping curricular reforms emphasizing science and mathematics in the public schools. Colleges, in turn, were expected to prepare the needed teachers. With the passage of the National Defense Education Act in 1958, the government served notice that higher education was to be used as an instrument of public policy, to further national manpower needs and foreign-policy goals. Massive government infusion of money for facilities, faculty, and programs, rising to even greater volume in the 1960s, made it almost impossible for colleges not to participate.

During this decade Lutheran college teachers thought seriously about the future of their institutions. The Washington office of the National Lutheran Educational Conference warned of the possible subversive effects of government largesse upon both the character and the curriculum of church-related liberal arts colleges. Five- and Ten-Year Master Plans were developed at every college, projecting enrollment, facilities, faculties, finances, and educational goals for the new age. Growth and expansion became the hallmarks of the times. Private gifts and church support rose to supplement government generosity. Lutheran college campuses blossomed with new science buildings, classrooms, athletic plants, libraries, student centers, and residence halls. The number of faculty members and the quality of their preparation increased. So, belatedly, did the levels of compensation. With such expansion, operational costs rose, and tuition followed, but students still flocked in, armed with GI funds, scholarships, state and federal grants and loans, and work-study awards. In one respect the 1960s could be described as the "Golden Decade." Never had college and university enrollments been so large. Never had there been so much money available for expansion, both from public and private sources.

The 1960s: Growth and Turmoil

For the church bodies that supported most of the Lutheran colleges in the United States, the decade of the 1960s also opened on a note of optimism. Significant mergers in 1959 and 1960 brought together ethnically rooted groups into two major denominations. The Lutheran Church in America (LCA) united more than three million members of five ethnic strains: German, Swedish, Danish, Finnish, and Slovak. The American Lutheran Church (TALC) brought together more than two million people of German, Norwegian, and Danish origin. The constituting synods of the LCA brought eighteen colleges and three junior colleges into their new church; those forming the TALC brought nine colleges and two junior colleges. In 1959, a new college, California Lutheran, was launched through the cooperative efforts of the merging churches.

Although the mergers did not directly influence the internal operation of related colleges, they did affect the patterns of relationship with each other and with the new church bodies. Both churches established new boards. The ALC Board of College Education maintained close oversight of its colleges and made annual financial grants to each institution. The Constitution of the LCA assigned primary responsibility for college relations to its 33 constituent regional synods. The LCA Board of College Education and Church Vocations was given advisory powers, but financial grants came from the synods. Patterns and governance varied widely among the individual institutions. Relations between the boards of the two new church bodies, however, were very cordial. Regular consultations and frequent cooperative programs were established to encourage close relations between administrators and faculty of both LCA and TALC colleges.

While Lutheran colleges and churches experienced significant growth and prosperity during the early 1960s, the decade was to establish its place in history on quite other grounds. It would become known as the decade of social revolution, anti-war protests, and racial conflict -- and the Lutheran colleges would share in its struggles. As late as 1965 there were virtually no black students on Lutheran campuses. But as the civil rights movement gained in intensity, most colleges launched recruitment and exchange programs to increase black enrollments. Numbers did increase, and instances of black activism on Lutheran campuses served to raise consciousness on the issues of civil rights. Campus protests against the military draft and the Vietnam War were more common. But Lutheran colleges, mostly small in size and located outside of urban centers, escaped the violence that exploded on many large university campuses. Demands for greater student autonomy and participation in college governance were more frequent causes for demonstrations and occasional sit-ins.

As the decade of the 1960s neared its close, the traditional climate of college support among the congregations of the church seemed to waver. Some thought they sensed a feeling among the colleges that government aid was more important than their ties with the church. Two colleges, Hartwick and Waterloo (in Canada), took the unprecedented step of severing their formal ties with the church. Rising tuitions, declining percentages of Lutheran students and faculty, evidences of the "new morality" on campuses, student demonstrations and occasional campus violence, the disappearance of required religion courses -- all tended to dim the image of the church college as a Christian oasis in an increasingly secularized and even violent society.[20]

Re-assessment of Church Relationships

As the 1970s began, campus violence subsided, but public enthusiasm for higher education also faded. Colleges began to pay the price of overexpansion. Red ink, observed one analyst, replaced broken glass as the hallmark of American higher education. Lutheran colleges, too, felt both the financial constraints and the erosion of confidence. In 1970, the Lutheran Educational Conference of North America (LECNA) commissioned an analysis of the status and prospects of Lutheran colleges and universities.

From this analysis emerged a Master Plan, urging greater cooperation among Lutheran colleges in the study of their history, their goals and purposes as Lutheran institutions, and the ways in which they could carry out their programs in the future. In response to the master plan, LECNA appointed a Commission on the Future that sponsored studies and publications throughout the 1970s dealing with church relationships, public policy, and the roots of Lutheran higher education.

In 1976 the LCA Department for Higher Education commissioned a comprehensive survey of the constituencies of its 18 colleges. More than 6,000 questionnaires were sent to pastors, lay persons, students, faculty, trustees, and administrators, asking whether the colleges were fulfilling expectations academically and as church-related institutions. Results reflected many of the concerns and critiques voiced during the 1960s and 1970s, but generally reaffirmed confidence in the colleges. In the same year, the biennial assembly of the LCA approved a theologically based statement defining the relation between the church and the colleges as a "partnership" of colleague institutions sharing a common concern.[21]

These documents provided an agenda for a churchwide series of regional forums involving colleges and representatives of their constituencies. At the same time, similar concerns were being pursued by the LCA and by other denominations and their colleges. The decade closed with a National Congress on Church-Related Colleges and Universities, which convened educators of twenty-three denominations in assemblies in Washington in 1978 and at Notre Dame University in 1980.

The same year, the Lutheran Educational Conference of North America devoted its annual meeting to a review of the multi-ethnic roots of the fifty colleges (including Canada) that were represented in its combined Lutheran membership. Sufficient interest in this theme was generated during subsequent meetings that in 1982 LECNA commissioned the first comprehensive history of Lutheran Higher Education in North America. The volume was published in 1985.

Recent Reorganizations of College Systems

Because of their primary character as schools for the preparation of church workers, the colleges of the Missouri system were not as directly affected by government educational policies and programs as other Lutheran institutions. Nor were the social conflicts of the 1960s felt as directly on their campuses. Of greatest significance for the Missouri system were the persistent challenges to the single-purpose character of its higher education program. Some inroads had been made during the depression years of the 1930s, when enrollments had declined sharply. But by 1970 the two-year prep colleges, already recruiting increasing numbers of general students, were requesting permission to become four-year institutions. By 1981, only two junior colleges remained. In addition, Christ College, a new four-year college, had been established in 1975 at Irvine, California.

Confronted by the fact that its colleges were no longer functioning solely for the preparation of church workers, but were assuming the character of liberal arts colleges, the Missouri Synod appointed a presidential commission in 1983 to review its entire system of higher education and to propose appropriate guidelines and structural revisions. The commission reported in 1986, offering proposals redefining the mission of the colleges, and strengthening the role of boards of regents in student recruitment and fund raising. Included in its report were criteria for college viability, according to which it recommended that two colleges be closed: St. John's in Winfield, Kansas, and St. Paul's in Concordia, Missouri.

Following the adoption and implementation of the commission report, the synod concluded that a completely new governance structure was needed to coordinate programs and effect economies of operation. A special task force was appointed for this purpose, and in 1990 it proposed a comprehensive plan for the Concordia University System. As adopted in 1992, it created a separate corporation, with the synod's Board of Higher Education serving as the corporate Board of Directors, bearing responsibility for the financial oversight of the colleges and universities and their church constituents. Individual colleges retained their administrative structures and their Boards of Regents.[22]

At present, the Concordia University System operates eleven degree-granting institutions, including seven four-year colleges: Concordia College in Ann Arbor, Michigan; Concordia Lutheran College in Austin, Texas; Concordia College in Bronxville, New York; Christ College Irvine in Irvine, California; Concordia College in Portland, Oregon; Concordia College in St. Paul, Minnesota; and Concordia College in Selma, Alabama. It also operates Concordia Teachers College in Seward, Nebraska, and two universities: Concordia University in River Forest, Illinois, and Concordia University Wisconsin in Mequon, Wisconsin. Valparaiso University, in Valparaiso, Indiana, continues to operate independently of synod control.

Some changes are taking place in the higher education system of the Wisconsin Synod during 1995. After a 130-year history, Northwestern College, its oldest degree-granting institution, is being merged with Martin Luther College in New Ulm, Minnesota. Wisconsin Lutheran College, formerly a two-year institution in Milwaukee, Wisconsin, has been elevated to four-year status.

The decade of the 1980s formed the backdrop for the most far-reaching merger of Lutheran church bodies in 250 years of North American history. Long-simmering resolves came to a head in 1980, when conventions of the LCA, the TALC, and a small offshoot of the Missouri Synod voted overwhelmingly to form a "new" Lutheran church. By 1987 the structure had been finalized, and on January 1, 1988, the Evangelical Lutheran Church in America (ELCA) came into being. With its 5,200,000 members, it became the fourth largest Protestant church body in the United States.

Twenty-nine colleges and universities became affiliates of the ELCA. The merger effected no changes in the internal administration of individual institutions, but patterns of church relationship assumed a variety of new forms. Financial support is now provided both by the national church and by groups of geographical synods. Patterns of governance follow previously established institutional practices. Some boards of regents are elected by associations of congregations, some by synods, some by the national church assembly. Some boards are self-perpetuating. Relations with the national church are maintained through the Division of Higher Education and Schools, which provides consultative and other services to colleges and universities. In 1991 student enrollment in the twenty-nine ELCA institutions totaled 53,216, of which 43,589 were full-time and 9,627 were part-time.[23]

Following is a list of colleges and universities affiliated with the Evangelical Lutheran Church in America, according to their founding dates: Gettysburg College in Gettysburg, Pennsylvania, 1832; Roanoke College in Salem, Virginia, 1842; Wittenberg University in Springfield, Ohio, 1845; Carthage College in Kenosha, Wisconsin, 1847; Muhlenberg College in Allentown, Pennsylvania, 1848; Capital University in Columbus, Ohio, 1850; Wartburg College in Waverly, Iowa, 1852; Newberry College in Newberry, South Carolina, 1856; Susquehanna University in Selinsgrove, Pennsylvania, 1868; Augustana College in Rock Island, Illinois, 1860; Augustana College in Sioux Falls, South Dakota, 1860; Luther College in Decorah, Iowa, 1861; Gustavus Adolphus College in St. Peter, Minnesota, 1852; Thiel College in Greenville, Pennsylvania, 1866; Augsburg College in Minneapolis, Minnesota, 1869; St. Olaf College in Northfield, Minnesota; 1874; Bethany College in Lindsborg, Kansas, 1881; Midland Lutheran College in Fremont, Nebraska, 1883; Wagner College in Staten Island, New York, 1883; Dana College in Blair, Nebraska, 1884; Concordia College in Moorhead, Minnesota,

1891; Lenoir-Rhyne College, Hickory, North Carolina, 1891; Pacific Lutheran University in Tacoma, Washington, 1891; Texas Lutheran College in Seguin, Texas, 1891; Upsala College in East Orange, New Jersey, 1893; Grand View College in Des Moines, Iowa, 1896; Suomi College in Hancock, Michigan, 1896; Waldorf College in Forest City, Iowa, 1903; and California Lutheran University in Thousand Oaks, California, 1959.

This essay is based upon material first published in *Lutheran Higher Education in North America* by Richard W. Solberg, copyright © 1985 Lutheran Educational Conference of North America. Used by permission of Augsburg Fortress.

Endnotes

1. Richard W. Solberg, *Lutheran Higher Education in North America*. Minneapolis: Augsburg Publishing House, 1985, pp. 12-20.
2. Joseph Henry Dubbs, *History of Franklin and Marshall College*. Lancaster, PA: Franklin and Marshall College Alumni Association, 1903, pp. 18-19.
3. Charles H. Glatfelter and Michael Bezilla, *A Salutary Influence: Gettysburg College, 1832-1985*, 2 vols. Gettysburg, PA: Gettysburg College, 1987.
4. Solberg, *Lutheran Higher Education*, pp. 94-112.
5. Donald L. Huber, *Educating Lutheran Pastors in Ohio, 1830-1980: A History of Trinity Lutheran Seminary and Its Predecessors* (Studies in American Religion, vol. 33). Lewiston, NY: The Edwin Millen Press, 1989; William A. Kinnison, *Wittenberg: A Concise History*. Springfield, OH: Wittenberg University, 1976.
6. For histories of many individual Lutheran colleges, see appended bibliography, and Thomas C. Hunt and James C. Carper, eds., *Religious Colleges and Universities in America: A Selected Bibliography*. New York and London: Garland Publishing, Inc., 1988, pp. 222-32.

7. Richard W. Solberg, "Foundations of the Missouri System of Higher Education," *Essays and Reports of the Lutheran Historical Conference* 11 (1984): 76-96.

8. Solberg, *Lutheran Higher Education*, pp. 122-36.

9. *Ibid.*, pp. 177-80.

10. Conrad Bergendoff, *Augustana: A Profession of Faith.* Rock Island, IL: Augustana College, 1969, pp. 29-49.

11. Ronald Sneen, *Through Trials and Triumphs: The History of Augustana College.* Sioux Falls, SD: Center for Western Studies, 1985.

12. David T. Nelson, *Luther College, 1861-1961.* Decorah, IA: Luther College Press, 1961, pp. 45-60.

13. Solberg, *Lutheran Higher Education*, pp. 225-48.

14. Doniver A. Lund, *Gustavus Adolphus College: A Centennial History.* St. Peter, MN: Gustavus Adolphus Press, 1963.

15. Thorvald Hansen, *We Laid Foundations Here: The Early History of Grand View College.* Des Moines, IA: Grand View College, 1972.

16. Arnold Stadius, "Suomi College and Seminary," in *The Finns in North America: A Social Symposium,* ed. by Ralph J. Jalkanen. East Lansing, MI: Michigan State University Press, 1969.

17. Solberg, *Lutheran Higher Education*, pp. 264-80.

18. *Ibid.*, pp. 280-91.

19. *Ibid.*, pp. 298-302.

20. *Ibid.*, pp. 303-10.

21. Richard W. Solberg and Merton P. Strommen, *How Church-Related Are Church-Related Colleges?* Philadelphia: Board of Publications, Lutheran Church in America, 1980; Arthur L. Olsen, ed., *Cooperation for the Future.* A Report of the Commission on the Future. Washington, DC: Lutheran Educational Conference of North America, 1976, pp. 6-12.

22. Lutheran Church-Missouri Synod, *Convention Proceedings, 1986,* pp. 189-93; *Convention Workbook, 1992,* pp. 265-68; *Convention Proceedings, 1922,* pp. 160-61.

23. Evangelical Lutheran Church in America, "Higher Education Trends Analysis, 1992," Division of Higher Education and Schools.

Bibliographic Entries

I. Institutional Histories

55.   Brolander, Glen E. *An Historical Survey of the Augustana College Campus*. Rock Island, IL: Augustana Historical Society, 1985.

Contains an historical atlas of Augustana College campus, detailing the growth of campus land and buildings during defined periods in college history from 1875 to 1985. A second part presents an extended descriptive commentary on each campus structure, past and present, including photographs.

56.   Butler, William, and William Strode, eds. *St. Olaf College -- A Pictorial History*. Lexington, KY: Harmony House Publishers, 1990.

Depicts the year 1988-89 in the life of St. Olaf College, through black-and-white and color photographs taken by Mitch Kezar of Black Star Photography. Also features a 36-page section of historical articles and photographs from St. Olaf archives.

57.   Engelhardt, Carroll. *On Firm Foundation Grounded: The First Century of Concordia College, 1891-1991*. Moorhead, MN: Concordia College, 1991.

Describes the founding and growth of a liberal arts college with a strong tradition of church relationship and Christian service. Reflects the religious and cultural context of the upper midwest and the historic commitment of Lutherans in that region to higher education.

58. Glatfelter, Charles H. and Michael Bezilla. *A Salutary Influence: Gettysburg College, 1832-1985.* 2 vols. Gettysburg, PA: Gettysburg College, 1987.

Offers a definitive treatment of the founding and history of the oldest Lutheran college in the United States. Includes a thorough study of the cultural climate in which Lutheran higher education emerged. Supersedes earlier histories of Gettysburg College and describes its significant development since World War II.

59. Halm, Dennis Ray. "A History of Christ College Irvine -- The First Thirty Years." Ed.D. dissertation, Pepperdine University, 1986.

Presents the story of the founding and early years of the Lutheran Church-Missouri Synod's youngest college. Also contains extensive bibliographic information.

60. Hansen, Thorvald. *Church Divided.* DesMoines, IA: Grand View College, 1992.

Chronicles the early stages of Danish-American Lutheranism and the division between followers of Grundtvig and Danish Lutheran Pietists. Provides the background for the founding of Grand View College and Dana College, representing each of the two opposing traditions.

61. Hiebert, Gary. *My Years at St. Olaf -- From Mellby to Mel.* Northfield, MN: Northfield Printing, 1988.

Contains 37 selected columns written by Hiebert and published in the *St. Paul Pioneer Press* from 1956 to 1986. Features St. Olaf faculty, staff, and programs. Illustrated.

62.   Huber, Donald L. *Educating Lutheran Pastors in Ohio, 1830-1980: A History of Trinity Lutheran Seminary and Its Predecessors.* Vol. 33 of *Studies in American Religion.* Lewiston, NY: The Edwin Millen Press, 1989.

63.   Jordahl, Leigh and Harris Kaasa. *Stability and Change: Luther College in its Second Century.* Decorah, IA: Luther College, 1986.

Deals with the growth of Luther College following its centennial year, 1961. Following a brief review of the first century, critical changes of the 1960s and the two most recent presidential administrations are examined.

64.   Kaden, Kenneth P. *A Century of Service: A Centennial History of Concordia College, St. Paul.* St. Louis, MO: Concordia Publishing House, 1992.

Contains brief capsule history in opening chapter, followed by a special historical review of student life. Records major institutional developments through eight successive presidential administrations. Appendix has complete list of faculty, boards, and administrators.

65.   Kinnison, William A. "Wittenberg: Prototype of the Mature Church-Related College." In *Tradition and Change: A Wittenberg Sesquicentennial Symposium.* Springfield, OH: Wittenberg University, 1992, pp. 1-20.

Traces the history and church-relationship of Wittenberg University from its founding in 1845 as an effort to interpret Lutheran theology and learning in a distinctively American context. Concludes by citing five distinguishing features of a mature church-relationship as developed in the experience of Wittenberg University.

66. Kunze, Johann Christopher. *Autobiography.* trans. by Donald H. Mill. Syracuse, NY: Bicentennial Joint Synodical Committee of the Ministerium of New York, the Lutheran Church in America Synods of Metropolitan New York, New England, New Jersey, and Upper New York, 1986.

Presents a personal account of the European background of a pioneer Lutheran educational missionary, and the founder of the "Seminarium," one of the earliest Lutheran institutions of advanced learning in America in 1773.

67. Lee, Art, and Alumni Board. *The Rise and Demise of Scandinavia Academy and Central Wisconsin College.* Scandinavia, WI: Scandinavia Academy/Central Wisconsin College Alumni Association, 1992.

68. Lund, Doniver A. *Gustavus Adolphus College: Celebrating 125 Years.* St. Peter, MN: Gustavus Adolphus College, 1987.

Traces the 125-year history of Gustavus Adolphus, a college with a strong Swedish-American tradition. Updates an earlier centennial account, focusing on the modern development of the college as one of Minnesota's strongest liberal arts institutions.

69. Miller, Mark F. *Dear Old Roanoke: A Sesquicentennial Portrait 1842-1992.* Macon, GA: Mercer University Press, 1992.

Traces the history of Roanoke College from its beginning as a prep school in 1842, its chartering in 1853, its survival of the Civil War crisis, and its growth in the 20th century. Contains over 400 photographs, as well as vignettes of significant persons and events.

70. Nordquist, Philip A. *Educating for Service: Pacific Lutheran University, 1890-1990.* Tacoma, WA: Pacific Lutheran University, 1990.

Relates the history of the only Lutheran university in the Pacific Northwest, with special emphasis on its growth in size and maturity since World War II. Emphasizes its institutional commitment of service to community and church.

71. Norris, Jeff L. and Ellis G. Boatmon. *Fair Star: A Centennial History of Lenoir-Rhyne College.* Norfolk: VA: The Donning Company, 1990.

Presents a pictorial and narrative history of Lenoir-Rhyne College through 100 years. Includes 300 photographs, a variety of tables reflecting college development, lists of distinguished alumni, current and past faculty and staff.

72. Oyos, Lynwood E. *A Noble Calling: Teacher Education Programs at Lutheran Normal School and Augustana College, 1889-1989.* Sioux Falls, SD: Center for Western Studies, 1989.

Provides a history of the teacher training program at Lutheran Normal School in Sioux Falls, SD, from 1889 to its merger with Augustana College in 1918, and the subsequent development of similar programs at Augustana College through 1989.

73. Park, James B., ed. *A History of the Lutheran Church in South Carolina, 1971-1987*. Columbia, SC: The South Carolina Synod of the Evangelical Lutheran Church in America, 1988.

    Supplements an earlier volume edited by Paul G. McCullough, *et al.*, and published by the Synod in 1971. Contains a sketch updating the history of Newberry College, on pages 90-95 and 351-52.

74. Schmidt, Allan H. *A College on a Mission: Leadership of Concordia College, Seward, Nebraska, 1941-1991*. Lincoln, NB: University of Nebraska, 1992.

    Examines the roles and experiences of presidents and professors in developing the mission of the college over a 50-year period.

75. Shaw, Joseph M. *Dear Old Hill*. Northfield, MN: St. Olaf College, 1992.

    Traces the development of the physical campus, grounds, and buildings of St. Olaf College, from the college's founding in 1874 to the present. Contains much informal college history and lore, anecdotes, glimpses of campus life and tradition, and vignettes of campus personalities. Narrative enriched by a pleasing selection of historical photographs.

76. Sneen, Donald J. *Through Trials and Triumphs: A History of Augustana College*. Sioux Falls, SD: Center for Western Studies, 1985.

    Traces the 125-year history of Augustana College from its beginnings in Illinois, its early odyssey through Wisconsin, Iowa, and South Dakota, and its development as the largest four-year liberal arts college in South Dakota since its location in Sioux Falls in 1920.

77. Toppe, Carleton. *Holding the Course: Northwestern College 125.* Milwaukee, WI: Northwestern Publishing House, 1990.

78. Wahlers, Mark Edward. "A Cloud of Witnesses: The History of Concordia Lutheran College of Texas." Ph.D. dissertation, University of Texas, 1989.

Presents college history with special reference to educational trends reflecting changes in the higher education system of the Missouri Synod: toward more local control, more liberal curriculum, and a broader student spectrum.

79. Wiederaenders, Arthur G. *TLC's First Century: An Age of Growing Excellence, 1891-1991.* Lubbock, TX, Craftsman Printers, 1990.

Updates an earlier volume by the same author, commemorating the centennial of Texas Lutheran College. Contains résumé of early years and chronologies of recent presidencies, together with a topical treatment of recent developments.

II. General Literature

80. *Affirming the Origins and Value of Lutheran Higher Education.* In *Papers and Proceedings, LECNA.* Washington, DC: Lutheran Educational Conference of North America, 1986.

Includes addresses delivered on the occasion of the publication of the first general history of Lutheran higher education in North America. Critiques and reflections by three leading Lutheran church historians follow.

81. Anderson, Philip J. "Swedish-American 'College Mania' in the Nineteenth Century." In *Nordics in America: The Future of Their Past*. Edited by Odd S. Lovoll. Northfield, MN: Norwegian-American Historical Association, 1993, pp. 26-36.

Describes the proliferation of religious-cultural academies and colleges among Swedish-Americans after 1880.

82. Benne, Robert. "Recovering a Christian College From Suspicious Tension, Toward Christian Presence." *Lutheran Forum*, 27, 2 (May 1993): 58-70.

Provides a typology of Christian colleges, ranging between the extremes of a "Christian cocoon" and "amicable or bitter divorce." Contrasts this with the preponderant decline of Christian character among church-related colleges. Followed by a symposium of responses from ten representatives of ELCA colleges and universities.

83. Benson, Paul. "A Cappella Choirs in Scandinavian-American Lutheran Colleges." *Norwegian-American Studies* 32. Northfield, MN: NAHA, 1989, pp. 221-45.

Cites the distinctive contribution of Scandinavian Lutheran colleges to the development of unaccompanied chorale singing in the U.S. Recognizes F. Melius Christiansen, founder of the St. Olaf Choir, as pioneer and model for choir masters in Lutheran colleges. In addition to the St. Olaf Choir, special mention is given to those of Concordia College, Moorhead, MN; Pacific Lutheran; Augsburg; Luther; and Augustana College, Rock Island, IL.

84.   Berger, David O. "Whither Higher Education in Missouri?" *Lutheran Education* 127 (January/February 1992): 124-41; 128 (November/December 1992): 64-80.

Places the higher education system of the Lutheran Church-Missouri Synod under scrutiny in the light of contemporary critiques of church colleges. By extending its program beyond the preparation of church workers to general and liberal arts education, it becomes more vulnerable to the hazards of secularization. Recommends instead "a distinctive approach to the academic disciplines and our western heritage from the perspective of biblical faith as reflected in the Lutheran confessions."

85.   Brauer, Jerald C. "Context and Tradition in Higher Education." In *Tradition and Change: A Wittenberg Sesquicentennial Symposium*. Springfield, OH: Wittenberg University, 1992, pp. 21-34.

Deals with the tension in contemporary higher education between those who wish to eliminate or ignore the role of tradition and those who argue for creative interplay between context and tradition. Affirms a special role for church-related colleges in the latter group and sees the Lutheran conception of the Christian faith as especially suited to embrace such an inclusive view of higher education.

86.   Christopherson, Myrvin F. "When is a College a College of the Church?" *Lutheran Partners* (March/April 1993): 13-16.

Compares the religious and social climate of Lutheran colleges in the 1950s and 1990s. Broader clientele and broader mission demand stronger and more religiously committed leadership.

87. Clark, Kenneth, *et al.* "Strengthening Presidential Leadership." *Papers and Proceedings of LECNA*, 1987, pp. 7-45.

88. Dovre, Paul J. "Through a Glass Darkly: Mission in the 21st Century." *The Cresset* (December 1991).

89. Gengenbach, Connie (ed). *Faith, Learning, and the Church College.* Northfield, MN: St. Olaf College, 1989.

Contains the substance of three sermons on education delivered by Dr. Sittler, expounding the biblical and theological foundations for the church's involvement in higher education. Includes introductory essay by Dr. Harold Ditmanson.

90. Glatfelter, Charles. "Gettysburg Seminary and College during the Battle of Gettysburg." *Essays and Reports of the Lutheran Historical Conference* 14 (1992): pp. 184-90.

91. Hamre, James S. *Georg Sverdrup: Educator, Theologian, Churchman.* Northfield, MN: Norwegian-American Historical Association, 1986.

Interprets the life and work of Georg Sverdrup, a leading Norwegian American theologian, educator, and churchman. As President of Augsburg Seminary and College, Sverdrup championed an approach to theological education that sought to break away from an elitist classical curriculum and to prepare clergy oriented to the life of free congregations in a free society. His strong theological bent slowed the development of Augsburg as a liberal arts college.

92. Hamre, James S. "Three Spokesmen for Norwegian Lutheran Academies: Schools for Church, Heritage, Society." *Norwegian American Studies* 30. Northfield, MN: NAHA, 1985, pp. 221-46.

Provides useful background for understanding the origins of several Norwegian American church colleges as preparatory schools for young immigrants.

93. Huegli, Albert G. and William Lehmann, Jr. "New Directions for Lutheran Higher Education." *Lutheran Education* 128 (November/December 1992): 81-95.

Supports the trend toward general and liberal arts education in the Missouri system. Recognizes dangers of secularization, but opposes limiting scope of system to church vocations.

94. Johnson, K. Glen. "The Marks of a Lutheran College or University." Lina R. Meyer Lecture, Lutheran Educational Conference of North America, 1994. *Papers and Proceedings, LECNA,* 1994.

Reviews current literature on church-related colleges and proposes six essential characteristics for Lutheran institutions.

95. Johnston, Paul I. "What Reu Thought About Contemporary Education." *Concordia Historical Institute Quarterly* 65 (Fall 1992): 106-25.

Describes the educational philosophy of Johann Michael Reu, 1869-1943, pioneer theologian and educator of the Iowa Synod and the American Lutheran Church. Includes his rationale for the liberal arts college, both for general education and as preparation for theological study.

96. Kinnison, William A. "The Past as Prologue in Lutheran Higher Education: The Pursuit of Opportunity." *Papers and Proceedings of LECNA*, 1985, pp. 7-20.

97. Klein, Christa Ressmeyer. "Perspectives on the Current Status of and Emerging Policy Issues for Theological Schools and Seminaries." Available from Association of Governing Boards of Universities and Colleges, One Dupont Circle, Suite 400, Washington, DC 20036.

98. Lagerquist, DeAne. "As Sister, Wife, and Mother: Education for Young Norwegian-American Lutheran Women." *Norwegian-American Studies* 33 (1992): 99-138.

   Compares the educational experiences of women from 1874 to 1920 in three Lutheran schools: St. Olaf College, Lutheran Ladies' Seminary at Red Wing, MN, and Lutheran Normal School at Madison, MN. Cites differences and similarities in philosophy and practice.

99. Lutheran Educational Conference of North America. *Papers and Proceedings, 1987-1994.* In archives of the Evangelical Lutheran Church in America, 8765 West Higgins Road, Chicago, IL 60631.

   Comprises valuable repository of papers and addresses dealing with contemporary concerns of Lutheran higher education. Annual volumes contain papers and commentaries delivered at annual meetings dealing with college history, church-related identity, international consciousness, leadership, and public policy.

100. *Lutheran Higher Education -- Facing Three Great Challenges,* in *Papers and Proceedings, LECNA.* Washington, DC: Lutheran Educational Conference of North America, 1991.

Contains essays and addresses by educational leaders dealing with sources of financial support, the fulfilling of a global mission, and church relationships.

101. Marty, Martin, *et al.* "Teaching and Research at CU: A New Symposium on an Old Conundrum." *The Cresset* (April 1989): 12-20.

Presents the views of five Lutheran college professors from five different disciplines on the issue of scholarly research versus undergraduate teaching in liberal arts colleges.

102. McGinn, Bernard. "The Letter and the Spirit: Spirituality as an Academic Discipline." *The Cresset* (June 1993): 13-22.

Offers an historical definition of spirituality, and claims that it is possible to teach spirituality in and through traditional academic disciplines such as theology, ethics, and history.

103. *Mission of the Evangelical Lutheran Church in American Colleges and Universities: The Joseph A. Sittler Symposium.* Chicago: The Evangelical Lutheran Church in America, Division for Education, and the Council of College Presidents, 1989.

Includes a tribute to Joseph Sittler by ELCA Bishop Herbert Chilstrom, and four substantive papers on the mission of ELCA colleges and universities: Martin Marty on the historical perspective, Robert W. Jenson on the theological, Will H. Herzfeld on the sociological, and Mary Hull Mohr on the liberal arts.

104. Nielsen, John Mark. "Tracing Threads: N.F.S. Grundtvig, the Danish Folk High School Movement, and the Elderhostel Experience." In *Nordics in America: The Future of Their Past*. Edited by Odd S. Lovoll. Northfield, MN: NAHA, 1993, pp. 7-46.

Identifies a close relationship between the Folk High School Movement brought to the U.S. by Danish immigrants, and the recent development of the Elderhostel program by American colleges.

105. Nordquist, Philip. "You Must Raise Your Own Crop: Lutheran Higher Education on the Pacific Coast." *Essays and Reports of the Lutheran Historical Conference* 12 (1986): 122-47.

Describes the variety of ventures, some successful and many unsuccessful, into higher education by Lutheran synods on the Pacific Coast, beginning in 1888. Highlights the emergence of four Lutheran colleges and universities from Washington state to southern California.

106. Parsonage, Robert Rue. "The Lutheran Contribution to Church-Related Higher Education: A Comparative Perspective." *Papers and Proceedings, LECNA*, 1986, pp. 13-24.

107. Pelikan, Jaroslav. *The Idea of the University: A Reexamination*. New Haven, CT: Yale University Press, 1992.

108. Ruppe, Loret Miller, *et al*. "Increasing International Dimensions of Luther Higher Education." *Papers and Proceedings, LECNA*, 1988, pp. 7-32.

109. Sernett, Gilbert. "Intellectual and Social History of Lutheran Education." *Lutheran Education* 128 (September/October 1992): 17-28.

     Traces Lutheran educational thought from Luther to C.F.W. Walther to the Missouri ideal of parochial education.

110. *Seventy-five Years of LECNA: The Pursuit of Opportunity*, in *Papers and Proceedings, LECNA*. Washington, DC: Lutheran Educational Conference of North America, 1985.

     Views the history and future potential of LECNA as a forum for the discussion of major issues in Lutheran higher education and for promoting institutional cooperation.

111. Solberg, Richard W. "Footnotes from Page 400." *Papers and Proceedings*. LECNA, 1986, pp. 7-12.

     Introduces the publication of the LECNA history, *Lutheran Higher Education in North America*, acknowledges its sponsors and contributors, and states its purposes.

112. Solberg, Richard W. "Foundations of the Missouri System of Higher Education." *Essays and Reports of the Lutheran Historical Conference* 11, 1984, 76-96.

    Traces the historical development of the Missouri system of higher education, primarily focused on the preparation of pastors and church workers. Beginning as the projection of the German "gymnasium," it gradually moved toward the prevalent American model of the four-year baccalaureate college, yet retaining a strong program of theological education.

113. Stadwalt, Kurt. "Luther Among the Humanists: Religion Meets the Liberal Arts." *Lutheran Education* 128 (March/April 1992): 217ff.

    Sees Luther's support of the humanism of Melanchthon and Erasmus, and his own strong recommendation for the study of history, languages, literature, and music as seeds of modern Lutheran liberal arts education.

114. *Tradition and Change: Toward a Mature Relationship Between Church and College: A Wittenberg Sesquicentennial Symposium.* Springfield, OH: Wittenberg University, 1992.

    Contains a series of three addresses delivered by William Kinnison, Jerald Brauer, and George M. Marsden on the 150th anniversary of the founding of Wittenberg University. Traces the history of Wittenberg's relationship with the Lutheran church and the effort to find balance between tradition and the contemporary context in church-related higher education without succumbing to the mounting threat of secularization.

115. Trusty, Lance. "All Talk and No Kash: Valparaiso University and the Ku Klux Klan [How Lutherans Outbid the KKK to Buy Valparaiso University]." *Indiana Magazine of History* 82 (1986): 1-36.

116. Wisnefske, Ned. "The Lutheran College: A Community of Learning, A Community of Faith." Lina R. Meyer Lecture, Lutheran Educational Conference of North America, 1993. *Papers and Proceedings, LECNA.* Washington, DC: LECNA, 1993, pp. 6-13.

CHAPTER 5
Reformed Colleges and Seminaries

Peter P. DeBoer

What is it that marks colleges and theological seminaries in North America as "Reformed"?

In the history of at least some of those who would call themselves Reformed, a single crisp answer is not easy to come by. For example, James Bratt suggests that the intellectual history of the Dutch in America, at least early in the twentieth century, is the story of debate over the meaning of "Reformed" or "American Reformed." And the debate resulted in at least four "warring" factions[1] whose differences still play a discernible role in contemporary Reformed Christian affairs.

Surely any respectable answer to our question about Reformed colleges and seminaries must indicate ties to the Protestant Reformation of the sixteenth century in western Europe. Hence, if certain churches are "Reformed" because they are rooted in the Reformation, then schools that are the offshoots of such churches should be considered Reformed. "Reformed" denotes something Protestant in the Calvinist tradition in distinction from something Protestant in the Lutheran tradition. And within the Calvinist tradition, "Reformed" suggests continental origins in Switzerland, Germany, France, and especially the Netherlands, whereas "Presbyterian" denotes origins in England and Scotland.[2]

Their theology based on the Belgic, Heidelberg, and Dort confessions, the Reformers -- according to Philip Schaff -- declared that the canonical Scriptures are the only source and rule of faith. They therefore affirmed (a) the absolute supremacy of the Word of God, (b) the absolute supremacy of the grace of Christ, and (c) the universal priesthood of believers (by which they declared the right and duty of laity not only to read the Bible but to take part in the government and all public offices of the church).[3] Within the Reformed Christian ecclesiastical tradition, the triple stress on the importance of the sermon as "preached Word," on sound doctrine, and an educated clergy led Reformers everywhere to establish schools, colleges, and seminaries.

This chapter is testimony to the vigor of that enduring Reformed legacy in North America. In the following essay the institutions are listed from the earliest to the most recent. For the most part, the schools describe themselves since the descriptors chosen are from college and seminary catalogs and other promotional resources.

New Brunswick Theological Seminary, located in New Brunswick, New Jersey, was founded in 1784 to train ministers for the Reformed Church in America. As such it is the oldest of the Reformed Christian colleges and seminaries and, in fact, it is the first theological seminary established in the United States. In 1810 the seminary was moved from New York City to the campus of Queens College (now Rutgers University). Queens College was established in 1766 by the Reformed Church and, for half a century, the two institutions shared the same facilities. The present seminary campus was established in 1856. Today the seminary offers theological education both at New Brunswick and at St. John's University at Jamaica in Queens, New York. The seminary is sponsored by the Reformed Church in America and "serves the sovereign God who in Christ, by the power of the

Spirit, is redeeming the creation, reconciling a divided humanity, and establishing righteousness on earth." Its mission is to prepare men and women for educated and faithful leadership in the church, particularly in congregations of the Reformed Church (though not limited to these), but also in specialized ministries serving church and society. New Brunswick Theological Seminary is accredited by the Association of Theological Schools, with its two divisions licensed respectively by the states of New Jersey and New York.

Geneva College, in Beaver Falls, Pennsylvania, was opened for the first time in 1848 when the Reverend J.B. Johnston -- a pastor in the Reformed Presbyterian Church -- built a small brick building with the assistance of a couple of theological students in Northwood, Ohio, and called it Geneva Hall. The name was changed to Geneva College in 1873, and in 1880 it moved from Northwood to Beaver Falls. The college, now enrolling approximately 1,400 students, has been accredited by the Middle States Association since 1923 to offer bachelor's degrees and a master of arts in professional psychology. Geneva College, established by the Reformed Presbyterian Church, is governed by a Board of Corporators elected by that Church who, in turn, elect the Trustees who manage and administer the college. The mission of the college is to educate and minister to a diverse community of students for the purpose of developing servant-leaders able to transform society for the Kingdom of Christ.

Central College, at Pella, Iowa, was founded in 1853 by pioneer settlers and officially opened for classes in the fall of 1854. Originally a Baptist institution, Central was transferred from Baptist control to the Reformed Church in America in 1916 and continues close ties to the Reformed Church. Central College, "a liberal arts college in the Christian tradition," aims to promote dialog between the Christian faith and the perspectives, values, and methodologies of the various disciplines, and through teaching and modeling to provide the members of the Central community assistance in their private and corporate lives. The college is accredited by the North Central Association and enrolls approximately 1,500 students on its 130-acre campus. The college is governed by a board, a majority of whose members are from the Reformed Church in America.

Hope College, located in Holland, Michigan, marks its beginnings in 1851, only four years after immigrants from the Netherlands founded the city of Holland. They built a Pioneer School that soon evolved into the Holland Academy. By 1862, the academy enrolled its first college class, which led to the chartering of Hope College in 1866. Today, Hope College, with a student body of just under 3,000, is a four-year liberal arts undergraduate college that is affiliated, like Central of Iowa and Northwestern in Orange City, Iowa, with the Reformed Church of America. It is accredited by a variety of agencies, including the North Central Association. It believes "that a vital faith, which provides both the incentive and dynamic for learning and living, is central to education and life."

Western Theological Seminary, located in Holland, Michigan, marks 1866 as its natal year. For it was then that several members of the senior class of Hope College petitioned and received permission from the Reformed Church in America to pursue theological studies within a Theological Department of Hope College. Though theological education was suspended at Hope College in 1877 due to disastrous fires and difficult economic conditions, the program was reintroduced in 1884. By action of the General Synod, Western Seminary began a separate and independent status in 1885. Today, approximately 150 students are enrolled in a variety of programs at the seminary, still operated and controlled by the General Synod of the Reformed Church in America through its Board of Theological Education.

Calvin College, in Grand Rapids, Michigan, marks 1876 as its founding date. In that year the Christian Reformed Church adopted a six-year curriculum for ministerial training. Students spent the first four years in the Literary Department and the last two years in the Theological Department within an institution then called the Theological School. In 1894, students who were not pre-theological were permitted to enroll, though the expanded curriculum and the staff to teach it were not added until 1900. By 1900, the Theological School was divided into a Literary Department which provided four years of preparatory work of a secondary nature for all students, plus an additional "collegiate" year for theological students, and a three-year Theological Department (or seminary, proper). By 1906, a second "collegiate" year was added, the four years of preparatory work and the two college-level years now constituting officially a John Calvin Junior College. By 1910, a third year of college work was added (and the "junior" college label dropped), though it was not until 1920 that the fourth year came into existence. Calvin has been awarding bachelor of arts degrees regularly since 1921. Calvin is owned and operated by the Christian Reformed Church, enrolls approximately 3,600 students, and is accredited by the North Central Association. It offers a variety of programs of a general, professional, and pre-professional nature at the bachelor's and master's levels that reflect a strong commitment to the liberal arts and sciences. At Calvin College, students are encouraged to develop value judgments grounded in a knowledge of their relationship to God, to themselves, to their fellow human beings, and to the world, and to acknowledge the Lordship of Jesus Christ in all areas of life.

Calvin Theological Seminary (CTS) is owned, supported, and governed by the Christian Reformed Church in North America. Located in Grand Rapids, Michigan, the seminary is named "Calvin" after the sixteenth-century reformer who was a dominant influence on subsequent Reformed, Congregational, Presbyterian, and other churches. His beliefs, which he shared with others, are expressed in three confessions accepted as foundational by the Christian Reformed Church: "The Belgic Confession" (1561), the "Heidelberg Catechism" (1563), and the "Canons of Dort" (1618-1619), and are basic to the seminary's existence. The term "theological" intends to express the premium placed on an intellectually superior education. As a "seminary" CTS is a professional school where experience and skill in ministering the Word are fostered through diverse field education experiences. CTS began in 1876 with one professor and several students who met in rented quarters. Closely knit with Calvin as college, the theological school has moved several times, and is now located with the college, though independent in organization from the college, on the Knollcrest campus. Accredited by the Association of Theological Schools, CTS offers several degree programs: the Master of Divinity program for those intending an ordained ministry in the churches; several Master of Arts programs aimed at church education, missions, church growth, and the like; and two advanced-degree programs, the Master of Theology and the Ph.D. program designed for deepening understanding in theological disciplines and preparation for teaching at college, university, or seminary levels.

Northwestern College, located in Orange City, Iowa, is sponsored by the Reformed Church in America, and now enrolls more than a thousand students. The college, begun in 1928, was originally incorporated as Northwestern Classical Academy in 1882. The academy and college coexisted until 1961, the year that marked the first graduating class of the now four-year college and the last class of the academy. Over time the emphasis of the institution has been shaped by changing needs. Early on, the academy aimed chiefly to prepare young men for ministry in the Reformed Church in America. Later, the academy and the two-year college accented teacher preparation. Since the mid-1960s, a broader program of liberal studies was introduced, leading to North Central accreditation in 1970. Today the college offers the associate and bachelor of arts degrees, and the master of arts in elementary education. Embracing the belief that Jesus Christ is Lord of all, the college promotes a comprehensive integration of faith, learning, and living to prepare students for lives of service to God and humankind.

The Theological School of the Protestant Reformed Churches, now located on Ivanrest Avenue in Grandville, Michigan, began shortly after several consistories and their pastors had been deposed, in January, 1925, by both Classis Grand Rapids West and Classis Grand Rapids East of the Christian Reformed Church. While still operating under the temporarily adopted name of Protesting Christian Reformed Churches, this *ad hoc* organization decided in March, 1925, that it needed a theological school. The Theological School opened in June, 1925, at its Eastern Avenue location in Grand Rapids. After another temporary location, the school moved to rather permanent quarters within the basement of the large First Protestant Reformed Church on Fuller Avenue in Grand Rapids. Recently the school moved to a ten-acre suburban campus on Ivanrest Avenue in Grandville, Michigan. The basis of instruction at the seminary is these truths: the infallible inspiration of the Scriptures and their authority in doctrine and life; the five points of Calvinism (unconditional election; total depravity; particular atonement; irresistible grace; and the preservation of the saints); and the unconditional covenant of grace made by God with his elect people. The Three Forms of Unity (the "Heidelberg Catechism," the "Belgic Confession," and the "Canons of Dort"), historically maintained by Reformed churches, are the confessional basis of the Theological School of the Protestant Reformed Churches.

The Reformed Bible College was chartered in 1939 and enrolled its first students in January, 1940. It is located in Grand Rapids, Michigan, though its location within the city has changed over time, from rented quarters on Wealthy Street, S.E., to Eastern Avenue, to more permanent quarters on Robinson Road, and most recently to the East Beltline campus. It began as the Reformed Bible Institute with an evangelism and missionary emphasis, chiefly focused on the formal study of the Bible. Since the early 1960s, after becoming accredited by the American Association of Bible Colleges, the Institute became the Reformed Bible College. Collegiate status was solidified when, in 1970, the state of Michigan approved its Bachelor of Religious Education program, the first graduates receiving their bachelor's degrees in 1972. The institution is supported largely by members of the

Christian Reformed Church and governed by a board whose members are from the CRC.

Covenant College, located on Lookout Mountain in Dade County, Georgia, overlooks Chattanooga, Tennessee. The college was organized as a Christian liberal arts college in 1955 by the Bible Presbyterian Synod, and began operations that fall at the Pasadena City Church in Pasadena, California. In 1956 the college moved to a suburb of St. Louis, Missouri, where, aided by an influx of professors from Faith Theological Seminary near Philadelphia, Covenant became a four-year liberal arts college and a three-year theological seminary. By 1963, growth of both institutions made the St. Louis facilities inadequate, permitting the college -- now an agency of the Reformed Presbyterian Church, Evangelical Synod -- to purchase in 1964 a former luxury hotel on the crest of Lookout Mountain for the opening of classes that fall. In 1982 the Reformed Presbyterian Church, Evangelical Synod joined the Presbyterian Church in America. Covenant College is now an agency of the PCA. Today this 250-acre campus enrolls approximately 600 students in a variety of bachelor and associate degree programs that are accredited by the Southern Association.

Dordt College, at Sioux Center in northwest Iowa, was organized in 1953 as the Midwest Christian Junior College. Classes began in the fall of 1955. In 1956 the name was changed to Dordt College, and in 1961 the decision was made to expand the two-year college to four. In September 1963, the first class of third-year students was added, and 1965 saw the first class of graduates receive the bachelor's degree. Today, Dordt, accredited by the North Central Association, enrolls about 1,100 students on a 45-acre campus. Founded primarily to train teachers, Dordt now graduates students from a wide variety of liberal and applied-arts fields, including master's work in education. The chief means for achieving the educational task at Dordt is a curriculum intent on revealing a kingdom perspective and serviceable insights to students expected to carry out their tasks in loving obedience.

Trinity Christian College, Palos Heights, Illinois, looks back to April, 1956, when a group of interested business and professional persons drafted a constitution and incorporated as the Trinity Christian College Association. In 1959 the association purchased the Navajo Hills Golf Course in Palos Heights to serve as a campus, and classes began -- after the college was granted a charter by the State of Illinois -- in the fall of that year. A third year of studies was introduced in the fall of 1969, and a fourth in 1970. The first baccalaureate degrees were awarded in May, 1971. This Christian college aims to provide biblically informed liberal arts education at the undergraduate level in the Reformed tradition for its more than 600 students. While maintaining a theoretical approach to the disciplines, undergirded with a strong core curriculum in philosophy, history, English, and theology, the college has enhanced its offerings to provide students with a broad base of programs in professional areas such as business, education, and nursing, in addition to the traditional liberal arts. The college is accredited by the North Central Association.

The *Reformed Theological Seminary* (RTS), begun in Jackson, Mississippi, in 1966, is today a multi-campus, independent institution intending to serve the church in all branches of evangelical Christianity, though especially those of the Presbyterian and Reformed family. Besides the Jackson campus, the seminary is now located at Orlando, Florida (1989), and Charlotte, North Carolina (1992), as well as serving students at three extension sites: in Los Angeles, California; Washington, D.C.; and Vienna, Austria. The seminary was born in the midst of a "modernist controversy" out of concern that the Presbyterian Church in the U.S. and its seminaries had become less and less loyal to the Bible and its inerrancy, with an equal concern that the general church membership was not aware of this "insidious assault" on an infallible Word. Therefore, to insure that the original purpose and doctrinal distinctives of the seminary be maintained, each member of the Board of Trustees, faculty, and other advisors is required to subscribe annually to statements of belief and covenant that affirm something of the following: (a) that all Scripture is verbally inspired and without error, and (b) that Reformed theology as set forth in the "Westminster Confession of Faith" and the Larger and Shorter Catechisms is a system of doctrine taught in the Scripture. RTS from its beginnings has attempted to tie together Scriptural integrity, academic excellence, and evangelistic zeal. It offers a variety of master's programs in biblical studies, theological studies, Christian Education, missiology, marriage and family therapy, divinity, and theology; and it offers doctrinal programs in ministry and missiology. It is accredited by both the Association of Theological Schools in the United States and Canada and the Commission on Colleges of the Southern Association of Colleges and Schools.

Mid-America Reformed Seminary (MARS), located in Orange City, Iowa, opened its doors to students for the first time in the fall of 1982. As such, it is the youngest of all the institutions described in this chapter. Given an eagerness to stress the high calling of preaching and teaching the gospel of the Lord Jesus Christ as the principal means of grace for the conversion of sinners, the founders decided that ministerial students at MARS (a) must be trained to proclaim that gospel fearlessly and faithfully, in exegesis and pulpit style, (b) must be aware of the Reformed biblical and confessional heritage as well as having knowledge of the spirits of the present age, and (c) they must develop sensitivity to non-Reformed world views that continue to shape the world. Closely associated with the Christian Reformed Church, the seminary is not governed by the rules of that church nor any other. Its education is therefore marked by confessional allegiances (to the "Belgic Confession," the "Canons of Dort," the "Heidelberg Catechism," and the Westminster Standards) rather than denominational affiliation. The seminary offers the Master of Divinity degree program (for which a bachelor's degree is required) and a Theological Diploma (for students with limited undergraduate preparation). Recent developments suggest a likely move in location from Iowa to Dyer, Indiana, by 1995.

Given such brief histories, it may be difficult for the reader to comprehend something of the dynamics that constitute the very life of these institutions. For they share much in common and yet differ in important ways.

Clearly all of these schools, in the tradition of the Reformation, indicate an enormous respect for the intellect, for the liberal arts and sciences, for high standards of achievement, and the like. The fact that most of them have sought and achieved accreditation by the most appropriate accrediting agencies would reinforce the point.

Yet that, though supportive of being Reformed, would not get to the heart of the matter. Deep down and rather uniformly these schools give evidence of zeal for developing and maintaining a rational historical Christian faith that addresses contemporary challenges while being self-consciously rooted in the Word and in the creeds associated with the Reformed tradition. Many of them, acknowledging the lordship of Jesus Christ, show maturing signs of servanthood, sensitivity to social issues, to issues of justice and peace.

But there are also differences, some of which are related to differences in function between colleges and seminaries. The seminaries would be centrally concerned with disclosing such fundamental theological matters as the doctrines of God, Christ, man, the church, the Christian life, the second coming, and the like, as well as the art of preaching the gospel and the science of missions. The colleges, in light of such theology, would concentrate on understanding the creation including the task(s) to which mankind has been called, the ways in which faith illumines knowledge, the relation of Christ and culture.

Not only are the colleges different from the seminaries, but Reformed colleges will likely differ from each other in a variety of areas. For one, there may be lifestyle differences that would lift up contrasting expectations as to such matters as chapel attendance, or dress, drinking, dancing, smoking, and the like, differences that may make the college seem more "evangelical" and less "Reformed" in the eyes of others. There are likely differences related to governance insofar as the community of supporters (be it a church or a society of laypersons) may be more or less confessionally unified. For another, some colleges may have church membership and/or confessional standards that faculty must uniformly meet, whereas other schools may have hiring policies that welcome greater diversity.

Among the seminaries, there would be some fundamental differences related to the Word and how one interprets it. Is it inerrant and infallible? Is it infallible (i.e., trustworthy) but not without error? And what does one mean by these terms, anyway? These questions, for starters, can lead to a variety of entailments such as those recently swirling about explosive issues like the relation of the Bible, science, and creation; or homosexuality; or gender-inclusive language for God; or the ordination of women to ecclesiastical offices.

Such differences can become magnified in the eyes of those promoting the differences, and lead to separations of churches. This separation occurred in 1857 with the Christian Reformed Church in North America seceding from the Reformed Church in America, in the 1920s when the Protestant Reformed Church and the Christian Reformed Church went their separate ways, and in the 1990s with growing numbers of congregations declaring their independence from the Christian Reformed denomination.

Internal to these institutions, as undoubtedly is true of other confessional organizations, is the ever-present tendency -- and this is especially true among the seminaries -- to wonder whether others are as "Reformed" or orthodox as they ought to be. After all, if something is "Reformed," it is supposed to be constantly reforming. Yet one senses that even here there are differences, probably chiefly in the degree to which they are willing to test the spirits to see whether they are of God, among colleges and seminaries who would otherwise appear to have rather similarly expressed ideals of responsive discipleship.

Endnotes

1. In *Dutch Calvinism in Modern America: A History of a Conservative Subculture.* Grand Rapids, MI: Eerdmans Publishing Co., 1984, p. 43. (Bratt divides the four factions into two sides, Pietists and Seceders versus neo-Calvinists or Kuyperians, with the Reformed Church of America in its "western" or Michigan manifestation then being one pietist group, and the Christian Reformed "Confessionalists" another like-minded group; opposing these [though also opposing each other] are the Christian Reformed Antithetical Calvinists and the Christian Reformed Positive Calvinists. See pp. 43 ff.)

2. See Frank S. Mead, *Handbook of Denominations in the United States.* New 9th edition, revised by Samuel S. Hill. Nashville, TN: Abingdon Press, 1990, p. 210.

3. See "Reformation" in *A Religious Encyclopedia: or Dictionary of Biblical, Historical, Doctrinal and Practical Theology.* Philip Schaaf, ed. 3rd ed. Vol. III. New York: Funk and Wagnalls Co., 1894, p. 2005.

Bibliographic Entries

117. Boelkins, Dawn. "Western Theological Seminary as Potter's Wheel." *Reformed Review* 44 (Spring 1991): 246-54.

   Seeks to assess how well Western Theological Seminary prepares pastors for church ministry via the reflections of four graduates who have served churches for approximately five years.

118. Bruggink, Donald J. "Beginning the Second Century." *Reformed Review* 44 (Spring 1991): 185-202.

   Recounts, in a special issue dedicated to the 125th anniversary of Western Theological Seminary, the significant events that characterized the administrations of seminary presidents Herman J. Ridder, I. John Hesselink, and Marvin D. Hoff.

119.   DeBoer, Peter P. *Origins of Teacher Education at Calvin College, 1900-1930.* Lewiston, NY: Edwin Mellen Press, 1991.

Argues that the training of teachers at Calvin, first in preparatory school and later in the college, at both elementary and secondary levels, played a significant part in helping the Calvinist day-school movement to develop. Also points out that the training of teachers played a more important role than recognized in helping Calvin mature as a college.

120.   De Jong, Peter Y. "Training Men for our Reformed Pulpits." *The Reformed Witness*, March, 1992, p. 17.

Facing the "ever-deepening crisis" in the Christian Reformed Church, one of the founding faculty of the Mid-America Reformed Seminary lifts up the aim and focus of the seminary with a brief history of the same as a help to conservatives in the CRC who are concerned about recent challenges to doctrinal, ethical, and church governmental principles and practices.

121.   Eddings, Greg. "Mid-America on the Move." *The Reformed Witness*, April 1994, p. 7.

Explains the methods for determining and the reasons justifying a move of the Mid-America Reformed Seminary from northwest Iowa to Dyer, Indiana.

122.   "Emeritus President Passes Away." *Calvin Seminary in Focus* 11 (Spring 1994): 1.

Presents a tribute upon the death on March 3, 1994, of John H. Kromminga, president emeritus of Calvin Theological Seminary. Kromminga, appointed to teach history at CTS in 1952, was named president in 1956, and held that post until his retirement in 1983.

123. Gasero, Russell L. "The Origins of the Theological Library at New Brunswick." In *Servant Gladly: Essays in Honor of John W. Beardslee III*, pp. 73-88. Edited by Jack D. Klunder and Russell L. Gasero. Grand Rapids, MI: Eerdmans Publishing Co., 1989.

Examines the long, complex, and difficult process by which the Reformed Church in America established a theological library at New Brunswick. Gasero, seminary activist, lists some of the library's rare manuscript collections while suggesting that New Brunswick could be a major center for theological research.

124. Geertsema, J. "The Purpose of the College." *Clarion* (The Canadian Reformed Magazine), 24 September 1993, pp. 398-400.

Presents a brief account of the history of the Theological College of the Canadian Reformed Churches, especially stressing the nearly twenty-five years of close ties between the college and the churches.

125. Haan, Bernard J. *A Zeal for Christian Education: The Memoirs of B.J. Haan*. Sioux Center, IA: Dordt College Press, 1992.

Tells the story of Dordt's first president, including his family background in Grand Rapids, Michigan, his first ministerial charge at Ridott, Illinois, and his subsequent call to Sioux Center, Iowa, where while pastor of a large congregation he became unofficially the area's leading advocate for Christian day school at all levels, including helping to establish Dordt College. These memoirs describe the exciting early years, and provide an insider's view of several significant controversies.

126. Kansfield, Norman J. "'Study the Most Approved Authors': The Role of the Seminary Library in Nineteenth-Century American Protestant Ministerial Education." Ph.D. dissertation. University of Chicago, 1981.

   Concerned with (1) the image of the ideal Protestant pastor in 19th-century America and its effect on theological scholarship, (2) seminary library ideals, (3) seminary library development, and (4) student use of 19th-century seminary libraries. The study focuses mainly, though not exclusively, on three major theological libraries: Andover, Princeton, and New Brunswick.

127. Klunder, Jack D., and Russell L. Gasero, eds. *Servant Gladly: Essays in Honor of John W. Beardslee III.* Historical Series of the Reformed Church in America, No. 19. Grand Rapids, MI: Eerdmans Publishing Co., 1989.

   Constitutes a *Festschrift* in honor of Professor John V. Beardslee III, for over forty years a distinguished minister, missionary, ecumenist, teacher, prophet, consultant, archivist, theologian, and social activist in the Reformed Church of America, with a record of academic service at both Central College of Iowa and New Brunswick Theological Seminary.

128. Larsen, David Alan. "Evangelical Christian Higher Education, Culture, and Social Conflict: a Niebuhrian Analysis of Three Colleges in the 1960's." Ph.D. dissertation. Loyola University of Chicago, 1992.

Attempts, through a comparative study of three evangelical Christian colleges (Calvin, Goshen, and Wheaton), to determine the impact of the social movement of the 1960s on evangelical higher education. Using the analytical paradigm of H. Richard Niebuhr's *Christ and Culture*, Larsen compares and contrasts the colleges, paying particular attention to the impact of the cultural/historical movements of the decade on the development of student leadership, institutional policies, and the process of character formation.

129. Meeter, Daniel James. "The Gardner A. Sage Theological Library." *The Journal of the Rutgers University Libraries* 45 (December 1983): 65-81.

Details the story of the Gardner A. Sage Library of the New Brunswick Theological Seminary of the Reformed Church in America. This article was prepared upon the 200th anniversary of the founding of the nation's first theological seminary, established 1784. The bicentennial celebration itself prompted new interest in both the Sage Library's collection and the century-old building housing the collection. This richly embroidered piece allows the outsider an insider's view of a treasured building and collection that rivals in certain respects and significantly supplements the nearby collections at both Princeton Seminary and New York's Union Theological Seminary.

130. Vanden Bosch, Mike. *A History of Dordt College: The B.J. Haan Years*. Sioux Center, IA: Dordt College Press, 1990.

Popularizes the early history of Dordt College, accenting student opinion expressed in the college's student newspaper, faculty growth and change, developing campus life, and the maturing relations between town and gown.

131. Wagenaar, Larry J., Craig G. Wright, and Rebecca A. O'Shesky, eds. *Supplement to the Guide to the Collections of the Joint Archives of Holland.* Holland, MI: The Joint Archives of Holland, 1991.

Integrates the three institutional collections of the city of Holland, Hope College, and Western Theological Seminary and presents an inventory or listing of particular information such as the contents of the photographic collections, vertical, biographic, pamphlet, and church files.

132. Wagenaar, Larry J., ed. *The Joint Archives of Holland: Guide to the Collections.* Holland, MI: The Joint Archives of Holland, 1989.

Catalogues the archives of the Holland Historical Trust (for the city of Holland), Hope College, and Western Theological Seminary collected by the Joint Archives of Holland and housed within the Van Wylen library on the Hope College campus.

133. Wing, William G. "Central College." Pella Historical Society, *History of Pella, Iowa: 1847-1987*, Vol. II, pp. 129-40. Dallas, TX: Curtis Media Corp., 1988.

Celebrates 140 years of collegiate history, concentrating on changes in administrative and faculty personnel, the physical plant, and academic programs.

134. Wolters, A.M. "The Reformational-Evangelical Worldview and the Future Mission of Institutions for Christian Higher Education in a North American Context." In *Vision and Mission: The Reformational-Evangelical Vision of Life and the Future Mission of Christian Higher Educational Institutions in World Perspective (1962-1987)*, edited by B. Vander Walt. Potchefstroom, South Africa: Potchefstroom University, 1989, pp. 84-95.

   Emphasizing the crucial importance of Christian theoretical insight, Wolters argues the continuing need for Christian scholars to develop a worldview that is an alternative to Marxism and liberalism, one that is orthodox, has philosophical depth, and literary finesse. "We must insist," he writes, "that ... the entire theoretical or scientific enterprise is praxis, and as much part of authentic human God-service as cultivating the soil, making music, doing justice, and singing praises to God."

135. Wolterstorff, Nicholas P. *Keeping Faith: Talks to New Faculty at Calvin College*. Grand Rapids, MI: Occasional Papers from Calvin College, 1989.

   Attempts to describe the identity and purpose of Calvin College and the challenges to which the college must address itself in light of that identity and purpose by (1) elaborating on the tradition of Christianity (the Reformed tradition) within which the college is located; (2) describing "who we are in this college" (including its history, important educational figures, dominant institutional characteristics, and underlying philosophy of education); and (3) projecting future challenges pertaining to the college's identity, program, and mission.

136. Wolterstorff, Nicholas P. "The Mission of the Christian College at the End of the 20th Century." *Faculty Dialogue* 10 (Winter-Spring 1988): 37-42.

Describes, within the purview of American Christian colleges, the relationship of scholarship to Christian faith in three stages: (1) a late-19th- to mid-20th-century stage marked by piety, evangelism, anti-intellectualism, and defensiveness; (2) a second stage begun after World War II, still in full bloom, of interaction with the stream of high culture, and the fruitful uniting of faith and culture; and (3) a stage that is now unfolding which, without repudiating stage two, seeks engagement of the Christian in the midst of society in socially responsible reformist acts.

CHAPTER 6
Higher Education Among Churches of Christ

Robert E. Hooper

Churches of Christ, one of the three streams of the Stone-Campbell Movement of the nineteenth century, trace their educational origins to Bacon College, a school begun in 1836 by J.T. and T.F. Johnson in Georgetown, Kentucky. Four years later, Alexander Campbell established Bethany College. Tolbert Fanning, who taught briefly at Bacon College, founded Franklin College in Nashville, Tennessee, in 1844. From these early beginnings, schools have flourished within the confines of the Stone-Campbell heritage.[1]

In addition to Franklin College, another small college operated in Tennessee. From 1849 until 1939, Burritt College, located in Spencer, Tennessee, flourished under W.D. Carnes, a graduate of the state university in Knoxville and a professor of English at the university, from 1850 to 1858 and from 1872 to 1878. In the 1906 school year, Burritt College had 231 students enrolled. The Great Depression of the 1930s spelled the death of the school.[2]

Schools Specifically Associated with Churches of Christ

In 1906, the United States Religious Census listed Churches of Christ as a separate body from the larger Disciples of Christ. Indicative of the division that would come, David Lipscomb and James A. Harding established the Nashville Bible School in 1891. Although it had the name Bible College, David Lipscomb had always favored a school where all students studied all facets of education. Thus Bible was at the core of education, but education was not complete with only a study of the Bible. This would become the model for schools established within the fellowship of Churches of Christ.

The Board of Directors changed the name of the school to David Lipscomb College in 1918. It remained a junior college until 1946 when the Board initiated a massive building program under the leadership of Athens Clay Pullias and began offering baccalaureate degrees. The first class graduated in 1948.[3]

In Henderson, Tennessee, a series of schools with roots to 1869 took the name Freed-Hardeman College in 1919. A.G. Freed, a graduate of Valparaiso University, teamed with N.B. Hardeman, a student of Freed's at Georgie Roberson Christian College, to establish in 1908 National Teachers' Normal and Business College. In 1919, members of Churches of Christ purchased the charter of the school from Freed and Hardeman. They, in turn, named the school Freed-Hardeman College. After 1925, N.B. Hardeman became the driving force behind the college until his retirement in 1950.

Out West in Abilene, Texas, a graduate of the Nashville Bible School, A.B. Barret, persuaded members of the local Church of Christ to sponsor a new school. As a result, Childers Classical Institute opened in the fall of 1906. Beginning primarily as a preparatory school, it became Abilene Christian College in 1912 under the direction of Jesse P. Sewell, its new president who was also a graduate of the Nashville Bible School. Sewell presided over the changes that soon made the school an accredited junior college. In 1919, Abilene Christian College became the first four-year standard senior college among Churches of Christ. The school moved to its present campus in 1929 just as the Great Depression humbled the United States. Under the leadership of James F. Cox, the college, with difficulty, made it through the 1930s.

Heir to the educational philosophy of James A. Harding, co-founder of the Nashville Bible School, Harding College became a reality in Morrilton, Arkansas, in 1924. James Harding left the Nashville Bible School in 1901 to organize the Potter Bible College in Bowling Green, Kentucky. This college would continue until 1913. Joining him on the faculty was J.N. Armstrong, Harding's son-in-law. Armstrong moved in 1905 to Odessa, Missouri, where, among others, he was instrumental in forming Western Bible and Literary College. (The school would continue until 1916.) Resigning the presidency after two years, he became president of Cordell Christian College in Cordell, Oklahoma, a school that would continue until 1931. After serving Cordell College until 1919, he moved to Harper College in Kansas, a school founded in 1915. Harper joined a junior college in Morrilton, Arkansas, in 1924 to become Harding College. J.N. Armstrong became president of the combined schools. In 1934, the school moved to its present campus in Searcy, Arkansas.[4]

George Pepperdine, founder of Western Auto Supply Company, gave his name and money in 1937 to a new college in Los Angeles. In need of a seasoned administrator, the Board of Trustees encouraged Batsell Baxter, a graduate of the Nashville Bible School and a former president of both David Lipscomb College and Abilene Christian College, to become the first president of Pepperdine. Pepperdine moved quickly toward accreditation, the first of the schools operated by members of Churches of Christ to be accredited. The west-coast school was the first college within the fellowship to offer a graduate degree. A master's program in religion, under the direction of W.B. West, Jr., began in 1944-1945 with the first degree conferred in 1947.[5]

The Established Schools and Higher Education after World War II

The five colleges specifically founded by members of Churches of Christ made great plans for growth following World War II. There were two major goals for the schools: expanded facilities to care for the pent-up demand for education following the world conflict and accreditation -- a goal reached previously only by Pepperdine. To gain accreditation the colleges had to add numerous Ph.D.s to their faculties.[6]

Abilene Christian College led the way in expansion and the pursuit of accreditation. Led by Don Morris for twenty-nine years, the school launched a $3,000,000 campaign to construct new facilities. At the end of his tenure in 1969, he could count a faculty that included sixty-eight who held the Ph.D. where he had only six in 1940. The student body had grown from 661 to 3,110. On December 9, 1951, Abilene Christian College received its accreditation. Three years later, it added its first graduate program.

David Lipscomb College, under the leadership of Athens Clay Pullias, reached a goal that had been elusive for many years -- senior college status. Raising a million dollars for new construction, the college also began to develop a faculty with increased numbers of Ph.D.s. As a result, the school received its accreditation in December 1954 from the Southern Association of Colleges and Schools. From 1955 through the end of the 1960s, the school increased enrollment and continued to add to its physical plant. There were 1,298 students enrolled in 1960-61. In 1970-71, the college counted 2,237 students. Lipscomb developed a positive reputation in pre-medicine, pre-law, and business administration. With its growing emphasis on liberal arts and professional education, each student continued to study the Bible each day.

Harding College had impressive growth under the leadership of Dr. George S. Benson. When he became president of the college in 1936, the school had a substantial indebtedness. In

1965, at his retirement, the school had assets of $25,000,000, including an endowment of $13,000,000 -- a large sum for colleges among Churches of Christ. Harding received its accreditation in 1953. A major move of Harding was the establishment of the Harding Graduate School of Religion in Memphis. Clifton L. Ganus, Jr., succeeded Benson as president, serving in this capacity from 1965 until 1987. Growth in the student body, the addition of new programs of study, and the building of new facilities highlighted his administration.

In 1972, George Pepperdine University opened its new Seaver College campus at Malibu. This was the culmination of nearly forty years of growth since World War II. From 1937 to the late 1960s, Pepperdine remained a rather small, for-the-most-part undergraduate college in the heart of Los Angeles. In 1970, it achieved university status at which time it added graduate and professional schools. The Seaver campus included its undergraduate program and a school of law. The development of Pepperdine during these growth years was under the direction of M. Norvel Young, William Bronowsky, and Howard White. All three men were graduates of David Lipscomb College.

Freed-Hardeman College remained a junior college until 1974. The school was under the direction of N.B. Hardeman from 1925 until 1950. In his place, the Board of Directors selected H.A. Dixon, who served until his death in 1969. A major change under Dixon was the awarding of associate degrees in the place of diplomas. Equally as important was the addition of junior-level Bible courses in 1953 for those who desired to enter the ministry. E. Claude Gardner gave leadership to the college as it moved from junior college status to a standard senior liberal arts college in 1974.

New Colleges Among Churches of Christ

A growing fellowship encouraged the formation of many new colleges beginning in the 1940s. Rex Turner, Sr., and Leonard Johnson founded Montgomery (Alabama) Bible School in 1942.

By 1950, the school had 200 students. After attempting to offer senior college classes in Bible and business, the college opted to remain a junior college. To increase its influence and better describe its area of outreach, the Bible school became Alabama Christian College in 1953. The institution continued to grow, needing new facilities by 1964. It received accreditation as a junior college in 1971. An identifying characteristic of Alabama Christian has always been its extensive educational centers across the state of Alabama. In 1978, Alabama Christian applied for senior college status. On December 11, 1984, the school received full accreditation as a senior college. In 1985, the Board of Trustees changed the name of the college to Faulkner University.[7]

Representing a special emphasis in Churches of Christ, Florida College resulted from planning that began in 1944. Located in Tampa, the school opened in the fall of 1946 with L.R. Wilson as chief administrator. James R. Cope became president in 1948 and remained in the position until the early 1980s. The school continues to this day as a junior college with an enrollment of 381 students during 1993-94. Florida College represents those in Churches of Christ who do not support orphan homes, homes of the aged, and cooperative mission programs. The president of the college is Dr. Charles G. Caldwell.

Southwestern Christian College in Terrell, Texas, is the only college among churches of Christ that is predominantly African-American. Developing out of the influence of G.P. Bowser, a leader among black Churches of Christ and an advocate of a W.E.B. DuBois approach to education, Southwestern Christian College had its beginning during the fall of 1948 as Southern Bible Institute in Fort Worth, Texas. The following year, a campus in Terrell became available. Purchasing the campus, the school opened for classes in 1950. Presidents of the school were all white until Jack Evans accepted the position in 1963. Although many doubted the school could survive, Southwestern has made its greatest strides under the leadership of Evans. It received accreditation as a junior college in 1973. In 1994, the college was accredited as a senior college in Bible and Religious Education. The 1993-94 enrollment was 235.[8]

L.R. Wilson had not planned to serve again as a college president, but the Board of Trustees for a college not yet organized chose him to be the first president of Central Christian College in Bartlesville, Oklahoma. The junior college accepted its first students in 1950. Dr. James O. Baird, who had served on the faculty of David Lipscomb College, became president in 1954. The Board of Trustees in 1958 moved the school to a new campus in Oklahoma City. One year later, the Board changed the name of the school to Oklahoma Christian College. On the new campus and with a new name, the college quickly moved toward a senior college status, graduating its first class in 1962. The school received full accreditation in 1966. In 1974, James O. Baird stepped down as president, welcoming Dr. Terry Johnson to the position.

The 1950s continued to be a time for founding new schools, stretching from Philadelphia to Portland, Oregon, and many places in between. York College, located in York, Nebraska, was opened in 1890 by local people who wanted a college for their community. From that date until 1956, the college operated under the administration of the United Brethren in Christ and, as a result of a merger, the Evangelical United Brethren Church. In 1956, Churches of Christ assumed control of the college. Harvey Childress served as the first president of the school. The junior college received accreditation in 1970. In recent years the college began offering Bachelor's Degrees in Biblical Studies and Religious Education. Under the leadership of Dr. Larry Roberts, York College had 350 students enrolled in 1993-94.

Beginning in Parkersburg, West Virginia, in 1956, a plan was set in motion to establish Ohio Valley College as a junior college under the leadership of Don Gardner. In the fall of 1960, the college opened in the facilities of the South Parkersburg Church of Christ. Three years later, the college moved to its own campus. In July 1978, the college received accreditation as a junior college. Since 1983 the college has awarded baccalaureate degrees in Bible. The college is offering four years of college preparation leading to B.A. and B.S. degrees in a number of disciplines. Enrollment during 1993-94 was 243 students. Dr. E. Keith Stotts serves the college as president.

In September of 1959, with Otis Gatewood serving as president, North Central Christian College welcomed its first students. Located in Rochester, Michigan, the Board of Trustees changed the name of the school to Michigan Christian College in 1961. After applying for candidate status in 1969, Michigan Christian College became fully accredited as a junior college in 1974. In 1980, the North Central Association authorized the college to offer baccalaureate degrees. Presently, the college offers majors in some twenty areas. There were 319 students enrolled at Michigan Christian during the 1993-94 school year.[9]

The state of Texas in 1954 authorized a Board of Directors to operate a private educational institution in Lubbock, Texas. Beginning at first as an elementary school, the Board established Lubbock Christian College, a junior college, in 1957. Dr. F.W. Mattox, formerly of Harding College, served as the first president. The college quickly received accreditation as a junior college. By 1968 the Board of Trustees authorized two additional years of education thus making Lubbock Christian College a four-year senior college. Accreditation came for the senior college in 1972. Enrollment during the 1993-94 school year was 1,154 students. The current president of Lubbock Christian is Dr. Kenneth Jones.

In the Pacific Northwest, members of the Churches of Christ, because of the great distances to other Christian colleges, opted to establish Columbia Christian College. Begun as elementary and secondary schools in 1947, a junior college opened in 1956. L.D. Webb served the school as its first president. The third and fourth years were added to the college in 1971. The Northwest Association of Schools and Colleges accredited the school as a senior college in 1975.

J. Harold Thomas served as the first president of Northeastern Christian Junior College in Villanova, Pennsylvania. The school began operation in 1959, serving young people in the northeastern section of the United States. The school never attracted great numbers of students, enrolling only 138 in 1965. The school merged in 1993 with Ohio Valley College on the campus in Parkersburg, West Virginia.

Crowley's Ridge College is a small junior college in Paragould, Arkansas. Founded in 1964, the school has always had a small enrollment. Now headed by Larry M. Bills, Crowley's Ridge College is seeking accreditation from the North Central accrediting agency. During the fall semester in 1993, the college had an enrollment of 185 students.

Special Educational Institutions Among Churches of Christ

Not all post-secondary educational institutions are liberal arts colleges with strong professional components. On the opposite end of the spectrum are the preacher training schools, including Sunset School of Preaching in Lubbock, Texas (the oldest such school among Churches of Christ, founded in 1949); Brown's Trail School of Preaching in Hurst, Texas (founded in 1965); Memphis, Tennessee, School of Preaching (founded in 1966); and the East Tennessee School of Preaching in Knoxville (founded in 1971). Between these schools of preaching and liberal arts colleges are several special types of schools. The International Bible College in Florence, Alabama, and the Magnolia Bible College in Kosciusko, Mississippi, represent the four-year college with special emphasis on training of preachers and Christian workers. International Bible College began operation in 1971 with nine students. The college holds membership in the American Association of Bible Colleges. This membership requires thirty-six hours in humanities, social science, and physical science. The enrollment ranges from 150 to 200 students each year.

Magnolia Bible College began with nine students in the fall of 1977. Magnolia offers a Bachelor of Arts degree in Bible. With sixty-one students enrolled in the 1993-94 school year, the school is now accredited by the Southern Association and the American Association of Bible Colleges. Carl Mays, Jr., serves the college as president.

Southern Christian University shares the same beginnings as Faulkner University. In 1966, Alabama Christian School of Religion emerged as a result of the inability of Alabama Christian College to offer the third and fourth years of Bible and keep its accreditation. The schools remained under Dr. Rex Turner until 1973 when Alabama Christian School of Religion became a separate school under its own Board of Regents. Turner remained president of the latter school. The college began offering a master's degree in 1973. By 1977 the school began offering a three-year Master of Divinity degree. The School of Religion received its accreditation in 1989. In 1991, the Board of Regents approved a name change to Southern Christian University. Its major emphasis is the training of preachers. The university has about 115 students. The president of Southern Christian University is Dr. Rex Turner, Jr.

The Institute for Christian Studies in Austin, Texas, began as a Bible Chair at the University of Texas in 1917. In 1975, the program underwent a revision that provided for third- and fourth-year Bible classes that would lead to a Bachelor's degree at Abilene Christian University. The program continued to expand to include the training of church leaders and ministers. This expansion culminated in 1983 with the Institute offering a bachelor's degree. However, students must complete their general education requirements at another accredited institution. In 1987, the Institute received recognition by the Southern Association of Colleges and Schools. There are approximately ninety students enrolled.

Current Status of Higher Education
Among Churches of Christ

Liberal arts colleges and universities among Churches of Christ have expanded their educational offerings since the 1970s. No longer strictly liberal arts, most four-year senior colleges began offering professional and advanced degrees. The one thing that ties them to their origins is an emphasis on the Christian religion and the offering of Bible as an important component of the curriculum.

Pepperdine University, the largest of the schools with 7,500 students, offers graduate work in law, business, education, and psychology. Doctor's degrees are offered in both education and psychology. The Sever campus in Malibu, California, is home of its undergraduate college, the law school, and its MBA program. The president of the university is Dr. David Davenport.

Abilene Christian University currently has 4,000 students in five undergraduate colleges and the graduate school. It also operates the Abilene Intercollegiate School of Nursing. The graduate program is accredited to offer both master's and doctor's degrees. The university offers M.A. degrees in thirty-two academic fields and a Doctor of Ministry in Biblical Studies. Much of this growth took place under the direction of Dr. John C. Stevens from 1969 to 1981. Following the administration of William J. Teague, Dr. Royce Money became president in 1991.

Harding University has grown at a faster rate in recent years than any of the colleges among Churches of Christ. The enrollment is presently about 3,600 students. The Searcy campus offers a Master of Education degree. The school also offers a degree in nursing. The Harding Graduate School of Religion in Memphis, under the direction of Dean Bill Flatt, continues to upgrade its program. Presently it offers three master's degrees and a Doctor of Ministry. The graduate school of religion has approximately 200 students. Dr. David Burks became president of Harding University in 1987.

David Lipscomb University changed its status from college to university in 1988 when graduate degrees in Bible were first offered. The university has 2,400 students in its undergraduate and graduate programs. In recent years, the school initiated an adult studies program, mainly focused on students who can only attend classes in the evenings and on the weekends. A master's degree in education began in 1993. The university operates a kindergarten through high school program for over 1,500 students, making it the largest private elementary and secondary school in Nashville. Following the presidency of Willard Collins, Dr. Harold Hazelip became president of Lipscomb in 1986.

Led by Dr. Terry Johnson, Oklahoma Christian College became Oklahoma Christian University of Arts and Sciences in 1990. Within its academic restructuring, Oklahoma Christian began offering a degree in engineering in 1986. The school has also initiated two very unique programs with two other colleges. Until recently, Oklahoma Christian offered a B.S. degree in business for Ohio Valley College. The students complete their program by video classes and classes taught by Oklahoma Christian faculty on the campus of Ohio Valley. In the fall of 1994, Cascade College, formerly Columbia Christian College, began operating under the umbrella of Oklahoma Christian University. The university also offers an M.A. degree in Bible. There are over 4,600 students enrolled on the Oklahoma City campus.

Freed-Hardeman University, under the presidency of Dr. Milton Sewell, has moved in recent years from a four-year senior college to university status offering graduate degrees. In 1990, the university began offering a Master of Education and Master of Ministry degrees. Freed-Hardeman University has an enrollment of 1,235.

Faulkner University has a rather unique system of education. Its Montgomery campus is home to less than a third of the university's students. The university operates centers in Birmingham, Mobile, Florence, and Huntsville. Faulkner also operates Jones Law School, an evening program in Montgomery.

In the four centers, the main campus in Montgomery, and the Jones Law School, the larger university enrolled 2,275 students during the 1993-94 school year. The school is under the presidency of Dr. Billy Hilyer.

The major change during the late 1980s and the 1990s among the senior colleges operated by members of Churches of Christ has been the addition of graduate programs, especially in biblical studies and education. Abilene Christian and Harding graduate schools now offer Doctor of Ministry degrees. Heretofore, only Pepperdine offered any degrees beyond the M.A. Oklahoma Christian has been the only school to venture in a substantial way into engineering, although only on the undergraduate level. All senior colleges emphasize programs in business and other non-traditional liberal arts. There is every indication that additional graduate and special courses will be added at many of the schools in the near future as the colleges and universities reflect the mainstream of higher education in the United States.

Endnotes

1. For the impact of Franklin College, see James E. Scobey, ed., *Franklin College and Its Influences*. Nashville: Gospel Advocate Company, reprint 1954.

2. The history of early developments in higher education in the Stone-Campbell Movement and Churches of Christ is based on M. Norvel Young, *A History of Colleges Established and Controlled by Members of Churches of Christ*. Kansas City, MO: Old Paths Book Club, 1949.

3. For a lengthy history of David Lipscomb University, see Robert E. Hooper and David England, *A Century of Memories: A Centennial Celebration*. Nashville: David Lipscomb University, 1992.

4. For a comprehensive history of Harding's educational background, see L.C. Sears, *For Freedom: The Biography of John Nelson Armstrong*. Austin: Sweet Publishing Company, 1969.

5.   See Jerry Rushford, ed. Text by Howard A. White, *Crest of a Golden Wave: A Pictorial History of Pepperdine University, 1937-1987*. Malibu, CA: Pepperdine University, 1987.

6.   For a survey of liberal arts colleges among Churches of Christ in the years after World War II, see Robert E. Hooper, *A Distinct People: A History of the Churches of Christ in the Twentieth Century*. West Monroe, LA: Howard Publishing Company, 1993, pp. 199-205.

7.   For the more recent history and status of higher education among Churches of Christ, I have relied on the most recent catalogs and bulletins from the various schools.

8.   The enrollment figures for all schools were taken from Mary Pat Rodenhouse, ed., *1994 Higher Education Directory*. Falls Church, VA: Higher Education Publications, Inc., 1994.

9.   Larry Stewart, *Michigan Christian College, 1959-1984*. Rochester, MN: Michigan Christian College, 1984.

Bibliographic Entries

137.   Brown, Larry. "Think on these Things: Reflections on the Place of the Humanities in Christian Education"; Goad, William P. "The Church Related University: Values and the Resource Dependence Theory"; Gross, Jerry. "Worshipping the Gods of a Beaten Enemy: The Responsibility of the Christian University to Address the Commitments of Christians to Live Non-violent Lives in a Violent Culture"; Kooi, William. "The Legitimacy of the Voice of Christian Tradition in the University"; Pulley, Kathy J. "Future Trends Facing Bible Departments"; Tippens, Darryl. "'On the Top of Golden Hours': The Future of the Christian University"; Tucker, David. "The Integration of Biblical Truth in the Curriculum of the University: Economics and Business"; Weed, Michael R. "Academic Freedom and the Christian University"; and Wilson, Jim. "The Impact of the Bible on the Teaching of History, or, Can a University History Teacher Go to

Heaven." Papers presented at Christian Scholars Conference, Oklahoma Christian University, Oklahoma City, OK, July 18-20, 1992.

Present current thinking within Churches of Christ on the status of higher education, both on a broad level and within various disciplines. These nine papers were responses to a call for papers on higher education among Churches of Christ by Oklahoma Christian University.

138. Cosgrove, Owen. *Morris: The Administration of Don Heath Morris at Abilene Christian College*. Fort Worth: Star Bible Publications, 1993.

Shows Don Heath Morris as the lead administrator of Abilene Christian College during its most formative years, including the era following World War II when the college earned its accreditation. The book provides source material at the end of the chapters.

139. Hayes, Franklin Delano. "An Administrative History of Harding University, 1924-1987." M.A. Thesis, University of Arkansas at Little Rock, 1989.

Looks at the administration of Harding from its formal founding at Morrilton, Arkansas, in 1924, with J.N. Armstrong as president, until 1987, the last year of the administration of Clifton L. Ganus, Jr. Between the administrations of these two men, George Benson placed his stamp on the school, beginning in 1936, after serving ten years as a missionary to China.

140. Hooper, Robert E. *A Distinct People: A History of the Churches of Christ in the Twentieth Century*. West Monroe, LA: Howard Publishing Company, 1993.

Develops the place of higher education among Churches of Christ within the growth and development of the fellowship in the twentieth century. As Churches of Christ have matured and become more middle class, the schools reflect this maturity by becoming regionally recognized colleges and universities.

141. Hooper, Robert E. and David England. *A Century of Memories: A Centennial Celebration*. Nashville: David Lipscomb University, 1992.

Traces the history of David Lipscomb University through narrative, recollections, and photographs from its founding in 1891 as the Nashville Bible School, through its years as David Lipscomb College, to university status. The emphasis of the book is upon people: administrators, faculty, and students.

142. McKelvain, Robert and Scott Perkins. *Excellence: A Christian Commitment*. New York: McGraw-Hill, Inc., 1992.

Serves as a handbook for the University Seminar at Abilene Christian University (ACU). It includes chapters on the ACU mission, ACU history, and the ACU library as it introduces the incoming student to the university setting.

143. McNicoll, Allan J. "Dismantling the Bible Chairs in Texas: A Church-State Struggle in Historical Context." *Institute of Christian Studies Faculty Bulletin* 9 (Fall 1988): 51-79.

Argues that the University of Texas in 1987 acted unconstitutionally by disbanding Bible chairs. Furthermore, the state overstepped its legitimate mandate in supporting a university that does not allow instruction in the Bible and teaching about Jesus, Paul, and other biblical personalities, especially when the same university includes instruction in Islam, Judaism, and Buddhism in various departments across the campus.

144. Richardson, William J. "Models of Ministerial Preparation Among Christian Churches/Churches of Christ and Churches of Christ." *Discipliana* 54 (Summer 1994): 49-63.

Presents a study of biblical teaching in schools operated by Christian Churches/Churches of Christ and Churches of Christ to prepare men for the ministry. Specifically, the author emphasizes that in Churches of Christ the model most often has been liberal arts with Bible being an integral part of the curriculum. In recent years, these same schools have added graduate degrees with special emphasis in theology and languages. This, in turn, has led to the rise of Bible colleges and even preacher training schools sponsored by individual congregations. The Bible colleges, however, have moved toward accreditation thus requiring a minimum of thirty-six hours in the humanities, social science, and physical science.

145. Rowland, Rick. *Campus Ministries: A Historical Study of Churches of Christ Campus Ministries and Selected College Ministries from 1706 to 1990.* Fort Worth: Star Bible Publications, 1991.

Surveys the work done by Churches of Christ on college and university campuses since the original program began at the University of Texas in 1918. In order to place the movement in its larger context,

Rowland traces the movement of campus ministries in the United States from 1706 to the present. The study began as a dissertation for a Doctor of Ministry at California Graduate School of Theology in 1990.

146.   Stevens, John C. *Before Any Were Willing: The Story of George S. Benson*. Searcy, AR: Harding University Press, 1991.

Examines the life and work of George S. Benson, president of Harding University from 1936 to 1965. Written by John C. Stevens, president of Abilene Christian University, 1969-1981. Stevens surveys Benson's work at Harding University and other Christian colleges and universities, the National Education Program, his missionary experiences in China, and the building of schools in Zambia.

147.   Womack, Morris M. *J.P. Sanders: A Champion of Christian Education*. Agoura and Malibu, CA: Professional Communication Services, Inc., in cooperation with Pepperdine University Press, 1988.

Traces the life and work of Joel Pilant Sanders from his birth in Fort Worth, Texas, in 1906, through his personal education, culminating in a Ph.D. from the University of Southern California. Sanders served as a minister for churches in Tennessee, Texas, and California. He served many years as dean of David Lipscomb College and Pepperdine University. He also served as president of Columbia Christian College.

CHAPTER 7
Moravian Colleges and Universities

Daniel R. Gilbert

The *Unitas Fratrum*, the Unity of the Brethren, commonly called the Moravians, a religious reform movement that developed in the 15th century in Bohemia and Moravia, underwent severe repression in the Thirty Years War. Only a "hidden seed" kept the movement alive with some of the parishes absorbed into other denominations; apostolic succession was kept alive through the Reformed Church.[1]

In the early 18th century, remnants of the Bohemian Brethren moved into Saxony and began the development of a "Renewed Church" on the estate of the pious Lutheran nobleman, Nicolaus Ludwig Count von Zinzendorf. To this center at Herrnhut were drawn Pietists from all over Europe, and in time there developed a new denomination. Moravians of this "Renewed Church" stressed missions and before long itinerant evangelists were moving through much of northern Europe, Switzerland, and the British Isles. The Diaspora eventually reached all areas of the known world including Africa, South America, Central America, and Labrador; there was even to be a mission in Tibet.

The desire to bring the Word to the heathen and others left "unchurched" inevitably drew the Moravians to North America. They were in the West Indies by 1732 and made a settlement in Georgia in 1735. But Pennsylvania was to become the center of their work and in 1741 they had established a "home congregation" at Bethlehem. From this base of operations they soon spread out through Pennsylvania and New Jersey, up into the Hudson Valley and New England, and down into Maryland and the back country of the South. Moravians established congregations and preaching stations at various locations, and in 1753 they created a new base of operations at what was to become Salem in the back country of North Carolina.[2]

The Moravians brought with them to America a tradition of education. Their great Bohemian leader and martyr, John Hus, who was burned at the stake in 1415, had been a popular professor in Prague. There had been Moravian nursery schools, secondary schools, colleges, and theological seminaries in Bohemia, Moravia, and Poland. One of the greatest Moravian leaders of that era, the Bishop John Amos Comenius, the "Father of Modern Education," was a school master in Moravia and Poland and came to be known internationally for his writings in educational philosophy and pedagogical theory.[3] The leaders of the Renewed Church were also learned men and graduates of such great universities as Jena, Halle, and Tubingen.[4]

While often referred to as a "missionary church," it is clear that the Moravians were an educational church as well. In the words of one of their early Bishops, "Whithersoever we bring the Gospel there we establish a school."[5] Some have suggested that the Moravians in America were at most literate people and not particularly interested in "higher education." These critics miss the point that the Church preached a doctrine of preparing everyone -- men and women -- over their entire lifetime for any and all vocations to which the Lord had called them. It is not surprising therefore that the Moravians in America had their own schools, libraries, a press, an advanced musical culture featuring both performance and composition, and were sophisticated linguists. The Moravian tradition, in contrast with much of Colonial America, placed the responsibility for education with the community rather than with the family.

In 1742 the Moravians began their formal educational program for young boys with the founding of what came to be known after 1759 as Nazareth Hall. This well-known boarding school prepared young men for either the ministry or teaching with those seeking further training before ordination going back to Europe. By the early 19th century, Church leaders began to express concern over their growing need for more "teachers and preachers" and the problems the Napoleonic Wars presented for those being sent abroad. Also there was concern that the German-trained clergy did not always provide the proper leadership for congregations and schools in a new and growing nation. Discussion as early as 1802 led to the establishment at Nazareth Hall in 1807 of a school of theology which was in time to become Moravian College and Theological Seminary.[6] Consistent with their belief that liberal studies were the best preparation for the ministry and for teaching, instruction was to be given in "Latin, Greek, Hebrew, French, German Composition, Mathematics, General History, Ecclesiastical History, Exegesis, Geography, Drawing."[7]

This small seminary moved frequently in the early years, but by action of the Synod of 1858 it was permanently located in Bethlehem. Church leaders also decided at that time to create a Moravian college under Church auspices to provide "...an institution in which the youths of our congregation can pursue a collegiate course of studies, either with a view to fit themselves for the various avocations of life, or with the ultimate object of entering the ministry...."[8] Opened in 1858, the institution was formally chartered as Moravian College and Theological Seminary in 1863, and granted its first degrees in 1870. Its 1868 catalog noted that it offered a four-year graded curriculum with a clear distinction between the collegiate and theological studies. The school remained under the close control of the Church up to

1893 when, as part of a general reorganization of Church programs, a separate board of trustees was established.

In the late 1880s, Church leaders made a historic decision to keep the institution in Bethlehem and to develop a new campus in a pastoral setting on what was then the northern limits of the town. These new buildings were opened in 1892, and, four years later, a new Latin-Scientific curriculum was added to broaden the appeal to prospective undergraduate students.

By the centennial of 1907, the College and Seminary had educated over 500 young men but it was to remain relatively small in enrollment and faculty through the 1940s.[9] World War I brought lower enrollments but the College survived through the presence on campus of a Student Army Training Corps. Benefactors helped meet a mounting deficit in the 1920s and paradoxically enrollment actually improved in the Depression years. By the onset of World War II, the College and Seminary had a combined enrollment of about 200 students, a combined faculty and administration of 18, and had developed a vigorous small-college culture.

World War II brought new challenges. Church leaders were determined to keep the Theological Seminary and the supporting College open in spite of declining enrollments and the nagging problem of a deficit. There was discussion of establishing a jointure with the nearby Moravian College for Women, but the latter, in spite of its problems, was not interested. Salvation came for the College by bringing students from Navy V-5 and V-12 programs to campus.

The post-war years brought dramatic changes. Veterans attending college under the GI Bill brought enrollment to an all-time high. Efforts begun even before the war led to the retirement of the debt by the late 1950s. In the same decade, the Moravian College and Theological Seminary was to merge with the Moravian College for Women (see below), and, in 1954, a new Moravian College was chartered to operate both a coeducational, undergraduate liberal arts college and a graduate-level theological seminary.

Coeducation brought a new culture to the campus. New buildings were added, including dormitories, a student union, a new gymnasium, new science facilities, and a new library. Enrollment gradually increased to about 1,200 students, most of whom were, in contrast to earlier years, in residence on campus. The older buildings of the former Seminary and College for Women were rebuilt to provide new dormitory facilities as well as a Center for Art and Music. At the same time, faculty and admissions standards were upgraded and the academic program changed to include a new honors program, a 4-1-4 calendar (since abandoned), and in recent years a core curriculum. There were expanded extracurricular programs including intercollegiate athletic competition for women, and the music program was upgraded to achieve national recognition. In 1961 a Division of Continuing Studies was developed to respond to community needs and to bring in added income. The College currently grants the B.A., B.S., B.Mus., and M.B.A. degrees.

The Theological Seminary has also undergone significant changes in the 20th century. Operating under its own administration since 1930, and granted full accreditation by the Association of Theological Schools in 1953, it moved to new facilities on campus in 1976. Its curriculum, board of trustees (under the Moravian College corporation), faculty, and student body are now separate from the undergraduate College although it does share a number of administrative functions. While it remains today committed to providing leadership for the Moravian Church, it has in recent years moved to have a more ecumenical faculty and serve other denominations as well. It currently enrolls about 85 full- and part-time students and offers the M.Div., M.A. in Pastoral Counseling, Theological Studies, and Christian Education degrees.[10]

The relationship of both the undergraduate College and Theological Seminary to the Moravian Church has also undergone significant change in the late 20th century. As late as in the years following World War II, Moravian College and Theological Seminary still proclaimed in its catalog that it was

"...an educational institution of the Moravian Church in America" and that its twofold task was to prepare men for "the study of theology" and to provide "...training of high quality in a Christian atmosphere for young men who wish to enter other fields of activity." The majority of the trustees were either ordained Moravian ministers or active Moravian laymen. But today the undergraduate College declares itself to be "an independent liberal arts college," and the Church elects less than one-third of the trustees with the rest drawn from a variety of backgrounds. It is significant that today the Church contributes less than 1% of the College's annual income. The Theological Seminary of necessity has closer ties to the Church. Yet only about half of the Seminary board of trustees is elected by the Church, and the latter contributes less than 20% of the annual income of the institution.

Two months before the founding of a school for young boys in 1742, the Moravians opened the Seminary for Young Ladies, the forerunner of the Moravian College for Women.[11] Founded by the Countess Benigna, Zinzendorf's daughter, in Germantown, Pennsylvania, it soon moved to Bethlehem where it was to serve the daughters of Moravian congregations for the next forty-five years. Then, in response to requests from those outside the Moravian community and with the blessings of Countess Benigna, it was opened to the general public in 1785. By the early 20th century, over 8,000 young women had been enrolled in its programs. Closely tied to the Church in the early years, it did not receive its own charter until 1863, at which time it was given its own board of trustees and granted the right to award degrees.

Some have claimed that the Seminary was primarily a finishing school for daughters of the American elite. But it was in fact one of those few institutions that provided young women with an opportunity for advanced training prior to the 20th century.[12] And while it is true that there were courses in drawing, painting, music, and ornamental needlework, there was also a strong core of traditional, liberal studies, including (by the mid-19th century) courses in philosophy, natural philosophy, astronomy, and what was called a program of "higher collegiate studies."[13]

In its first century, most of the young women came to the Seminary from all over North America and the Moravian mission fields, and had left by the time they were age fifteen. But in the later years of the 19th century, some stayed on to take post-graduate work. By 1888, the Seminary was offering degrees in a collegiate course that included study of "Latin (Virgil and Cicero); Higher Literature (including the History of Classic Greek and Latin, German and Scandinavian Literatures, and some acquaintance with Anglo-Saxon); the Philosophy of History; Contemporary History; Mental and Moral Science (including Ethics and Aesthetics); History of Art and Architecture; a survey of the legal status of women (with references to the elements of property and contract law); Political and Social Economy; Logic; Evidences of Christianity."[14] Up to the 20th century, however, the school granted only one advanced degree, a Bachelor of Arts in Literature, in 1896.

A general reorganization of Church auxiliary programs gave the Seminary a more autonomous board of trustees in 1893, and that body in 1908 moved to introduce more advanced course work. Finally recognized as a college for women, its name was changed in 1913 to the Moravian Seminary and College for Women.[15]

The progress of the collegiate program was slow up to the 1930s, with the several presidents (two of them former members of the staff of Salem Academy and College in North Carolina) struggling to separate the secondary and collegiate programs and achieve financial stability. The secondary school program achieved accreditation by the Middle States Association for Colleges and Secondary Schools in 1941, but the College for Women never achieved similar status because of continuing problems with low faculty salaries and an inadequate library. Yet, even with these problems, a genuine women's-college culture had developed at the Seminary and College for Women in its teas, drama programs (often in conjunction with nearby Lehigh University), musical and athletic programs, and a strong YWCA.

Some Moravian leaders, concerned with the financial problems of their Theological Seminary, thought that the College for Women was not truly "church related" or vital to the future of the Church. But it is fair to say that the Moravian Seminary and College for Women, located in the center of the historic Bethlehem community, did much to sustain the traditions of the Moravians including their music, unique forms of worship and celebration of religious holidays.

The Seminary and College for Women, however, continued to have problems with finances, low enrollment, and aging facilities. An offer to join with nearby all-male Moravian College during World War II was rejected and the College for Women proudly proclaimed itself a single-sex institution to its end. In 1949 a significant gift of land and buildings on a tract east of Bethlehem gave new life to the upper grades of the secondary program, but declining enrollment forced the closing of its lower grades in 1951. In 1953 the college trustees, unable to find new financing, voted to merge the women's collegiate program with the previously all-male Moravian College and Theological Seminary. In 1954 this new Moravian College was chartered to operate the now fully accredited coeducational undergraduate liberal arts college, a graduate-level Theological Seminary, and, at least temporarily, the Moravian Seminary for Girls. The formal separation of the latter was completed in 1956, and it would in time combine with another Bethlehem Moravian school to produce the present K-12 Moravian Academy.

Salem Academy, the forerunner of Salem College, was modeled after Bethlehem's Seminary for Young Ladies and the two institutions had much in common well into the 20th century.[16] Both reflected the Moravian commitment to education of young women as well as young men. In the words of Comenius, "No reason can be shown why the female sex ... should be kept from a knowledge of languages and wisdom."[17]

Begun in 1772 as a school for the young girls of that early Moravian community, Salem Academy became after 1802 a well-known boarding school for young women from all over the South. It was subsequently chartered in 1866 as Salem Female Academy and added the name Salem College in 1890.

In its first century it offered what one scholar called "a formal education of polite accomplishment."[18] But others have pointed out that it also offered a rigorous program of traditional liberal studies. It sought "...to furnish young woman [sic] an education in classics, mathematics, and sciences equal to that obtained in our best college for young men, and to add to these special training in social culture, music, art, and conversation."[19] Stressing a system of socialization through the "room company" and requiring all students to engage in "minor household services," the school's aim was "...to preserve and perfect every characteristic of complete womanhood" while also teaching southern girls "...order, frugality, and the use of their own limbs."[20]

After surviving the turmoil of the Civil War years and receiving its charter, Salem was by 1878 offering instruction at four grade levels. Post-graduate study was now possible under "The Advanced Course" and six young women received certificates under this program in 1878. In the next decade additional academic departments were added, the program was expanded to four years, and the first Bachelor of Arts degree was awarded in 1890. In 1907 the name was changed to Salem Academy and College to reflect the addition of this new level of study.

During the long presidency of the Rev. Dr. Howard Rondthaler from 1909 to 1949, Salem continued to expand its collegiate program. By 1912 the College had been formally separated from the secondary school although a 1914 report to a Southern Provincial Synod noted that one administration was still operating an Elementary Academy, a High School, and a College.[21] In the 1915-1916 academic year, the College was included in a controversial list of "approximate colleges" by a southern accrediting agency which cited problems of a weak library, inadequacies in laboratory equipment, and low faculty salaries.[22] But in the 1922-1923 academic year, full accreditation was given to the College by the Association of Colleges and Secondary Schools of the Southern States, and it had received American Association of University Women (AAUW) sanction by 1932. By that time Salem offered a Bachelor of Arts degree and a Bachelor of Science degree which included those majoring in Home Economics. The College also offered a number of special programs offering a Bachelor of Music degree after the 1925-1926 school year. Over the years several presidents complained of inadequate support of the Moravian Church.[23] But the College was able over the years to expand the campus, increase its endowment, and build new facilities through the generosity of alumnae and friends.

World War II brought additional changes. During the war there was some adjustment of program to meet government needs and there was some discussion of introducing coeducation. But while it would enroll 55 men under the GI Bill in the immediate post-war years and eventually admit men to its evening division courses, Salem would, to the present, remain a women's college. In doing so, it avoided the fate of some other women's college programs in the mid-20th century, including that of its sister institution in Bethlehem. Instead Salem was able to maintain enrollment, upgrade admission standards and its academic program (including the introduction of an Honors program), and take steps to continue to improve its endowment and facilities.

Today Salem offers an undergraduate program to about 700 women in a residential setting and to men and women in a Continuing Studies Program. It grants a B.A., a B.Mus., a B.S., a B.S. in Business Administration, and both a Master of Arts in Teaching and a Master of Education degree. It declares itself to be an "independent college committed to the liberal arts and quality professional preparation." In defining its present relationship with the Moravian Church, one of its leaders notes that it has in recent years moved "...from an institution controlled almost completely by the Southern Province (of the Moravian Church) to that of an independent academy and college conscious of its Moravian heritage but autonomous in terms of academic program and fiscal affairs."[24] Today that Southern Province elects only one-third of the trustees of the institution and gives financial support only to the College Chaplaincy and the program of religious studies. The location of the College adjacent to the historic Old Salem restoration gives it an opportunity to incorporate the unique Moravian traditions into its programs.

In conclusion, both Salem College and Moravian College have maintained ties to the Moravian Church, but in recent years they have become independent liberal arts colleges drawing their support from a variety of sources. Yet both colleges also continue to reflect and sustain in their academic programs and extra-curricular activities an awareness and sensitivity to the unique traditions of the Moravians.

Endnotes

1.   The definitive history of the Moravian Church is J. Taylor and Kenneth G. Hamilton, *History of the Moravian Church.* Bethlehem, PA and Winston-Salem, NC: Interprovincial Board of Christian Education, 1967. For a brief introduction see John R. Weinlick and Albert H. Frank, *The Moravian Church Through the Ages.* Bethlehem, PA and Winston-Salem, NC: The Moravian Church, 1966.

2.   Gillian K. Gollin, *The Moravians in Two Worlds.* New York: Columbia University Press, 1967.

3.   While successive generations at both Salem and Moravian Colleges have paid homage to the Comenius legacy, there is little evidence that either institution has consciously tried to build its program upon his idea. Instead, both have chosen to follow the model of the American liberal arts college. Moravian College has its Comenius Hall and the student newspaper is

named for him. There have also been occasional lecture series and Comenius Medallion Awards focusing on his legacy. Both Salem College and Moravian College do reflect his ideals in that they are both *teaching* institutions and educate both men and women (Salem's evening division is open to men). Both also place emphasis on language training and physical education and show a concern for life-long learning in their continuing education programs. For further comment see Paul C. Roberts, "Comenian Philosophy and Moravian Education to the Present Day." Ph.D. dissertation, Rutgers University, 1979.

4.   William N. Schwarze, *History of the Moravian College and Theological Seminary*. Bethlehem, PA: Moravian Historical Society, 1909, p. 10.

5.   Quoted in Mabel Haller, "Early Moravian Education in Pennsylvania," *Transactions of the Moravian Historical Society* 15 (1953): 213. Her Chapter VII contains an excellent introduction to Moravian education in Colonial America, and her Chapter VIII gives an analysis of Moravian educational theory and practice.

6.   Schwarze, *History of Moravian College*, Ch. II.

7.   Quoted in Saul Sack, *History of Higher Education in Pennsylvania*. Harrisburg, PA: PA Hist. & Mus. Com., 1963, I, p. 233.

8.   *Ibid.*, p. 233.

9.   John R. Weinlick, *Twentieth Century Moravian College: Challenge and Response*. Bethlehem, PA: Alumni Assoc., 1977. Picks up the narrative history of the College and Theological Seminary from Schwarze's history at the time of the 1907 Centennial.

10.   An unpublished "Moravian Theological Seminary Factbook, 1992-3."

11.   William C. Reichel and William H. Bigler, *A History of the Moravian Seminary for Young Ladies at Bethlehem, Pa.*, 4th Edition. Bethlehem, PA: Moravian Seminary, 1901. These histories of the Seminary are commonly called "Souvenirs" and focus almost exclusively on the early years. But this 1901

education does include a list of the students and faculty up through the mid-19th century.

12. For comments on the role of these women's seminaries in the development of women's higher education, see Thomas Woody, *A History of Women's Education in the United States*. New York: Octagon Press, 1966, II, p. 143.

13. Sack, *History of Higher Education*, II, p. 578.

14. *Ibid.*, p. 579.

15. Weinlick, *Twentieth Century Moravian College*, Chapter VIII, is the only published history of the collegiate program of the Moravian Seminary and College for Women.

16. Francis Griffin, *Less Time for Meddling: A History of Salem Academy and College, 1772-1866*. Winston-Salem, NC: John Blair, 1979; and Woody, *Women's Education*, II, p. 380ff.

17. Quoted in Griffin, *Less Time for Meddling*, p. 7.

18. Woody, *Women's Education*, I, p. 108.

19. *Ibid.*, II, p. 381.

20. *Ibid.*

21. Unpublished report of the President of Salem Academy and College to the Triennial Synod of the Southern Province of the Moravian Church, 1914.

22. Woody, *Women's Education*, II, p. 187.

23. Dale G. Gramley in his *Remembrances of Salem's 13th President*. Salem, NC: Salem Academy and College, 1985, p. 257, makes this charge, and the unpublished reports of other presidents to Provincial Synods tend to confirm his observation.

24. From a letter from Salem's Chaplain to the author, June 28, 1994.

Bibliographic Entries

148. Blair, Marian. "Contemporary Evidence -- Salem Boarding School, 1834-1844." *North Carolina Historical Review* 27 (1950): 142-61.

Uses letters received by Academy principal to portray life within the school and suggest factors explaining its growth.*

149.   Fries, Adelaide. *Historical Sketch of Salem Female Academy*. Salem, NC: Crist and Kehlin, 1902.

Describes the beginnings and development of the school that became Salem College. Written from primary sources by the long-standing archivist and historian of the Southern Province of the Moravian Church.

150.   Gramley, Dale G. *Remembrances of Salem's 13th President*. Salem, NC: Salem Academy and College, 1985.

Describes in a lively, personal style the experiences of a former president at Salem in a crucial period of the college's development, 1949-1971.

151.   Griffin, Francis. *Less Time for Meddling: A History of Salem Academy and College, 1772-1866*. Winston-Salem, NC: John Blair, 1979.

Contains a well-written narrative of the founding of Salem Academy and its development up through the American Civil War. Unfortunately, it contains little on the creation of a collegiate program in the 20th century.

152.   Haller, Mabel. "Early Moravian Education in Pennsylvania." *Transactions of the Moravian Historical Society* 15 (1953): 1-409.

Uses the rich resources of the Moravian Archives in Bethlehem to analyze in detail the development in the colonial era of Moravian schools in Bethlehem, Nazareth, Lititz, and other Moravian communities. Includes an in-depth study of Moravian educational philosophy and pedagogical principles and an exhaustive bibliography.

153. Hamilton, J. Taylor and Kenneth G. *History of the Moravian Church.* Bethlehem, PA and Winston-Salem, NC: Interprovincial Board of Christian Education, 1967.

Examines in detail the development of the Moravian movement in both Europe and America.

154. Hamilton, Kenneth, ed. *Records of the Moravians in North Carolina.* Raleigh, NC: 1966.

Contains volumes of historical information on Moravian life in North Carolina. Volumes 10 and 11 include information on education and Salem College.

155. Hickson, Shirley Ann. "The Development of Higher Education for Women in the Antebellum South." Ph.D. dissertation, University of South Carolina, 1985.

Includes Salem in its study of five institutions, but focuses on the Academy prior to its development of a collegiate program.

156. Hixon, Ivy. "Academic Requirements of Salem College, 1854-1909." *North Carolina Historical Review* 27 (1950): 419-29.

Uses college catalogues and issues of *The Academy* as well as Moravian histories to study the era in which Salem expanded its secondary program to include college-level courses.*

157. Monroe, Will. *Comenius and the Beginnings of Educational Reform.* New York: Charles Scribner's Sons, 1912.

Analyzes the impact Comenius had on European educational reformers including Francke, Rousseau, Pestalozzi, Froebel, and Herbart.

158.   *The Moravian Archives*, Winston-Salem, NC.

Contains a wealth of unpublished material on Salem Academy and College including detailed reports of the College to the Triennial Synods of the Southern Province of the Moravian Church.

159.   Reichel, William C. and William H. Bigler. *A History of the Moravian Seminary for Young Ladies at Bethlehem, PA. With a Catalogue of its Pupils, 1785-1870. With a Sketch of the School from 1742 to 1785, By Bishop J. Mortimer Levering, and a Continuation of the History and Catalogue to the Year 1900.* Fourth Edition, Bethlehem, PA: Published for the Seminary, 1901.

Includes a list of students from 1785-1870, a brief sketch of the school 1742-1785, and some additional material on the institution up to 1900. Labeled a "Souvenir" on the book cover and in some bibliographical listings.

160.   Rights, Douglas L. "Salem in the War Between the States." *North Carolina Historical Review* 27 (1950): 277-88.

Shows how Salem was able to remain open during the Civil War.*

161.   Roberts, Paul C. "Comenian Philosophy and Moravian Education from 1850 to the Present Day." Ph.D. dissertation, Rutgers University, 1979.

On the basis of documents and interviews, concludes that Comenius' philosophy and pedagogical techniques have not always been the basis for modern Moravian higher education but that his influence is present in the elementary and secondary schools.

162. Rondthaler, Howard E. "New Plans Against an Old Background, Salem College, 1866-1884." *North Carolina Historical Review* 27 (1950): 430-36.

Focuses on the transitional period in which Salem began to add college-level courses to its program.*

163. Schwarze, William N. *History of the Moravian College and Theological Seminary Founded at Nazareth, Penna., October 2, 1807. Reorganized at Bethlehem, Penna., August 30, 1958.* Bethlehem, PA: Times Publishing Company, Printers, 1910.

Includes a definitive study of the creation and development of Moravian higher education in what is now the Northern Province of the Moravian Church. Based on primary sources and written by a former president of Moravian College and Theological Seminary and a former Archivist of the Moravian Church.

164. Spinka, Matthew. *John Amos Comenius: That Incomparable Moravian.* Chicago, IL: The University of Chicago Press, 1943 (UMI reprint 1960).

Reflects the mid-twentieth century rediscovery of Comenius and his position in the Moravian Church.

165. Weinlick, John R. *Twentieth Century Moravian College: Challenge and Response.* Bethlehem, PA: Alumni Assoc. of Moravian College, 1977.

Uses documentary sources, interviews, and personal reminiscences to survey the dramatic changes in Moravian higher education in Bethlehem in the 20th century. Written by a former dean of the Theological Seminary and well-known church historian, it includes a rare chapter on the history of the former Moravian College for Women, now part of modern Moravian College.

166. Weinlick, John R. and Albert H. Frank. *The Moravian Church through the Ages.* Bethlehem, PA and Winston-Salem, NC: The Moravian Church in America, 1966.

Provides a readable introduction to the history of the Old Unitas Fratrum and the Renewed Church in Europe and America. Includes chapters on John Hus and Comenius.

167. Wenhold, Lucy. "The Salem Boarding School Between 1892 and 1822." *North Carolina Historical Review* 27 (1950): 32-46.

Reconstructs the intimate life of the Academy in the first two decades.*

168. Woody, Thomas. *A History of Women's Education in the United States.* 2 vols. New York: Octagon Books, 1966.

Gives an overview of the development of elementary, secondary, and higher education of women from the colonial era up through the first quarter of the twentieth century.

169. Young, Elizabeth Barber. *A Study of the Curricula of Seven Selected Women's Colleges of the Southern States.* New

York: Teacher's College, Columbia University, 1932, Chapter I, pp. 9-21.

Contains a careful analysis of the development of Salem Academy and its gradual evolution of a collegiate program in the late 19th and early 20th centuries. Includes a unique perspective in its comparison of Salem to other southern women's colleges.

*The five starred items in this section were reprinted as *Salem Academy and Colleges Through the Years*. Salem, Alumnae Association, 1951.

CHAPTER 8
United Church of Christ
Colleges, Universities, and Seminaries

Lowell H. Zuck

This chapter is divided into two parts. The first describes briefly the complicated history of religion and higher education in the United Church of Christ (UCC). The second presents annotated bibliographies of recent institutional materials arranged alphabetically by twenty-six college names within prior denominational frames and ten seminary names. It then concludes with an unannotated listing of recent general works regarding higher education both within and beyond the UCC, since the Congregational tradition within the UCC has maintained a strong conviction that colleges should *not* be under the control of an ecclesiastical body.

The History of United Church of Christ Higher Education: Transplanting the Covenant

At least four streams of ecclesiastical history have come together to form the educational enterprise of the United Church of Christ. The UCC was formed in 1957 with the union of the Congregational Christian Churches and the Evangelical and Reformed Church. Each of the two churches had already joined two other separate traditions in 1931 and 1934.[1]

The clearest single tradition uniting the UCC is the combined influence of continental European Reformed covenant theology, brought to abortive fruition within the English Puritan Revolution, but allowing its colonial anticipation as New England Puritanism to become the most powerful initial American religious/educational paradigm.[2] Puritanism in America more clearly than in England distinguished the mutual and interrelated roles of the church committed to the rule of faith, the college dependent upon reason, and the political commonwealth based upon law.

Reformation influences dominated Puritan educational ideals. Puritans saw themselves as heirs of a medieval university tradition conceiving of the whole of human society as unified in Christ in terms of his royal, priestly, and prophetic roles. Thus, the state was based on law; the church was founded on revelation; and the university was upheld by reason. To this day this symbolism is upheld in the Western world by gowns worn by justices in court, ministers in church, and professors/graduates at commencement.

At the first colonial college, Harvard, this tradition was derived from Calvin and English clergymen like William Ames, who was a thorough covenant theologian. Zwingli's successor in Zurich, Switzerland, Heinrich Bullinger, wrote the pioneer treatise on the covenant of God in 1534, stressing the freedom of God's election along with human responsibility to fulfill covenant conditions. Ursinus, a German Reformed theologian, developed a covenant of works scheme in 1562, which English Puritans developed further in the 1580s.[3]

Thus, the New England Puritans regarded themselves as a people under a covenant with God to continue here on these shores the covenant God had established with Abraham and Isaac extending into the covenant of grace. In 1643 they said:

"After God had carried us safe to New England and we had builded our houses, provided necessities for our livelihood, rear'd convenient places for God's worship, and settled the Civil Government, one of the next things we longed for and looked after was to advance learning."

In the three-fold system, the college part descended from the school of the prophets under Elijah, through the Court schools of Charlemagne, the Genevan academy, Leyden University, Scottish universities, and especially Emmanuel College, Cambridge, until the mantle was placed upon the president of Harvard in 1636. Like the ancient prophets, the college was to bring the judgment of God upon both priest and king.[4]

The curriculum emphasized classical and biblical languages, catechetical divinity, and rhetoric. Its administrators and tutors, and many of its overseers, were clergymen. Yet from the earliest days, Harvard and its successors were also interested in educating magistrates and merchants, and over half of Harvard's graduates between 1642 and 1689 did *not* enter the ministry. Though all studied the same classical disciplines, it was assumed that the college needed academic freedom from both the church and the government, even though it had a close relationship, even dependency, upon both institutions.

When the Massachusetts Cambridge Platform in 1648 outlined the dispersal of church authority into local congregations, that establishment of the New England Way assured the college of academic freedom within the Reformed system of church, state, and academy.[5] Similar situations effected the character of the other eight colleges founded by several traditions during colonial times. Only the University of Pennsylvania had nonreligious origins, although by the time of the Revolution it was also under Anglican auspices.

Among Congregationalists, the second colonial college, Yale, from its founding in 1701 also flourished under the leadership of clergy, although it had difficulty deciding what town to call its home. A degree of rivalry and dissatisfaction with incipient liberalism at Harvard figured in its origin. More than Harvard,

Yale through the early nineteenth century came to be the leading conservative college. Its size and influence fell behind Harvard around the 1870s.

Dartmouth was begun by Congregationalists as a clerical Indian school in 1769. It, however, also came to follow the legally independent plan of the other colonial colleges, refusing religious tests for students.

Like all other colonial colleges, the Congregational schools focused upon pagan Greek, Roman, and Christian literature. After the Civil War, they slowly changed due to the impact of science and new knowledge.

After the Revolution, the transition to completely private status caused some anxiety for colleges, although Harvard continued to enjoy a monopoly in Massachusetts until Tufts was founded by Universalists in 1852. But over 250 new colleges were established in the nation between the Revolution and the Civil War, marking the emergence of denominationalism as a new basis for college founding.

Legally, the Dartmouth College case in 1819 established the right for chartered private institutions to conduct instruction without state interference. The Second Great Awakening also led to a peak of new college founding between 1856 and 1861. The religious revival also was accompanied by fears of Roman Catholic schooling and the felt need for literate ministers on the Western frontier.

Although Congregationalists long resisted becoming a denomination, they aided Western college founding considerably with their 1843 Society for the Promotion of Collegiate and Theological Education at the West (SPCTEW).[6] Contributing as much as $74,000 in a single year to new colleges, the influence of the SPCTEW stretched from coast to coast with the founding of Pomona College in California in 1887. Common efforts with the Presbyterians in that same society resulted in colleges begun in twenty-one of the thirty-four states prior to the Civil War.[7]

The 1801 Plan of Union (church cooperation between Presbyterians and Congregationalists) allowed Congregational missionaries to begin twenty-one colleges. After its failure, Congregationalists established eight colleges in the upper Mississippi valley, including Illinois (1829), Knox (1837), Northland (1842), Olivet (1844), Grinnel (1846), Beloit (1846), Pacific (1849), and Ripon (1851). Wheaton College was founded in 1860 in Illinois when Congregationalists protested Presbyterian domination of Knox and Illinois Colleges. Two colleges on the West Coast, including the College of California (1855) -- which became the secular University of California in 1868 -- were Congregationalist-related prior to the Civil War.

From about 1860 through 1900 a new period in higher education brought about the emergence of the university and the dominance of impersonal research motivations. If an early covenantal ordering of education had been gravely challenged by denominational or sectarian religious rivalries (with positive missionary outreach also manifesting itself), the third period of university dominance also threatened religious perspectives, while it also derived to some extent from the same covenantal motivation.

The departure of southern legislators from Congress enabled passage of the Morrill Act in 1862, which gave federal land to the states in support of technical and agricultural education. The A & M era in public education had emerged. Since money derived from sale of these lands could be distributed in a variety of ways, even some private colleges with religious roots became "land-grant" schools, including Yale and Dartmouth.

Long before that, renewed graduate education in German universities had appealed to American scholars able to study abroad. In 1876, a century after the Declaration of Independence and 240 years after Harvard's founding, Johns Hopkins University opened in Baltimore, with a concentration upon graduate students and the production of research.[8] The new universities with their professionalism and their later skepticism about the compatibility of science and religion tended to separate their identities from the older religious colleges of the previous age, which had stressed liberal education for undergraduates along with the development of piety and virtue.

Even though the new Baptist-oriented University of Chicago developed a divinity school of significance for later UCC theological education, it quickly moved in university directions that appeared to be more secular than religious. Most four-year colleges drifted beyond religious orbits in the post-Civil War years. Harvard, Yale, and California severed whatever Congregational ties they had previously maintained. The 1905 Carnegie Foundation for the Advancement of Teaching tended to encourage secularization since colleges had to sacrifice most denominational ties in order to qualify faculty for Carnegie pension benefits.

Since Congregationalism had in the meantime itself become a denomination, church support established the American Education Society in 1893, and the Congregational Education Society in the following year. Then in 1921 the Congregational Foundation for Education assumed responsibility for church-related colleges, providing $200,000 in aid during its first year. An uneasy period followed that attempted to combine support without control. That uncertain situation continues right up to the present.

Along more missionary-oriented lines, however, the contributions of Congregationalists to support of African-American education in the South following the Civil War was considerable. For instance, currently, the Council for Higher Education of the UCC and especially the continuing American Missionary Association (AMA), founded in 1846, relate to six post-Civil War African-American colleges they helped found: Fisk (1866), Talladega (1867), Dillard (1869), Tougaloo (1869), LeMoyne Owen (1871), and Huston-Tillotson (1876). The School of Religion of Howard University (1867) is also a seminary related to the UCC. In addition, the AMA was instrumental in founding Hampton Normal and Agricultural Institute in 1861, the first school planted by the North to educate the children of slavery.[9]

Wesley Hotchkiss has offered a helpful interpretation of the secular era in education. He says that in this period not only was a wall built between the church and the state but walls were being built inside the secular academy. The older tripartite division was effective so long as the sovereignty of God kept them in relationship. But the academy enthroned reason as its sovereign, becoming the technological and scientific center for the new nation.

The academy, extricated from the church, and free from the state, became the empirical servant of technology. When the rule of reason, the rule of law, and the rule of faith become separated from each other in a secularized society, the result is an arrogant, dehumanized rationalism, law without mercy or equal justice, and an isolated, fragmented sectarianism.

Thus, Hotchkiss argues, integration and synthesis are necessary for us. The institution in our society that can best do this, he thinks, is the church-related college, and, presumably, the church-related seminary. It is this perspective that currently informs the interest of the UCC in church-related higher education.[10]

Thus far, we have discussed only Congregational higher education institutions. Other people within the UCC, because of their time of settlement in the U.S. and their different ethnic characteristics, have developed varying patterns of support for higher education. Many of them participate, however, in an understanding of a common continental European Reformed and English Puritan tradition, which provides a unifying perspective in spite of notable differences.

An alternative outlook on church-related higher education is provided by the German Reformed tradition within the UCC.[11] When Germans began arriving in colonial Pennsylvania a century later than the Puritans in New England, they were unable to implement the covenantal structures originated by their ancestors in Germany and Switzerland. The Quaker "establishment" in Pennsylvania modeled a sectarian or denominational alternative to covenanted New England. A less uniform population was allowed to settle on the shores of the Delaware and the Schuylkill Rivers, and no pretensions assuming churchly domination by majority Lutherans or Reformed were possible in that colony. Moreover, the Lutherans and Reformed alike suffered from lack of clerical supervision or ordained clergy available to serve scattered immigrants having to establish their own homesteads in isolated and uncoordinated communities.

Higher education, therefore, was unavailable to immigrant Germans, poverty-stricken and struggling with what now appears to have been a foreign language. To be sure, literacy was high among immigrant Swiss and Germans. But educational and church institutions were not easy to come by. And the unfamiliarity of what we now know as a normal American religious way of life was difficult for churchly immigrants having few leaders in their midst.

Though about 15,000 German Reformed people were scattered throughout eastern Pennsylvania and surrounding areas in the early eighteenth century, no churches and no pastors were available for them until about 1725. Michael Schlatter, one of their organizing immigrant pastors, lost favor with his churches in the 1750s because of his willingness to support "charity schools," which the Germans suspected were instruments of Anglican conversion, supported as they were by ample gifts of English people to help "poor Germans."

Thus, higher education remained out of reach for German-speaking Pennsylvania immigrants until the founding of a joint Lutheran/Reformed Franklin College at Lancaster in 1787. In spite of widespread support, the German college did not flourish, and the German Reformed Church had to wait for organized training of its pastors until 1825, when it was able to begin a struggling seminary at Carlisle, moving later to Mercersberg and Lancaster.[12]

The union principle at Franklin College did not work well because of lack of financial support and because Lutherans and Reformed tended to quarrel with each other in spite of their similarities. When the seminary began and when Franklin and

Marshall Colleges were combined later into a single Reformed institution after 1853, the organizational principle used by the German Reformed Church was to place financial and administrative control firmly in the hands of the denomination, a viewpoint never fully accepted by Congregationalists.

Glen T. Miller has pointed out two directions that continental European Protestant immigrants followed in nineteenth-century America: a desire to begin anew the state churches they knew in the homeland, and a more discontented effort to improve their theology and piety in the new world.[13] The German Reformed people were largely of the first type. But their seminary leaders, John W. Nevin and Philip Schaff (the latter himself a German/Swiss immigrant professor/pastor), began an innovative liturgical/catholic movement that brought about inner-churchly controversy between 1843 and 1863, and also provided the liveliest theological conversation in the country.

The Mercersburg theology manifested discontent with American (including Congregational) revivalism while at the same time it was catholic and ecumenical. Its sense of tradition was deeper than that of other American Protestants of the time. It also resembled somewhat the views of a quite different innovative linguistic and nurturing theological tradition derived from Congregationalism and developed in Hartford by Horace Bushnell.

While the Mercersburg battle continued, with the oppositional establishment of a new college, Ursinus, in 1869, and comparable institutions more adapted to the West in Ohio and Wisconsin, Heidelberg (1850) and Mission House (1862), a third denominational root of the UCC was taking shape in Missouri, as a result of efforts in Germany on the part of the Prussian monarch to unite the Lutheran and Reformed churches.[14]

All of the German Reformed people so far described thought of themselves primarily as *Reformed* (including Schaff who had himself been ordained by the Prussian Union Evangelical Church). A sizable group of other German immigrants in the West and in areas such as Buffalo desired to relate to

Evangelical, that is, Lutheran and/or Reformed union church patterns.

Already in 1840, in what is now suburban St. Louis, an Evangelical Church Association of the West was begun as a pastoral conference, which grew into a large denomination known after the 1870s as the Evangelical Synod of North America. Although led initially by German-speaking immigrant pastors commissioned by Swiss or German mission societies, beginning with Friedrich Schmid, at Ann Arbor, Michigan, in 1833, the missionaries cooperated with university-trained clergy, especially Adolf Baltzer from Berlin, in establishing Evangelical institutions on the frontier.[15]

The Evangelical clerical leaders demanded high educational standards for ordaining clergy, although education for the young was also regarded as a major responsibility, since instruction in the German language was not provided in the public schools. Thus, the Evangelicals began a theological seminary at Marthasville, Missouri, in 1850. A journal, the *Friedensbote* (Messenger of Peace) began appearing the same year, and a bi-weekly newssheet for children, the *Christliche Kinder-Zeitung*, began in 1867. The Evangelicals published their own revision of Luther's and the Heidelberg Catechism, the *Evangelical Catechism*, in 1847, and a dignified and unifying *Evangelische Agenda* (Book of Worship) in 1857.

In 1871 the Evangelicals took over what became Elmhurst College, near Chicago, which served for a long time as a pre-ministerial school in preparation for Marthasville/Eden Seminary. By 1883, out of 557 Evangelical congregations, 266 were supporting parochial schools, employing 110 full-time teachers, in addition to the pastors who taught them. With Americanization, the parochial schools faded, so that the more conservative Missouri Synod Lutherans were left with the largest parochial school system next to the Catholics in America.

In a real sense, the Evangelicals, like the Reformed to a slightly lesser extent, had also transplanted the covenant to the New World, although they had little specific knowledge of

Congregational traditions. Their people combined a conservative desire to maintain old established church patterns along with an innovative willingness to engage in diaconal church-related services derived from German Pietism.

They suffered educational deficiencies while they maintained a strong commitment to preparation of educated, committed ministers. It is no accident, perhaps, that the strongest members of the theological family of twentieth-century Protestantism, including Reinhold and H. Richard Niebuhr, were born and educated within the Evangelical tradition, while at the same time they were always eager to improve their own educational institutions.[16]

In conclusion, we turn back to look at the educational contributions of the fourth UCC tradition, the Christian Connection, which is important though little known. Unlike the three other main branches of the UCC, the Christians relate more directly to American-frontier experiences, as restorationist movements emerged in three late-eighteenth-century areas: the South, New England, and Kentucky.

In 1792 James O'Kelly, rejecting episcopal authority, withdrew from the early Methodist church. Two years after leaving Methodism in Virginia, O'Kelly and his followers moved against sectarian labels, desiring to be known only as "Christians." A similar movement arose about the same time among New England Baptists, when Abner Jones organized a "Christian Fellowship" in 1800, abandoning sectarian names and human creeds and making piety alone the test of Christian fellowship.[17] Finally, Western followers of the Cane Ridge, Kentucky, revivalist Barton W. Stone continued a separate existence of many "Christians" who were not able to unite with the similar Campbellite "Disciples."

Appealing to popular piety of the time, Christians sprang up in many places, stressing that Christ was the only head of the church, that the New Testament was the only rule of faith, and that "Christian" was their sole name. Unitive in spirit (and divisive in practice), various churches calling themselves

"Christian" in 1819 held a general conference in Portsmouth, New Hampshire. By 1833 a general convention was organized which in effect formed a Christian Church. Christians combined a somewhat anti-intellectual approach to faith issues with innovative publication and education ventures, including the first religious journal, *The Herald of Gospel Liberty* (1800), openness toward female ordination, and willingness to experiment with educational ventures.

Antioch College in Ohio began in 1852 as a nonsegregated coeducational institution under Christian auspices, which as late as the twentieth century came to be recognized for its successful cooperative education plan. Its first president was the notable educational reformer, Horace Mann.[18] Mann had previously contributed significantly to the American public school movement and was the clearest advocate of education for freedom. Defiance College in Ohio was chartered as a non-sectarian institution in 1850, and came to be affiliated with the Christian Churches in 1900. Among other Christian colleges, Elon College (begun in 1889 in North Carolina) remains a strong Southern educational institution.

An interesting reform movement of the early nineteenth century which touched upon Christian educational interests was the so-called "Friends of Education," including among its number Horace Mann, Alexander Campbell (founder of the Disciples who united with other Christians), William McGuffey (Ohio public school organizer and compiler of the famous McGuffey readers), and Catharine Beecher (Congregational founder of the celebrated Hartford Female Seminary in 1831). The Friends of Education worked to create systems of free elementary schools, promoted education of women, encouraged teacher training, and helped increase the number of academies and colleges.[19]

Thus, the four traditions that came to unite as the UCC each in their own way found higher education to be significant in their program for church life. As higher education entered the post-World-War-II boom period, UCC institutions (like many others) grew, experienced troubles, and went through many crises.

It had taken more than a century before many colleges followed the example of Yale in appointing the Rev. Naphtali Daggett in 1755 as America's first college chaplain. As late as 1920, fewer than twenty-five full-time college chaplains served in U.S. colleges. Between 1880 and 1910, Congregationalists established many full-time campus pastorates at secular universities. The Disciples of Christ attempted their own college teaching ministry, establishing Bible chairs at five state universities by 1909.

After 1910, Congregationalists established national funding for campus ministry. Following World War II, different directions became advisable. The dramatic increase in number of students, combined with a lack of funding, has encouraged interchurch ventures, in which UCC clergy and laypeople have banded together with Presbyterians, American Baptists, Disciples of Christ, Episcopalians, and others to provide campus religious services. The percentage of full-time campus ministers has increased at a significantly faster rate than that of the clergy at large, and the style of campus ministry has broadened. The Disciples of Christ have increased the number of Bible chairs at state universities to fifty.

Student-led religious groups on campus have also been strengthened, and efforts have been made to give students the responsibility for local evangelism. But more conservative organizations than the UCC feel comfortable with having been more successful in making use of these efforts.

Twenty years ago, Wesley Hotchkiss summarized four critical issues in our society affecting the UCC. They appear to be equally relevant today.[20]

First, he said, is the question of meaning and purpose. When the question of what knowledge means is asked, "the fusion of traditions of church relationships in our colleges has uniquely prepared them to deal with those questions inside the curriculum of the colleges."

Second, is the question of the integration of the disciplines around the basic purposes of education. Our colleges "believe that to educate is to *e-duce*, to bring out the best that is in the human spirit…. Therefore to educate whole human beings, the curriculum and method must be whole."

Third, is the question of "…the rising interest of this generation in the 'new vocationalism.' Many educators are misinterpreting this interest as a new demand for job training…. The real question is: 'What shall I do with my life?' That is a vocational question and it has to do with 'calling' (vocare) and human destiny."

Fourth, "…is the difficult matter of dealing with religion, both in the curriculum and outside the curriculum…. The ultimate source of freedom of the academy is religious. The same public posture of the college which frees it from the church and sectarianism frees it from the state, but it is a freedom arising from the covenant with a sovereignty higher than any human institution …. The church-related colleges, particularly those of the United Church of Christ, are obligated to 'own their covenant' and to make a new statement of academic freedom and purpose which will speak with power and persuasion to the crucial problems of education for our time."

Endnotes

1.   For Congregational-Christian history, see John von Rohl, *The Shaping of American Congregationalism, 1620-1957*. Cleveland: Pilgrim Press, 1992. For Evangelical and Reformed history, see David Dunn, ed., *A History of the Evangelical and Reformed Church*. Reissued with new introduction by Lowell H. Zuck. Cleveland: Pilgrim Press, 1990.

2.   Consult John von Rohl, *The Covenant of Grace and Puritan Thought*. Atlanta: Scholars Press, 1986.

3.   David A. Weir, *The Origins of the Federal Theology in Sixteenth Century Reformed Thought*. New York: Oxford University Press, 1990.

4. George H. Williams, *Wilderness and Paradise in Christian Thought*. New York: Harper & Brothers, 1962, Part II.

5. Williston Walker, *Creeds and Platforms of Congregationalism*. Reissued with new introduction by Elizabeth Norbeck. Cleveland: Pilgrim Press, 1991, pp. 157-237.

6. James Findlay, "Agency, Denominations and the Western Colleges, 1830-1860: Some Connections between Evangelicalism and American Higher Education," *Church History* 50 (March 1981): 64-80; "The SPCTEW and Western Colleges: Religion and Higher Education in Mid-Nineteenth Century America," *History of Education Quarterly* 17 (1977): 31-62.

7. A brief summary of Western college founding is by F. Michael Perko, "Religion and Collegiate Education," in Charles H. Lippy and Peter W. Williams, eds., *Encyclopedia of the American Religious Experience*. New York: Charles Scribner's Sons, 1968, III, pp. 1613-15.

8. W.H. Cowley and Don Williams, *International and Historical Roots of American Higher Education*. New York: Garland Publishing, Inc., 1991, pp. 136-41.

9. Joe Martin Richardson, *Christian Reconstruction: The American Missionary Association and Southern Blacks, 1861-1890*. Athens, GA: University of Georgia Press, 1986.

10. Wesley A. Hotchkiss, "The Prophetic Academy: An Historical Perspective on U.C.C. Related Colleges," Supplement to *Journal of Current Social Issues* (1977): 66-71. A publication of the United Church Board for Homeland Ministries.

11. See Louis W. Gunnemann, *The Shaping of the United Church of Christ: An Essay on the History of American Christianity*. New York: Pilgrim Press, 1977.

12. George W. Richards, *History of the Theological Seminary of the Reformed Church in the U.S., 1825-1934*. Lancaster, PA: n.p., 1952.

13. Glenn T. Miller, *Piety and Intellect: The Aims and Purposes of Ante-Bellum Theological Education*. Atlanta: Scholars Press, 1990, p. 344.

14.   Carl E. Schneider, *The German Church on the American Frontier: A Study in the Rise of Religion Among the Germans of the West: Based on the History of the Evangelischer Kirchenverein des Westens, 1840-1866*. St. Louis: Eden Publishing House, 1939.

15.   Consult articles by Lowell H. Zuck on the Evangelical Synod, Louis Nollau, George Wall, Adolf Baltzer, Andreas Irion, Samuel D. Press, and Louis Goebel, in *Dictionary of the Presbyterian and Reformed Tradition in America*, D.G. Hart and Mark Noll, eds., Downers Grover, IL: InterVarsity Press, 1995.

16.   Donald H. Stone, *Reinhold Niebuhr: A Mentor to the Twentieth Century*. Louisville: Westminster/John Knox Press, 1992.

17.   Note the discussion concerning New England Christians in Nathan O. Hatch, *Democratization of American Christianity*. New Haven: Yale University Press, 1989.

18.   On Horace Mann, see Lawrence A. Cremin, *American Education: The National Experience, 1783-1876*. New York: Harper & Row, 1980, pp. 133-42.

19.   Miller, "Piety and Intellect," p. 419.

20.   Hotchkiss, "The Prophetic Academy," pp. 70-71.

Bibliographic Entries

Institutional Materials

A. Related to Congregational Churches

Amherst College (1821)

170.   Brennan, Robert T. "The Making of the Liberal College: Alexander Meiklejohn at Amherst." *History of Education Quarterly* 28 (Winter 1988): 569-97.

Analyzes the introduction of coherent undergraduate learning experience at Amherst.

Beloit College (1846)

171. Savage, Chuck. *Beloit College: A Contemporary Portrait, A Timeless Testament.* Beloit, WI: Beloit College, 1992.

A 112-page history and contemporary sketch.

Carleton College (1866)

172. Jarchow, Merrill E. *Carleton Moves Confidently Into Its Second Century, 1966-1992.* Northfield, MN: Carleton College, 1992.

A 177-page introduction to Carleton's recent history.

Dartmouth College (1769)

173. Whitehead, John S., and Herbst, Jurgen. "How to Think About the Dartmouth College Case." *History of Education Quarterly* 26 (Fall 1986): 333-49.

Analyzes the 1819 victory of Federalists and religionists which kept higher education in private hands.

Doane College (1872)

174. Ziegler, Donald Jenks. *A College on a Hill: Life at Doane, 1872-1987.* Lincoln, NB: Media Publishing, 1990.

A comprehensive history of Doane College.

Grinnell College (1846)

175.   Haas, Dennis W. *Sermons for Seekers: Preaching to a College Community, 1966-1986.* Grinnell, IA: Grinnell College, 1988.

Twenty sermons preached by a college chaplain.

176.   Wall, Joseph Frazier. *The History of Grinnell College.* Grinnell, IA: Grinnell College, 1988.

A recent history of Grinnell College.

Harvard University (1636)

177.   Keller, Phyllis. *Getting at the Core: Curricular Reform at Harvard.* Cambridge: Harvard University Press, 1982.

Outlines the development of Harvard's core curriculum during the 1970s.

178.   Rosovsky, Henry. *The University: An Owner's Manual.* New York: W.W. Norton, 1990.

Provides an inside view of Harvard as an American research university of the 1980s.

Howard University (1867)

179.   Brown, Peggy, ed. "Educational Equity for Minorities," in *Forum for Liberal Education.* Washington, DC: Association of American Colleges, January-February, 1983.

Evaluates several minority enrichment programs including Howard University's summer enrichment program for gifted elementary youth.

Illinois College (1829)

180. Yeager, Iver F. *Illinois College 160th Anniversary Papers: A Legacy of Excellence, 1829-1989.* Jacksonville, IL: Illinois College, 1990.

Numerous papers celebrating a pioneer Illinois college.

Northland College (1892)

181. Lachecki, Marina Denise. *Building an Ecumenical Campus Ministry.* Ashland, WI: Northland College, 1993.

An internship project of the institute in pastoral ministries at Northland.

Pacific University (1849)

182. Dressler, June L. *Pacific University Alumni: Participation in the Annual Fund.* Forest Grove, OR: Pacific University, 1993.

A recent account of financial support efforts at a northwestern college.

Ripon College (1851)

183. Ashley, Robert Paul. *Ripon College: A History.* Ripon, WI: Ripon College Press, 1990.

A substantial history representing Congregationalism in Wisconsin's educational history.

Westminster College of Salt Lake City (1875)

184. Mott, Adam Joseph. *A New Library/Resource Center for Westminster College*. Salt Lake City, UT: Westminster College, 1990.

A brief account of literary efforts in Salt Lake City.

Yale University (1701)

185. Lane, Jack C. "The Yale Report of 1828 and Liberal Education." *History of Education Quarterly* 27 (Fall 1987): 325-38.

A classic conservative statement reconsidered, showing the contributions that Yale's liberal education could make to society during a time of change.

186. Pierson, George W. *The Founding of Yale: The Legend of the Forty Folios*. New Haven: Yale University Press, 1989.

Shows how claims during colonial times for Yale's freedom continued to be echoed after the Revolution.

B. Related to the Christian Church (not to be confused with the Christian Church, Disciples of Christ)

Antioch College (1852)

187. Morrison, Jack. *The Maturing of the Arts on the American Campus: A Commentary*. Lanham, MD: University Press of America, 1985.

Studies the growth of the arts in seventeen colleges, including Antioch College, Dartmouth, and Harvard.

Elon College (1889)

188. Waggoner, James M. *The Fighting Christians: Elon College Athletics Through the Years*. Greensboro, NC: Greensboro Printing Co., 1989.

An extensive record of a college athletic department.

C. Related to the Reformed Church in the U.S. (German Reformed Church)

Catawba College (1851)

189. Dedmond, Francis B. *Catawba: The Story of a College*. Boone, NC: Arromondt House, 1989.

A recent history telling the story of the only Southern German Reformed college.

Franklin and Marshall College (1787)

190. Leslie, W. Bruce. *Gentlemen and Scholars: College and Community in the "Age of the University."* University Park, PA: Pennsylvania State University Press, 1992.

Describes the social role of the American college between the Civil War and World War I, looking at Franklin and Marshall, as well as Bucknell, Princeton, and Swarthmore.

Heidelberg College (1850)

191. Cassell, William C. "A Small College Opens a Window on the World." *Educational Record* 68 (Spring 1987): 12-16.

Development of a range of international opportunities arising from a handful of juniors studying abroad.

192. Kolehmainen, John I. *Remembering Bygone Days*. Tiffin, OH: Computer Works, 1991.

A beloved professor remembers his Heidelberg teaching days from 1938 to 1980.

Hood College (1893)

193. *Hood: Answers in Action*. Frederick, MD: Hood College, 1988. 37 pp.

What one women's liberal arts college is doing to meet the challenges confronting American higher education.

Ursinus College (1869)

194. Staiger, Margaret B. *Ursinus College Faculty: 1869-1988*. Collegeville, PA: Ursinus College, 1988.

An account of faculty at a German Reformed college.

D. Related to the Evangelical Synod of North America

Elmhurst College (1871)

195. Crocco, Stephen. "Institutional Identity and Change: Lessons from H. Richard Niebuhr," Columbus, OH: *Summary and Proceedings*, American Theological Library Association, 1989, pp. 113-27.

 Reflections upon Niebuhr's leadership of Elmhurst College from 1924 to 1927.

196. Westermeyer, Paul. "H. Richard Niebuhr, Music, and Elmhurst College." 1990. Sixty-four-page typewritten lecture; copy in Eden Archives, St. Louis.

 A critical analysis of the teaching of music at Elmhurst, with special reference to the period when H. Richard Niebuhr was president.

E. Related to the American Missionary Association

Dillard University (1869)

197. Dent, Jessie Covington. *Reminiscences of Dillard University: The Early Years.* New Orleans: J.C. Dent, 1991.

 A full account of Dillard beginnings.

Fisk University

198. Richardson, Joe M. *History of Fisk University, 1865-1946.* Tuscaloosa: University of Alabama Press, 1980.

 A scholarly history of Fisk University.

LeMoyne Owen College (1862)

199.   Faith, Ellen. *Strategy, Culture and Renewal: An Interpretive Case Study of LeMoyne Owen College.* Ann Arbor, MI: UMI Dissertation Services, 1993.

An extensive dissertation concerning an African-American college.

Talladega College (1867)

200.   Jones, Maxine Deloris. *Talledega College: The First Century.* Tuscaloosa: University of Alabama Press, 1990.

An extensive anniversary history.

F. Seminaries Related to the United Church of Christ

Andover-Newton Theological School (1807)

201.   Jensen, Robin. "Starting an Arts and Theology Program from Scratch: A Case Study in Faculty Cooperation." *ARTS* 6 (Spring 1994-95): 26-27.

Getting programs in arts started in theological schools, including Andover-Newton and United Seminary in the Twin Cities.

Chicago Theological Seminary

202.   Bass, Dorothy C. "The Congregational Training School for Women." In *Hidden Histories in the United Church of Christ.* Vol. 2, pp. 149-67. Edited by Barbara Brown Zikmund. New York: United Church Press, 1987.

The story of a Chicago Congregational seminary for women, which did not ordain, between 1909 and 1926.

Eden Theological Seminary (1850)

203. Zuck, Lowell H. "Evangelical Pietism and Biblical Criticism: The Story of Karl Emil Otto." In *Hidden Histories of the United Church of Christ*. Vol. 2, pp. 66-79. Edited by Barbara Brown Zikmund. New York: United Church Press, 1987.

An early heresy trial of an Eden Seminary President by his own Evangelical Synod for teaching biblical criticism in the liberal German way.

204. Laaser, Robert O. *Our Beloved Eden: The Story of the Seminary*. St. Louis: Eden Theological Seminary, 1993.

A popular history of Eden Seminary, written by a minister member of the Board of Directors.

Harvard Divinity School (1811)

205. Thiemann, Ronald F. "University Divinity Schools: Communities of Connected Critics." Address at the installation of T.W. Ogletree as Dean of Yale Divinity School. *Harvard Divinity Bulletin* 20 (1990-91): 9-10.

The Dean of Harvard Divinity School comments on the nature of contemporary divinity schools.

The Interdenominational Theological Center (1958)

206. Richardson, Harry V. *Walk Together, Children: The Story of the Birth and Growth of the Interdenominational Theological Center*. Atlanta, GA: ITC Press, 1987.

A recent history of the Atlanta Afro-American seminary complex, begun in 1958.

Lancaster Theological Seminary (1825)

207. Hartley, Loyde H. *Cities and Churches: An International Bibliography.* Metuchen, NJ: Scarecrow Press, 1992. See index under "theological education" and "theological seminaries."

A project of the research center in religion and society, related to Lancaster Seminary.

Union Theological Seminary, New York (1836)

208. Handy, Robert T. *A History of Union Theological Seminary in New York.* New York: Columbia University Press, 1987.

A candid and interestingly written history of Union, bringing its development up to date through the troubled 1960s and beyond.

United Theological Seminary of the Twin Cities (1960)

209. Merrill, Arthur L. *United Theological Seminary of the Twin Cities: An Ecumenical Venture.* Lewiston, NY: Edwin Mellen Press, 1993.

A careful history of a Minneapolis seminary that united the Wisconsin Reformed Mission House seminary in 1960 with the Yankton, South Dakota, German Congregational seminary.

Vanderbilt Divinity School (1875)

210. Conkin, Paul Keith. *Gone With the Ivy: A Biography of Vanderbilt University*. Knoxville: University of Tennessee Press, 1985.

    A recent scholarly history of the university and seminary.

211. Thompson, Bard. *Vanderbilt Divinity School: A History*. Nashville: Vanderbilt University, 1960.

    A brief history of the divinity school.

Yale Divinity School (1822)

212. Gritsch, Ruth C.L., ed. *Roly: Chronicle of a Stubborn Non-Conformist*. New Haven, CT: Yale Divinity School, 1988.

    The inimitable memoirs of a favorite church history professor at Yale Divinity School, centering in a personal way upon the seminary.

213. Marty, Martin E. "A Scripted Nation." (1987 Bartlett Lecture at Yale Divinity School) *Reflections* (Winter 1990): 17-20.

    A spirited tribute to the nature and character of Yale Divinity School by a noted church historian.

B. UCC Higher Education, General

214. Acosta, Samuel. "The Hispanic Council of the United Church of Christ: Its History, Impact, and Ability to Motivate Policy." *Chicago Theological Seminary Register* 79 (Summer 1989): 28-41.

215. Bass, Dorothy C. and Smith, Kenneth B., eds. *The United Church of Christ: Studies in Identity and Policy*. Chicago: Exploration Press, 1987.

216. Brown, Charles C. *Niebuhr and His Age: Reinhold Niebuhr's Prophetic Role in the Twentieth Century*. Philadelphia: Trinity Press International, 1992.

217. Cooper, Charles W., Jr. "The New Ecumenical Partnership of the U.C.C. and the Disciples of Christ." *Ecumenical Trends* 17 (September 1988): 113-15.

218. Dunn, David, ed., *A History of the Evangelical and Reformed Church*. Reissued with new introduction by Lowell H. Zuck. Cleveland: Pilgrim Press, 1990.

219. Findlay, James. "Agency, Denominations and the Western Colleges, 1830-1860: Some Connections between Evangelicalism and American Higher Education." *Church History* 50 (March 1981): 64-80.

220. Fukuyama, Yoshio. "The United Church of Christ and Human Sexuality: The Life Cycle of a Social Concern." *Chicago Theological Seminary* 76 (Fall 1986): 1-10.

221. Hatch, Nathan O. *Democratization of American Christianity*. New Haven: Yale University Press, 1989.

222. Neeval, Mary Ann. "Global Religious Diversity and the U.C.C." *Chicago Theological Seminary Register* 79 (June 1989): 68-78.

223. Paul, Robert S. *Freedom With Order: The Doctrine of the Church in the United Church of Christ*. New York: United Church Press, 1987.

224. Richardson, Joe M. *Christian Reconstruction: The American Missionary Association and Southern Blacks, 1861-1890.* Athens, GA: University of Georgia Press, 1986.

225. Riggs, John W. "Traditions, Tradition and Liturgical Norms: The U.C.C. *Book of Worship." Worship* 17 (January 1988): 113-15.

226. Smith, Sally Stevens. "Women in the U.C.C. Parish Ministry, An Inquiry and Handbook." D.Min. dissertation, San Francisco Theological Seminary, 1982.

227. Smith, Sheldon Treat. "The United Church of Christ: An Introduction for Persons with Roman Catholic Backgrounds." Ph.D. dissertation, Andover-Newton Theological School, 1987.

228. Stackhouse, Max L. *Apologia: Contextualization, Globalization, and Mission in Theological Education.* Grand Rapids, MI: Eerdmans, 1988.

229. Stone, Donald H. *Reinhold Niebuhr: A Mentor to the Twentieth Century.* Louisville: Westminster/J. Knox, 1992.

230. Throckmorton, Ansley Coe. "The Minister as Teacher." *Chicago Theological Seminary* 77 (Fall 1987): 20-25.

231. Tyson, Stuart William. "Perceptions of Identity in the United Church of Christ." D.Min. dissertation, Lancaster Theological Seminary, 1986.

232. von Rohr, John. *The Shaping of American Congregationalism, 1620-1957.* Cleveland: Pilgrim Press, 1992.

233. Walker, Williston. *The Creeds and Platforms of Congregationalism.* Reissued with a new introduction by Elizabeth C. Nordbeck. Cleveland: Pilgrim Press, 1991.

234. Youngs, J. William T. *The Congregationalists.* New York: Greenwood Press, 1990.

235. Zikmund, Barbara Brown. *Hidden Histories in the United Church of Christ.* Vols. 1 and 2, New York: United Church Press, 1984, 1987.

236. Zuck, Lowell H. "Four Centuries of Evangelism in the United Church of Christ." New York: United Church Board for Homeland Ministries, 1987.

CHAPTER 9
Disciples of Christ
Colleges, Universities, and Seminaries

John M. Imbler

I

Disciples of Christ came into being at a time of transition in many public arenas. Colonialism was giving way to Jacksonian democracy. Sectarianism was settling in as denominations sought to stake their claims on industrializing urban centers and developing rural communities. Growing interests in scientific knowledge were replacing academic studies in the classics. And, a new revivalist spirit was emerging that resulted in the Second Great Awakening in the mid-part of the 19th century. All of this and more blended to color a curious complexion on the indigenous Restoration Movement that became the Christian Church (Disciples of Christ).

Barton Warren Stone's *Last Will and Testament of the Springfield Presbytery* (1804) and Thomas Campbell's *Declaration and Address* (1809) were foundational documents that set a standard by which Disciples judged contemporary religious expressions. Recently immigrated Presbyterian minister Thomas Campbell could no longer adhere to particular tenets of the church, specifically those relating to authority of the clergy and restrictions on who was welcome at the Lord's table. Informed solely by the New Testament, interpreted by both reason and revelation, his critique of ecclesiastical organizations afforded the opportunity to rethink all religious matters in light of the scriptures. A rejection of creeds, a disdain for church hierarchies, and a call for the unity of the Church of Christ became the marks of the Restoration Movement. These marks remain with the denomination today, albeit to a lesser degree.

Barton Warren Stone, a Presbyterian preacher and teacher in Kentucky, was educated in one of the popular "log colleges" in North Carolina. Thomas Campbell's son, Alexander, landed from Ireland and settled in western Pennsylvania (now West Virginia), was quickly acknowledged as the voice and intellectual force of the movement. Having studied at Glasgow, he had little in common culturally or educationally with Stone, and their personalities certainly were different. Their affinity, however, clearly was in the unity of Christianity, the role of the laity in the leadership of the church, the restoration of the New Testament as the guide for all things ecclesial, and reliance on the New Testament for all things theological. On January 1, 1832, Stone's Christians and Campbell's Disciples formally merged during a Sunday worship service at Hill Street Church in Lexington, Kentucky.[1]

Progress had been independently by both Disciples and Christians building churches and claiming converts between 1804 and 1832. The merger, however, increased membership and expanded the geographical distribution of churches, which also extended religious influence and solidified public confidence. The Christian Church (Disciples of Christ) eagerly followed America's westward migrations to the South, the Northwest Territory, and the other territories in the southern plains.

New congregation establishment is the oldest form of Disciples outreach ministry. Education is the second oldest. The founding of colleges was a popular enterprise of settled denominations like the Baptists, Congregationalists, Methodists, and Presbyterians. Although still in their infancy, Disciples were no less aggressive. In the decade of the 1850s, for example, eighty institutions were created.[2] New county-seat towns claimed their place on the map with newspapers, hotels, rail stations, and political organizations. Colleges and academies similarly were regarded as significant enterprises of the community. While founded for religious purposes by religious people, these schools were readily appropriated by the citizens as additional signs of the town's importance. Colleges appreciated this kind of partnership, and some eventually took the name of the towns in which they were located, e.g., Columbia (Missouri), Eureka (Illinois), Hiram (Ohio), and Lynchburg (Virginia).

II

It was a symbiotic relationship -- one which was quite productive. From the ranks of the schools' graduates, towns enjoyed a supply of able merchants, bankers, teachers, and lawyers even though the principal purpose of many Disciples institutions was to train ministers. The school benefitted from community allegiance, not the least of which was financial support. The story of Disciples educational enterprises in the middle part of the 1800s is "the preacher and the promoter."[3] With but a few exceptions these schools were founded by ministers and financed by entrepreneurs who seized the opportunity to improve their status, perhaps realize a profit, and/or do good for the town and the church.

One exception to the preacher-and-promoter schema is Butler University and Christian Theological Seminary in Indianapolis.[4] Organized in 1854 as North Western Christian University, it was created as a post-secondary institution through the cooperative efforts of the churches in Indiana as a special project of the state meeting.[5] A second exception is Texas Christian University in Fort Worth.[6] Add-Ran College in Thorp Springs was the vision of the Clark family. Chartered in 1873, the Clarks received the endorsement of the Texas Organization of Disciples only four months after the charter papers were drawn.[7]

Near and after the turn of the century, church organizations and societies became more active than individuals in building institutions. Disciples Divinity House at the University of Chicago was founded in 1894 by the Christian Woman's Board of Missions. Atlantic Christian College (now Barton College), was established in Wilson, North Carolina, in 1900, by the Disciples North Carolina Missionary Society. Oklahoma Christian College (now Phillips University in Enid) and Phillips Graduate Seminary in Enid and Tulsa were founded in 1906 under the aegis of the missionary societies of both the Oklahoma and Indiana territories. And Jarvis Christian College in Hawkins, Texas, was founded in 1912 by the Christian Woman's Board of Missions in cooperation with the Black Disciples of East Texas.[8]

Whatever the source, Disciples' interest in and commitment to education was deep, fostering a breadth of schools across the land. By the end of World War II, more than 450 institutions of learning had been established through the efforts of Disciples.[9] Of those 450 plus, only a small percentage were four-year degree-granting institutions. Many were secondary schools, academies, institutes, and junior colleges. Few were graduate schools or had graduate departments. Thirty-two schools and specialized institutions are listed in the *1994 Yearbook of the Christian Church (Disciples of Christ)* engaged in some form of educational mission.

The rapid proliferation of schools was short-lived; many soon closed due to lack of funds and low enrollments. Some merged with other schools. Some chose to sever their relationship to the church and become independent institutions. Still others changed their mission and became different entities. A final group maintains a relationship with the now-independent Churches of Christ (*a capella*) or Christian Churches and Churches of Christ (undenominational) both of which have their roots in the Restoration Movement.

III

As impressive as the numbers may seem in denominational annals, more significant is the educational philosophy that brought them into existence. In addition to being one of the founders of the Disciples of Christ, Alexander Campbell was its chief educational architect. He believed that knowledge is power and that educated citizens promote a responsible society. Furthermore, all education must be infused with moral values based on the reason and revelation of biblical interpretation. Sectarian education, he argued, is a contradiction in terms. "Education properly defined is the full development of man to himself, in his whole physical, intellectual and moral constitution with a proper reference to his whole destiny in the Universe of God."[10]

Campbell's opinions were drawn from Bacon's rationalism, Locke's empiricism, and Newton's scientific method all tempered by Scottish common sense. While Campbell was not an uncritical disciple of Locke, Locke's notions of sensory and experiential learning formed the base from which Campbell's educational philosophy was derived.[11] Wholeness of person, moral formation of character, biblical studies, non-sectarianism, perfectibility of the individual, and life-long learning were six propositions that defined the mission and directed the curriculum of his own school, Bethany College in Bethany, West Virginia, in 1840. These propositions also were embraced in numerous other school foundings.

In any Disciples educational enterprise, whether grammar school or college, the Bible was regarded as the finest primer since it contained the core of humanities: languages, history, literature, geography, anthropology -- and, of course, moral formation. "With respect to the Bible, concern focused not on the principle of authority but upon its application. Free recourse to the Bible was to be granted to all, and clear biblical teaching alone was to bind the conscience."[12] The problem with church-related schools in general in Campbell's view was that the faculty promoted or defended denominationalism not Christianity. A proper focus on the Bible was one step toward countering that practice.

Disciples' attraction to rationalism combined nicely with biblical restoration and the revivalistic spirit to fuse faith and reason. Although schools were designed to educate ministers for the growing number of churches, this was no cause to prevent any student pursuing any course of study from access to biblical inquiry and understanding.

Not all Disciples schools were chartered for ministerial preparation even though moral formation remained central. Bacon College in Georgetown, Kentucky, opened just four years after the 1832 union of Christians and Disciples. Under the presidency of Walter Scott, the fourth of the recognized Disciples founders, its curriculum focused on civil engineering and mathematics.[13] Although there were professors of moral and intellectual philosophy and classical languages, most of the faculty consisted of those who could prepare graduates to design and construct the highways, waterways, and railways to the west, including offering courses in surveying and cartography. The founders of Bacon College were not merely accommodating the nation's migration patterns, but giving direction to them.

In 1839, the college was moved to Harrodsburg, Kentucky, in response to declining enrollments, and in 1858 it was rechartered as the University of Kentucky. During 1865, it entered into a new agreement with Transylvania University in Lexington and became affiliated with the College of the Bible as well.[14]

As numbers and philosophy claim attention on Disciples education, so does innovation -- and innovation is not without risk. Some Disciples educational ventures were directed to what today would be described as the disenfranchised.

Culver-Stockton College (Canton, Missouri) was chartered as Christian University in 1853, the first co-educational, post-secondary school west of the Mississippi. This was a bold step in an era and an environment where the education of women beyond basic literacy was not valued. The curriculum reflected the Campbelliam model of moral philosophy, languages, and mathematics.[15]

Midway College (Midway, Kentucky) began in 1849 as Kentucky Female Orphan School under the direction of Dr. L.L. Pinkerton, who later served in the Union Army as a surgeon and chaplain.[16] His intent was to establish not an orphanage but an educational institution for orphaned girls where academic subjects as well as social graces would be learned. Midway College remained a two-year college until 1989 when its first baccalaureate class was enrolled.

Butler University (1854) had abolitionist leanings. This was in many circles neither a popular position nor a popular institution considering the numerical strength of Disciples in southern and border states. First- and second-generation leaders maneuvered around the tensions of slavery and states rights, but Butler's notoriety made the issue difficult to ignore.

Regardless of particular political dispositions, Disciples generally were sensitive to the religious orientation and educational needs of slaves and freed blacks. Southern Christian Institute was founded in 1874 near Edwards, Mississippi, as an elementary and secondary school for black people.[17] Toward the end of the century it achieved junior college status, and in 1954, as blacks were accorded more opportunity in education, it merged with Tougaloo College located outside of Jackson.

Jarvis Christian College was established in 1912 with a gift of land in Hawkins, Texas, by Major and Mrs. J.J. Jarvis of Fort Worth with the express purpose that land be used for Negro education.[18] Under the leadership of the Christian Women's Board of Missions and with the support of funds contributed by the Negro churches of Texas, Jarvis developed from a junior college to a recognized four-year school in 1937.

V

Competing with the church-sponsored liberal arts colleges in the latter part of the nineteenth century were the state universities. Although they were attracting students away from the church colleges, of greater concern was the secular curriculum and the lack of church connection.

The Morrill Land Grant Act of 1862 and the Morrill Act of 1890 provided land and money directly to the states from the federal government for the construction of public universities.[19] With the growth of the state schools came a renewed interest in the separation of church and state. While the charge of secularism was leveled at the public institutions, the charge of sectarianism was leveled at the denominational institutions. It was argued that state schools must be free of religious control; so, in defense, churches tightened their control on their schools. A new era was approaching which Disciples quickly recognized.

In response to the curricula of state universities, a Bible Chair was envisioned. Founded by the Christian Woman's Board of Missions, the first Bible Chair was established at University of Michigan in Ann Arbor to offer "what the university could not: courses and lectures on such subjects as the history of Israel, the life of Christ, Prophecy, and New Testament Greek."[20] Instructors were provided by the church not the university, and in addition to supplementing the curriculum with non-credit courses and lectures in religion, the Bible Chair afforded the students opportunities for community life and church fellowship.

The experimental program at Ann Arbor generated seven more such Chairs: University of Missouri, Columbia, 1896; University of Virginia, Charlottesville, 1897; University of Georgia, Athens, 1897; University of Kansas, Lawrence, 1901; University of Texas, Austin, 1905; Tri-State College, Angola, Indiana, 1908; and Indiana University, Bloomington, 1910. Four Bible Chairs in modified form developed at: Eugene Divinity School, Eugene, Oregon, 1895; Washington State College, Pullman, 1908; University of California, Berkeley, 1898; and

University of Nebraska, Lincoln, 1946.[21] From the Bible Chair programs emerged the concept of campus ministry where churches and church leaders in state university towns ministered to students, faculties, and staffs.

VI

Considering Disciples' emphasis on biblical studies and moral formation, it is interesting that graduate schools for ministerial education, i.e., theological seminaries, were so late developing. The same year the first of what was to become a Disciples seminary opened its doors in Lexington, Kentucky, editor Charles L. Loos commented, "No schools for ministerial education should be established apart from our colleges" (*Millennial Harbinger*, September 1865). Indeed, all five Disciples seminaries began as departments of religion or Bible colleges of undergraduate schools and provided religious instruction not only for ministerial students but other students as well.

Of those five, three have incorporated themselves as independent institutions. Lexington Theological Seminary separated from the University of Kentucky and Transylvania University by relocating to its present facility in 1950. Christian Theological Seminary separated from Butler University in 1958. Phillips Graduate Seminary separated from Phillips University in 1987. Drake Divinity School closed its doors in 1967 while still under the auspices of Drake University.[22] Brite Divinity School remains one of the graduate schools affiliated with Texas Christian University.

Before graduate theological education was widely accepted by Disciples, another innovation occurred. Again it was the Christian Woman's Board of Missions that took the initiative by responding to an invitation from the newly established Baptist institution, the University of Chicago, by organizing a divinity house. The divinity-house concept was a denominational presence on the campus of a university supported by another denomination as a non-degree-granting entity that provided community, financial support, denominational orientation, and subsequently residential facilities while academic instruction was taken and degrees were granted at the host university.

The Disciples Divinity House at the University of Chicago opened in 1894. A Disciples Foundation was established at Vanderbilt University (Nashville, Tennessee) in 1927 with the Divinity House formally organized in 1942. A house came into being at Yale University (New Haven, Connecticut) in 1958 but closed in 1972 due to decreasing enrollments. The last of this kind was the Disciples Seminary Foundation that aligned with the School of Theology at Claremont, California, in 1960. In the fall of 1987 the Foundation created a second service area in Berkeley in affiliation with Pacific School of Religion.

VII

From 1836 to 1890, the flurry of school foundings was, as previously noted, largely independent ventures. In 1894 the national convention meeting in Chicago formed a Board of Education under the control of the American Christian Missionary Society.[23] No financial support was provided for its operation, and it struggled until 1910 as a loose confederation of schools functioning primarily for the purpose of collecting statistical data and producing interpretive literature to assist in the recruitment of students. In 1914 at the St. Louis convention, the Board was reorganized to promote the training of leaders for the church and to assist the colleges in fund raising with finances for its work coming as dues paid by the member institutions.[24] In 1977 the Board of Higher Education of Disciples of Christ became the Division of Higher Education, one of the eleven general administrative units of the Christian Church (Disciples of Christ) funded through the church's outreach program, Basic Mission Finance.

VIII

The history of Disciples higher education meanders across the educational landscape, although not without purpose or direction. It seemed particularly responsive adjusting to the changes in society, meeting standards of new accrediting bodies, and addressing the needs of the church.

Those undergraduate schools that survived their often-meager beginnings and hard financial times emerged stronger, and with academic programs of high quality and a campus environment that appreciated the Campbellian tradition -- physical, intellectual, and moral constitution. The Bible was no longer the primer in the 20th century, but neither was it taken out of the curriculum.

By the end of World War II, post-baccalaureate degrees were expected of Disciples ministers; however, the Bible colleges and departments of the universities had begun offering B.D. and M.A. degrees well before World War I. Drake Divinity School conferred its first Bachelor of Divinity degree in 1882.[25]

The question that confronts Disciples in the 1990s is one with which many denominations are struggling: what it means for a college or university to be church-related. The health of Disciples colleges and universities is adversely affected by several factors: a highly competitive educational market where technological courses are more in demand than humanities; a shrinking denominational income affecting the direct and indirect financial support given to schools; and the location of many Disciples institutions in the rural county-seat towns of America at a time when many students prefer to locate in urban centers. Just a couple of generations ago, college presidents first were ministers, even though some held Ph.D.s. Today, they are largely secular academicians or corporate executive types bringing the concerns of technical administration, institutional promotion, non-church capital development, and financial management to their jobs. This shift in leadership has changed the character of the schools even to the extent of changing the nature of the trustees who are selected. This is not to imply that presidents and trustees are disinterested in the church relationships, but this leadership shift certainly causes the schools to take on a different character and appeal to a broader constituency. The potential for more closures and mergers is imminent at the turn of next century unless the church and administrators can recapture that innovative spirit that produced the heyday of Disciples educational achievements in the past century and a half.

Endnotes

1.   Lester G. McAllister and William E. Tucker, *Journey in Faith: A History of the Christian Church (Disciples of Christ)*. St. Louis: CBP Press, 1975, p. 151.

2.   D. Duane Cummins, "The Preacher and the Promoter," *Discipliana* 44:1 (Spring 1984): 5.

3.   *Ibid.*, 3.

4.   Now an independent graduate theological institution, Christian Theological Seminary was formed as the Butler School of Religion.

5.   Henry K. Shaw, *Hoosier Disciples*. St. Louis: Bethany Press, 1966, p. 112.

6.   Along with TCU is Brite Divinity School which was formed as the University's College of the Bible.

7.   Carter Boren, *Religion on the Texas Frontier*. San Antonio: Naylor Co., 1951, p. 222.

8.   Cummins, *The Disciples Colleges: A History*, pp. 92f.

9.   Cummins, "The Preacher and the Promoter," 5.

10.   *Millennial Harbinger* VII:4 (March 1850): 123.

11.   John M. Imbler, *Beyond Buffalo: Alexander Campbell on Education for Ministry*. Nashville, TN: Disciples of Christ Historical Society, 1992, pp. 13-16.

12.   James O. Duke, "Scholarship in the Disciples of Christ Tradition," *Disciples Theological Digest* 1, 1 (1986): 9.

13.   D. Duane Cummins, *The Disciples Colleges: A History*. St. Louis: CBP Press, 1987, pp. 1f.

14. *Ibid.*, p. 20.
15. McAllister/Tucker, p. 165.
16. *Ibid.*, p. 164.
17. Kenneth E. Henry, "Faith and Learning Among African American Disciples of Christ," *Discipliana* 53:4 (Winter 1993): 112.
18. *Ibid.*, 114.
19. Thomas R. McCormick, *Campus Ministry in the Coming Age*. St. Louis: CBP Press, 1987, pp. 2f.
20. Lawrence S. Steinmetz, "A Century of Witness: Celebrating Campus Ministry," *Disciples Theological Digest* 8:2 (1993): 5.
21. McCormick, p. 174.
22. McAllister/Tucker, p. 433.
23. Cummins, *The Disciples College: A History*, p. 97.
24. *Ibid.*, p. 100.
25. Charles J. Ritchey, *Drake University Through Seventy-Five Years, 1881-1956*. Des Moines: Drake University, 1956, p. 39.

Bibliographic Entries

237. Andrews, Linda L. and Cindy L. Munro. "Builder of Colleges and Character." *The Disciple*, January 1989, pp. 12-14.

   Presents a short biography of Josephus Hopwood, early Disciples leader, founder, and first president of Lynchburg College (Virginia Christian College).

238. Bean, Dottie. "Transylvania: The Shearer Years." *Lexington Herald-Leader*, July, 1993, pp. B1-2.

   Acknowledges the financial stability, academic quality, and enrollment growth of Transylvania University during the tenure of its president Charles L.

Shearer (1983-present). Founded in 1780, Transylvania is the 16th oldest university in the United States.

239.   Beaver, A. Alton, ed. *The Call and Nurture of Ministers: A Manual for Church Elders*. Enid, OK: PGS Press in cooperation with the Christian Church (Disciples of Christ) in Oklahoma, 1992.

Promotes the role of local church elders in the process of ministerial enlistment and support, particularly giving emphasis to enrollment in Disciples-related undergraduate schools and theological education institutions.

240.   Becker, Edwin L. *Yale Divinity School and the Disciples of Christ, 1872-1989*. Nashville, TN: Disciples of Christ Historical Society, 1990.

Depicts Disciples of Christ relationships at Yale from the early "Campbell Club," an association of Disciples seminarians, to a divinity school that entered associate status with the denomination due to the impact those students and Disciples faculty had on the institution and its curriculum.

241.   Botkin, Robert R. "Midway College: Employing Strategic Imagination to Survive and Excel." *Management Issues*, September 1991, pp. 1-4.

Describes the process by which the struggling Midway College (Kentucky) in the mid-1980s discovered its "natural mission" resulting in retained health and new respectability through the dedicated efforts of administrators, trustees, and faculty.

242. Cummins, D. Duane. "Black Disciples and Higher Education." *Discipliana* 47:1 (Spring 1987): 3-6.

Relates the modest but important successes of establishing academies and schools for American blacks during the latter part of the 19th and early part of the 20th centuries. Credits the shifting of Disciples of Christ missional orientation of second generation leaders from salvation to education.

243. England, George. *In A Tall Shadow*. Enid, OK: Phillips Graduate Seminary. George England, 1990.

Reminisces about the life of his father, Stephen, the first dean of Phillips Graduate Seminary (College of the Bible) in Enid, Oklahoma. Focuses on the relationship of the academy and the church.

244. Flowers, Ronald B. "Disciples of Christ as Educators." *Disciples Theological Digest* 5 (1990): 5-22.

Investigates the value Disciples put on higher education through the establishment of colleges, academies, and institutes, based on the educational philosophy of Alexander Campbell as a means of preparing the laity to take leadership in the church.

245. Gilpin, W. Clark. "Education on Behalf of Hope." *Encounter* 50:1 (Winter 1989): 79-85.

Suggests that Disciples of Christ seminaries take seriously the wealth of material on theological education published in the last decade as a guide for establishing new directions for ministerial education toward the 21st century.

246.   Harrison, Richard L., Jr. *From Camp Meeting to Church: A History of the Christian Church (Disciples of Christ) in Kentucky.* St. Louis: Christian Board of Publication, 1992.

Gives attention to Lexington Theological Seminary (College of the Bible), Midway College (Kentucky Female Orphans Schools), and Transylvania University in their own rights and in the context of the formation of the regional structure of the Christian Church (Disciples of Christ).

247.   Henry, Kenneth E. "Faith and Learning Among African American Disciples of Christ." *Discipliana* 53:4 (Winter 1993): 99-118.

Highlights the persons, places, and programs that were involved in developing educational institutions for blacks. Noted are Southern Christian Institute, Northeast Texas Christian Theological and Industrial College, and Jarvis Christian College, of which only the latter exists.

248.   Hull, Debra. "Lavina and Clarinda: The Campbell-Pendleton Bridge." *Discipliana* 50:2 (Summer 1990): 25-28.

Portrays the contributions of two of Alexander Campbell's daughters to the building of Bethany College. Living in a family dedicated to education, each woman was also, in turn, a wife of W.K. Pendleton, the college's second president.

249.   Hull, John H. "Jane Campbell McKeever." *Discipliana* 52:1 (Spring 1992): 7-11.

Illustrates the efforts of Jane McKeever who, in 1819, founded and directed Pleasant Hill Seminary in West Middletown, Pennsylvania. Reorganized in 1842, it was noted as the first female academy associated with the Restoration Movement.

250. Imbler, John M. *Beyond Buffalo: Alexander Campbell on Education for Ministry.* Nashville, Tennessee: Disciples of Christ Historical Society, 1992.

Traces the development of theological education from colonial America into the 19th century and analyzes Campbell's attitudes toward it. Introduces Campbell's educational philosophy in ways that shaped the curriculum of Bethany College as an "anti-seminary" model.

251. Jeter, Joseph R., Jr. *Brite Divinity School: An Historical Sketch.* Fort Worth, TX: Brite Divinity School, Texas Christian University, 1990.

Celebrates the diamond anniversary of this university-affiliated seminary, chartered in 1914, through a chronological overview of the personalities and events which gave it life and shaped its mission.

252. Kirkpatrick, Forrest H. "Cloyd Goodnight." *Discipliana* 52:2 (Summer 1992): 25-27.

Outlines the strategy by President Cloyd Goodnight (1919-1932) to improve the educational standards of Bethany College at a time when the college was facing serious enrollment and academic problems.

253. McAllister, Lester G. *Bethany: The First 150 Years.* Bethany, WV: Bethany College Press, 1991.

Offers a detailed history of the college founded by Alexander Campbell (1840) based on his educational principles. Lists courses, personalities, events, and resources that make this school unique and able to survive when so many other colleges during this time failed.

254. McCormick, Thomas R. "The Bible Chair Movement: The Foundation of Disciples Campus Ministry." *Discipliana* 47:2 (Summer 1987): 19-23.

Connects the origins of campus ministries to the establishment of the English Bible Chair at the University of Michigan in Ann Arbor, 1893. Attention is focused on controversies and motivations around the Bible Chair Movement.

255. McCoy, Jerry D. "What Does It Mean to Be a Church-Related College?" *Disciples Theological Digest* 5 (1990): 23-36.

Questions what is distinctive about a church-related school and how it can express its relatedness in positive ways. The author concludes from his experiences as a faculty member and department chair at a small Midwestern Disciples liberal arts college that church-relatedness is an ongoing struggle that involves the whole community.

256. McDonald, William H. "Whatever Others Might Do: A Look at the Principles of L.L. Pinkerton." *Discipliana* 53:2 (Summer 1993): 35-46.

Observes that educating women was not well accepted in the mid-part of the 19th century. Pinkerton, minister of the Midway Christian Church, defied convention by opening the Kentucky Female Orphans School which was to become Midway College.

257. Morgan, Peter M. *Two Villages: A Brief History of One Bethanian's Ministry of Hope.* Nashville, TN: Disciples of Christ Historical Society, 1993.

Tells the story of how two alumni from Bethany College -- one a home missionary, the other an industrialist -- positively impacted the immigrant workers in the coke industry around Republic, Pennsylvania, with the gospel and social progress during the early part of this century.

258. Osborn, Ronald E. "Education for Ministry Among Disciples of Christ." *Discipliana* 47:3 (Fall 1987): 40-45.

Emphasizes that Disciples founders acknowledged the need for an educated clergy, but were resistant to the existing structures of formalized theological education programs because they feared the influence of sectarianism. Establishing permanent churches on the western frontier, however, demanded settled clergy with a specialized knowledge which caused second-generation leaders to engage in the founding of theological seminaries.

259. Pittas, Peggy. *Blow Your Little Tin Whistle: A Biography of Richard Clarke Sommerville.* Lanham, MD: University Press of America, 1992.

Captures the history of the institution and the community in which it is situated by reviewing the life of a professor who taught at Lynchburg College (Virginia) from 1928 to 1946.

260. "Remembering Herman Norton (1921-1992)." *The Spire,* Summer/Fall, 1992, cover editorial.

Honors the contributions of Dr. Herman A. Norton as the first dean of the Disciples Divinity House, Vanderbilt University Divinity School, and Drucilla Moore Buffington, Professor of Church History at the Divinity School, and friend and mentor of generations of students, pastors, and academicians.

261.   Santos, Michael W., ed. *Through the Years: Essays in Lynchburg College History, 1903-1984.* Lynchburg, VA: Alpha Beta Upsilon Chapter of Phi Alpha Theta, Lynchburg College, printed by H.E. Howard, 1988.

Interprets the history of the college from students' perspectives through a collection of seven papers prepared as class assignments for a course on historical research and writing.

262.   Stevenson, Dwight E. "Writing Our Centennial History." *Lexington Theological Quarterly* 25:2 (April 1990): 44-49.

Recounts writing the history of Lexington Theological Seminary for its 1865-1965 Centennial, and offers four observations in the approach to organizing institutional histories.

CHAPTER 10
Episcopal Colleges and Universities

Donald S. Armentrout

This essay builds on the seminal work done on Episcopal Colleges and Universities by Arthur Ben Chitty, historiographer of the University of the South and former president of the Association of Episcopal Colleges. Others who have assisted are: Sue E. Armentrout (head of Interlibrary Loans), Anne Armour (head of Archives and Special Collections), John Capellaro, John L. Janeway (Library Assistant), Wayne C. Maxson (Public Services and Reference Coordinator), Mary P. O'Neill (Reference-Documents Librarian), Deneen Patton, Susan P. Sloan, Susalee Spruill, and the Rev. Keith Talbert, all of the University of the South; Julia E. Randle (Archivist at Bishop Payne Library, Virginia Theological Seminary), Andrea Matlak (Assistant Archivist for Reference), and Stephanie Walker (Assistant Archivist for Reference Services), and others at the Archives of the Episcopal Church in Austin, Texas.

The sketches of the colleges and universities in this essay are somewhat uneven in that very little material is available on many of the schools. Also, the bibliography not only updates the bibliography published by Garland in 1988, but adds some pre-1988 titles that were omitted in that book.

All Saints' Episcopal College (Vicksburg, Mississippi)

All Saints' Episcopal College was founded by Theodore DuBose Bratton (November 1, 1862-June 26, 1944), the third Bishop of Mississippi, 1903-1938, to educate young women. The original charter was granted on August 26, 1907, and the school opened on September 16, 1907, with the Rev. William Mercer Green II (July 12, 1876-November 12, 1942) as dean. In reality it was a junior college and high school for women. The original building was called William Mercer Green Hall after the first bishop of the diocese. The second dean, 1911-1913, was the Rev. Thomas Pierce Bailey (August 18, 1867-February 7, 1949), who was succeeded by two women who held the title of principal: Jennie Graham Baker Trapier, 1913-1916; and Mary Leslie Newton, 1916-1937. On May 30, 1937, the Rev. William Gerow Christian (b. September 28, 1902) became rector and served until 1958. In 1943 the Dioceses of Arkansas and Louisiana joined Mississippi in ownership of the school. The Rev. John Maury Allin was rector from July 1, 1958 until 1961. The Rev. John Stone Jenkins was rector from February 1, 1962 until August 1967. In 1962 the name was changed from All Saints' Junior College to All Saints' School, and college work was discontinued. The Rev. Alec Dockery Dickson, Jr., was rector from July 1, 1978 until May 1983. In 1970, males were enrolled for the first time, and blacks were admitted. The present rector is the Rev. David Stafford Luckett, Jr., who took office in 1984. The school is presently co-educational, boarding and day, for grades 8-12.

Andalusia College (Bucks County, Pennsylvania)

About 1859, the Rev. Horatio Thomas Wells (May 29, 1816-December 19, 1871) bought the property in Bucks County, Pennsylvania, where Dr. William Chapman operated a boarding school for boys with speech defects, known as a "stammering school." Here Wells opened a boarding school for boys, and in 1865-1866 the state legislature granted a charter naming the school Andalusia College. A primary department was housed in Potter Hall, named after the third Bishop of Pennsylvania, Alonzo Potter. In 1871 the school had four professors and twelve teachers in the three courses of study -- classical, scientific, and commercial -- and 85 students. The school never granted any degrees and did not long survive its founder, although Adam H. Fetterolf (November 24, 1841-December 2, 1912), later president of Girard College, gave it a try.

Bard College [formerly St. Stephen's] (Annandale-on-Hudson, New York)

As early as 1852, Bishop Jonathan Mayhew Wainwright (February 24, 1792-September 21, 1854) of New York expressed the need for a training college for the ministry in his diocese. In 1856 the Rev. John McVickar (August 10, 1787-October 29, 1868), superintendent of the Society for Promoting Religion and Learning, urged the diocesan convention to establish a church school to prepare young men for entrance to the General Theological Seminary in New York City. John Bard (1819-February 12, 1899), president of the New York Life Insurance and Trust Company, and his wife, Margaret Johnston Bard (d. April 10, 1875) gave part of their estate to establish a college at Annandale in 1860, and on March 20, 1860, St. Stephen's College was chartered by the New York state legislature. It was founded for the "...education and Christian training of young men, who desire to enter the sacred ministry in the Protestant Episcopal Church."[1]

On May 1, 1928, St. Stephens entered a cooperative agreement with Columbia University, in which the president of Columbia was the president of St. Stephens. This relationship was terminated on May 1, 1944, and in September of that year the first women students were admitted. On May 24, 1934, the name was changed to Bard College in honor of the original benefactors. Bard is a coeducational, liberal arts college and is a member of the Association of Episcopal Schools.

Bethany, College of the Sisters of (Topeka, Kansas)

On January 19, 1857, the Rev. Charles M. Callaway (1827-April 11, 1877) arrived in Tecumseh, Kansas, to organize a school for girls. Some Episcopalians in Topeka convinced him to establish the school there, and this he did, then leaving Kansas for Missouri on November 16, 1860. The Rev. Nathaniel Ogden Preston (December 22, 1809-February 14, 1866) succeeded Calloway as rector of Grace Church, Topeka, and principal of the school in 1861. On February 2, 1861, the legislature granted a charter for "The Episcopal Female Seminary of Topeka." On June 10, 1861, the school opened with 33 students. In 1864 Preston left Topeka, and the Rev. John Newton Lee (d. September 1, 1899) served as rector, 1865-1873. On July 9, 1872, Bishop Thomas Hubbard Vail (October 21, 1812-October 6, 1899) obtained a new charter that changed the name to the College of the Sisters of Bethany. Bishop Vail explained the name: "We aim to make this Institution like that sweet home of Bethany, which Jesus visited and so hallowed by His frequent presence ... that Home where the younger Mary sat at Jesus' feet, while the elder Mary, not forgetful of His Divine teachings, but occupied with her household cares, ministered to His temporal comfort -- that Home, which contained the representative women of the two great classes of Christian womanhood, the contemplative and the active...."[2] In 1897 the first Bachelor of Arts degrees were awarded, and on July 2, 1924, the name was changed to Vail College. The school closed in 1928. Its motto was "That Our Daughters May Be As the Polished Corners of the Temple."

Bristol College (Bristol, Pennsylvania)

In 1825, the Rev. Drs. Gregory Townsend Bedell (October 28, 1793-August 30, 1834), James Milnor (June 20, 1773-April 8, 1844), and Stephen Higginson Tyng (March 1, 1800-September 3, 1885) founded the Episcopal Education Society of Philadelphia, and began a manual labor college for prospective ministers near Wilmington, Delaware. It moved to Bristol in Bucks County, Pennsylvania, and reopened as Bristol College on October 2, 1833. It promoted the idea of "united manual labor with mental improvement, and converting the hours of recreation into a source of pecuniary profit." The Rev. Chauncey Colton (d. January 12, 1876) was its only president, and it closed in February 1837 for lack of financial support.

Buckner College (Witcherville, Arkansas)

Buckner College only operated from 1887 to 1889 under the Rev. David Ferguson MacDonald (d. August 19, 1894).

Burlington College (Burlington, New Jersey)

Burlington College was granted a charter on February 27, 1846, and was adjacent to and affiliated with St. Mary's Hall for girls, which was founded in 1837. By 1870, the college had awarded 73 degrees but had been forced to close the divinity department. It closed around 1881 and by 1900 was being listed as Burlington Academy.

Canterbury College (Danville, Indiana)

Canterbury College was established in 1946 using the gift of the buildings and campus of Central Normal College, which was founded on September 5, 1876. Edgar C. Cumings (b. November 27, 1909) was installed as president on November 17, 1946, and served until 1948. On July 15, 1948, the Rev. Douglas Robert MacLaury (August 7, 1914-March 23, 1971) became acting president. He served until 1951 when the school closed.

Charleston, College of (Charleston, South Carolina)

The College of Charleston was established by a group of Charleston citizens including the Rev. Robert Smith (August 25, 1732-October 28, 1801) who was later the first Bishop of South Carolina, 1795-1801. A charter was granted on March 19, 1785, and classes began on July 3, 1785 in Smith's home. On February 6, 1786, Smith was elected president of the board of trustees and served in that capacity until 1789. The college was officially opened in 1790 and Smith served as principal from then until 1797. The school had its first graduation in 1794, and one of the six members of that class was the Rev. Nathaniel Bowen (June 29, 1779-August 25, 1839), president of the school, 1823-1824 and 1827-1828, and third Bishop of South Carolina. A third Episcopal priest to serve as president was the Rev. Jasper Adams (August 27, 1793-October 25, 1841) who served 1824-1826 and 1828-1836. The school was not really Episcopal, but did have these three Episcopal clergy as presidents.

Clarkson College (Omaha, Nebraska)

The Bishop Clarkson School of Nursing was founded in 1888 in memory of Bishop Robert Harper Clarkson (November 19, 1826-March 10, 1884). It became the Bishop Clarkson College of Nursing, and became a degree-granting institution in 1981. In

1993 it became a comprehensive, four-year college offering the bachelor's degree. It is a member of the Association of Episcopal Colleges.

Colorado School of Mines (Golden, Colorado)

The Rt. Rev. George Maxwell Randall (November 23, 1810-September 28, 1873), the first Bishop of Nebraska, received a gift of $5,000 in 1868 from a Brooklyn merchant, George A. Jarvis, to establish a school. With this gift plus ten acres of land in Golden, he laid the cornerstone of Jarvis Hall, named for the Rt. Rev. Abraham Jarvis, the second Bishop of Connecticut, on August 25, 1869. This was to be a School of Mines and the school was known as Jarvis Hall. On November 17, 1869, a storm destroyed Jarvis Hall, but on October 19, 1870, a resurrected Jarvis Hall opened. On February 9, 1874, the School of Mines was deeded to the Territory of Nebraska.

Columbia University [King's College] (New York, New York)

As early as 1703, the rector, William Vesey (October 10, 1674-July 11, 1747), and the wardens of Trinity Church had plans for the establishment of a college in New York City. On October 31, 1754, King George II granted the charter of King's College. On May 13, 1755, the corporation of Trinity Church conveyed to the governors of the college a piece of land with the express condition that "the President of the said College forever for the time being shall be Member of and in communion with the Church of England as by law established and that the Morning and Evening Service in the said College be the Liturgy of the said Church...."[3]

Prior to this, on November 22, 1753, the trustees had invited the Rev. Samuel Johnson (October 14, 1696-January 6, 1772), rector of Stratford Parish in Connecticut, to be president. On July

17, 1754, Johnson began instruction in the vestry room of the schoolhouse of Trinity Church. The first commencement was held on June 21, 1758, when eight students received the B.A. degree. Johnson resigned on March 1, 1763, and the Rev. Miles Cooper (February 1737-May 20, 1785) was elected president on April 12, 1763. Cooper, a loyalist, fled in the night on May 10, 1775, and on May 16, 1775, the Rev. Benjamin Moore, later the second Bishop of New York, was named president *pro tempore*.

On May 1, 1784, the name was changed to Columbia College. William Samuel Johnson (October 7, 1727-November 14, 1819), the son of Samuel Johnson, was president from November 12, 1787 to July 16, 1800, and was succeeded by the Rev. Charles Henry Wharton (June 5, 1748-July 23, 1833), who only served several months, August 3-December 11, 1801. Benjamin Moore (October 5, 1748-February 27, 1816), Assistant Bishop at the time, was president from December 31, 1801 to May 1811. He was succeeded by the Rev. William Harris (April 29, 1765-October 18, 1829), who was president from June 17, 1811 until his death. In 1896 the name was changed to Columbia University of the City of New York. Columbia no longer has any connection with the Episcopal Church.

Daniel Baker College (Brownwood, Texas)

The Presbyterians in 1888 established Daniel Baker College, named for one of its great revival preachers, Daniel Baker (August 17, 1791-December 10, 1857). In 1930 the school became an independent, self-maintaining institution. On June 1, 1950, the Right Rev. Charles Avery Mason (August 2, 1904-March 6, 1970), Bishop of Dallas, took over the school, and the Rev. Richard Alden Hayes (August 13, 1909-July 16, 1978), rector of St. John's parish, Brownwood, became president. In 1951 the Rev. Wilford Oakland Cross (July 26, 1901-September 12, 1978) became president. When Canterbury College in Danville, Indiana, closed in 1950 some of its students transferred to Daniel Baker. In June 1953, the last Episcopal-connected class graduated. So Daniel

Baker College, sometimes called "The Episcopal College of the Southwest," ran from June 1, 1950 to June 1953.

De Veaux College (Niagara Falls, New York)

Judge Samuel De Veaux (De Voe) (May 12, 1789-August 3, 1852) left a bequest of all his residuary estate for the foundation of "a benevolent Institution under the supervision of the Convention" of the Diocese of Western New York. Under the provisions of this will, De Veaux College was founded, and it was incorporated on April 15, 1853. The board of trustees, of which the Rt. Rev. William Heathcote DeLancey (October 8, 1797-April 5, 1865), the first Bishop of Western New York, was president, began the erection of a building in 1855, and the school opened on May 20, 1857, on a domain of 300 acres with thirty pupils. There were a number of Episcopal presidents of the school, the last being the Rev. William Samuel Barrows (November 16, 1861-January 26, 1940), 1897-1934. Under Barrows the college curriculum was dropped and he was listed as headmaster. The preparatory school closed in 1973.

Doane College (Crete, Nebraska)

Doane College had extremely tenuous Episcopal connections. It was founded in 1872, and endorsed by the Diocese of Nebraska in 1931, when Bishop Ernest Vincent Shaylor (October 1, 1898-June 26, 1947) was elected to its board of trustees. It remained related in this superficial way to the diocese for twenty years, until March 15, 1951, when Bishop Howard Rasmus Brinker (October 20, 1893-May 19, 1965) resigned from the board.

Episcopal Academy of Connecticut (Cheshire, Connecticut)

On June 4, 1794, the convention of the Diocese of Connecticut appointed a committee to prepare an address "pointing out the importance of establishing an Episcopal Academy in this state." The school "was intended to be not only a preparatory school of high order, but a college and a nursery of theological learning." Cheshire was chosen as the site, and, on May 6, 1796, a constitution was adopted by the convention. The cornerstone for the first building had been laid on April 28, 1796. The first three principals of the schools were the Rev. John Bowden (January 7, 1751-July 31, 1817), June 1796-April 1802; the Rev. William Smith (c. 1754-April 6, 1821), April 1802-October 1, 1806; and the Rev. Tillotson Bronson (January 8, 1762-September 6, 1826), October 8, 1806-September 6, 1826.

This school was America's first junior college and the Episcopal Church's first theological seminary, but it never became a real college. The legislature refused to change its name to the "Episcopal College of Connecticut," and the founding of Washington College (later Trinity) at Hartford meant that the academy would always be a preparatory school. The academy went out of existence in June 1917 as an Episcopal school.

Florida Diocesan College (Auburndale, Florida)

This school for women was proposed in 1888, some land and money were given, but the school never opened.

Florida Episcopal College (Deland, Florida)

This school was a proposed ecumenical venture with Stetson University, and lasted only from 1970 to 1973.

Fort Valley College (Fort Valley, Georgia)

The Fort Valley High and Industrial School was chartered in 1895. Under its second principal, Henry A. Hunt (d. October 1, 1938), the trustees voted on November 11, 1918 to place the school under the auspices of the Diocese of Atlanta, with the Bishop of Atlanta as chairman of the board of trustees. In 1919 the school affiliated with the American Church Institute for Negroes of the Episcopal Church. The Diocese of Georgia joined the Diocese of Atlanta in 1928 in partial support of the school. Affiliation with the American Church Institute was discontinued in 1939 with the passage of the school from church to state control. On July 1, 1939, the State Teachers and Agricultural College at Forsyth, founded on May 9, 1902 by William Merida Hubbard (d. May 19, 1941), merged with the Fort Valley High and Industrial School to create Fort Valley State College. The first class to receive degrees was graduated in 1941.

Griswold College (Davenport, Iowa)

Around 1858 the Rt. Rev. Henry Washington Lee (July 29, 1815-September 26, 1874) bought the property of Iowa College, Davenport, and in 1859 secured a charter for Griswold College, named after the great evangelical bishop Alexander Viets Griswold of the Eastern Diocese. This venture was called "the college of the Trans Mississippi bishops and sees" but this interdiocesan aspect was never realized. A theological department opened in 1861 and after Bishop Lee's death was called Lee Hall. Kemper Hall for boys served as a preparatory department until it closed in 1895. The Rev. Willis Hervey Barris (d. June 10, 1901) taught classes in the college until it closed in 1897. Under the Rt. Rev. William Stevens Perry (January 22, 1832-May 13, 1898) St. Katherine's School for Girls was established. The college, the boys' school, and the seminary closed in the 1890s.

Henrico College (Henrico, Virginia)

Henrico, sometimes called Henricus or Henricopolis, was named in honor of Henry, Prince of Wales. In 1618 the Virginia Company of London ratified a former grant whereby a suitable place at Henrico should be set aside to establish a university. Ten thousand acres was allotted for endowing the university. George Thorpe was sent over from England to supervise the construction, and the Rev. Thomas Bargrave (d. 1621), rector of the Henrico parish, donated his library. On March 22, 1622 (Good Friday), Chief Opechancanough and his Indians massacred George Thorpe along with about 400 colonists. The charter for the school was revoked on June 16, 1624. This would have been the first college in the American colonies.

Hobart and William Smith College (Geneva, New York)

Hobart College, first called Geneva College, grew out of the Geneva Academy that was in operation prior to 1800. The Rt. Rev. John Henry Hobart (September 14, 1775-September 12, 1830), third Bishop of New York, was the primary founder. A provisional charter was granted on April 10, 1822, and the school's existence dates from that year. On August 5, 1822, ten students began their studies in Geneva Hall. The first commencement was held on August 1, 1826. A medical college opened in 1835, and, on January 23, 1839, Elizabeth Blackwell (February 3, 1821-May 31, 1910) graduated from it, the first woman in the United States to receive the Doctor of Medicine degree. In 1852 the name was changed to Hobart College. William Smith College for women, named after a Geneva nurseryman, opened in 1908 with eighteen students. Hobart and William Smith College is a member of the Association of Episcopal Colleges.

Jefferson College (Washington, Mississippi)

Jefferson is the oldest chartered college in Mississippi. The charter was granted on May 13, 1802. It operated as an academy from 1805 to 1810, as a college from 1816 to 1821, and then reverted to academy status. Little information is available on it, including the precise date it closed. Among the Episcopal priests who were its presidents are James Angel Fox (March 19, 1794-July 1, 1881), Charles Reighley (?), and Abednego Stephens (July 24, 1812-February 27, 1841).

Jubilee College (Robin's Nest, Illinois)

Jubilee College was founded by the Rt. Rev. Philander Chase (December 13, 1775-September 20, 1852), the first Bishop of Illinois, 1835-1852. He was convinced that the best way to establish and maintain the Episcopal Church on the frontier was to build a college where "sons of the soil" could be prepared under the same conditions as those in which they were to labor. In 1836 he moved to Peoria County and erected a log cabin that he named "Robin's Nest" because, he said, it was "made of mud and sticks and full of young ones." He decided to call the school "Jubilee" as an expression of his thankfulness and joy. On April 3, 1839, the cornerstone of the chapel was laid, and the preparatory department opened on January 1, 1840. The Theology Department was established early, and, on December 18, 1842, there was the first ordination in Jubilee Chapel. On that day Fredrick Southgate was ordained deacon. On July 7, 1847, five students received the B.A. degree at the schools' first commencement. All faculty members were required to be members of the Episcopal Church. All professors "must be in full orders and all other teachers pious communicants."

The Rev. Samuel Chase (d. January 15, 1878), a grand-nephew of the Bishop, was in charge of the school. At its peak, Jubilee had a Preparatory Department, a Theological Department, a Collegiate Course, and a girls' school. The school published a magazine, *The Motto of Jubilee College*, and the motto was "Jehovah Jireh, God Will Provide." By 1862 the burden of indebtedness was so great that the school closed. There were several efforts to re-open including one by the Rev. Thomas Wilson Haskins (d. September 1, 1895), who opened the "Homewood School" for Indians. In 1933 the property was given to the state of Illinois for a park.

Keble College (Pass Christian, Mississippi)

In 1951 the Rev. Hewitt Breneman Vinnedge (June 26, 1898-March 15, 1957) and some Episcopal lay persons attempted to open a co-educational, liberal arts, pre-professional school. In 1952 Vinnedge resigned as president and the school closed. The school was named after John Keble, one of the founders of the Oxford Movement.

Kemper College (St. Louis, Missouri)

The Rt. Rev. Jackson Kemper (December 24, 1789-May 24, 1870) was consecrated the first Missionary Bishop of the Episcopal Church on September 25, 1835. He reached the conclusion that the only hope of supplying the West with clergy was to provide means to train them at home. By January 1, 1837, the trustees had been elected, and had submitted a request for a charter to the Missouri legislature. On January 13, 1837, the charter was granted with the qualification that they would not use the name, Missouri College, which the Bishop and the trustees had agreed upon. In the Bishop's absence, the trustees named the school Kemper College. In April, the 125-acre site five miles from St. Louis was purchased for $2,000. The college opened its doors on October 15, 1838, with the Rev. Peter Raynard Minard (d. August 27, 1846) as acting president and principal of the grammar school. Students paid $180 per academic year for tuition, room, board, bedding, fuel, and lights. In the fall of 1839, the Rev. Silas Axtell Crane (October 21, 1799-

July 16, 1872) took over as president and served until 1841. In 1840 a medical school was established. The Rev. Eleazar Carter Hutchinson (d. July 27, 1876) assumed the presidency on November 1, 1841 and served until January 15, 1845. The Rev. Henry Caswall (May 11, 1810-December 17, 1870) served as professor of divinity. Because of indebtedness the school closed on April 1, 1845, and in November of that year the debts were liquidated by the sale of the property to the county of St. Louis. The county used the buildings for many years as a poor house.

Kenyon College (Gambier, Ohio)

The Rt. Rev. Philander Chase (December 14, 1775-September 20, 1852), the first Bishop of Ohio, 1819-1831, wanted to establish "a school for the education of young men for the ministry." He went to England to raise money and met two of his greatest benefactors, Lord Gambier, James Gambier (October 13, 1756-April 19, 1833), and London Kenyon, George Kenyon (July 22, 1776-February 25, 1855). On November 3, 1824, Bishop Chase and the Diocese founded "The Theological Seminary of the Protestant Episcopal Church in the Diocese of Ohio" at Worthington, and the school received its charter on December 29, 1824. In 1828 the school the moved to Gambier as Kenyon College and Bexley Hall Theological Seminary. Kenyon is a four-year liberal arts college and is a member of the Association of Episcopal Colleges.

Lambeth College (Kittanning, Pennsylvania)

Lambeth College, first known as Kittanning Collegiate School, was granted a charter on September 7, 1868. The nine trustees were Episcopalians, and the Bishop of Pittsburgh was *ex officio* chancellor of the corporation. It was to promote "liberal learning on a distinctive church basis." The head of the school was the Rev. Bryan Bernard Killikelly, Jr. (d. October 16, 1887). It was named after the first Lambeth Conference, September 24-28, 1867, which was called by the Archbishop of Canterbury. The college never awarded any degrees and closed in 1876.

Lehigh University (Bethlehem, Pennsylvania)

In 1865 Judge Asa Packer (December 29, 1805-May 17, 1879) asked the Rt. Rev. William Bacon Stevens (July 13, 1815-June 11, 1887), the fourth Bishop of Pennsylvania, to help him plan a university. On February 9, 1866, a charter was granted, and the school opened on September 1, 1866, with 40 students. "Lehigh has no official connection with any Church. But incidental relations between the Episcopal Church and the University have always been close and significant."[4]

Nebraska College (Nebraska City, Nebraska)

Nebraska College and Divinity School was started at Nebraska City in 1861, the second year of the episcopate of the Rt. Rev. Joseph Cruikshank Talbot (September 5, 1816-January 15, 1883), Bishop of the Northwest Diocese. Later the name was changed to Talbot Hall in his honor. The Rev. John Godfrey Gasmann (1833-December 17, 1915) was the first president, and the Rev. Robert W. Oliver (d. June 23, 1899) was dean of the divinity school. Gasmann was succeeded by the Rev. John McNamara (d. October 21, 1885). The trustees voted to close the college on April 21, 1885, the last president being the Rev. M.F. Carey (d. April 3, 1903).

Norwich University (Northfield, Vermont)

On August 6, 1819, Captain Alden Partridge (February 12, 1785-January 16, 1854) founded "The American Literary, Scientific, and Military Academy" at Norwich, Vermont. Instruction began on September 4, 1820, and on November 6, 1834, it was chartered as Norwich University as an Episcopal institution. On October 1, 1866, the trustees voted to move the school to Northfield, Vermont.

Okolona College (Okolona, Mississippi)

Okolona Industrial School was founded in 1902 by Wallace A. Battle as a high school and junior college for black students to prepare for vocations in manual work. In 1920 the Diocese of Mississippi took over the school to "develop it along church lines." In 1921, the American Church Institute for Negroes accepted it. In 1965 the trustees voted to close the school.

Philadelphia, College of (Philadelphia, Pennsylvania)

In 1740 a charity school was founded in Philadelphia by the Rev. George Whitefield, and on November 13, 1749, trustees for an Academy were named. Among them were Benjamin Franklin (January 17, 1706-April 17, 1790), who was president, and the Rev. Richard Peters (c. 1704-July 10, 1776). In December 1749, the trustees of the Academy bought the Charity School building, and on September 16, 1751, classes began. Only July 13, 1753, the legislature granted a charter of incorporation for "Trustees of the Academy and Charitable School in the Province on Pennsylvania." On July 16, 1755, a new charter was granted and the name was changed to "The Trustees of the College, Academy, and Charitable School of Philadelphia."

The Rev. William Smith (September 7, 1727-May 14, 1803) had written in 1753 *A General Idea of the College of Mirania* in which he described what a college should be. He sent a copy to Franklin and Peters, and in 1755 he was named provost of the school. The first commencement was held on May 17, 1757, when seven persons graduated. On November 27, 1779, the legislature voided the charter of the college and created the Trustees of the University of the State of Pennsylvania, and Smith resigned as provost. Thus there were two institutions, and, on September 30, 1791, an act of the legislature united the University of the State of Pennsylvania and the College of Philadelphia as the University of Pennsylvania.

While this school was not exclusively a church institution, the Anglican influence dominated until the Revolution. Among the Episcopal leaders were two presidents of the board of trustees: Richard Peters, 1756-1764, and the Rt. Rev. William White (April 4, 1748-July 17, 1836), 1790-1791.

Racine College (Racine, Wisconsin)

In 1852 the Rev. Joseph Hurlbut Nichols (August 20, 1805-December 13, 1862), rector of St. Luke's Church, Racine, joined the Rev. Azel Dow Cole (December 1, 1818-October 15, 1885), president of Nashotah House, in an appeal to Bishop Jackson Kemper to establish a college. A charter was granted on March 3, 1852, and the college opened in November. The president was the Rev. Roswell Park (October 1, 1807-July 16, 1869), who served from 1852 to 1859. In 1859 the college was combined with St. John's Hall, Delafield, and the Rev. James DeKoven (September 19, 1831-March 19, 1879), headmaster of St. John's, became president. This was its golden age. After DeKoven's death, the school declined; it closed in 1929. It was revived on March 19, 1930, as the Racine Military Academy, but on August 8, 1933, it was announced that it would not open that September. The Sisters of St. Mary bought the property and in December 1935 opened the DeKoven Foundation for Church Work.

Rose Gates College (Okolona, Mississippi)

Rose Gates College opened in 1859 with Bishop William Mercer Green as president of the board of trustees. It was named after Rose Gates, daughter of Col. Charles Gates, who bought the property. The headmaster was the Rev. William S. Lacey (d. 1867), who served until the school closed in 1862.

Shelby College (Shelbyville, Kentucky)

Shelby College was incorporated on February 29, 1836, and transferred to the Episcopal Church in 1841. Sometimes the school was called St. James College. Information about Shelby College is very sketchy.

Shimer College (Mt. Carroll and Waukegan, Illinois)

Shimer College was established as Mount Carroll Seminary by Frances Wood Shimer and opened on May 11, 1853. In July 1896 the name was changed to the Francis Shimer Academy of the University of Chicago. In 1951 Shimer College began admitting students who had only completed the tenth or eleventh grades. In 1959 eight bishops of the Dioceses of Chicago, Eau Claire, Fond du Lac, Indianapolis, Iowa, Milwaukee, Quincy, and Northern Indiana took over the school. In 1973 Shimer College withdrew from the Association of Episcopal Colleges.

South, University of the (Sewanee, Tennessee)

The University of the South was founded on July 4, 1857, at a meeting at Lookout Mountain, Tennessee. The leaders in its founding were: the Rt. Rev. James Hervey Otey (January 27, 1800-April 23, 1863), the first Bishop of Tennessee; the Rt. Rev. Stephen Elliott (August 31, 1806-December 21, 1866), the first Bishop of Georgia; and the Rt. Rev. Leonidas Polk (April 10, 1806-June 14, 1864), the first Bishop of Louisiana. On October 10, 1860, the cornerstone of the central building was laid, but because of the war the school did not officially open until September 18, 1868. The three main parts of the University have been the College of Arts and Sciences, the School of Theology, and the Sewanee Grammar School (in 1902 called the Sewanee Grammar Academy, in 1908 the Sewanee Military Academy, in 1971 the Sewanee Academy). The Sewanee Academy merged in

1980 with St. Andrew's school to form St. Andrew's-Sewanee School. The University of the South is a four-year, co-educational, liberal arts college and is a member of the Association of Episcopal Colleges.

St. Andrew's College (Jackson, Mississippi)

St. Andrew's College opened on January 1, 1852, with the Rev. Meyer Lewin (August 16, 1816-May 29, 1886), rector of St. Andrew's Church, as president. It received its charter on October 16, 1852. Other presidents were the Rev. A. D. Corbin (d. October 19, 1855) and the Rev. Josiah Swett (August 14, 1814-January 4, 1890). The school closed on February 1, 1856.

St. Augustine College (Chicago, Illinois)

St. Augustine College was chartered by the State of Illinois on October 7, 1980, as a bilingual (Spanish-English) institution of higher learning. Its name is to perpetuate the memory of St. Augustine, Florida, the first permanent city in this nation. The city of St. Augustine was founded by Pedro Menendez de Airlez, on September 8, 1565. The college was founded by the Rev. Carlos Alberto Plazas (b. May 12, 1931). It is a two-year, co-educational school and is a member of the Association of Episcopal Colleges.

St. Augustine, Missionary College of (Benicia, California)

The Missionary College of St. Augustine was one of several schools founded by the Rev. James Lloyd Breck (June 27, 1818-March 30, 1876). In December 1867 he bought the 20-acre tract and buildings which had belonged to the recently closed Benicia Collegiate Institute and Law School, and the school opened in 1868. Breck also established St. Mary's School for girls on the same campus. Upon Breck's death, the Rt. Rev. John Henry Ducachet Wingfield (September 24, 1833-July 27, 1898), first Missionary Bishop of Northern California, became head of the school. St. Mary's closed in 1885 and St. Augustine's in 1889. St. Augustine's had 713 matriculants in its history, and granted 78 diplomas.

St. Augustine's College (Raleigh, North Carolina)

St. Augustine's College was founded by the Rev. Joseph Brinton Smith (March 1, 1822-October 1, 1872), the first head of the Freedmen's Commission of the Episcopal Church. It was chartered on July 19, 1867, and opened with four students on January 13, 1868. It opened as the St. Augustine Normal School and Collegiate Institution, and in 1919 became St. Augustine's Junior College. In 1928 it became St. Augustine's College, and in 1931 the first twelve B.A. degrees were awarded. In 1896 St. Agnes' Hospital was established, and in 1925 the Bishop Tuttle School for religious and social workers began. In January 1907 the school affiliated with the American Church Institute for Negroes, and in 1949 it joined the United Negro College Fund. St. Augustine's is an historically black, four-year, liberal arts college, and is a member of the Association of Episcopal Colleges.

St. James College (Hagerstown, Maryland)

St. James College was founded by the Rt. Rev. William Rollinson Whittingham (December 2, 1805-October 17, 1879), the fourth Bishop of Maryland, and the Rev. Theodore Benedict Lyman (November 27, 1815-December 13, 1893), rector of St. John's Church, Hagerstown. St. James was to be patterned after St. Paul's School, College Point, New York. Bishop Whittingham arranged for the Rev. John Barrett Kerfoot (March 1, 1816-July 10, 1881) to leave St. Paul's School and to head the new school. On October 2, 1842, St. James College opened in Claggett Hall, named after Thomas John Claggett, the first Bishop of Maryland. The final commencement was held on July 12, 1864, and on September 1, 1864, an announcement was made that "The College of St. James is forced by the perils of war to suspend its work." It continues as St. James School.

St. John's College (Annapolis, Maryland)

In 1696 "King William's School" opened as a free school at Annapolis "to instruct youth in Arithmetick, Navigation and all useful learning, but chiefly for the fitting such as are disposed to study divinity." Governor Nicholson gave the land for a school building which completed in 1701. In November 1784 the Maryland legislature passed a bill with the following title: "An act for founding a college on the Western Shore of this state and constituting the same, together with Washington College on the Eastern Shore, into one university by the name of the University of Maryland."[5] The first meeting of the Board of Governors of St. James College, among whom was the Rev. Thomas John Claggett, later the first Bishop of Maryland, was held on February 28, 1786. On March 2, 1786, King William's School was amalgamated with the proposed St. John's College, which opened on November 11, 1789. In reality St. John's, which exists today, was never a college.

St. John the Evangelist, College of (Denver and Greeley, Colorado)

The College of St. John the Evangelist was more aspiration than realization. Jarvis Hall for boys, Wolfe Hall for girls, and Matthews Hall for theological students operated off-and-on from 1879 to 1937. No degrees were ever awarded.

St. John's College (Spartanburg, South Carolina)

St. John's College opened in January 1852 as St. John's School for Boys, under the leadership of the Rev. John DeWitt McCollough (December 8, 1822-January 23, 1902). It was never really a college, and closed in 1862 because of the war. In October 1866 the Theological Seminary of South Carolina re-opened on St. John's campus but closed on May 16, 1868. The property was sold to Converse College in 1889.

St. Mark's College (Grand Rapids, Michigan)

In 1850 a charter was obtained for the establishment of an institution for academic, collegiate, and theological learning, to be known as St. Mark's College. The only president was the Rev. Charles C. Taylor (d. February 2, 1955). The enterprise was abandoned in 1851.

St. Mary's College (Dallas, Texas)

The Rt. Rev. Alexander Charles Garrett (November 4, 1832-February 19, 1924), the first Bishop of Dallas, founded this school for women. A cornerstone was laid on July 4, 1876, but classes did not begin until September 10, 1889. By 1900 the school offered a four-year program leading to a Bachelor of Arts degree. With the exception of Bishop Garrett, the faculty was female. The school closed in June 1930.

St. Mary's Junior College (Raleigh, North Carolina)

St. Mary's College opened on May 12, 1842, and has been in operation ever since. It is a two-year school with a liberal arts curriculum for women. In 1954 the name was changed to St. Mary's Junior College.

St. Paul's College (College Point [Flushing], New York)

The cornerstone of St. Paul's College was laid on October 15, 1836 by the Rev. William Augustus Muhlenberg (September 16, 1796-April 8, 1877). The Christian religion was the center of education for Muhlenberg, and the school was to train missionaries and teachers. The school closed in 1848.

St. Paul's College (Lawrenceville, Virginia)

St Paul's Normal and Industrial School was founded on September 24, 1888, by the Rev. James Solomon Russell (December 20, 1857-March 28, 1935). In 1906 it became a part of the American Church Institute for Negroes. On December 30, 1941, the name was changed to St. Paul's Polytechnic Institute, and on February 27, 1957, to St. Paul's College. St. Paul's is a four-year, historically black college, and is a member of the Association of Episcopal Colleges.

St. Paul's College (Palmyra, Missouri)

The Governor Clark Mission was established in February 1848 on 57 acres of land in Marion County that had been purchased by the Rt. Rev. Cicero Stephens Hawks (May 26, 1812-April 19, 1868), the second Bishop of Missouri. On February 24, 1853, the legislature incorporated the school as St. Paul's College. In June 1889 St. Paul's College graduated its last class, and, because of inadequate funding, the school did not re-open.

St. Paul's College (Anderson, Austin, Brenham, and Hempstead, Texas)

The Rev. Charles Gillette (1813-March 6, 1869) was the founder of St. Paul's College, which opened on January 5, 1852, at Anderson, as the Anderson Female Institute and Texas Diocesan School. It received a charter on February 4, 1853, with the name of St. Paul's College. Gillette resigned as president (principal) in June 1854, and was succeeded by the Rev. Hannibal Pratt (November 15, 1827-December 16, 1857), who resigned sometime in 1855. Pratt was succeeded by the Rev. Jonathan B.T. Smith (d. 1867?). On April 5, 1855, the board of trustees voted to move the school to Austin, but it closed in 1856.

St. Paul's was re-established at Brenham and opened on January 1, 1868, under the presidency of the Rev. Lindsey Powell Rucker (d. January 4 or 11, 1890). It closed in 1870, and failed to re-open at Hempstead as suggested by some citizens.

St. Philip's College (San Antonio, Texas)

St. Philip's School was founded in 1898 by the Rt. Rev. James Steptoe Johnston (June 9, 1843-November 4, 1924), the second Bishop of West Texas, to prepare Black people for the responsibilities of citizenship. In September 1902, Artemisia Bowden (January 1, 1884-August 18, 1969) became principal of St. Philip's Normal and Industrial School, and in 1927 she became president of St. Philip's Junior College. In 1921 St. Philip's began being supported by the American Church Institute for Negroes. By 1940 the diocese had relinquished all ties with the school, and in August 1942 St. Philip's ceased to function as a private institution and became a municipal junior college through an affiliation with San Antonio College.

Trinity College (Hartford, Connecticut)

Trinity College began as Washington College. The charter for Washington College was granted on May 16, 1823, and on September 23, 1824, it opened with nine students. The first commencement was held on August 1, 1827, when the B.A. degree was conferred on ten men. The founder and first president, 1823-1831, was the Rt. Rev. Thomas Church Brownell

(October 19, 1779-January 13, 1865), the third Bishop of Connecticut. In 1845 the name was changed to Trinity College. In 1968 the trustees voted to withdraw from the Association of Episcopal Colleges.

Voorhees College (Denmark, South Carolina)

Voorhees College was founded on April 14, 1897, by Elizabeth Evelyn Wright (April 3, 1872-December 14, 1906), as the Denmark Industrial School. In 1902 the name was changed to Voorhees Industrial School in honor of the generosity of Ralph (d. April 1, 1907) and Elizabeth Rodman (d. September 21, 1924) Voorhees. On February 25, 1904, the school was incorporated as Voorhees Industrial School for Colored Youths. In 1916 the name was changed to Voorhees Normal and Industrial School. In 1924 the Dioceses of South Carolina and Upper South Carolina and the American Church Institute for Negroes joined in supporting the school. Since 1963 it has been called Voorhees College, and is a historically black, four-year liberal arts college. Voorhees is a member of the United Negro College Fund and the Association of Episcopal Colleges.

Washington College (Chestertown, Maryland)

The Rev. William Smith (September 7, 1727-May 14, 1803) left the College of Philadelphia in 1779, and, early in 1780, became the principal of Kent County Free School, which had begun instruction around 1729-1730. On May 24, 1782, the Maryland General Assembly granted a charter that made Kent School Washington College "in honorable and perpetual memory of his *Excellency General Washington* the illustrious and virtuous commander-in-chief of the armies of the U.S." It held its first commencement on May 14, 1783. Smith returned to Philadelphia in 1789, and was succeeded by the Rev. Colin Ferguson (December 8, 1751-March 10, 1806), 1789-1806. Two other Episcopal principals were the Rev. Jacob Goldsmith Cooper (deposed in 1820), September 1, 1816-September 1, 1817, and the Rev. Timothy Clowes (?), October 1823-June 9, 1829. The school no longer is associated with the Episcopal Church.

Wharton College (Austin, Texas)

Wharton College was founded in 1858 by the Rev. Charles Gillette (1813-March 6, 1869) and named after his wife Mary Ann Wharton. It received its charter on February 11, 1860, and closed in 1865.

William and Mary, College of (Williamsburg, Virginia)

William and Mary College was founded by the Rev. James Blair (1656?-May 18, 1743), the first commissary to Virginia. In 1690 Blair convened the clergy of the colony and proposed that for the "better encouragement of learning" there be founded a college "to consist of three schools, viz., Grammar, Philosophy, and Divinity." On February 8, 1693, King William III and Queen Mary II granted a charter, and on December 20, 1693, a total of 330 acres was purchased at "Middle Plantation" (now Williamsburg) for the school. The cornerstone of the first building was laid on August 8, 1695. For nearly ninety years William and Mary continued as the "nursery of pious ministers" for the Church in Virginia. On December 4, 1779, under the leadership of Thomas Jefferson, the governor of Virginia, the college became a university and the Grammar and Divinity schools were discontinued. In 1820 a chair of theology was established and the Rev. Reuel Keith (June 26, 1792-September 3, 1842) was named professor, but when no students came he moved to Alexandria in 1823 to teach at the newly established Virginia Theological Seminary. For 135 of the first 160 years of the life of the school, all of its presidents were clergy. On March 5, 1860, the property of the college was transferred from "The

President and Masters or Professors of the College of William and Mary in Virginia" to "The College of William and Mary in Virginia," and the school became a state institution.

Worthington College (Worthington, Ohio)

In the summer of 1817 the Rev. Philander Chase (December 14, 1775-September 20, 1852) located in Worthington and soon became principal of the academy there. On February 8, 1819, the legislature gave the academy a college charter and Chase became president. In 1821 Chase moved to Cincinnati, and in 1828 the teachers and students moved to Kenyon College. In 1830 it became the "Reformed Medical College" with no Episcopal connection.

York College (York, Pennsylvania)

York College traces its origins to an academy founded in 1787 by the Rev. John Andrews (April 4, 1746-March 29, 1813), rector of St. John's Church. The Diocese of Central Pennsylvania took over the school in 1873. The first two principals were the Rev. Octavius Perinchief (d. April 29, 1877) and the Rev. Henry Lafayette Phillips (August 4, 1830-July 6, 1906). It no longer has any connection with the Episcopal Church.

Endnotes

1. Brian R. O'Connor, Jr., "A Descriptive Survey of Colleges in the United States Belonging to the Association of Episcopal Colleges." Ph.D. dissertation, University of Denver, 1969, p. 39.
    2. *Journal of the Diocese of Kansas, 1873*, pp. 34-35.
    3. *A History of Columbia University 1754-1904, Published in Commemoration of the One Hundred and Fiftieth Anniversary of*

the Founding of King's College. New York: Columbia University Press, 1904, p. 11.

    4. Catherine Drinker Bowen, *A History of Lehigh University*. Bethlehem, PA: Lehigh Alumni Bulletin, 1924, p. 26.

    5. Tench Francis Tilghman. "The Founding of St. John's College, 1784-1789," *Maryland Historical Magazine* 44 (June 1949): 78.

Bibliographic Entries

All Saints' School (formerly All Saints' Episcopal College)

263.   *The Episcopal Church in Mississippi, 1763-1992*. Jackson, MS: Episcopal Diocese of Mississippi, 1992.

    Describes briefly All Saints' School.

264.   Turner, Mary Ellen. *For All the Saints: A Chronicle of All Saints' Episcopal School, 1908-1983*. Vicksburg, MS: All Saints' Episcopal School, 1983.

    Presents a complete history of the school with lists of trustees, faculty, staff, and graduates.

Bethany, College of the Sisters of

265.   *The First Hundred Years, Being an Historical Review of the Diocese of Kansas of the Protestant Episcopal Church from Its Formation in 1859 to Its Centennial in 1959*. Topeka: Diocese of Kansas, 1959.

    Describes the college very briefly.

266.   Blackmar, Frank W. *Higher Education in Kansas*. No. 27 of Contributions to American Educational History. Edited

by Herbert R. Adams. Washington: Government Printing Office, 1900.

Provides a very brief sketch of the college.

Canterbury College

267. Beeler, Kent D. "Canterbury College, 1946-1951: Its Decline and Demise." Ed.D. dissertation. Indiana University, 1969.

Describes fully the development and demise of the school.

268. *Central Normal College, 1876-1945; Canterbury College, 1945-1951.* N.p.; n.p., n.d.

Provides a detailed history of both institutions.

Clarkson College

269. Oderkirk, Wendell W. *Learning to Care: A Century of Nursing Education at Bishop Clarkson College.* Omaha: By the Author, 1988.

Traces the history of this school in great detail from 1888 to 1988.

De Veaux College

270. Hayes, Charles Wells. *The Diocese of Western New York: History and Recollections.* Rochester: By the Author: 1904.

Treats briefly the De Veaux School.

271. Locker, Donald E. *A History of De Veaux School, 1853-1953.* Niagara Falls, NY: Board of Trustees, De Veaux School, 1963.

    Gives a very complete history of the school.

Jubilee College

272. Lefflingwell, Charles W. "Bishop Chase and Jubilee College." *Illinois State Historical Society Transactions* (1905): 82-100.

    Gives much primary information.

273. Martin, Lorene. "Old Jubilee College and Its Founder, Bishop Chase." *Illinois State Historical Society Transactions* (1934): 121-52.

    Treats the school in a full and helpful way.

274. Norwood, Percy V. "Jubilee College, Illinois." *Historical Magazine of the Protestant Episcopal Church* 12 (March 1943): 44-58.

    Provides solid information about the founding of the school.

275. Pischaske, David R. "Jubilee College: Bishop Chase's School of Prophets." *The Old Northwest* 2 (1976): 281-97.

    Tells several interesting stories about Bishop Chase and the school.

276. Shively, Roma Louise. *Jubilee: A Pioneer College.* Elmwood, IL: Elmwood Gazette, 1935.

Presents a full history of the college.

Kenyon College

277.   Kennedy, Gerald. "Kenyon College." *Scribners Monthly* 15 (March 1878): 698-706.

Gives brief information about its early history.

Lehigh University

278.   Haskins, Charles H. *A History of Higher Education in Pennsylvania*. No. 39 of Contributions to American Educational History. Edited by Herbert B. Adams. Washington, DC: Government Printing Office, 1902.

Treats the founding and early history of the school.

279.   Yates, W. Ross. *Lehigh University: A History of Education in Engineering, Business, and the Human Condition*. Bethlehem: Lehigh University Press, 1992.

Treats the entire history of Lehigh from 1866 to 1980.

280.   Yates, W. Ross. *Sermon in Stone: Packer Memorial Church. An Historical Essay*. Bethlehem, PA: Lehigh University, 1988.

Provides a detailed history of the Lehigh chapel and briefly discusses Lehigh's relationship with the Episcopal Church.

Norwich University

281. Bush, George Gary. *History of Education in Vermont.* No. 29 of Contributions to American Educational History. Edited by Herbert B. Adams. Washington, DC: Government Printing Office, 1900.

   Gives a full history of the school until 1900.

St. Andrew's College, Jackson, Mississippi

282. *The Episcopal Church in Mississippi, 1763-1992.* Jackson, MS: Episcopal Diocese of Mississippi, 1992.

   Treats the school briefly.

St. James' College

283. Brand, William Francis. *Life of William Rollinson Whittingham, Fourth Bishop of Maryland.* 2 vols. New York: E. & J.B. Young & Co., 1886.

   Treats St. James' College from the perspective of the founder.

284. Duncan, Richard R. "The College of St. James and the Civil War: A Casualty of War." *Historical Magazine of the Protestant Episcopal Church* 39 (September 1970): 267-86.

   Describes the problems that rector John B. Kerfoot had during the Civil War and the school's closing on September 1, 1864.

285. Harrison, Hall. *Life of the Right Rev. John Barrett Kerfoot.* 2 vols. New York: James Pott & Co., 1886.

Contains correspondence about the school by its only rector.

286. Hein, David, ed. *A Student's View of the College of St. James on the Eve of the Civil War: The Letters of W. Wilkins Davis (1842-1866)*. Studies in American Religion 30. New York: Edwin Mellen Press, 1988.

   Presents a view of the school from a student's perspective.

St. John's College

287. Middleton, Arthur Pierce. "William Smith: Godfather and First President of St. John's College." *Maryland Historical Magazine* 84 (Fall 1989): 235-41.

   Treats the outstanding career of Smith as an educator.

288. Tilghman, Tench Francis. "The Founding of St. John's College, 1784-1789." *Maryland Historical Magazine* 44 (June 1949): 75-92.

   Provides great detail about the founding of the school.

Washington College

289. Barroll, L. Wethered. "Washington College, 1872." *Maryland Historical Magazine* 6 (June 1911): 164-79.

   Treats the founding of the school and lists the original subscribers.

290. Dumschott, Fred W. *Washington College*. Chestertown, MD: Washington College, 1980.

    Provides a full history of the school from its establishment.

General

291. "Episcopal Colleges." *Episcopal Life* 5 (February 1994): 15-22.

    Provides helpful, current information about all twelve schools in the Association of Episcopal Colleges.

292. Holmes, Dwight Oliver Wendell. *The Evolution of the Negro College*. New York: Teachers College, Columbia University, 1932.

    Discusses the American Church Institute for Negroes.

293. Mead, Gilbert W. "William Smith -- Father of Colleges." *Association of American Colleges Bulletin* 27 (May 1941): 270-85.

    Describes the many contributions of this great educator.

CHAPTER 11
Higher Education Institutions of the Church of the Brethren

Kenneth M. Shaffer

The Church of the Brethren is one of several Brethren groups that originated with the baptism of eight people in 1708 at Schwarzenau, Germany. The early Brethren were Radical Pietists in that they separated from the state churches in Germany to form their own sect. They were greatly influenced by the Anabaptists in that they sought to live their lives according to New Testament patterns, including pacifism, nonconformity to the world, and a morally upright lifestyle. Because of persecution and economic conditions, all of the early Brethren migrated to colonial Pennsylvania from Europe within thirty years of their origin. Between 1750 and 1900, they spread across the continent as far as California. The Brethren have experienced both external and internal struggles. Because of their pacifism, some of the most difficult external struggles have occurred when the United States has been at war. Internally their struggles take place when they confront changes in the culture around them. The development of higher education presented them with one such internal struggle.

The Controversy Over Higher Education

Given the importance Brethren place on the authority of the Scriptures for faith and practice, they have always emphasized the need for each member to be able to read the Bible. Thus, Brethren have sought to teach their children to read and write since the founding of the denomination. In the United States, they welcomed the development of local grade schools, which in the 1800s were often known as *common schools*. For the first 150 years of their existence, however, Brethren opposed higher education -- high school, college, etc. When the 1831 Annual Meeting was asked if members should educate their children in college, the answer was: "Considered not advisable, inasmuch as experience has taught that such very seldom will come back afterward to the humble ways of the Lord."[1] The Brethren emphasis on nonconformity to the world meant that higher education was taboo. "High schools and beyond were worldly places where the young would at best puff up with proud knowledge and at worst desert the church."[2]

Nothing more was said about higher education in the minutes of Annual Meeting until the 1850s. The minutes of 1852 and 1853 both contain statements in opposition to high schools and colleges. This opposition was reiterated in an article that appeared in the March 1854 issue of *The Monthly Gospel Visiter*, the only Brethren periodical in existence at that time. Henry Kurtz, the editor, began the article with the question: "Are Academies, College &c., safe places for young brethren and brethren's children?"[3] In the article he supported the decision of the 1853 Annual Meeting and warned youth of the dangers of higher education. Also, he noted that he had received some articles favoring advanced education but refused to publish them. Interestingly, in December of 1854 Kurtz did print three articles in favor of higher education.

The three articles were followed the next month by an article opposing higher education. The article was in the form of a long letter to the *Visiter* from a conservative using the name "Rufus."

Then there was over a year of silence in the *Visiter* on the topic. Suddenly, in the March 1856 issue, Kurtz printed a letter proposing a school to prepare Brethren teachers to teach in common schools. The letter was written by James Quinter, a friend of Kurtz who would soon join him as an editor of the *Visiter*. In an editorial comment to the letter, Kurtz explained how the idea of the need for a school to train school teachers had come to Quinter and himself. Three months later Kurtz himself wrote a fuller explanation of the need for a school. Obviously, Kurtz changed his position between March 1854 and March 1856. Whereas he had formerly warned how Brethren young people who attended college would lose their faith, now he called for Brethren to be trained as teachers so as to be a good influence on the children they taught.

While Kurtz and Quinter were merely proposing that the Brethren begin what were then known as normal schools to train teachers for common (elementary) schools, their opponents saw where such schools could lead. In a letter published in the September issue, Brother Rufus responded to the proposed school saying "the cure will be worse than the disease."[4] He went on to point out what would happen. First, while the proposed school is meant only to prepare teachers, it will lead to full colleges. Second, young ministers will begin to feel the need for higher education and so will seek out theological education. The concept of theological education was rejected by almost all Brethren of that day since it implied that the word of God was not simple enough for the ordinary person to understand. James Quinter replied to Brother Rufus in the same issue. Quinter argued that the school was needed in order to save Brethren youth from going to non-Brethren schools where they would lose their faith. This argument was the primary reason given for Brethren colleges in the years to come.[5]

At the next Annual Meeting (1857), a question was raised about the proposed school. The answer pointed out that such a school involved conforming to the world and quoted First Corinthians 8:1: "Knowledge puffs up, but love builds up." But debates continued in the pages of *The Gospel Visitor*,[6] and the 1858 Annual Meeting took a neutral stance to the school: "We think we have no right to interfere with an individual enterprise so long as there is no departure from gospel principles."[7]

The First Schools

Even though Kurtz and Quinter had received the freedom to begin a school, they did not act on their proposal for some time. In the meantime, a small group of Brethren in Virginia ushered the Brethren into the new era. John Kline was the most prominent of these Virginia Brethren. A minister who traveled extensively from church to church on horseback, he was well-known in several states. During the Civil War he would serve four times as moderator of Annual Meeting. Near the end of the Civil War, he was killed by a Confederate sympathizer. In 1859 Kline, along with four other Brethren, established the Cedar Grove Academy in Broadway, Virginia, on land that Kline himself donated from a corner of his farm. Though the school was not owned by the denomination, its primary sponsors were Brethren. It "was the first instance where a school of higher grade [beyond primary or common school] was initiated by a group of Brethren who became the directors for its governance."[8] The school closed not long after the Civil War, perhaps in part due to the death of Kline.

Kurtz and Quinter were also preempted in their plans by yet another school. In the summer of 1861, Solomon Z. Sharp opened his normal school in Lewistown, Pennsylvania. Sharp, who had just recently received his Bachelor of English degree, purchased the Kishacoquillas Seminary and opened it for a summer term. Thirty-six students enrolled. As with the Cedar Grove Academy, this school was not sponsored by the denomination; but it was run by a member of the denomination who understood his school as being Brethren. The school was probably closer to being a college than Cedar Grove in that Sharp intended that the school would prepare people to enter the sophomore college classes. The school survived the Civil War, but in 1866 Sharp sold it. This was the first of four schools that Sharp would help found during his lifetime.

Finally, on 14 October 1861, Quinter and Kurtz opened their school. It was located near New Vienna, Ohio, and named the New Vienna Educational Institute. Announced as being a school for Brethren, it was sponsored by members of the nearby Fall Creek congregation. Quinter served as the superintendent. The school lasted only two-and-a-half years, closing primarily because of the difficulties of running a school during the war years.

While precedents had been set, the Brethren had no school by 1867. Then in 1870 the District of Northern Indiana[9] agreed to begin a college using buildings and land donated by the town of Bourbon, Indiana. "This was the first instance where an official Brethren body initiated a school."[10] According to the 1871 articles of association, the purpose of the college was "the diffusing of useful, religious, moral and scientific knowledge, under the control of the German Baptist Church [the name of the Church of the Brethren at that time] of the Northern District of Indiana."[11] It was to be "an institution under the control and patronage of the church, that shall be a school where the Brethren can safely place their children."[12] The school was named Salem College and was to be modelled after Oberlin College in Ohio. Classes began in December 1871 and plans were made to raise an endowment of $100,000. Unfortunately, the school lasted only three years. It failed in part because it was too ambitious for the Brethren of the day and in part because of a quarrel between the president and the trustees.

Juniata -- the First Brethren School to Survive

On 17 April 1876, the Huntingdon Normal School opened with three students on the second floor of a printing shop in Huntingdon, Pennsylvania. Three men -- two brothers and a cousin all with the last name of Brumbaugh -- initiated the project. The two brothers were Henry B. and John B. Brumbaugh. They were the publishers of the *Pilgrim*, one of three Brethren periodicals then in existence. Their cousin Andrew B. Brumbaugh held an M.D. degree from the University of Pennsylvania. The Brumbaughs engaged Jacob M. Zuck to serve as principal of the school. They provided his room and board; his income was to be provided by tuition fees. The purpose of the school was to prepare its graduates "for teaching, for life, and for entering college."[13]

After weathering two crises -- a small pox epidemic in 1878 and the death of Zuck in 1879 -- the school gradually developed into a fully accredited four-year liberal arts college. When it was chartered as a joint-stock company in 1879, the school changed its name to Brethren's Normal College. Then, in 1894, after Martin G. Brumbaugh, former governor of Pennsylvania, became president, the school changed its name to Juniata College. Today Juniata has approximately 1,150 students and 31 buildings on 100 acres of land. The college also owns land used for a nature preserve and a conference center and leases land that it uses as an environmental studies field station. According to Early Kaylor, "Among colleges of its size, it enjoys a national reputation, ranking high in the percentage of graduates who earn doctoral degrees. Its curriculum is strong in several preprofessional fields, most notably in the health sciences."[14]

Ashland and Mount Morris

In 1879, within less than a month of each other, two more schools began holding classes. On August 20th, August Mount Morris Seminary and Collegiate Institute in northern Illinois opened with 60 students; and on September 17th, Ashland College in Ohio opened with 55 students. Both schools viewed themselves as Brethren schools and aimed to enter the first rank of colleges in the nation. Both flourished in their early days with Mount Morris having 260 students by the beginning of its second year and Ashland having almost 200 students at the end of its first year. In 1881 Ashland became the first Brethren school to confer the B.A. degree.

Soon, however, both schools began experiencing financial difficulties. Ashland's problems began with the schisms that occurred among the Brethren in the early 1880s. These schisms involved three groups: the progressives, now known as the Brethren Church; the conservatives, now the Church of the Brethren; and the old orders, now the Old German Baptist Brethren. While there were major theological differences between the three groups, other important differences included their attitudes toward higher education, the salaried ministry, and Sunday schools. After the schisms, control of Ashland went to the progressive Brethren. Today Ashland bears the name Ashland University and has an enrollment of over 5,000 students. Mount Morris existed until 1932 when, due to financial problems, it merged with Manchester College.

Bridgewater College

On 6 September 1880, Daniel C. Flory opened the Spring Creek Normal School in Rockingham County, Virginia. Among the first group of students was a woman. Thus, the school is known as "the first co-educational liberal arts college in Virginia."[15] Influenced by his schooling at the University of Virginia and by what he saw happening at Huntingdon Normal School, Flory began the school as a private venture. Within a year, however, a board of thirty trustees was formed. Members of this board included the Brethren leaders in the area, but the school was not under official Brethren sponsorship. After two years in Spring Creek, the school was moved to the nearby town of Bridgewater, and renamed Virginia Normal School. In 1889 the name was again changed -- this time to Bridgewater College. While the school faced many trials in its early years (including a fire and a scandal), it developed a strong curriculum, faculty, and endowment, and received the appropriate accreditation over the years. Particularly helpful to Bridgewater was its consolidation with Daleville College (Virginia) in 1923 and its association with Blue Ridge College (Maryland) in 1930. Both of these colleges had also been begun as Brethren schools -- Blue Ridge in 1899 and Daleville in 1910. Today Bridgewater has approximately 1,000 students and offers degrees in 27 major fields.

McPherson College

After the founding of Bridgewater, two other schools (both of which were short-lived) were attempted in the early 1880s, and then nothing occurred until 1887. One writer has suggested that the Brethren were "resting up for the most extraordinary run on education in their history -- a new set of schools under new auspices."[16] While it is indeed true that with the founding of McPherson College in 1887 the Brethren began a new era in higher education, it is more likely that the lull was caused by the schisms, in which debates over higher education figured prominently.

Chartered in 1887 in Kansas, McPherson College and Industrial Association (shortened in 1898 to McPherson College) "manifested three unique characteristics at its founding. It was the first of the Brethren undergraduate educational institutions to seek a direct relationship with the church; it was the first to include in its initial conception an academic program specifically devoted to the study of the Bible; and it was the first to offer a curriculum in agriculture."[17] While two other schools -- Mount Morris and Juniata -- already had Bible departments, McPherson was the first to have such a department from its founding. The idea of theological education of ministers was still unacceptable among the Brethren, but the idea of studying the Bible in college was becoming acceptable. S.Z. Sharp was called to be the first president of McPherson, and the college began classes in September of 1888. Since the founding of the school in Lewistown, Pennsylvania, Sharp had served as the first president of Ashland and taught at Mount Morris. Thus, he was a veteran of Brethren higher education. Today, McPherson has a 23-acre campus with 15 major buildings, and maintains an enrollment of between 400 and 500 students. Its commitment to vocational and technical training continues with programs in industrial education, home economics, business administration, and agriculture.

University of La Verne

The first Brethren congregation in California was organized in 1852, and by 1880 there were six congregations in northern California. Most of these Brethren joined with the Progressive Brethren during the schisms of 1881-83. Then, in 1889, members of the German Baptist Brethren (now Church of the Brethren) began coming to southern California as a result of being employed by the Santa Fe Railroad. In 1890 the Lordsburg congregation was founded, and in September 1891 Lordsburg College was opened in a large hotel that the Brethren had purchased when it closed due to a business collapse in the area. M.M. Eshelman, who had been involved in the founding of both Mount Morris and McPherson, was the prime organizer of this new venture. The school was intended to provide only college-level courses, but actually offered primarily high-school-level courses to train teachers. Even though there were few Brethren in southern California, the college managed to survive for ten years before announcing its closing. Fortunately, W. C. Hanawalt, a Brethren school principal, came from Pennsylvania to lease the college.

While many more struggles were to come, Lordsburg developed into a full college, and granted its first B.A. degree in 1914. In 1917 the town was renamed La Verne, and the college was likewise renamed. The college continued to develop over the next several decades, but after 1967 changes came at a startling pace. In 1969, degree programs were begun on military bases in Greece, Italy, and the Philippines, as well as in California. In 1970, a law school was opened and in-service teacher training was offered in several areas around the United States. The college changed its name to the University of La Verne in 1977 because by then several master's degrees and a doctorate in education were being offered.

Manchester College

While the majority of Brethren remained opposed to theological education for ministers, by the mid-1890s all surviving Brethren schools had a Bible department. Then, in 1895, E.S. Young, a Bible professor at Mount Morris College, became the first president of the new Manchester College and Bible School. This was the first instance of the founding of a Bible school by Brethren. Manchester opened on what had been the campus of a United Brethren Church school in North Manchester, Indiana. It was a private venture that was granted permission by Annual Meeting to continue the year after it opened. "Under the leadership of Gladdys E. Muir, Manchester College began in 1948 the first college or university program in peace studies."[18] Today the college is located on a 100-acre campus and is accredited to grant the B.A., B.S., and A.A. plus a master's degree in accounting. Currently, student enrollment is approximately 1,000.

Elizabethtown College

Finally, in the late 1890s, the tradition-minded Brethren of eastern Pennsylvania decided they needed a college. On 29 November 1898, at a meeting called by J.G. Francis, a minister of the Green Tree congregation, a group of elders decided to organize a school. After almost two years of planning, the school, named Elizabethtown College, opened on 13 November 1900 in Elizabethtown, Pennsylvania. Located in Lancaster County, a veritable Brethren mecca, the college tended to be less secularly oriented than some of the other Brethren colleges had become. Musical instruments were even banned for a time.

Today the school offers two residence degrees (B.A. and B.S.) and three continuing education degrees. All are accredited. Several new buildings have been added to the 15 major buildings which already existed on the campus in 1980. Among the new buildings is one housing the Center for the Study of Anabaptist and Pietist Groups. Over 1,500 students were enrolled in 1994.

Bethany Theological Seminary

By the early twentieth century the Brethren had colleges with Bible departments and one school that was both a college and a Bible school. Perhaps they were ready for a full-fledged Bible school. In 1905 Albert Cassel Wieand and Emmanuel B. Hoff opened the Bethany Bible School in Chicago. This was the first Brethren school founded solely for theological education. It was both "a seminary to educate college graduates for the ministry, and a training school to give a basic education to those with limited secondary education, preparing them for church leadership."[19] It was popular and grew quickly -- from 12 students in 1905, to 150 students in 1908, to 376 students in 1919. Opposition came not from conservatives in the church, but from the colleges which felt that Bethany was usurping the role of their Bible departments. After much debate, the 1925 Annual Conference decided "to assume full ownership and governance of Bethany."[20] Thus, Bethany is the first, and to this day only, school to be owned and operated by the Church of the Brethren. The colleges began as private ventures, were sometimes owned/controlled by districts in the denomination, and today are only affiliated with the denomination.

In 1931 Bethany changed its name to Bethany Biblical Seminary. Then in 1963 it moved from Chicago to suburban Oak Brook, Illinois, and changed its name to Bethany Theological Seminary. That same year the training school was closed. In the summer of 1994, Bethany moved from Illinois to Richmond, Indiana, to affiliate with the Earlham School of Religion, a Quaker seminary. Today Bethany is an accredited graduate school of theology granting the M.Div. and M.A.Th. degrees. The seminary also offers nondegree work through the Bethany Academy for Ministry Training.

Endnotes

1.   *Minutes of the Annual Meetings of the Church of the Brethren: Containing All Available Minutes from 1778 to 1909.* Elgin, IL: Brethren Publishing House, 1909, p. 54.

2.   James H. Lehman, *Beyond Anything Foreseen: A Study of the History of Higher Education in the Church of the Brethren.* Prepared for the Conference on Higher Education and the Church of the Brethren, June 24-27, 1976, at Earlham College, Richmond, IN, p. 2.

3.   Henry Kurtz, "To Our Young Aspirants After Learning," *The Monthly Gospel-Visiter* March 1853 (*sic*) p. 238. (After its early years, the publication changed the spelling of "Visiter" to "Visitor.")

4.   Rufus, "The Contemplated School," *The Monthly Gospel-Visiter* September 1856, 247.

5.   Lehman, p. 14.

6.   The name of the periodical changed in 1857 to *The Gospel Visitor*; note change in spelling.

7.   *Minutes*, 178.

8.   Lehman, p. 2.

9.   A district is a group of congregations in a given geographical area.

10.   Lehman, p. 21.

11.   K. Heckman, "Bourbon (Ind.) Correspondence," *Christian Family Companion*, 28 November 1871, p. 752.

12.   *Ibid.*

13.   Donald F. Durnbaugh, ed., *The Brethren Encyclopedia.* Philadelphia: The Brethren Encyclopedia, Inc., 1983, s.v. "Juniata College," by Earl C. Kaylor, Jr.

14.   *Ibid.*

15. "Bridgewater Past and Present," *Bulletin of Bridgewater College* 19 (October 1992): 7.

16. Lehman, 36.

17. *Brethren Encyclopedia,* s.v. "McPherson College," by Leland L. Lengel.

18. *Brethren Encyclopedia,* s.v. "Peace Studies Institute," by Allen C. Deeter.

19. *Brethren Encyclopedia,* s.v. "Bethany Theological Seminary," by Murray L. Wagner, Jr.

20. *Ibid.*

Bibliographic Entries

294. Bowers, Stephen E. "Institutions." In *Planing the Faith in a New Land: The History of the Church of the Brethren in Indiana,* 131-50. Nappanee, IN: Evangel Press, 1992.

    Includes discussions of the Brethren attitude toward higher education in the 1800s, the founding of Salem College, and the development of Manchester College.

295. *The Brethren Heritage of Elizabethtown College.* Elizabethtown, PA: Elizabethtown College, 1993.

    Reviews Brethren beliefs and practices and describes Brethren programs and historical collections on the campus. There are special sections in this twelve-page booklet on the Brethren peace position and the educational philosophy of the college.

296. Fitzkee, Don. "Bucher Center Teaches Brethren Who They Are." *Messenger,* August/September 1987, pp. 10-11.

    Describes Elizabethtown College's plans to create the Rufus P. Bucher Center for the Study of Anabaptist and

Pietist Groups. The focus of the center is on groups such as the Brethren, Mennonites, and Amish. Bucher was one of the first six students enrolled at the college when it officially opened in 1900 and later chaired the board for fifteen years.

297. Gardner, Richard B., guest ed. *Brethren Life and Thought*, Winter 1994.

Presents a collection of essays and recollections on the occasion of the relocation of the Bethany Theological Seminary from Oak Brook, Illinois, to Richmond, Indiana. Contributors include current and former faculty and staff members as well as former students.

298. Heckman, Marlin L. *The Gem of Lordsburg: The Lordsburg Hotel/College, 1887-1927*. La Verne, CA: University of La Verne Press, 1987.

Describes the construction and use of the first building on the campus of the University of La Verne. Built during the land boom of the 1880s in southern California, the 130-room hotel never opened. In 1891, it was sold to several Brethren who used it for a college until 1927 when it was demolished.

299. Hogan, Herbert W. and Gladdys E. Muir. *The University of La Verne: A Centennial History, 1891-1991*. La Verne, CA: University of La Verne, 1990.

Updates Muir's *La Verne College: Seventy-five Years of Service* (1967). New material is also incorporated into the section originally written by Muir.

300. Jones, Timothy K. *Manchester College: A Century of Faith, Learning and Service.* North Manchester, IN: Manchester College, 1989.

Presents the history of the college from 1889 through 1989. Originally founded as a United Brethren Church school, the college became a Church of the Brethren school in 1895. The book is intended as a popular history that emphasizes vision and personalities as well as historical facts.

301. Jones, Timothy K. "Otho Winger: He Lived 'With the Throttle Wide Open.'" *Messenger*, October 1989, pp. 24-27.

Profiles the man who served as president of Manchester College for thirty years (1911-1941). The article focuses on both Winger's accomplishments at the college and his leadership in the denomination.

302. McFadden, Wendy Chamberlain. "Windows on God." *Messenger*, December 1988, pp. 16-19.

Explains how and why two professors at Juniata College developed a major exhibit of Russian icons. The exhibit of 45 icons from Russia's golden age of icons (1400-1700) opened at the college in April 1988. Later it traveled to several other locations in the eastern United States.

303. Miller, Donald E. "Bethany: A Seminary in Search of its Mission." *Messenger*, April 1990, pp.14-16.

Describes how Bethany's mission in 1905, when it was founded, is still its mission today. After reviewing Bethany's record of leadership training for the Church of the Brethren, the author makes recommendations for the future.

304. Mines, Cynthia. *McPherson College: The First Century, 1887-1987*. McPherson, KS: McPherson College, 1987.

Presents a short history of the college on the occasion of its centennial. Numerous old photographs are included in the 28-page booklet.

305. Ramirez, Frank. "Gene Roop: Leading Bethany on a Journey." *Messenger*, May 1992, pp. 24-28.

Profiles Eugene F. Roop on becoming president of Bethany Theological Seminary in 1992. Included are Roop's reflections on the decision of the seminary to relocate in Richmond, Indiana, and affiliate with the Earlham School of Religion.

306. Thomasson, Kermon. "Bethany and the Brethren." *Messenger*, April 1990, pp. 17-19.

Reports an interview with Wayne L. Miller, president of Bethany Theological Seminary from 1989 to 1992. The interview provides biographical data about Miller as well as his reflections on the problems facing Bethany when he took office.

307. Wayland, Francis Fry. *Bridgewater College: The First Hundred Years, 1880-1980*. Bridgewater, VA: Bridgewater College, 1993.

Provides an in-depth (979 pages) history of the college. Commissioned in 1972 as the centennial history, the project took over twenty years. Also noteworthy are the twelve wood engravings by Isaac J. Sanger, an alumnus of the college.

CHAPTER 12
Foursquare Gospel Church Colleges

John C. Holmes

The International Church of the Foursquare Gospel is a Protestant Evangelical Pentecostal denomination with membership in the National Association of Evangelicals. The Foursquare denominational headquarters are in Los Angeles, California, and it has two Bible colleges in the United States: L.I.F.E. Bible College at Los Angeles in San Dimas, California, and L.I.F.E. Bible College East in Christiansburg, Virginia.

L.I.F.E. Bible College at Los Angeles is accredited by the American Association of Bible Colleges and was incorporated in 1924 by Evangelist Aimee Semple McPherson. L.I.F.E. Bible College moved to its own campus in San Dimas, California, after being located in the educational facilities of Angelus Temple, the headquarters church of the International Church of the Foursquare Gospel, for over six decades.

L.I.F.E. Bible College East was originally known as Mount Vernon Bible College, and was located in Mount Vernon, Ohio, from its founding in 1956 until 1988. In 1988, the Bible college relocated to Christiansburg, Virginia, and changed its name. In both of the colleges' names, the letters "L.I.F.E." stand for Lighthouse of International Foursquare Evangelism.

Bibliographic Entries

308. Blumhofer, Edith L. *Aimee Semple McPherson: Everybody's Sister*. Grand Rapids, MI. Erdmanns Publishing, 1993.

An Evangelical Christian history professor at Wheaton College (Illinois) and director of the Institute for the Study of American Evangelicals presents an overview of the life of evangelist Aimee Semple McPherson. Blumhofer deals with the dynamics that caused McPherson to found L.I.F.E. Bible College at Los Angeles. The school's first term began February 1, 1923, thirteen months after Angeles Temple opened its doors. Incorporated in September, 1924, as "Angeles Temple Training School," the stated purpose of the school was "'hands-on' training in evangelism" (p. 253).

309. Epstein, Daniel Mark. *Sister Aimee: The Life of Aimee Semple McPherson*. New York: Harcourt Brace Jovanovich, 1993.

Baltimore poet, who makes no pretense of being an Evangelical and/or Pentecostal Christian, reviews the life of evangelist Aimee Semple McPherson. Contains background as to the founding of L.I.F.E. Bible College at Los Angeles in 1924.

CHAPTER 13
Wesleyan Colleges and University

John C. Holmes

In 1968, the Wesleyan Methodist Church, which was organized in 1843, merged with the Pilgrim Holiness Church, which was founded in 1897. The result of the merger was The Wesleyan Church, whose denominational headquarters are situated in Indianapolis, Indiana. The Wesleyan Church is a member of the National Association of Evangelicals and is theologically Protestant Evangelical Wesleyan-Arminian with a holiness tradition.

Postsecondary institutions of The Wesleyan Church include one university and one seminary foundation. Indiana Wesleyan University of Marion, Indiana, was formerly known as Marion College and was founded in 1919. Indiana Wesleyan University changed its name officially on July 1, 1988, and offers Associate, Bachelor, and Master degrees. The Wesleyan Seminary Foundation is located in Indianapolis, Indiana.

Wesleyan four-year Christian liberal arts colleges include Houghton College in Houghton, New York (1883); Central Wesleyan College (1906) in Central, South Carolina; and Bartlesville Wesleyan College (1972) in Bartlesville, Oklahoma.

All of the Wesleyan postsecondary institutions that offer a Bachelor's degree are members of the Christian College Coalition and are regionally accredited. Acceptance into membership in the Christian College Coalition assumes the following: regional accreditation; integration of the Christian faith with learning and student life; and the maintaining of a faculty and administration who profess a "personal commitment to Christ."

Bibliographic Entries

310. Dixon, Ruth A. *Improving Reading Comprehension: A Key to University Retention?* Arlington, VA: ERIC Document Reproduction Service, ED 359 498, 1993.

    Studies first-time freshmen at Indiana Wesleyan University who entered in school years 1989-90 and 1990-91. Compares retention rates at Indiana Wesleyan University of those required to take a computer-assisted instruction developmental reading course versus those who scored high enough on the Nelson-Denny Reading Test to not be required to enroll. Retention rates for those taking the course were 59% and 65% versus 35% and 36% of the students who did not. Findings suggest that reading comprehension can be increased and retention can be aided by computer-assisted instruction in developmental reading. Presented at the 6th Annual Midwest Regional Reading and Skills Conference (3/93) in Kansas City, Missouri.

311. Sykes, Charles, and Brad Miner, eds. "Unforsaken Values," In *The National Review College Guide: America's 50 Top Liberal Arts Schools*, pp. 83-86. New York: Wolgemuth & Hyatt Publishers. 1991.

    Houghton College is ranked highly by political conservative editors because of its academic standards and "strong affiliation with the Wesleyan Church." Even though most of Houghton's students are Evangelical Protestant, less than 20% of its student body is Wesleyan. The college has shown its independence and "religious identity" by refusing New York State Bundy aid in 1990. General education requirements are critiqued.

CHAPTER 14
Free Methodist Colleges

John C. Holmes

The Free Methodist Church of North America was organized in 1860 as an anti-slavery movement that broke away from the Methodist church. Its denominational headquarters are located in Indianapolis, Indiana. The Free Methodist Church is a member of the National Association of Evangelicals and is theologically Protestant Evangelical and Wesleyan-Arminian.

Postsecondary institutions of the Free Methodist Church include one two-year college, Central College in McPherson, Kansas, founded in 1884. The Free Methodist four-year, Bachelor-degree-granting colleges include: Greenville College in Greenville, Illinois, established in 1892; Spring Arbor College in Spring Arbor, Michigan, founded in 1873; and Roberts Wesleyan College in Rochester, New York, founded in 1866.

All of the Free Methodist colleges that offer a Bachelor's degree are members of the Christian College Coalition. Acceptance into membership in the Christian College Coalition assumes the following: regional accreditation; integration of the Christian faith with learning and student life; and the maintaining of a faculty and administration who attest to a "personal commitment to Jesus Christ."

CHAPTER 15
Catholic Higher Education in the United States: An Historical Perspective

Gerald P. Fogarty, S.J.
Mary A. Grant
Anna M. Donnelly

Catholic higher education in the United States has undergone a dramatic sea change in the past thirty years. Some fear that the change is at the cost of the loss of Catholic identity. Others embrace the new-found status of Catholic colleges and universities as a sign that Catholics have been assimilated into American culture. Some voice concern that what happened to institutions like Harvard, Yale, and Duke, founded under Protestant auspices, will also occur with Georgetown, Notre Dame, and Fordham. Still others reject the recent Vatican overtures to have the local bishop oversee the Catholic nature of a wide spectrum of Catholic institutions. What complicates the discussion is the realization that the vast majority of these institutions were founded, not by the hierarchy, but by religious orders at a period when the church in the United States, unlike that in Europe, resorted to colleges and universities to preserve the religious identity of an immigrant population and enable it to move socio-economically into the middle class. The American Catholic university was not until recently the locus of research and scholarship, and teaching of Catholic doctrine took second place to the inculcation of Catholic values and practice. The institutions reflected the changing needs of the Catholic population.

To grasp the evolution of Catholic higher education in the United States, this essay will present an overview of the history in three periods: first, from John Carroll to the end of the nineteenth century; second, the period after Modernism up to the 1950s; and finally, the post-war years.

I. The Origins of Catholic Higher Education

John Carroll addressed Father Ferdinand Farmer, a trustee of the University of Pennsylvania, on the possibility of the school and other institutions being potential sources for future clergymen. At this point, he felt that

> The R. Catholics are too inconsiderable in point of wealth to erect & support a college; & we Clergymen are too few to supply a sufficient number of masters for the entire education of youth, if even such a College existed. In this situation the only reasonable prospect of raising a succession of ministers for the service of Religion here is, that in the number of Catholic Youth who receive their Grammar education in the College of Philad, & in those of Maryland, there may be perhaps one or two every year, desirous of engaging themselves in the service of the Church to which will much contribute a good deal of attention on the part of the priest destined to attend these youths either in the Colleges, or in the towns, where they are or may

> be: it being an intended stipulation that
> provision be made, from the College funds, if
> necessary, to procure them opportunities to
> frequent their particular forms of worship.

Carroll's reference to the colleges in Maryland was to Washington and St. John's Colleges, to whose boards of directors he was named. Carroll recognized that there might be "inconveniences & danger of immorality in these mixed colleges," but he felt it better "to consider the advantages to be made of new institutions, rather than study to find out the objections which beset them."[1]

In the early days of the republic, Carroll saw the advantages of Catholics being fully integrated into American society. "Being admitted to equal toleration," he continued,

> must we not concur in public measures, & avoid
> separating ourselves from the Community? Shall
> we not otherwise be marked, as forming distinct
> views, & raise a dislike which may terminate in
> consequences very disagreeable to us?[2]

While Carroll believed that these schools could be feeder schools for the future seminary he envisioned, he hoped for more. St. John's College and Washington College were to be "open to Professors & Scholars of all denominations," he wrote Joseph Edenshink, then teaching at the academy of Liege and soon to be ordained a priest. Carroll reflected "that it may be of much service not only to learning, but to true religion, to have some of these professorships filled by R.C. men of letters & virtue: and if one of them were in orders, it would be so much the better." Since he himself expected "that I may possibly have some interest with the Governors of these Colleges, & that my recommendation would have some weight," he requested Edenshink to submit to him the names of any potential professors.[3] Carroll was not to realize his desire to have a Catholic professor at either of the two colleges. In fact, he later somewhat regretted his involvement with the institutions, as he saw them draining support from the nascent Georgetown academy.[4]

Georgetown came into being as part of the movement toward the clergy's requesting an ordinary bishop for the United States. At the end of the American Revolution, the only priests in the thirteen United States had been members of the Society of Jesus, which Pope Clement XIV suppressed in 1773. John Carroll, who had been originally scheduled to be a professor of theology in one of the English Province's houses of studies on the continent, returned to his native Maryland and rapidly emerged as the leader of the American ex-Jesuits. The impetus for requesting a bishop for the United States was directly related to opening a seminary for the training of future priests. Carroll had already envisioned St. John's College, Washington College, and the University of Pennsylvania as schools preparing students for later seminary education, but now he made Georgetown the major focus for such training. The clergy decided to open an academy at the same meeting in 1786 where they also petitioned the Holy See to allow them to elect one of their number as the first bishop. Carroll, however, still retained his vision of a "mixed" school. The original prospectus for Georgetown stated that the school was to "be open to Students of every Religious Profession." Non-Catholic students were to "be at Liberty to frequent the places of Worship and Instruction appointed by their Parents."[5]

What Carroll had in mind with these "mixed" colleges, whether Georgetown, founded under Catholic auspices but open to non-Catholics, or the other colleges, open to all denominations, was basically the classical and philosophical preparation of students who would then go into law or medicine or, when a seminary was established, the study of theology in preparation for the priesthood. Even when seminaries had been established, they retained a sharp distinction between "philosophy," the years of college leading to a bachelor's degree, and "theology," the years after college leading to ordination. This situation prevailed until well into the twentieth century. When theology was introduced into the undergraduate curriculum in Catholic colleges in the 1940s, it produced an anomaly. The graduate of a Catholic college would have studied theology; a young man who left the seminary after philosophy would not have studied the subject.

As Carroll focused his vision on Georgetown as "our Main Sheet Anchor for Religion,"[6] others continued to look toward "mixed" schools. In New York, Dutch-born Father Anthony Kohlmann, S.J., pastor of St. Peter's Church on Barclay Street and administrator of the new diocese of New York from 1808 to 1814, opened the New York Literary Institute. Columbia College -- later Columbia University -- was then located near his church. Kohlmann established the Literary Institute uptown on ground now occupied by Rockefeller Center. It included among its early students the sons of DeWitt Clinton and Robert Livingston. Kohlmann saw it as a preparatory school for Columbia College and the two schools even held joint commencements. Unfortunately, Kohlmann's vision was short-lived. In 1805, the ex-Jesuits in Maryland and Pennsylvania were allowed to affiliate themselves with the Society of Jesus in Russia, where it had not been suppressed. Carroll complained that they would have to make up their minds where to place their emphasis -- on Georgetown or the Literary Institute. There was obviously insufficient manpower, he pointed out, to staff both schools. His own preference was clearly for Georgetown.[7] In 1813, Father Anthony Grassi, S.J., superior of the American Mission of the Jesuits, ordered Kohlmann to close the school and sell the property. Georgetown now became the exclusive focus of Jesuit education in the East for the next generation.

Even without the shortage of manpower, however, there were other factors that soon forced a change in Carroll's early vision. First and most apparent was the beginning of immigration that changed the composition and increased the numbers of Carroll's church. The nativist response to immigration took the form of anti-Catholicism. The Catholic counter-response was to develop a defensive posture. Debates over the Protestant character of public schools, particularly in New York and Philadelphia, led to the creation of a separate parochial school system on the elementary level.[8] The new composition of the Church and the nativist environment influenced higher education. In 1843, Bishop Benedict Fenwick, S.J., of Boston, a native of Maryland, founded the College of the Holy Cross in Worchester, Massachusetts. Because of the anti-Catholicism of the Massachusetts legislature, the new college could not be chartered and for more than twenty years granted degrees through Georgetown. Fenwick, for his part, stated that his college was not to be open to non-Catholics -- a sharp contrast to Georgetown's earliest days. He now envisioned the "philosophy" training as not only preparing students for future professions, but also preserving the faith in a hostile culture.[9]

By the time Holy Cross was founded, it was part of what Emmett Curran had called "a Catholic Educational Empire." Between 1829 and 1849, thirty-one Catholic colleges were founded, including Xavier in Cincinnati (1831), Fordham (1841), Notre Dame (1842), Villanova (1842), and Mt. St. Vincent (1847). Although occasionally these institutions were founded at the initiative of the bishop, as was the case of Fordham, they were principally the work of religious orders, particularly the Jesuits, Holy Cross Fathers, Augustinians, and Vincentians -- only in the 1890s were institutions of higher learning established for women. Only seventeen of these schools, however, would survive the Civil War.[10] While an avowed purpose of the Catholic college by the 1840s was to preserve the faith of Catholic students, Protestant students continued to make up a substantial portion of the student body of the new Catholic colleges until 1850. In California, the Italian Jesuits who founded the University of Santa Clara in 1852 were astounded to find half their boarding students were Protestant.[11] What attracted Protestants to these schools was the discipline offered by the priest-teachers and the religious emphasis.

Catholic colleges, almost by design, were not centers of scholarly research, although extraordinary individuals did from time to time emerge in Catholic colleges -- Benedetto Sabetti, S.J., in astronomy at Georgetown and later Woodstock College, in the 1860s and 1870s; and John A. Zahm, C.S.C., in science at Notre Dame, at the end of the century. At the same time, seminaries evolved and expanded their curricula. The "minor seminary," totally independent from institutions for lay students, embraced what would later be called high school and the first two years of college, concentrating on classics. After completing the minor seminary, the student would then attend the "major seminary" for two years of philosophy and four years of theology.[12] Within this development of seminaries, however, there were some differences. The German immigrant clergy brought with them the experience of having studied in universities in preparation for the priesthood. The Irish and other ethnic groups, however, focused more on seminaries independent of a broader university training.[13] Among the diocesan seminaries in the nineteenth century, only St. Mary's Seminary in Baltimore, founded by the Sulpicians under John Carroll in 1791, was chartered to grant pontifical degrees in theology. The other seminaries granted no degrees, civil or ecclesiastical. Though there may well have been reasons for eschewing the trappings of the secular world, such as degrees, the policy did make a strong statement about how the American church envisioned academic achievement. This attitude toward seminary education, in turn, reflected the appreciation for scholarship in institutions for lay students.

Several factors conditioned the attitude toward scholarship, particularly theology, within Catholic institutions. From the time of Carroll, there was a dramatic shift in theological method. He and his early successors expressed a strong sense of episcopal collegiality and adhered to a notion of tradition as the lived and living experience of the Church. For this theological orientation, they relied heavily upon the Fathers of the Church, almost to the exclusion of the scholastics. This theological orientation dramatically changed in the years following the First Vatican

Council. First of all, the council emphasized tradition as a "deposit," as something far more static than the treatment of Carroll and his successors.[14] Its emphasis on papal primacy and infallibility, furthermore, gradually undermined the theology of episcopal collegiality. Second, Pope Leo XIII's Thomistic revival produced a type of theology that was decidely a-historical.[15] This new theological method caused a shift in the interpretation of magisterial pronouncements of councils and popes.

Using the older theological method, nineteenth-century American bishops had little hesitancy in explaining publicly that such papal condemnations as Pius IX's "Syllabus of Errors" did not apply to the United States.[16] In the new theological milieu, they would have greater difficulty in defending such a position, and it was in that milieu that they decided in 1884 to found the Catholic University of America, the most ambitious American Catholic undertaking in the realm of higher education up to that time.

Catholic University was originally conceived as a *seminarium principale*, a graduate school of theology and philosophy for priests who had already completed their seminary theological courses.[17] Only later did it expand its programs to include undergraduate education. As the bishops planned for the opening of the university, they displayed surprising naivete about the nature of higher education. At an early meeting of the trustees, they voted simply to hire "a German" as professor of Scripture.[18] Ultimately, the first professor to be hired was a Scripture scholar, not a German, however, but Henri Hyvernat, a classmate of M.-J. Lagrange, O.P., at the Sulpician Seminary at Issy in France. Hyvernat was primarily a specialist in ancient, near eastern languages. In 1895, he moved the Semitic Languages department from the School of Theology to the Graduate School -- perhaps to avoid the close scrutiny of biblical studies that might follow from the encyclical, *Providentissimus Deus*, in 1893.

The influence of new theological method was most evident in the choice of the first professor of dogmatic theology, Joseph Schroeder. Schroeder was a Thomist who soon became a thorn in the sides of the liberal bishops who were the university's principal supporters. He displayed his theological approach in a series of articles on "theological minimizing" in the *American Ecclesiastical Review* in 1891. The object of his concern was Canon Salvatore di Bartolo's *Criteri theologici*, which had won a warm endorsement from Cardinal James Gibbons, Archbishop of Baltimore and chancellor of the university, but which was later placed on the Index of Forbidden Books. Schroeder charged di Bartolo with "theological minimizing" because he denied that papal temporal power was a matter of official doctrine. For Schroeder, this clearly ran counter to a whole host of papal statements.[19] In 1896, Schroeder played a key role in the forced resignation of Bishop John J. Keane, the first rector of the university. The following year, John Ireland, Archbishop of St. Paul, led the liberal bishops on the board of trustees to force Schroeder's resignation. Schroeder was dismissed, not because of lack of orthodoxy or competence, however, but because of charges of personal immorality.[20]

Ireland was representative of the liberal bishops who were totally committed to making the university an intellectual center and naively optimistic about the academic freedom such an institution should have. In 1892, he chastised Keane for failing to hire St. George Mivart, an English layman and scientist. "I do not forgive you for the loss of Mivart," he wrote. "Don't be afraid of good sound liberalism. Confidence in self, & the support of the American people will carry us through." Within a year, Mivart would have several articles placed on the Index of Forbidden Books and would be excommunicated at the end of the century. Ireland was also annoyed that Keane had allowed Sebastian Messmer, the first professor of canon law, to become Bishop of Green Bay. His reaction revealed an interesting insight into the relationship he saw between bishops as members of the magisterium and scholarly life. "You must educate your professors," he instructed Keane, "& hold on to them -- making bishops only of those who are not worth keeping as professors."[21]

II. Romanization of Catholic Higher Education

Unfortunately, the enthusiasm of the founders of the university soon fell victim to the reaction to several movements in the Church. In the late 1890s, the hierarchy was divided into two camps on a series of issues. The liberals, led by Ireland, Gibbons, and Keane, promoted the Americanization of the Church. In Rome, they had the assistance of Denis J. O'Connell, rector of the American College until his dismissal in 1895. Gradually, their program became known as "Americanism," and was exported to France, Italy, and Germany. As formulated by O'Connell, Americanism showed the benefit to the Church of the American separation of Church and State. They found their position subjected to a new interpretation of the Syllabus of Errors and other papal statements, noted above.[22] In 1895, Leo XIII warned against their enthusiasm for the cherished American tradition and argued that some favorable treatment of the Church in the law would be preferable. In 1899, the pope formally condemned Americanism, largely construed in terms of a misreading of the thought of Isaac Hecker, the founder of the Paulists and the "spiritual father" of the movement. The pontiff also threw out a veiled warning that he considered the Americanists to be semi-Pelagians by condemning their praise of "natural virtues."[23]

Not only did the pope speak to the American Church, however; he also acted. The Holy See began appointing a new breed of bishops in the American hierarchy who would influence higher education in the twentieth century. This began a process of Romanization. The first of this new Roman orientation was William Henry O'Connell, who was named Bishop of Portland, Maine, in 1901, though he had not been on any of the canonical lists of candidates. In 1905, he was named coadjutor Archbishop of Boston, although, again, he had not been on any of the lists.[24] O'Connell and others who would follow him used their position to implement a new spirit into the American Church. One of the first signs of the change came at the Catholic University.

In the immediate aftermath of the condemnation of Americanism, the university seemed untouched. In 1903, Denis O'Connell returned to the good graces of Roman officials after his prominent role in the condemned movement and was named the rector of the university. But gone was the openness to new ideas that had characterized his Roman career. He soon alienated several of his supporters on the faculty, notably Charles Grannan, professor of Scripture. In 1904, the university hired Henry Poels, a student at Louvain of A. Van Hoonacker, as professor of Old Testament. Poels found himself caught in the battle between the faculty and the rector and became a victim of the feud through a case of mistaken identity. His case had all the characteristics of a very bad soap opera.

Poels was a consultor to the Biblical Commission, established in 1903. His difficulties began with the commission's "response" that Catholic exegetes had to consider Moses to be substantially the author of the Pentateuch. A man of deep piety, Poels went personally to see Pope Piux X in the summer of 1907. Through an interpreter, he explained his scholarly reservations about the response, but he promised never to teach or write contrary to it. The pope accepted this arrangement. All was fine for the next academic year, but then Poels' case became entangled with the personality conflict between O'Connell and Grannan. In the summer of 1908, Grannan, who was also a consultor of the Biblical Commission, had a personal audience with the pope, but they did not discuss biblical matters. Shortly later, O'Connell also met with the pope. He explained that he had a professor who raised critical questions about the Bible with his students, but did not give adequate answers. The pope stated that he had told the professor to resign. O'Connell then confronted Grannan with this information, only to learn that the pope was thinking of Poels. For the next year, Poels found himself defending not only his orthodoxy but also his integrity. He was accused of lying about the pope's instructions to him. The interpreter, present at his papal audience, wrote him a letter verifying his account, but then the pope himself wrote out a different account. Piux X later realized that he was wrong in his recollection of his conversation with Poels, and instructed Leopold Fonck, S.J., the first rector of the Biblical Institute, to write Poels. This was to no avail, for Cardinal Raffaele Merry del Val, the Secretary of State, insisted that Poels swear an oath that "in conscience" he believed Moses was the author of the Pentateuch. Poels refused and the university board of trustees demanded his resignation at the end of the academic year 1909-1910.[25]

Poels was clearly a victim of injustice. He had never dissented in public and was caught up in the American Church's desire, after the condemnation of Americanism, to show itself orthodox as the Church entered the lists against Modernism. For his own part, Poels wrote up an account of his case, "A Vindication of My Honor," which he distributed privately to the bishops on the university board of trustees and to several scholars in Europe. In was published only in 1982.[26] Paradoxically, however, Poels remained a consultor to the Biblical Commission until his death in 1946.

Schroeder in 1897 and Poels in 1910 were the only two professors in any Catholic institution of higher education up to that time forced to resign their posts. The Poels case, however, was more significant, for it represented the American Church's reaction to Modernism. In 1907, Piux X had issued his encyclical *Pascendi Dominici Gregis* condemning this "heresy of heresies." The pontiff also decreed that each bishop establish a diocesan committee of vigilance to be the watchdog against any deviation from orthodoxy. This mentality led to the "integrist" movement, a secret network of spies reporting on those suspect of heresy, especially on seminary faculties. In 1914, in one of his first acts as pope, Benedict XV strongly condemned the movement.[27]

But the harm had been done. Intellectual life in the American Catholic Church was then only in its infancy, and the anti-Modernist movement virtually destroyed it. The effect was most obvious in seminaries. Gone was the openness to new developments, characteristic of Kenrick and Ireland. Present were now the manuals of theology, usually written by Roman professors and always published with Roman approval. Professors of theology were not to be so much scholars as interpreters of the manuals. Seminarians were expected not to be exposed to various philosophical and theological systems in their contexts, but to be able to refute "adversaries" through the scholastic method.[28]

The Sulpician seminaries were especially hard hit. In the 1890s, John B. Hogan, who had been successively the president of St. John's Seminary, Brighton, Massachusetts, rector of Divinity College at the Catholic University, and then a professor at Brighton, outlined in *Clerical Studies* a program for theological education that was decidely historical and biblical. He was representative of a number of Sulpicians, whose seminaries would feel the brunt of the issues leading to the anti-Modernist reaction. In 1905, five Sulpicians at St. Joseph's Seminary, Dunwoodie, New York, withdrew from the society and became incardinated into the Archdiocese of New York. The issues were: the increasingly conservative censorship of biblical writings demanded by their superiors in Paris; and their founding without Sulpician authorization of the scholarly *New York Review*.[29] At Brighton, the Sulpicians fell victim to the personal vendetta of Archbishop O'Connell, who peremptorily ordered them to leave his seminary at the end of the academic year 1910-1911.[30]

The increasing intellectual isolation of seminaries was reflected in higher education. Here the Jesuits, who were dominant in the college and university apostolate, were largely responsible. In the late 1890s, they had engaged in debate with Charles W. Eliot, president of Harvard University. The controversy arose over the admission of graduates of Jesuit colleges to Harvard's medical and law schools. Harvard had agreed to accept students from Georgetown. Other Jesuit schools then argued that they had the same curriculum as Georgetown. Harvard then responded that the graduates of Georgetown and the other schools had not performed well because of their preparation. The Jesuits then challenged Eliot that the Jesuit system of required courses was superior to Harvard's elective system.[31] For the first sixty years of the twentieth century, Jesuit schools adhered to their curriculum with little deviation. They concentrated on the classics and on philosophy. Gradually some changes were grudgingly introduced -- not everyone had to take Latin. As late as 1960, this produced a strange anomaly -- a student who majored in English without taking Latin would receive a B.S., while a classically inclined Chemistry student would receive a B.A.[32]

Jesuits and their schools cherished their intellectual isolation, which they often construed as intellectual superiority. They welcomed the accolades of leading alumni, such as Cardinal William O'Connell who so fondly remembered his boyhood days at Boston College, where there was "competition" but not "antagonism." "For that," he declared, "was the distinctive spirit of this College, and I think of every Jesuit college." No Jesuit institution could have been more pleased than to hear the cardinal tell his Boston College audience that "I am proud to say that both here and in the American College at Rome, the training developed the sort of manhood which can win without elation and lose without peevishness."[33] The inference was clear that Jesuit schools were distinguished because their education approximated that which could be obtained in a Roman seminary. And that education focused primarily on neo-Thomastic philosophy, which now seemed synonymous with Catholic thought.[34]

As Catholic education was becoming permeated with a new spirit of isolation from American culture, there were other important developments in Catholic higher education. In 1895, the School Sisters of Notre Dame expanded their academy for girls in Baltimore, and established the College of Notre Dame of Maryland, the first Catholic institution of higher learning for women.[35] Five years later in Washington, the Sisters of Notre Dame de Namur laid the cornerstone of Trinity College, the first Catholic institution specifically founded for the higher education of women. Its location near the Catholic University, however, caused some Roman officials to fear that the new college would mean the admission of women to the university. These fears Cardinal Gibbons succeeded in dissuading.[36] But there were other reasons for opposition. The *Intermountain Catholic* in Salt Lake City put it this way:

> If the Catholic University opens its doors to the students of Trinity College and they are given equal opportunities with the students of the former, then little fear need be entertained for the success of the latter. But if this new institution is to be a sort of left-handed appendage to the Catholic University, nominally in connection with it, but really not fully enjoying its privileges, it seems to us fatuous to hope that Trinity College can draw to it Catholic young women who are now at such places as Chicago, Ann Arbor, Cornell, etc., where they know they enjoy opportunities not inferior to their non-Catholic sisters.... The day is gone when you can deprive our brainy, ambitious young women from the highest and the best in education. She insists in having all the advantages of her brother, and she is right. The world "do move."[37]

It was a surprisingly "feminist" observation for the Utah editor at the turn of the century. In 1901, there were only two Catholic colleges for women in the United States, but in the twentieth century, there would be many more, including St. Catherine's College in St. Paul, the only Catholic institution, other than the Catholic University of America, to have a chapter of Phi Beta Kappa prior to the mid-1960s.

The Utah editorialist, however, was also making another point. An increasing number of Catholic students were beginning to attend secular colleges and universities. Catholic higher education had gradually come to be seen as a safeguard against the dangers of secular institutions. In the early 1890s, the bishops had been divided over the issue of establishing parochial schools and of providing religious education for children in public schools. A decade later, they had to address the problem of Catholics attending non-Catholic universities. Bishop Bernard McQuaid of Rochester, regarded as one of the leaders of the conservatives in the earlier dispute, broached the problem with the archbishops of the country in 1906. In view of the large number of Catholic students attending state universities, he recommended "that for their benefit, there be associated with these Universities, Colleges having Catholic professors to conduct them; and these professors paid, if possible, from the State University funds." The archbishops took no action on the recommendation, because "divers laws, sentiments and view-points obtain in different States of the country."[38]

At the same time, Catholic educators debated the establishment of Newman Centers at non-Catholic universities. This proposal, too, met with opposition. The Jesuits, in particular, argued that the existence of Newman centers would encourage Catholic students to attend non-Catholic colleges. The Jesuits, of course, had a vested interest in preserving their own schools.[39]

From the time of Carroll, there had been a dramatic shift in Catholic higher education. By the beginning of the twentieth century, Catholic colleges played the role not so much of promoting scholarship as of preserving the faith of young Catholics. Catholics were intellectually and culturally isolated from the American mainstream -- and they were proud of it. In 1927, Mary McGill, associate editor of *The Catholic Girl*, commented to Wilfred Parsons, S.J., editor of *America*, about the impression Catholics made on their fellow Americans. "We are so sure," she said. "That characteristic would hurt me, if I didn't believe. I think I would hate people who are so certain and set apart...."[40]

Catholic universities consciously contributed to both the certitude and the isolation. In 1938, George Bull, S.J., dean of the Fordham University graduate school, argued that the purpose envisioned by the secular graduate school was "to add to the sum of human knowledge." Such a purpose, however, was antithetical to the Catholic graduate school, for it would mean "attempting the impossible of being Catholic in creed and anti-Catholic in culture." The Church and Catholic universities, he reasoned, were already in possession of the truth still pursued by secular universities. Bull summed up his position by stating that the starting point for understanding the "Catholic mind" and "its totality of mind" was

> the simple assumption that wisdom has been achieved by man, and that the humane use of the mind, the function proper to him as man, is contemplation and not research.... In sum, then, research cannot be the primary object of a Catholic graduate school, because it is at war with the whole Catholic life of the mind.[41]

Bull could not have better expressed the Catholic pride in cultural isolation. Research and scholarly productivity were not to be hallmarks of the Catholic university.

Even as Bull was writing, however, Catholic educators were beginning to change the characteristics of Catholic higher education. Colleges had previously been seen as providing "philosophical" training, a system that was modelled largely upon the seminary. Religious instruction was for the most part catechetical and devotional. It was not, except in some rare cases, part of the formal curriculum for which credit was given. In the 1940s, Catholic colleges began requiring theology courses -- usually one each semester -- for graduation. But the theology was largely that of the type of Thomism then being taught in seminaries.[42] Teaching theology for credit now became a hallmark of Catholic colleges and universities, but this was not intended to be scholarship or research. The theology taught was part of the re-enforcement of Catholic identity in a world still deemed to be hostile; it was a-historical and frequently induced in the student the mentality that change and development were un-Catholic, if not anti-Catholic. Moreover, college theology teachers were usually priests who had simply undergone their own seminary education as academic preparation. But change was in the offing, both in the type and numbers of Catholic students going to college and in theology itself.

III. The Post-War Years

The years after World War II witnessed increasing numbers of Catholics attending college. One reason was the GI Bill of Rights, which gave educational benefits to returning veterans. Catholics now had the same access to higher education as their non-Catholic counterparts. The enrollment at Jesuit colleges alone leapt from 22,191 in the fall of 1945 to 62,108 in the fall of 1946.[43] Catholic colleges expanded their facilities. But, as James Hennesey has pointed out, many administrators failed to realize that a Catholic university could not depend on tuitions, low-paid lay faculty, and unpaid members of male and female religious orders. No Catholic university has ever had an endowment approaching that of the leading secular institutions. To remain solvent, Catholic colleges increasingly depended on government subsidies, which brought with them increased secularization. Increased education also meant that Catholics were moving sociologically into the middle class and geographically into the new suburbs, away from the urban setting so characteristic of Catholicism in the northeast and midwest. The Catholic laity was well on its way to being better educated than the clergy, at least in secular fields.

Increased enrollments and expanded facilities of Catholic colleges, however, did not mean a renewal of Catholic intellectual life. In 1955, Monsignor John Tracy Ellis shattered the intellectual complacency of American Catholics. They could not merely argue that they were the victims of prejudice, he said. There were other causes for the poverty of Catholic intellectual life: lack of funding for higher education; the absence of a real love of learning among professors; the substitution of morality for intellectual endeavors in Catholic colleges; and an almost spiritual denigration of intellectual and scholarly pursuits.[44] Other Catholic educators raised their voices in agreement.[45]

In the meantime, the increased education of the laity had several long-range effects on American Catholicism. Many middle-class Catholics no longer sought a Catholic college education for their children, but sent them to prestigious secular institutions. Other Catholics, to be sure, continued to embrace Catholic higher education for their children, but some identified "Catholic" with the type of theology they may have learned prior to Vatican II. Life in the suburbs also altered the religious outlook of middle-class Catholics. For the working-class Catholic who attended an urban parish, ethnicity was a re-enforcement of religious identity. In the suburbs, no denomination was in prior possession. There was no turf to be won, and ethnic distinctions began to be blurred or even forgotten. This situation presented the danger that religion can become a strictly private affair. Catholic colleges have had to grapple with a much different type of religiously prepared student than they had up to the 1960s. In addition, they had to respond to new educational demands. Catholic institutions had traditionally emphasized the liberal arts as preparation for professions, particularly law and medicine. Many smaller Catholic colleges had to shift their focus to the emerging field of business as an undergraduate concentration. Few Catholic colleges or universities attempted to raise their endowments to promote scholarship.

Catholics had achieved a new social status that brought with it a new complacency. Many felt all the more secure with a sense of being finally accepted as truly American with the election of John F. Kennedy as President of the United States in 1960. But few seem to have looked closely enough at Kennedy's speech to the Houston Ministerial Association and realized that he was basically making his Catholicism a private matter with no influence on his political views.[46]

While all these changes were taking place among the laity, theology was itself undergoing a revolution, but it was confined to the realms of seminaries and the Catholic University of

America. In 1943, John Courtney Murray, S.J., professor of dogmatic theology at Woodstock College and editor of *Theological Studies*, began writing on the neuralgic American question of religious liberty and of the separation of Church and State. He soon met opposition from Monsignor Joseph C. Fenton, professor of dogmatic theology at the Catholic University and editor of the *American Ecclesiastical Review*. Fenton was almost a caricature of the type of theology so dominant in the twentieth century, but he had powerful Roman allies, notably Alfredo Ottaviani, who was named a cardinal in 1953 and placed in charge of the Holy Office. In the summer of 1955, Murray was told by his Roman superiors that the censors could not approve several articles for publication, because of some accusations made against him at the Holy Office. He voluntarily gave up writing on the topic -- at least for the moment.[47] He was the first American scholar since Henry Poels to be constrained to stop publishing.

With Murray silent, Fenton then began to attack biblical scholars, some of whom taught at the Catholic University. This battle mirrored a similar one then raging in Rome against the Pontifical Biblical Institute, a center for progressive scholarship. In 1958, Fenton received an additional ally in his campaign, the apostolic delegate, Archbishop Egidio Vagnozzi. At its annual meeting in 1961, the Catholic Biblical Association (CBA), founded in 1938, passed a resolution censuring the *American Ecclesiastical Review*. Vagnozzi intervened, however, to prevent any reference to the journal in the published resolution.[48]

Shortly thereafter, Edward Siegman, C.Pp.S., who was teaching at the Catholic University and who, as editor of the CBA's journal, the *Catholic Biblical Quarterly*, had brought it to a high level of scholarship, suffered a heart attack. While recovering, he received word that the rector of the university had hired someone else to replace him. The School of Theology and the Graduate School of the university both passed resolutions of protest, but to no avail. Officially, the reason given for his dismissal was his poor health. But Siegman and his supporters knew that the real reason was the combined opposition of

Fenton and Vagnozzi.[49] Siegman was the first professor at the Catholic University to be removed for scholarly reason since Poels.

At the opening of Vatican II in 1962, the American Church gave little indication of the role it would play in the council. Fenton was appointed to the preparatory commission drafting documents for discussion at the council, and was named a *peritus*, or expert, for the council itself. John Courtney Murray remained at home, "disinvited," to use his term, at the request of Ottaviani and Vagnozzi.[50] This was, however, only a temporary setback. For the second session, Murray was present as a *peritus*, through the intervention of Francis Cardinal Spellman, Archbishop of New York. At the council, the American bishops found themselves grappling with what seemed to be new theological concepts, such as episcopal collegiality. But the attention of most Americans, Catholic and non-Catholic alike, was drawn toward more pragmatic issues, such as religious liberty, ecumenism, and the statement on the Jews.[51]

At the end of the council, however, the American church was confronted with something new. Its cherished position on religious liberty, so long held suspect in Rome, was now part of the council's teaching. Its liturgy would soon be in the vernacular. The council's documents on collegiality of bishops with the pope and on the relationship between Scripture and Tradition seemed to many Catholics, including the clergy, to be something new, when in fact they would have quite familiar to the American bishops of the mid-nineteenth century. The council's supplement of the traditional hierarchical view of the Church with the concept of the "people of God" ushered in a new age of lay involvement with the Church. The council's teachings represented positive achievements. They also occasioned new problems.

In some ways, the American Church had little opportunity immediately to absorb the conciliar teaching, except the reforms in the liturgy. Simultaneously with the council, American society was undergoing a dramatic change, and Catholics played leading parts in it. The civil rights movement brought forth the new phenomenon of priests and nuns standing side by side with lay people and non-Catholics in demonstrations. The unpopular war in Vietnam spawned the unprecedented protests of Catholics against the policy of the government. Priests and nuns were not only arrested and put in jail, but also left their rectories, religious houses, and convents to get married. The 1960s and 1970s were a period of social, political, and religious upheaval. In 1968, the enthusiasm with which so many Catholics embraced the council was challenged when Paul VI reiterated the Church's ban on birth control. The papal action gave rise to the new debate over the right of theologians officially to dissent from official, non-infallible teaching -- an issue which the American bishops addressed in their pastoral of 1968.[52] All of these events, together with the new-found status of American Catholics, influenced the direction of American Catholic higher education.

American Catholic intellectual life had been undergoing self-criticism from the time of Ellis' address in 1955. Catholic learned societies, most of them formed at the beginning of the century, participated in this identity crisis. Was the American Catholic Historical Association, for example, an organization of Catholics who were historians or a society of historians who studied Catholicism? Catholics in universities wished increasingly to be identified with the academic mainstream. Catholic institutions decreased the theology requirements for their students, sometimes not requiring anything specifically Catholic in their curricula. At the same time, the requirement, at least for boarding students, of religious practice, long an emphasis in Catholic colleges, was also dropped. In July, 1967, a group of Catholic educators gathered at Land O'Lakes, Wisconsin, and issued a statement that "to perform its teaching and research functions adequately, the Catholic university must have a true autonomy and academic freedom in the face of authority of whatever kind, lay or clerical, external to the academic community itself."[53]

The Land O'Lakes statement coincided with a dramatic change in the composition of the faculty and governance of the Catholic college. In the early part of the century, most institutions were staffed by priests and religious. By the late 1960s, not only Catholic lay professors but also non-Catholic ones made up an increasing percentage of the faculty. Until the 1960s, the religious superior appointed the administration of Catholic colleges. This governance was replaced by "separate incorporation" of the religious community from the college or university, with the latter under a board of trustees, the majority of whom were lay people. Some Catholic colleges and universities became increasingly secularized in order to gain Federal funds. Others closed altogether. In 1965, there were 309 institutions of higher learning; in 1991, there were 235.[54] In some instances, notably in New York, Catholic institutions had to drop specific reference to Catholicism or face the danger of losing state funding.[55]

As Philip Gleason notes, this new situation for Catholic colleges led to two divergent approaches, reflecting ideological divisions in the American Church. The older and more established institutions replaced their theology requirements with an emphasis on doctrine, with an orientation toward faith and justice in practice. New colleges, such as Christendom in Virginia and St. Thomas Aquinas in California, came into being to stress the doctrinal orthodoxy that many felt had been lost since the council.[56]

This historical survey provides the context for a discussion of secularization and the future of American Catholic higher education as we approach the year 2000. First of all, there is a tendency to define a college as "Catholic," because it teaches Catholic theology. But theology was not a component of a Catholic college or university until the 1940s -- philosophy had previously been the integrating factor in providing an American Catholic vision of the world and culture. Second, most colleges and universities were founded by religious orders, and were largely independent of episcopal control -- and support. To institute episcopal oversight over these institutions would change their original character and might, as Father Theodore M. Hesburgh, C.S.C., has argued, jeopardize their receiving Federal funds, essential for their continued existence.[57]

The question of the Catholic identity of colleges and universities is related to the questions of authority and academic freedom. While the freedom of the professor should be preserved, should the institution not also have the freedom to maintain its identity? The answer to that question will have to come from the members of the religious orders and from their lay colleagues, Catholic and non-Catholic. It will have to be shaped in light of Catholicism's encounter with the secular culture of the present, not the religious pluralism of the past.

Endnotes

1.   Carroll to Farmer, Dec., 1784, in Thomas O. Hanley, S.J., ed., *The John Carroll Papers*. 3 vols.; Notre Dame, IN: University of Notre Dame Press, 1976, I, 158.

2.   *Ibid.*

3.   Carroll to Edenshink, Apr.-June, 1785, *Ibid.*, 186. For the background to the acceptance of Catholics at the University of Pennsylvania and at Washington College and St. John's, see R. Emmett Curran, S.J., *The Bicentennial History of Georgetown University: From Academy to University, 1789-1889.* Washington: Georgetown University Press, 1993, pp. 11-13.

4.   Carroll to Charles Plowden, Rock Creek, 24 February 1790, in *Ibid.*, 431.

5.   Archives of Georgetown University, "Proposals to establish an academy at George Town, Patomack River, Maryland," quoted in Joseph T. Durkin, S.J., *Georgetown University: First in the Nation's Capital.* Garden City, NY: Doubleday & Co., Inc., 1964, p. 5. See Curran, *Georgetown*, pp. 25-26.

6.   Carroll to Plowden, 23 October 1789, quoted in Curran, *Georgetown*, p. 13.

7.   Carroll to Charles Plowden, 12 December 1813, in *John Carroll Papers*, III, 247.

8.   James Hennesey, S.J., *American Catholics: A History of the Roman Catholic Community in the United States*. New York: Oxford University Press, 1981, p. 107.

9.   Archives of Georgetown University, Benedict Fenwick to George Fenwick, Boston, 29 November 1838.

10.   See Curran, *Georgetown*, pp. 127-29.

11.   Gerald McKevitt, S.J., *The University of Santa Clara: A History: 1851-1977*. Stanford: Stanford University Press, 1979, p. 40.

12.   It should also be noted that some seminaries provided education for young men who had no intention of studying for the priesthood. In 1852, Jesuits opened Loyola College in Baltimore to leave St. Mary's Seminary with those students who were seminarians in the strict sense.

13.   John Tracy Ellis, "The Formation of the American Priest: An Historical Perspective," in John Tracy Ellis, ed., *The Catholic Priest in the United States: Historical Investigations*. Collegeville, MN: St. John's University Press, 1971, pp. 20-21.

14.   DS, 3019. See also Yves M.-J. Congar, O.P., *Traditions and Tradition: An Historical and a Theological Essay*. New York: The Macmillan Company, 1967, p. 198.

15.   Gerald A. McCool, S.J., *Catholic Theology in the Nineteenth Century: The Quest for a Unitary Method*. New York: The Seabury Press, 1977, p. 23.

16.   I have developed the theme of the reinterpretation of papal statements in *Nova et Vetera: The Theology of Tradition in American Catholicism*. Milwaukee: Marquette University Press, 1987.

17.   *Acta et Decreta Concilii Plenarii Baltimorensis Tertii*. Baltimore: John Murphy & Co., 1886, nos. 186-187, pp. 54-55.

18.   Archives of the Catholic University of America, Minutes of Trustee Meetings, 22 January 1885, p. 4.

19.   Joseph Schroeder, "Theological Minimizing and its Latest Defenders," *American Ecclesiastical Review* 4 (1891): 115-32.

20.   See my *Vatican and the American Hierarchy from 1870 to 1965*, Stuttgart: Anton Hiersemann Verlag, 1982; paperback: Wilmington, DE: Michael Glazier, 1985, pp. 157-59.

21.   Archives of the Catholic University of America, Ireland to Keane, Rome, 26 April 1892.

22.   See my *Vatican and the American Hierarchy*, pp. 143-89.

23.   Leo XIII, *Testem Benevolentiae*, in John Tracy Ellis, ed., *Documents of American Catholic History*. Chicago: Henry Regnery Co., 1967, pp. 541-42.

24.   James Gaffey, "The Changing of the Guard: The Rise of William Henry Cardinal O'Connell," *Catholic Historical Review* 59 (1973): 225-44.

25.   For a popular account of the Poels' case, see my "Dissent at the Catholic University: The Case of Henry J. Poels," *America*, 156, 11 October 1986, pp. 180-84.

26.   Henry A. Poels, "A Vindication of My Honor," edited with an introduction by Frans Neirinck, *Annua Nuntia Lovaniensia*, 225 (1982).

27.   Roger Aubert, *et al., The Church in a Secularised Society*, Vol. V of *The Christian Centuries*. New York: Paulist Press, 1978, pp. 198-203.

28.   Michael V. Gannon, "Before and After Modernism: The Intellectual Isolation of the American Priest," in John Tracy Ellis, ed., *The Catholic Priest in the United States: Historical Investigations*. Collegeville, MN: St. John's University Press, 1971, pp. 350-56.

29.   See Gannon, pp. 341-48 and Michael J. De Vito, *Principles of Ecclesiastical Reform According to the New York Review*. New York: the United States Catholic Historical Society, 1977.

30.   Ellis, "The Formation of the American Priest," p. 77. The material on this affair can be found in the Sulpician Archives in Baltimore.

31.   See Archives of the Maryland Province of the Society of Jesus, Georgetown University, Brosnahan-Eliot correspondence.

32.   On the Jesuit curriculum during this period, see Joseph A. Tetlow, "The Jesuits' Mission in Higher Education: Perspectives and Contexts," *Studies in the Spirituality of Jesuits* 15-16 (November 1983, and January 1984): 24-27.

33.   *The Pilot* (Boston), 23 March 1912.

34.   See William M. Halsey, *The Survival of American Innocence: Catholicism in an Era of Disillusionment, 1920-1940.* Notre Dame: University of Notre Dame Press, 1980, pp. 138-68.

35.   Hennesey, p. 187.

36.   Peter E. Hogan, S.S.J., *The Catholic University of America, 1896-1903: The Rectorship of Thomas J. Conaty.* Washington, DC: The Catholic University of America Press, 1949, pp. 95-98.

37.   Quoted *ibid.*, p. 99.

38.   Archives of the Archdiocese of New York, Annual Meeting of the Archbishops, 26 April 1901.

39.   John Whitney Evans, *The Newman Movement: Roman Catholics in American Higher Education.* Notre Dame: University of Notre Dame Press, 1980.

40.   Quoted in Hennesey, p. 221.

41.   Quoted in Gannon, pp. 358-59.

42.   Philip Gleason, "In Search of Unity: American Catholic Thought, 1920-1960," *Catholic Historical Review* 65 (1979): 199-204.

43.   Tetlow, p. 32.

44.   John Tracy Ellis, "American Catholics and the Intellectual Life," *Thought* 30 (1955): 351-88.

45.   Hennesey, p. 301.

46.   *New York Times*, 13 September 1960.

47.   See Donald E. Pelotte, S.S.S., *John Courtney Murray: Theologian in Conflict.* New York: The Paulist Press, 1975, pp. 27-73.

48.   The information on this affair is contained in the Archives of the Catholic Biblical Association, the Catholic University of America, Washington, DC. This and related events

will be more extensively treated in my forthcoming book, *American Catholic Biblical Scholarship: A History.*

49.   Siegman memorandum, Archives of the Congregation of the Most Precious Blood, Carthagena, OH.

50.   See Pelotte, p. 77.

51.   See my "American Journals and Paul VI at Vatican II," *Paolo VI e i problemi ecclesiologici al concilio: colloquio internazionale di studio Brescia 19-20-21 settembre 1986.* Brescia: Pubblicazioni dell'istituto Paolo VI, 1989, pp. 547-59.

52.   Nolan, *Pastoral Letters*, pp. 687-88. See also Hennesey, pp. 307-31.

53.   Quoted in Hennesey, p. 322.

54.   *Ibid.*, p. 323. *The Official Catholic Directory, Anno Domini 1991.* New York: P.J. Kennedy & Sons, 1991, "General Summary."

55.   For an excellent survey of this issue, see Philip Gleason, "American Catholic Higher Education, 1940-1990: The Ideological Context," in George M. Marsden and Bradley J. Longfield, eds., *The Secularization of the Academy.* New York: Oxford University Press, 1992, especially pp. 247-49.

56.   Gleason, pp. 250-51.

57.   Theodore M. Hesburgh, "The Vatican and American Catholic Higher Education," *America*, 155, 1 November 1986, pp. 247-50, 263.

Bibliographic Entries

312.   Annarelli, James John. *Academic Freedom and Catholic Higher Education.* New York: Greenwood Press, 1987.

Examines academic freedom in Catholic institutions in a scholarly manner.

313.   Apczynski, John, ed. *Theology and the University.* Lanham, MD: University Press of America, 1989.

Inquires into dynamic tensions among the Church, the scholar, and the discipline of theology. Several of the 15 authors examine the U.S. context.

314.   Bautista, Edna R. *Baccalaureate Origins of Doctorates from U.S. Catholic Universities and Colleges during the 1960s, 1970s and 1980s*. Washington, DC: ERIC Document Reproduction Service, 1993. ERIC Document ED 364 129.

Ranks 155 Catholic institutions and offers trend information.

315.   Beisheim, Peter H. "Justice and Peace: Can Colleges and Universities Make a Difference?" *New Catholic World* 231 (September 1988): 212-19.

Reviews curriculum and campus developments, and U.S. bishops' statements concerned with peace and justice.

316.   Bonachea, Rolando E. (ed.). *Jesuit Higher Education: Essays on an American Tradition of Excellence*. Pittsburgh, PA: Duquesne University Press, 1989.

Gathers fourteen essays focusing on the Jesuit approach to education.

317.   Boughton, Lynn C. "Catholic Higher Education and the Vatican Proposal." *Homiletic & Pastoral Review* 88 (December 1987): 19-20.

Analyzes objections to 1985 Vatican commission of scholars' proposal that academically sound instruction in Catholic doctrine be offered at Church-related institutions to counter faulty teaching.

318. Buckley, Michael J. "The Catholic University and Its Inherent Promise." *America*, 168, 29 May 1993, pp. 14-16.

Deals with integrating the academic and the religious and the summons of *Ex Corde Ecclesiae*. Based on presentation in *Catholic Universities in Church and Society* (see below).

319. Burghardt, Walter J. "Intellectual and Catholic? Or Catholic Intellectual?" *America*, 160, 6 May 1989, pp. 420-25.

Feels the intellectual life must become a vocation for Catholics.

320. Byron, William J. "Between Church and Culture: A Role for Catholic Higher Education." *Thought* 66 (September 1991): 310-16.

Discusses the notion of culture and its relation to values in the light of *Ex Corde Ecclesiae*, and the role of Catholic higher education in relating the Church and culture.

321. Byron, William J. *Quadrangle Considerations*. Chicago: Loyola University Press, 1989.

Reflects upon experiences in and offers suggestions for Catholic higher education; author is Catholic University of America's former Jesuit president.

322. Byron, William J. "The Religious Purpose of Catholic Higher Education." *New Catholic World* 231 (September 1988): 196-200.

Argues social issues belong on Catholic educational agendas.

323. Cafardi, Nicholas P., ed. *Academic Freedom in a Pluralistic Society: The Catholic University.* Pittsburgh, PA: Duquesne University, 1990.

Includes papers, addresses and responses from a 1989 Duquesne symposium.

324. Conn, James Jerome. *Catholic Universities in the United States and Ecclesiastical Authority.* Rome: Editrice Pontificia Universita Gregoriana, 1991.

Studies the Church's teaching on Catholic universities and the relationship of those in the U.S. to ecclesiastical authority (1990 doctoral dissertation, Pontifical Gregorian University, Rome).

325. Curran, Charles E. *Catholic Higher Education, Theology, and Academic Freedom.* Notre Dame, IN: University of Notre Dame Press, 1990.

Reviews historical Catholic attitudes and presents personal ideas and struggles of Catholic University's former professor of moral theology.

326. Curran, Robert Emmett. *The Bicentennial History of Georgetown University: From Academy to University.* Vol. 1. Washington, DC: Georgetown University Press, 1993.

Sketches a detailed history of Georgetown University to 1889.

327. *Current Issues in Catholic Higher Education.* Vol. 1, (1980)-.

Contains several articles on current relevant topics in each semiannual theme issue. Published by the Association of Catholic Colleges and Universities.

328.   Daley, Brian E. "Christ and the Catholic University." *America*, 169, 11 September 1993, pp. 6-14.

Considers the person, work, and way of living of Christ, and the effect this understanding has on university life.

329.   Daly, Robert J., ed., *In All Things: Religious Faith and American Culture; Papers of the Inaugural Conference of the Jesuit Institute at Boston College*. Kansas City, MO: Sheed & Ward, 1990.

Highlights the family among concerns that should be part of the research profile of a Catholic university, but which often receive less attention.

330.   Davis, Bergram H., Richard G. Huber, and Schubert M. Ogden. "Academic Freedom and Tenure: The Catholic University of America." *Academe* 75 (September-October 1989): 27-40.

Reports on the Charles E. Curran controversy by a committee of The American Association of University Professors.

331.   Deuben, Caroll Ann Johnston. "Factors Facilitating or Inhibiting Institutional Merger Among Three Catholic Institutions of Higher Education." Ph.D. dissertation, Wayne State University, 1992. 2 vols.

Studies the University of Detroit, Marygrove College, and Mercy College of Detroit.

332. Dodge, Donna Marie. "Beyond the Mission Statement: What Makes a College Catholic?" Ed.D. dissertation, Columbia University Teachers College, 1991.

Identifies attention given to moral and spiritual development of students, and environment of Christian community in a case study at the College of Mount St. Vincent (NY) as essential elements in Catholic identity.

333. Dulles, Avery. "University Theology as a Service to the Church." *Thought* 64 (June 1989): 103-15.

Recommends that university theology contribute to the renewal of Catholic intellectual life.

334. Dumestre, Marcel Jacob, Jr. "The Contribution of Bernard Lonergan Toward the Recovery of a Catholic Philosophy of Education." Ed.D. dissertation, Peabody College for Teachers of Vanderbilt University, 1990.

Proposes recent conflicts between U.S. Catholic higher education and the U.S. hierarchy are due to lack of a clear philosophy of education. Applies Canadian Jesuit theologian Lonergan's thought in this regard.

335. Dunn, Catherine and Dorothy A. Moehler, eds. *Pioneering Women at the Catholic University of America: Papers Presented at a Centennial Symposium, November 11, 1988.* Hyattsville, MD: International Graphics; Washington, DC: distributed by the Catholic University of America Press, 1990.

Examines the role that Catholic University played in providing educational opportunities for women. Focuses on five individuals.

336.   Ellis, John Tracy. "The Catholic Church and Her
       Universities: A View from History." *Current Issues in
       Catholic Higher Education* 8 (Summer 1987): 3-9.

       Reviews historical academic-ecclesiastical
       controversies, academic freedom in the U.S., and
       addresses reasons for deficiencies in Catholic intellectual
       achievement.

337.   Evans, John Whitney. "Making Best of a Bad Job?
       Newman Chaplains Between Code and Council." *U.S.
       Catholic Historian* 11 (Winter 1993): 35-50.

       Tells the story of the development of U.S. Newman
       Clubs in the 20th century in the light of the 1917 Code
       of Canon Law.

338.   "'Ex Corde Ecclesiae' and Its Ordinances: A Discussion."
       Commonweal, 120, 10 November 1993, pp. 14-15, 22-26.

       Contains articles by Charles E. Curran, Joseph A.
       Komonchak, and Anita Pampusch, a review of *Catholic
       Universities in Church and Society* (see above), and the
       eight "Proposed Ordinances" by a committee of
       American bishops applying *Ex Corde Ecclesiae*'s norms in
       the U.S.

339.   Fellowship of Catholic Scholars. Convention (11th: 1988:
       Boston, MA). *Catholic Higher Education: Proceedings of the
       Fellowship of Catholic Scholars Eleventh Convention*. Edited
       by Paul L. Williams. Pittston, PA: Northeast Books, 1989.

       Presents two dozen papers on contemporary
       Catholic issues in higher education.

340. Fogarty, Gerald P. "Academic Freedom and American Higher Education: An Historical Analysis." *New Catholic World* 231 (September 1993): 220-25.

Discusses the origin, purpose, development, and characteristics of Catholic higher education in the U.S.

341. Gallin, Alice. "On the Road Toward a Definition of a Catholic University." *The Jurist* 48 (1988): 536-58.

Presents a scholarly review of Catholic higher education in the U.S., focusing on effects of culture on faith and the pastoral mission of the Church.

342. Gallin, Alice, ed. *American Catholic Higher Education: Essential Documents, 1967-1990*. Notre Dame, IN: University of Notre Dame Press, 1992.

Compiles over two dozen key documents issued by U.S. church officials and university presidents, and by the Vatican, in a collaborative effort to define the role and purpose of a Catholic university or college.

343. Gannon, Ann Ida. "Some Aspects of Catholic Higher Education Since Vatican II." *CCICA Annual* (1987): 11-32.

Traces interaction between Vatican and officials of U.S. Catholic higher education institutions; focuses on *Lumen Gentium*.

344. Gleason, Philip. "American Catholic Higher Education, 1940-1990: The Ideological Context." In *The Secularization of the Academy*, ed. George Marsden and Bradley J. Longfield, 234-58. New York: Oxford University Press, 1992.

Reviews underlying religious and cultural assumptions that shaped the perspectives of Catholic educators.

345.	Gleason, Philip. *Keeping the Faith*. Notre Dame, IN: University of Notre Dame Press, 1987.

Offers an overview of the progress of Catholic higher education in America within a larger cultural context.

346.	Heft, James L. "A Taste for the Other: the Moral Development of College Students and Young Adults." *Living Light* 29 (Spring 1993): 23-36.

Explores integration of moral formation with academic education. Note that the November 1992 lecture also in *Current Issues in Higher Education* 13 (Winter 1993): 5-13.

347.	Hesburgh, Theodore M. *The Challenge and Promise of a Catholic University*. Notre Dame, IN: University of Notre Dame Press, 1994.

348.	Hunt, George W. "American Catholic Intellectual Life." *America*, 160, 6 May 1991, pp. 412-19.

Examines the history of American Catholic intellectuals since John Tracy Ellis' 1955 essay "American Catholics and the Intellectual Life." Notes shift toward theology and biblical scholarship.

349.	Hunt, Michael J. *College Catholics: A New Counter-Culture*. New York: Paulist Press, 1993.

Written by a Paulist college chaplain. Recounts the stories of college students on their faith journeys.

350. Isetti, Ronald Eugene. "Americanization, Conflict and Convergence in Catholic Higher Education in Late Nineteenth Century California." In *Religion and Society in the American West: Historical Essays,* ed. Carl Guarneri and David Alvarez, 333-52. Lanham, MD: University Press of America, 1987.

Chronicles the history of and influences on Jesuit and Christian Brothers' schools in California.

351. Jacobs, Richard M. "A Modest Proposal for the Recruitment and Retention of Catholic Educators." *Momentum* 22 (September 1991): 58-61.

Suggests that dioceses finance training of quality teachers for Catholic schools.

352. John Paul II. *Apostolic Constitution Ex Corde Ecclesiae of the Supreme Pontiff John Paul II On Catholic Universities.* Washington, DC: United States Catholic Conference, 1990; Boston, MA: St. Paul Books & Media, 1990.

Establishes norms for the distinct character of Catholic universities and colleges world-wide. Document was ten years in preparation, and appears also in *Catholic Universities in Church and Society* (1993) and Gallin (1992) (see above).

353. Kelly, James R. "*Collegium* and the Futures of Catholic Higher Education." *America,* 169, 11 September 1993, pp. 15-17.

Reports on a 1993 summer institute on "Faith and Intellectual Life" held at Fairfield University, Connecticut.

354. Kennedy, Leonard A. *How to Keep Your University Catholic*. Toronto: Life Ethics Centre, 1992.

Deals with the Catholicity issue. Author feels Catholic universities in the U.S. aren't healthy, and he is critical of "values programs."

355. Kirby, Donald J., *et al. Ambitious Dreams: The Values Program at Le Moyne College*. Kansas City, MO: Sheed & Ward, 1990.

Concludes that the Program goal at New York State Jesuit college is to empower students as agents for community improvement.

356. Kolman, Eileen. "The Influence of Institutional Culture on Presidential Selection." *Review of Higher Education* 10 (Summer 1987): 319-32.

Examines dynamics of institutional culture in selecting a new president at three Catholic colleges. Based on 1986 thesis from Loyola University of Chicago.

357. LaMagdeleine, Donald R. *Foundational History in Catholic Higher Education: An Exploratory Typology with Implications*. Edited by James Reidy. Aquin Papers No. 15: 13-23. St. Paul, MN: College of St. Thomas, 1987.

Shows differences between a diocesan college and a university founded by a religious congregation as to changes and future policies.

358. Lane, Julia. "Returning Gospel Values and Nursing Education." *Health Progress* 72 (June 1993): 30-35.

Calls for renewed emphasis on Christian values as the basis for nursing service and education in Catholic institutions.

359. Langan, John P., ed. *Catholic Universities in Church and Society: A Dialogue on Ex Corde Ecclesiae.* Washington, DC: Georgetown University Press, 1993.

Contains symposium papers, comments and discussion summaries by 20 contributors on implications and implementation of the apostolic constitution in American Catholic colleges and universities.

360. Leahy, William P. *Adapting to America: Catholics, Jesuits, and Higher Education in the Twentieth Century.* Washington, DC: Georgetown University Press, 1991.

Investigates major developments in Catholic higher education since World War I. Also investigates effects of American culture on Catholicism in this century.

361. Lent, Craig S. "Can a University Be Both Great and Christian?" *New Oxford Review* 60 (September 1993): 10-14.

Weighs challenges of secularism to the Catholic character of the University of Notre Dame. Affirms that a Catholic intellectual community must be maintained at its core.

362. Loyola Symposium on Values and Ethics. *The Catholic University and the Urban Poor: The 1987 Loyola Symposium*

on Values and Ethics, February 19 and 26, and March 19, 1987. Chicago: Loyola University Press, 1988.

Examines the "preferential option for the poor" in 15 short papers.

363. Malloy, Edward A. *Culture and Commitment: The Challenge of Today's University.* Notre Dame, IN: University of Notre Dame Press, 1992.

Collects significant public addresses given in the author's first term as president of the University of Notre Dame.

364. May, William W., ed. *Vatican Authority and American Catholic Dissent: The Curran Case and Its Consequences.* NY: Crossroad, 1987.

Includes papers by 14 authors. Focuses on the proper role and vocation of the theologian, the limits of theological dissent, and academic freedom.

365. McBrien, Richard P. "Academic Freedom in Catholic Universities: The Emergence of a Party Line." *America*, 159, 3 December 1988, pp. 454-58.

Calls for balance in institutional autonomy, faculty academic freedom, and the requirements of Catholic faith.

366. McCrabb, Don. "Empowering the Spirit: Campus Ministry at Catholic Colleges and Universities." *New Catholic World* 231 (September 1988): 226-29.

Considers the work of campus ministry as a faith community, integrating faith and daily life, forming a Christian conscience, and educating for justice.

367. McFadden, William C., ed. *Georgetown at Two Hundred: Faculty Reflections on the University's Future*. Washington, DC: Georgetown University Press, 1990.

Details Georgetown's first century and its particular American adaptations.

368. McManus, Frederick R. "Academic Freedom and the Catholic University of America." *America*, 160, 27 May 1989, pp. 506-09.

Reviews major concerns in the Curran case; written by professor of canon law at Catholic University.

369. Mitrano, Tracy Beth. "The Rise and Fall of Catholic Women's Higher Education in New York State, 1890-1985." Ph.D. dissertation, State University of New York at Binghamton, 1989.

Charts the history of 13 colleges through four phases of development.

370. Morrisey, Francis G. "What Makes an Institution 'Catholic'?" *The Jurist* 47 (1987): 531-44.

Analyzes identity issue relative to the 1983 Code of Canon Law.

371. Murphy, J. Patrick, ed. *Visions and Values in Catholic Higher Education*. Kansas City, MO: Sheed & Ward, 1991.

Summarizes core values of five American Catholic colleges and universities, documents differences, and presents a model of value sharing.

372. Murray, Jean. "The Small Catholic College Today." *New Catholic World* 231 (September 1988): 206-11.

Presents advantages of small-college education. Covers issues of poverty and multicultural programs.

373. Nuesse, C. Joseph. *The Catholic University of America: A Centennial History.* Washington, DC: Catholic University of America Press, 1990.

Outlines in detail the history and development of the University prior to its 1889 inauguration to 1989.

374. Oats, Mary J., ed. *Higher Education for Catholic Women: An Historical Anthology.* New York: Garland Publishing., 1987.

Reprints 46 articles and other items published from 1890 to 1977 that document differences among and leadership in U.S. Catholic women's colleges.

375. O'Brien, David J. "The Church and Catholic Higher Education." *Horizons* 17 (Spring 1990): 7-29.

Reviews difficulties and dialogues concerning diverse understandings of the nature and purpose of the church and the university in the U.S.

376. O'Brien, David J. *From the Heart of the American Church: Catholic Higher Education and American Culture.* Maryknoll, NY: Orbis Books, 1994.

377. O'Brien, William J., ed. *Jesuit Education and the Cultivation of Virtue*. Washington, DC: Georgetown University Press, 1990.

    Assembles six authors' distinguished lectures based on development of character shaped by the gospel narrative.

378. O'Connell, David M. "An Analysis of Canon 810 of the 1983 Code of Canon Law." J.C.D. dissertation, Catholic University of America, 1990.

    Examines canonical regulations of Catholic universities and institutes of higher education in light of questioning by American Catholic educators. Canon 812 was examined by Sharon Ann Euart in a 1989 Catholic University thesis.

379. O'Hare, Joseph A. "The Vatican and Catholic Universities." *America*, 160, 27 May 1989, pp. 503-05.

    Reports on meeting of the Third International Congress of Catholic Universities, April 18-25, 1987.

380. O'Meara, Timothy. "The Evolution of a Catholic University -- the Next Challenge." *New Catholic World* 231 (September 1988): 201-05.

    Urges Catholic educators to assess progress and goals.

381. Ong, Walter J. "Yeast: A Parable for Catholic Higher Education." *America*, 162, 7 April 1990, pp. 347-49, 362-63.

Asserts Catholic identity can nevertheless be maintained in a pluralistic culture.

382. Orsy, Ladislas. "Bishops and Universities: Dominion or Communion." *America*, 169, 20 November 1993, pp. 11-16.

Argues that episcopal power should be used pastorally, not legally, and that the mandates of *Ex Corde Ecclesiae* are not workable in the U.S.

383. Orsy, Ladislas. *The Church: Learning and Teaching*. Wilmington, DE: Michael Glazier, 1987.

Examines the journey of the whole church, with Chapter 4 covering "Teaching Authority, Catholic Universities, Academic Freedom."

384. Pilarczyk, Daniel. "Academic Freedom: Church and University." *Origins* 18 (June 9, 1988): 57-59.

Outlines points of tension in address by the Archbishop of Cincinnati and chairman of the board of Catholic University of America.

385. Provost, James H. "The Canonical Aspects of Catholic Identity in Light of *Ex Corde Ecclesiae*." *Studia Canonica* 25 (1991): 155-91.

Explores Canons 807-814 of the 1983 Code of Canon Law in relation to the apostolic constitution.

386. *Recruitment and Retention of Minorities: Ten Case Studies from the Neylan Minorities Project*. Washington, DC: Association of Catholic Colleges and Universities, 1991.

Presents results of study by U.S. Catholic institutions of higher education founded by communities of women religious. Also available as ERIC Document ED 338 172.

387. Reher, Margaret Mary. *Catholic Intellectual Life in America: A Historical Study of Persons and Movements.* NY: Macmillan, 1989.

Explores the search for Catholic identity in the intellectual, spiritual, and devotional areas, 1780-1985. Chapter 4 examines "The Catholic University and Americanism, 1880-1900."

388. Reilly, Robert T. "Have Catholic Colleges Kept the Faith?" *U.S. Catholic*, 52, October 1987, pp. 34-40.

Surveys opinions of educational leaders on changing values and Catholic institutional character. Affirms that Catholic education unites the scholarly and the spiritual.

389. Salvaterra, Mary E. "Catholic Identity at Risk: Case Study of Two Colleges." Ph.D. dissertation, Syracuse University, 1990. See also presented paper in ERIC Document ED 330 259.

Demonstrates gradual changes in goals, governance, and mission.

390. Sasseen, Robert F. "Liberal Education and the Study of Politics in a Catholic University." *Perspectives on Political Science* 19 (Summer 1990): 146-52.

Calls on Catholic institutions to restore availability of a liberal education in the United States.

391. Sasseen, Robert F. and William F. Sasseen. "Controversial Student Organizations." *Crisis* 11 (October 1993): 38-41.

Argues against recognizing and legitimizing controversial groups that oppose institutional mission and Church teaching.

392. Scanlan, Michael. "Keeping Colleges Catholic." *Crisis* 11 (October 1993): 33-37.

Describes author's efforts, as president of Franciscan University (Steubenville, OH), to renew spirituality and develop his institution.

393. Schneider, Mary Lea. "The Social Ecology of the American Catholic College." *Horizons* 18 (Spring 1991): 63-73.

Addresses identity, character, and values of Catholic higher education in historical and social contexts.

394. Schubert, Frank D. *A Sociological Study of Secularization Trends in the American Catholic University; Decatholicizing the Catholic Religious Curriculum.* Lewiston, NY: The Edwin Mellen Press, 1990.

Analyzes the secularization of Catholic religious curricula at three universities from 1955 to 1985. Originally a 1987 Boston University thesis.

395. Sorin, Edward. *Chronicles of Notre Dame du Lac.* Edited and Annotated by James T. Connelly. Notre Dame, IN: University of Notre Dame Press, 1992.

Records personal account of the establishment of University of Notre Dame, Indiana, in 1842 by its founder who also guided sisters at nearby St. Mary's Academy (later College). For the latter story see *Priceless Spirit: A History of the Sisters of the Holy Cross, 1841-1893* (Notre Dame: University of Notre Dame Press, 1994).

396. Stritch, Thomas. *My Notre Dame: Memories and Reflections of Sixty Years.* Notre Dame, IN: University of Notre Dame Press, 1991.

Covers the history and growth of Notre Dame in a biographical account by the former head of its journalism department.

397. Sweeny, Stephen J. "State Financial Assistance and Selected Elements Influencing Religious Character in Catholic Colleges Sponsored by Women Religious." Ph.D. dissertation, New York University, 1991.

Examines similarities and differences between 1965 and 1986 among 104 four-year Catholic colleges sponsored by women religious. See also Sweeny's 1989 paper in ERIC Document ED 313 975.

398. Vigilanti, John Anthony. *Academic Freedom and the Adult Student in Catholic Higher Education.* Malabar, FL: Krieger Publishing Company, 1992.

Examines the idea of academic freedom from the point of view of the student's right to know and to learn. Based on 1991 thesis from Fordham University.

399. Whitehead, Kenneth D. *Catholic Colleges and Federal Funding.* San Francisco: Ignatius Press, 1988.

Refutes the claim that Catholic colleges were forced to secularize for public funds.

400. Witham, Larry. *Curran vs. Catholic University: A Study of Authority and Freedom in Conflict.* Riverdale, MD: Edington-Rand, 1991.

Reports in detail on Charles Curran's dispute with Catholic University.

401. Woodward, Kenneth L. "Catholic Higher Education: What Happened?" *Commonweal*, 120, 9 April 1993, pp. 13-16, 18.

Believes quality education in U.S. Catholic colleges has declined in a failure to stress love of learning.

402. Zagano, Phyllis. "Sectarian Universities, Federal Funding, and the Question of Academic Freedom." *Religious Education* 85 (Winter 1990): 136-48.

Considers sectarianism and academic freedom, canon law and juridic control, and American implications.

403. Zingg, Paul J. "Mission Fulfilled and Forfeited: American Catholic Higher Education and the Challenges of Diversity." *Educational Record* 72 (Summer 1991): 39-44.

Presents two hypothetical Catholic colleges illustrating racial diversity.

CHAPTER 16
Baptist Colleges and Universities

Jerry M. Self

Alderson-Broaddus College

Two institutions were united in 1932 to form Alderson-Broaddus College. The older of the two, Broaddus College, was founded in Winchester, Virginia, in 1871 by Edward Jefferson Willis who greatly admired the Reverend William Francis Ferguson Broaddus. The other institution, Alderson Junior College, was founded at Alderson, West Virginia, in 1901 by Emma Alderson as Alderson Academy. The financially depressed 1920s and 1930s brought the decision that the two colleges, both American Baptist supported, should be merged. Today Alderson-Broaddus is the only institution of higher education in West Virginia related to the American Baptist Churches, USA.[1]

Anderson College

Anderson College traces its origin to the Johnson Female Seminary opened in the village of Anderson in 1848. The founder was the Reverend William B. Johnson, a Baptist minister and the first president of the Southern Baptist Convention. The school was forced to close during the Civil War and did not reopen, but in time a new generation carried on what had been begun at that institution. A group of public-spirited citizens in Anderson offered 32 acres of land and $100,000 to the South Carolina Baptist Convention at its meeting in 1910. In 1912, Anderson College opened its doors and operated as a four-year college for women until 1929. In response to the harsh economic realities of the Great Depression, Anderson College trustees in 1929 restructured the school as a junior college. In 1989, trustees voted to return the college to its roots as a four-year institution.

Averett College

Most scholars trace the beginning of Averett to 1854 when young ladies began to gather for classes in William I. Berryman's Danville, Virginia, home. The school was known as the Baptist Female Institute until 1856 when, under the direction of Nathan Pennick, its name was changed to Baptist Female Seminary. Pennick successfully gathered support from the Dan River, Roanoke, and Concord Baptist Associations to form a college. The name of the college was changed again in 1859 to Union Female College. That same year, Mr. and Mrs. Joseph Averett came to teach at the Danville school. The property on which the college now stands was purchased in 1908. In 1917 the name of the college was officially changed to Averett College to honor two of its early principals and teachers.

Bacone College

For over 100 years, Bacone College has provided a Christian education for American Indian youth. Founded on February 9, 1880, in a one-room schoolhouse at Cherokee Baptist Mission in Tahlequah, Indian Territory, and known initially as Indian University, Bacone is Oklahoma's oldest continuing center of higher education. The Creek (Muscogee) Tribal Council donated 160 acres of land in Muskogee for a permanent site, and in 1885, the college moved to its present location. In 1910 it was renamed Bacone College after the founder and president. Today a large percentage of the full-time students is American Indian representing over 40 tribes. The college is governed by a 30-member board of trustees, ten of which are American Baptist, ten of which are Indian, and ten of which are undesignated positions.

Baylor University

Baylor University was established in 1845 by an act of the Texas Republic. In 1885, the unification of Texas Baptists' general conventions led to the merging of Waco and Baylor universities. The University's academic system is now comprised of the College of Arts and Sciences, the Graduate School, the Hankamer School of Business, the Schools of Education, Law, Nursing, and Music, and the affiliated graduate programs offered through the U.S. Army Academy of Health Sciences in San Antonio and the Baylor College of Dentistry in Dallas. The Baylor University Medical Center in Dallas is the headquarters for the Baylor Health Care System which operates seven satellite hospitals across Texas.

Belmont University

Belmont University has its origins in the 19th century when the grounds were known as Belle Monte estate. In 1890, two ladies from Philadelphia, Susan Heron and Ida Hood, purchased the mansion and opened Belmont College for Women. In 1913, Belmont College merged with a rival Nashville women's school, Ward Seminary, and became Ward-Belmont School. Because of a decreased demand for an exclusive girls' school and financial difficulty, Ward-Belmont was sold in 1951 to the Tennessee Baptist Convention Executive Board and again became known as Belmont College, a coed junior college. A junior year was added in 1953 and a senior year added in 1954.

Bethel College

Bethel College began as a junior college as an outgrowth of the success of Bethel Theological Seminary and Bethel Academy. These schools were founded to serve Swedish immigrants in the Chicago area. A junior college was developed in 1931 and in 1947 Bethel College expanded its academic program to become a four-year liberal arts institution. In 1961 land was purchased and a new campus was built in the present Arden Hills location. Bethel is owned and operated by the Baptist General Conference.[2]

Bluefield College

In 1919, the Baptist General Association of Virginia appointed a committee to study the need for a junior college in southwestern Virginia. Citizens from Bluefield and vicinity generously offered $75,000 and 65 acres of land if the Association would locate the proposed college in the Bluefield area. At the meeting of the Baptist General Association in Lynchburg in November the Bluefield offer was accepted. In 1972, the Board of Trustees decided Bluefield College should become a four-year college.

Blue Mountain College

Blue Mountain College was founded in 1873 by Mark Perrin Lowrey, a village preacher and Civil War veteran. Lowrey purchased an antebellum country home in Tippah County, Mississippi, and in 1873 opened Blue Mountain Female Institute. Between 1873 and 1960 three generations of the Lowrey family, including General Lowrey, two sons (Dr. W.T. Lowrey and Dr. B.G. Lowrey) and one grandson (Dr. Lawrence T. Lowrey), presided over the college. In 1877, the name of the school was changed to Blue Mountain Female College. Later the word *Female* was dropped and Blue Mountain College became the official name. Blue Mountain College was independently owned and administered until 1920 when control was turned over to the Mississippi Baptist Convention. The school began offering a coordinate academic program for men preparing for church-related vocations in 1956 at the request of the Convention.

Brewton-Parker College

Brewton-Parker College was founded in 1904 as Union Baptist Institute by Rev. J.C. Brewton, a pastor, and C.B. Parker, a local businessman. In 1912, Dr. Brewton asked the trustees to change the name to Parker Institute to honor the generosity of Mr. Parker. Instead, the trustees deemed it fitting and proper to change the name to Brewton-Parker Institute to honor both men who had contributed toward its establishment. In 1927 the school was renamed Brewton-Parker Junior College. In 1978, one year short of its 75th anniversary, the current name, Brewton-Parker College, was officially adopted.

California Baptist College

In 1950, the Los Angeles Baptist Association opened the doors of California Baptist College, located at First Southern Baptist Church, El Monte. In 1955, after four years of growth and a search throughout California for another location, the college relocated to Riverside in several Spanish-styled buildings.

Campbell University

Campbell University, located in Buies Creek, North Carolina, was founded as Buies Creek Academy in 1887 by James Archibald Campbell, a Baptist minister, to provide Christian education without regard to financial status. In 1925, Campbell deeded the property to the Baptist State Convention of North Carolina. A year later, Buies Creek Academy was elevated to junior-college status and the name was changed to Campbell College in honor of the founder. University status was achieved in 1979.

Campbellsville College

Because of the efforts of the Russell Creek Association of Baptists in Kentucky, the Russell Creek Academy was founded in 1906. Through continual growth, the Academy attained junior college status by 1923. The following year, the Academy became Campbellsville College. In 1960, Campbellsville College became a four-year school.

Carson-Newman College

Chartered by the state of Tennessee in 1851, the Mossy Creek Academy was born. Facing great debt in the wake of the Civil War, the college was placed on the auction block and sold to the only bidder for a down payment of $50 and a promise to pay

$950 within a year. The college was rescued in 1869 by a former college president who raised $5,250 in cash and pledges. The name was changed to Carson College, in honor of a benefactor. Newman College for girls was established in 1882. The two colleges merged in 1889 to become a co-educational institution, Carson-Newman College. On April 19, 1919, the college entered into a cooperative agreement with the Educational Board of the Tennessee Baptist Convention, establishing denominational affiliation and financial support of the college.

Charleston Southern University

In 1960 Baptist College at Charleston was chartered. But not until 1965 was land purchased outside the city limits of Charleston. The first semester of classes was held in the education building of the First Baptist Church of North Charleston. In November of 1990 the South Carolina Baptist Convention in Columbia officially voted to have the name changed to Charleston Southern University.

Chowan College

Chowan College, known as Chowan Baptist Female Institute until 1910, was founded in 1848 by Baptists of northeastern North Carolina and southeastern Virginia. Chowan, the second oldest of North Carolina's seven Baptist colleges, began enrolling men in 1931 and continued to operate as a four-year institution until 1937 when it became a two-year residential college. A shortage of students occasioned by World War II forced Chowan College to close its doors in 1943. The school reopened in 1949 as a private, two-year co-educational college owned and supported by the Baptist State Convention of North Carolina. Then, in 1990, the Board of Trustees voted for Chowan to return to four-year college status in August 1992.

Clear Creek Baptist Bible College

Clear Creek Mountain Preacher's Bible School was founded in 1926 in Kentucky by Dr. L.C. Kelly, pastor of the Pineville First Baptist Church, to bring Christian education to the mountains. In 1986 the name was changed to Clear Creek Baptist Bible College.

Cumberland College

A few short decades after the Civil War, in the mountains of Eastern Kentucky, the annual meeting of the Mount Zion Association resolved to pursue the founding of Williamsburg Institute. In 1889 the college opened its doors. In 1913, with the acquisition of Highland College, Williamsburg Institute's name was changed to Cumberland College. The General Association of Baptists of Kentucky voted in 1959 to allow Cumberland College to resume four-year status, having previously awarded the bachelor's degree until 1913.

Dallas Baptist University

Dallas Baptist University is affiliated with the Baptist General Convention of Texas. The forerunner of Dallas Baptist University was Decatur Baptist College, founded in the 1890s as the first two-year junior college in Texas. The institution became Dallas Baptist College when it was relocated to a 200-acre campus in southwest Dallas in 1965 at the invitation of the Dallas Baptist Association, representing local churches. The institution achieved university status in 1985.[3]

East Texas Baptist University

In 1911 the Rev. W.T. Tardy felt led to establish an educational institution under Baptist auspices. During September of 1913, the Education Board of the Baptist General Convention of Texas agreed to build and maintain a junior college in Marshall with the understanding that the College of Marshall provide a campus of 50 acres and $30,000 for the first building. In 1944 the name was changed from the College of Marshall to East Texas Baptist College. In November 1882, by a vote of the Baptist General Convention of Texas, East Texas Baptist College became East Texas Baptist University.

Florida Baptist Theological College

Florida Baptist Theological College was born from one man's desperate search for a training program that would help equip him for the ministry. Rev. Frank Faris, who served as pastor of the First Baptist Church in Dover, Florida, learned that others recognized a need for pastor training. From this desire emerged Florida Baptist Institute at Lakeland, Florida, which began classes in 1943. The college was relocated to its current site in Graceville, Florida, in 1953. The Florida Baptist State Convention assumed ownership and control in 1957. The college was known as Baptist Bible Institute from 1948 until 1988, at which time the name changed to Florida Baptist Theological College.

Florida Memorial College

In 1892, a group of Baptists sought and obtained financial assistance from the American Baptist Home Mission Society to establish the Florida Baptist Academy in Jacksonville. In 1918 the Florida Baptist Academy moved to St. Augustine, Florida. There, the institution became a junior college. Its name was changed to Florida Normal and Industrial Institute. In 1941, the Florida

Baptist Institute of Live Oak merged with its sister institution, Florida Normal and Industrial Institute, and immediately a four-year college curriculum was instituted and the school's name was changed to Florida Normal and Industrial College. In 1963, the College became Florida Memorial College. Finally, in 1968, the College moved to Miami, due to heightened racial tensions in St. Augustine, Florida.

Franklin College

Franklin College was founded in 1834 in Franklin, Indiana, by the Baptist Education Society. In 1844, the institution formally adopted the name Franklin College. Franklin maintains a voluntary affiliation with the American Baptist Churches/USA. Franklin endured some bumpy times during the Civil War. From 1864 to 1869, the college was forced to close its doors while its students went off to fight. Following the war, the college reopened and many of those who had fought returned to complete their education.[4]

Furman University

Furman University is named for Richard Furman of Charleston, South Carolina, a prominent pastor and president of the first Baptist Convention in America. Founded as the Furman Academy and Theological Institution at Edgefield, South Carolina, in 1825, the school was chartered as a full-fledged university in 1850 and moved to Greenville. Its theological school branched off in 1858 as the Southern Baptist Theological Seminary and moved to Louisville, Kentucky. In 1933 Furman was coordinated with the Greenville Woman's College, which had been founded by the South Carolina Baptist Convention in 1854. Operations continued on separate campuses until 1961, when the women students joined the men on a new campus five miles north of Greenville. In 1992, formal ties with the South

Carolina Baptist Convention were severed and the college became fully independent.

Gardner-Webb University

Boiling Springs High School, chartered in 1905, was transformed to Boiling Springs Junior College of North Carolina in 1928. In 1942, Governor O. Max Gardner began devoting his energy, time, and wealth to strengthen the College. The name of the institution was soon changed to Gardner-Webb College in honor of the governor, his wife, and their families. In January of 1993, the institution officially became Gardner-Webb University. That same year also marked the birth of the School of Divinity and the Masters of Business Administration programs. Gardner-Webb is affiliated with the Baptist State Convention of North Carolina.[5]

Georgetown College

When Elijah Craig arrived in Kentucky, one of his goals was to open a classical school for the instruction of young men. In 1788, Craig founded his academy in a small settlement that would later be named Georgetown. It was with this vision that Georgetown College was chartered in 1829 as a liberal arts college affiliated with the Kentucky Baptist Convention. It was the sixth Baptist college to be organized in the nation and the first located west of the Allegheny Mountains. The Georgetown Female Seminary merged with Georgetown College in 1892.

Grand Canyon University

In the late 1920s, two or three students and faculty of a failed small New Mexico Baptist college, Montezuma, cached away a dream of one day helping to build another school for the glory of God. That dream resurfaced in the mid-1940s in a business meeting of Arizona Southern Baptists. Pastor L.D. White of Calvary Baptist Church, Casa Grande, inspired the collecting of funds for a school. One of the Montezuma alumni became the first chairman of the board of trustees. Another became Grand Canyon University's first professor. The doors to the school were opened in 1949 in an abandoned armory building in Prescott, Arizona. Two years later Grand Canyon University opened its doors on its present campus in Phoenix.[6]

Hannibal-LaGrange College

Hannibal-LaGrange College continues the work and ideals of LaGrange College, for seventy years located at LaGrange, Missouri. LaGrange College was founded in 1858 by the Wyaconda Baptist Association, Missouri. For 61 years the college was maintained by this association; but in 1919, its charter was amended to enlist a large number of additional associations and churches in its support. Further provisions made in the charter of 1928 required that trustees be approved by the Missouri Baptist General Association. In 1928, the citizens of Hannibal pledged $232,000 for the establishment of a Baptist college at Hannibal. The merged school took the name Hannibal-LaGrange College. In 1957, Hannibal-LaGrange College received a new charter that conveyed the ownership and control of the college to the Missouri Baptist Convention.

Hardin-Simmons University

Hardin-Simmons University, located in Abilene, Texas, was founded in 1891 as Abilene Baptist College, renamed Simmons College in honor of the first major donor, Dr. James B. Simmons, a Baptist minister of New York City, and later named Hardin-Simmons University in recognition of gifts by Mr. and Mrs. John G. Hardin of Burkburnett, Texas. Originally founded by the Sweetwater Baptist Association, the University has been affiliated with the Baptist General Convention of Texas since 1941.

Houston Baptist University

In the 1950s, the Union Baptist Association, along with the Education Commission of the Baptist General Convention of Texas, approved the idea of establishing a college. In 1958, a campus site was acquired in southwest Houston, and, in 1960, the college charter was ratified. The College opened in September, 1963 and attained the four-year program in 1966-67. The College name officially became Houston Baptist University and the University adopted a quarter calendar that permitted multiple admission opportunities annually.

Howard Payne University

Howard Payne University, located in Brownwood, Texas, is owned and operated by the Baptist General Convention of Texas. Howard Payne College was founded by Dr. John David Robnett in 1889. The first session opened on September 16, 1890. In 1974, Howard Payne College became Howard Payne University upon approval of the Baptist General Convention of Texas.

Judson College (Elgin, Illinois)

Judson College is a four-year, American Baptist-affiliated college in Elgin, Illinois. Judson's roots extend back to the 1920s when the college division of Northern Baptist Theological Seminary was formed. In the early 1960s, the seminary moved from Chicago to Lombard, and it became necessary to move the college to a separate location. The college was named after Adoniram Judson, the first American missionary to foreign shores.[7]

Judson College (Marion, Alabama)

Judson College is a Christian, liberal arts college for women affiliated with the Alabama Baptist State Convention and located in Marion, Alabama. The college was founded in 1838 by Milo P. Jewett, later first president of Vassar College in New York, and member of historic Siloam Baptist Church where the Home Mission Board of the Southern Baptist Convention was formed. The College is named after Ann Hasseltine Judson, America's first female foreign missionary.

Kalamazoo College

Founded in 1833 as The Michigan and Huron Institute, Kalamazoo College was established by visionary Baptists. Although the College operates as an independent institution, it acknowledges its historic indebtedness to its Baptist founders and the American Baptist Church.[8]

Keuka College

Keuka College was founded in 1890 by the Freewill Baptist Churches of New York. Initially coeducational, a dramatic change occurred in 1920 when, with the cooperation of the Northern Baptist Convention, Keuka became a college for women. Dr. Katherine Gillette Blyley, Keuka College's first female president, initiated a distinctive education program for women committed to social responsibility.[9]

Linfield College

One of the oldest colleges in the Pacific Northwest, Linfield College was established in 1849. Linfield traces its roots to Oregon City, where it was founded as the Oregon City College in what was then the capital of the Oregon Territory. It later merged with a college in McMinnville and was chartered in 1858 by the Oregon Territorial Legislature as McMinnville College. In honor of Frances Ross Linfield's generosity, trustees renamed the college for her late husband, the Rev. George Fisher Linfield. The college maintains its American Baptist tradition, although faculty, students and staff are bound by no religious requirements.[10]

Louisiana College

Louisiana College, founded in Pineville, Louisiana, on October 3, 1906, is the successor of two earlier Louisiana Baptist schools. Mt. Lebanon University was founded in 1852 by the North Louisiana Baptist Convention as a college for men. Keatchie College was founded in 1857 by the Grand Cane Association of Baptist Churches. After a history beset by financial difficulties, both schools came under the control of the State Baptist Convention in 1899. An understanding noted both would be succeeded by a more centrally located college as soon as a suitable campus could be selected. When Louisiana College opened in 1906, Mt. Lebanon was closed, followed by Keatchie a few years later.

Mars Hill College

Mars Hill is the oldest educational institution in western North Carolina. It was founded in 1856 by descendants of the original settlers who opened the French Broad Baptist Academy. In 1859 the school became Mars Hill College. It remained in operation during the first two years of the Civil War but was closed from 1863 until 1865. During its early history the college operated as an academy, offering only a few college-level courses. In 1921 it was reorganized as a junior college. In 1960 the state Baptist convention approved plans for converting Mars Hill into a senior college.

University of Mary Hardin-Baylor

The Female Department of Baylor University was moved to Independence in 1866 and controlled by a separate board of trustees under the name of Baylor Female College. This made the institution the first women's college established west of the Mississippi River. As the population shifted inland in Texas, it was decided that the college must move as well. In 1886, the college moved to Belton, Texas. The college's name was subsequently changed to Baylor College for Women and then to Mary Hardin-Baylor College to honor the wife of the couple who became its first major benefactors. In 1968, the University of Mary Hardin-Baylor granted its first degree to a male student and became fully coeducational in 1971. It achieved university status in 1978.

Mercer University

Mercer University traces its origins to Mercer Institute, which opened on January 14, 1833, in Penfield, Georgia, as a manual labor school for boys. The University is named for Jesse Mercer, an eminent Georgian, a distinguished Baptist clergyman, and a principal organizer of the Georgia Baptist Convention. Mercer was incorporated in 1838 and its name was changed to Mercer University. Thirty-three years later, in 1871, the institution relocated to Macon, adding a law school in 1873. Today, Mercer is the second-largest Baptist university in the world.

Meredith College

The idea of Meredith College can be traced to 1835 when it became an unexpected item of business at the North Carolina Baptist Convention. Thomas Meredith was a committeeman appointed to study the feasibility of educating women, and his persistence linked years of progress and defeats to the school's reality. Long before its charter in 1891 as Baptist Female University, Meredith had a mission to provide the same high-quality liberal arts studies for women as those available to men. Since classes began in 1899, Meredith has offered women that education. Today Meredith is the largest private four-year college for women in the Southeast.

Mississippi College

Mississippi College, chartered by the state legislature in 1826, is the oldest institution of higher learning in Mississippi. Originally called Hampstead Academy and later Mississippi Academy, the College was named Mississippi College in 1830. The College came under the control of the Mississippi Baptist Convention in 1850. The school was the first coeducational college in the United States to grant degrees to women. The Female Department was discontinued in 1850 and in 1853 a Central Female Institute, later renamed Hillman College, was established in Clinton. Mississippi College purchased and absorbed Hillman College in 1942, and the institution has been coeducational ever since.[11]

Missouri Baptist College

Missouri Baptist College was founded during the mid-1950s, through the desire for an evangelical Christian institution in the St. Louis area. The institution began first as a seminary extension program, followed by its establishment as a Hannibal-LaGrange College extension center offering liberal arts courses. In 1964 Missouri Baptist College was chartered as a four-year liberal arts college. Classes met at Tower Grove Baptist Church until a campus could be constructed. Four years later, the Convention approved the consolidation of Missouri Baptist College with Hannibal-LaGrange College. In 1973, Missouri Baptist College was re-established as a separate institution and began granting its first baccalaureate degrees.

University of Mobile

The story of the University of Mobile began in 1952, when the Mobile Baptist Association appointed a committee to study the feasibility of starting a Baptist-affiliated college in Mobile. In 1959 the Alabama Baptist State Convention agreed to cooperate with the Mobile community in building and operating a college. Alabama Governor John Patterson signed the college's charter in 1961.[12]

North Greenville Junior College

At a meeting of the North Greenville Baptist Association in 1892, John Ballenger of the Tigerville, South Carolina, community urged that the time allotted for missions be used for the discussion of the need for a school. Soon plans were underway to begin North Greenville Baptist Academy. Tigerville was chosen as the location for a new high school because the citizens had offered ten acres of land and a donation of $2500 toward the expenses of the project. In 1934, the trustees voted to set up one year of college work and thus the junior college was launched. Years later the high school was dropped and all effort turned to North Greenville Junior College. Four-year programs were begun in 1992.

Oklahoma Baptist University

Baptists of Oklahoma Territory created two institutions before they pooled their efforts and founded Oklahoma Baptist University. In 1906 the State Baptist Convention appointed a commission to make plans for the founding of a Baptist university. In 1907, a board of trustees was elected, and in 1910 articles of incorporation were granted. The school opened in September of 1911 in the basement of the First Baptist Church and in the Convention Hall of Shawnee. The City of Shawnee contributed the original 60-acre campus and the first building, Shawnee Hall, which opened in 1915. Oklahoma Baptist University is the only higher education institution owned and supported by the Baptist General Convention of Oklahoma.

Ottawa University

Ottawa University arose from the commitment and dedication of many people working together to realize the common purpose of educating individuals for lives of service to humanity. By 1860, a charter had been obtained from the Kansas Legislature in the name of Roger Williams University. The turmoil and distress of the American Civil War, however, deterred founding action until 1865 when a second charter was obtained for the creation of Ottawa University. The name change was principally in recognition of a 20,000-acre grant of land by the Ottawa Indians living in the vicinity. The grant was made by this tribe to ensure the education of their children and other children interested in private Christian education. Additional land was granted in 1867 to further support the institution. The Board of Trustees sold much of the land to generate the income necessary to start the college.

Ouachita Baptist University

John Conger was selected as Ouachita Baptist University's first president, and classes began in September of 1886 with six faculty members and 166 students. In 1889, a growing enrollment and a joint financial effort of Arkansas Baptists and the city of Arkadelphia resulted in the construction of "Old Main," which served as Ouachita's administration building, library and classroom building. The campus grew around "Old Main," the University's focal point, until the building burned in 1949.

Palm Beach Atlantic College

In 1964, the John D. MacArthur Foundation offered to donate a 200-acre site, in Palm Beach Gardens, to the Education Commission of the Florida Baptist Convention. A steering committee was appointed to plan the school. Plans stalled when evangelist Billy Graham announced his intention to build a university in South Florida. In February 1968 he dropped the idea, and the plan was back into action but under the auspices of the Palm Lake Baptist Association instead of the Florida Baptist Convention. In April 1968, trustees approved the name of the new school, Palm Beach Atlantic College. Trustees opted to locate the college downtown, near First Baptist Church, to take advantage of facilities that could be borrowed or rented.[13]

University of Redlands

A peculiar set of circumstances led to the birth of University of Redlands, California: the devastating 1906 San Francisco earthquake that destroyed the hopes for success with educational plans there, the failure of an American Baptist college in Los Angeles, the determination of businessmen in Redlands, and the energetic skill of the Reverend Jasper Newton Field. Dr. Field urged first his parishioners at the First Baptist Church and then the Redlands Board of Trade to convince the American Baptist committee to locate its new university in Redlands. The University admitted its first students in September, 1909.

Samford University

Founded by a group of educational, economic, and religious leaders, Samford University was chartered in 1841 and opened its doors the following year in Marion, Alabama, as Howard College. It has survived two destructive fires and the partial paralysis of the Civil War. In 1887 it was relocated in

Birmingham, and in 1957 the institution was moved to its present campus.

Shaw University

Shaw University was founded in 1865 by Henry Martin Tupper, a native of Monson, Massachusetts, and a graduate of Amherst College and Newton Theological Seminary. The University was chartered by an Act of the North Carolina General Assembly in 1875. Elijah Shaw, a woolen goods manufacturer of Wales, Massachusetts, for whom the University is named, joined with others to contribute funds for the establishment of the school. Although established originally to train religious leaders, the institution has, over the years, initiated other programs to produce graduates in various professions. The University graduated its first college class in 1878. In 1881, the University established the Leonard Medical School, the first four-year medical school in the nation.

Shorter College

Combining the generosity and wealth of Alfred and Martha Shorter with the insight and vision of Luther Rice Gwaltney, Shorter College stands as a memorial to these three co-founders. Originally called the Cherokee Baptist Female College, it was chartered in 1873 by a group of Northwest Georgia Baptists. In 1877, Alfred Shorter, who was already president of the board of trustees, was induced to take a commanding role in the affairs of the institution. The name of the school was changed to honor him and his wife. First called Shorter Female College, in 1923 the name was changed to Shorter College.

Sioux Falls College

Sioux Falls College is a four-year, Christian liberal arts college located in Sioux Falls, South Dakota, and affiliated with the American Baptist Churches, USA. Founded in 1883, Sioux Falls College is the second largest and oldest private college in South Dakota.[14]

Southwest Baptist University

First established in Lebanon, Missouri, Southwest Baptist College was moved to Bolivar after one year because of the greater support and interest exhibited by local citizens. Early leaders of the college were constantly faced with hardships and near failures, but managed to keep the doors open until 1908 when it finally surrendered to creditors. In 1913 the institution was reopened as a junior college. In 1964, the Missouri Baptist Convention endorsed trustee plans for Southwest to become a senior liberal arts college once again. Bolivar area citizens reaffirmed their support by purchasing and donating a farm of approximately 100 acres. In 1980 approval was given for the name change to Southwest Baptist University.

Stetson University

Stetson University, Florida's oldest private university, was founded as DeLand Academy in 1883 by Henry A. DeLand, a New York philanthropist. In 1887, the State of Florida chartered DeLand University. The university name was changed in 1889 to honor John B. Stetson, the nationally known hat manufacturer who gave generously of his time and means to advance the institution, and who served, with Mr. DeLand and others, as a founding trustee of the university. Stetson University has been affiliated since 1887 with the churches of the Florida Baptist Convention.

Truett-McConnell College

The history of Truett-McConnell College goes back to 1887 when George W. Truett and his cousin, Fernando C. McConnell, established a private Christian academy at Hiawassee. Changing conditions led to the closing of that school, but the dream did not die in the hearts of area people. Georgia Baptists were led to establish Truett-McConnell to carry on the same high tradition inaugurated by those early Baptist leaders. On July 23, 1946, ceremonies in Cleveland heralded the establishment of the new college. Truett-McConnell, operating in temporary quarters, opened her doors to the first students in September 1947.

Union University

Two colleges were to be established, one each in East and West Tennessee, by a provision of the North Carolina Compact, which ceded Tennessee to the U.S. government. As a result, West Tennessee College was chartered by legislative enactment in 1844. West Tennessee College continued as such until 1874, when it was offered to and accepted by Tennessee Baptists. It was chartered as Southwestern Baptist University in 1875, and the name was changed to Union University in 1907. In 1925 the Board of Trustees deeded all of Union University's property to the Tennessee Baptist Convention. In 1975 Union moved to a new campus on 190 acres in the northwest section of Jackson. The unique campus design features a 225,000-square-foot "shopping mall" complex with most academic and student services under a single multi-level roof.

Virginia Intermont College

Virginia Intermont College began as the result of efforts by the Rev. J.R. Harrison, who for many years cherished the hope of establishing a school for the higher education of women. The hope became a reality with the opening of Southwest Virginia Institute in Glade Spring, Virginia, in 1884. In 1891, the college began its move to Bristol. Shortly after, the college's name was changed to Virginia Institute. In 1910 the college was the first two-year institution to be accredited by the Southern Association of Colleges and Schools. The name was changed in 1922 to Virginia Intermont College, "Intermont" being suggested by its location in the beautiful Appalachian Mountains of Southwest Virginia. In May of 1968, plans were approved for the development of a four-year institution. The first baccalaureate degrees were awarded in 1972, the same year that men were admitted to full status.[15]

Virginia Union University

Virginia Union University was founded to provide quality Education for young Black men and women in 1865. The name Virginia Union resulted from the merger in 1899 of two institutions (Wayland Seminary and Richmond Theological Seminary) which had been established by the American Baptist Home Mission Society. Later, Hartshorn Memorial College of Richmond and Storer College of Harper's Ferry, West Virginia, merged with Virginia Union as it became an even stronger "union" of educational institutions.

Wake Forest University

The beginnings of Wake Forest University and the formation of the Baptist State Convention of North Carolina were closely interwoven: a leading motive for the organization of the Convention was that it serve as an agency for establishing an institution that would provide education under Christian influences. Land near Raleigh was purchased and the North Carolina Legislature granted a charter in 1832. For three years of the Civil War, the College suspended operations. The buildings were used briefly for a girls' school; after 1863 the Confederate government used its facilities as a military hospital. During the bleak days of financial uncertainty following the Civil War, a Wake Forest student, James W. Denmark, proposed and founded the first college student loan fund in the United States. The Z. Smith Reynolds Foundation donated a significant fund to the school provided that the entire College be relocated to Winston-Salem and that other friends of the College provide a campus site and buildings. In 1946 the proposal was accepted.

Wayland Baptist University

Wayland Baptist University began in 1906 with a proposal to the Staked Plains Baptist Association to establish a college whose mission was to provide Christian education for the children of the region. In 1908 Dr. and Mrs. James Henry Wayland, a local physician and his wife, offered $10,000 and 25 acres of land toward the construction of a college, providing that the members of the association and the citizens of Plainview raise an additional $40,000. The association accepted both the gift and the challenge, and Wayland Literary and Technical Institute was chartered by the State of Texas in 1908. In 1910, the school's name was changed to Wayland Baptist College. In 1914, Wayland became affiliated with the Baptist General Convention of Texas. In 1981 the name of the institution was changed to Wayland Baptist University.

William Carey College

William Carey College was founded in 1906 as South Mississippi College, a private coeducational institution. The name became Mississippi Woman's College in 1911. In 1953 the Mississippi Baptist Convention voted to return the school to coeducational status, and in 1954 the name was changed to honor William Carey, the eighteenth-century British cobbler-linguist whose missionary work in India earned him the international recognition as the "Father of Modern Missions." In

1968 William Carey College entered a new dimension when it announced its merger with the prestigious Mather School of Nursing in New Orleans, Louisiana. Still another dimension opened for the college in 1976 when it opened its Gulfport, Mississippi, campus.

William Jewell College

William Jewell College has long been recognized as the "Campus of Achievement." Founded by the Baptists of Missouri in 1849 and named in honor of Dr. William Jewell, frontier statesman, physician, and benefactor, William Jewell was the first four-year men's college west of the Mississippi. In 1921 it became co-educational.

Williams Baptist College

In 1941, H.E. Williams, the pastor of First Baptist Church in Pocahontas, Arkansas, led in the establishment of Williams Baptist College. In 1947, the College was moved to the Marine Corps Air Base, near Walnut Ridge, Arkansas. In 1968, the Arkansas Baptist State Convention officially adopted Williams Baptist College into its family of institutions. The college is now owned and operated by the convention. The name of the school was changed in 1991 from Southern Baptist College to Williams Baptist College, in honor of the institution's founder and president emeritus.

Wingate College

Wingate College was established in 1895 by Baptist families in the Union County, North Carolina, and Lancaster, South Carolina, areas who wanted their children to receive an educational opportunity that included moral training. Wingate College was named in honor of Washington Manley Wingate, a well-known Baptist preacher and president of Wake Forest from 1856 to 1879. The Wingate campus was established in the small community of Ames Turnout, which was later renamed Wingate, North Carolina. Wingate College became a senior college in 1978.

Yellowstone Baptist College

Yellowstone Baptist College was begun in 1974 as a Bible institute with the purpose of providing a center for advanced Bible study and Christian education in the Northwest. In 1980 the board of directors added a junior college to the Institute. At the same time generous gifts made possible the purchase of a campus located on ten acres west of Billings, Montana. The Board voted to establish Yellowstone Baptist College as a senior Bible college with a four-year academic program in 1984.

Endnotes

1.   Unless otherwise indicated the material is excerpted from the school catalog as provided by the Public Relations office.

2.   Heidi Benson, Letter, 18 February 1994.

3.   Darrell W. Wood, Letter, 8 December 1993.

4.   Michael J. Aldrich, Letter, 17 November 1993.

5.   Matt Webber, Letter, 12 November 1993.

6.   Carl G. Paetz, Jr., Letter, 22 February 1994.

7.   James A. Tew, Letter, 6 January 1994.

8.   Dana Holton Hendrix, Letter, 18 March 1994.

9.   Amy Reed, Letter, n.d.

10.   Lee Howard, Letter, 22 November 1993.

11.   Norman H. Gough, Letter, 16 December 1993.

12.   Kathy Dean, Letter, 5 January 1994.

13.   Don Harp, Letter, 3 December 1993.

14.   Jaciel Keltgen-Pierson, Letter, 11 November 1993.

15.   Judy Bracher, Letter, 11 January 1994.

Bibliographic Entries

404. Armbrister, David M. *A History of Bluefield College.* Bluefield, VA: Bluefield College, n.d.

405. Arrington, Michael. *Ouachita Baptist University: The First 100 Years.* Little Rock: August House, 1985.

406. Arrington, Michael, and William D. Downs, Jr. *Once in a Hundred Years.* Arkadelphia: Ouachita Baptist University, 1986.

   Recounts pictorially the history of Ouachita Baptist University.

407. Baker, Eugene W. *To Light the Ways of Time, An Illustrated History of Baylor University, 1845-1986.* Waco, TX: Baylor University Press, 1987.

   Contains more than 500 pictures, illustrations, and documents related to the history of Baylor University. In addition to the narrative, there are vignettes of the University's namesake and the major presidents.

408. Bowman, Georgia. *The Distaff Side: Women at William Jewell.* Liberty, MO: William Jewell College, 1984.

409. Boyd, James Hubert. "History of The College of Marshall." Ph.D. dissertation. Baylor University, 1944.

410. Browne, B.P. *Comrades in an Adventure of Faith: A Somewhat Personal History of the Beginnings of Judson College.* Unpublished work.

   Refers personally to Alabama's Judson College.

411. Butler, William and William Strode, eds. *Stetson University*. Louisville: Harmony House, 1992.

Takes readers on a photographic visit.

412. Capp, Glenn R. *Excellence in Forensics: A Tradition at Baylor University*. Waco, TX: Baylor University, 1986.

413. Davison, Floyd Francis. *One Hundred Forty Years of Biology at Baylor University*. Waco, TX: Baylor University, 1991.

Contains information about the faculty and curriculum of the Department of Biology during its first 140 years of operation in Independence and Waco.

414. Fields, Carl R. and Robin Oldham. *A Sesquicentennial History of Georgetown College*. Georgetown, KY: Georgetown College Press, 1979.

415. Foster, Luther A. "A History of Missouri Baptist College, The College That Had To Be." Unpublished and undated.

Recounts Foster's tenure as president, his relationship with pastors and trustees, and the growth of the institution after his retirement.

416. Baghart, Herbert C. *Work: the Soul of Good Fortune: Memoirs of a Love Affair with Belmont College*. Nashville, TN: Broadman, 1989.

417. Gaskin, J.M., Helen Thames Raley, Eunice E. Short, and Slayden A. Yarbrough. *The View from Bison Hill: 75 Years of Remembrances*. Oklahoma City: Jostens, 1985.

Recounts Oklahoma Baptist University history.

418. Gaskin, J.M., ed. *The Oklahoma Baptist Chronicle*. Vol. 28, No. 1. Oklahoma City: Messenger Press, 1985.

 Honors Oklahoma Baptist University's 7th anniversary.

419. Griffin, Z.F. *The Builders of Keuka College*. Penn Yan, NY: The Penn Yan Press, 1937.

420. Hamilton, Frances Dew and Elizabeth Crabtree Wells. *Daughters of the Dream*. Marion, AL: Judson College, 1989.

 Tells the story of Alabama's Judson College.

421. Hayes, J.I. *A History of Averett College*. Danville, VA: Averett College Press, 1984.

422. Hester, Hubert Inman. *The Wingate College Story*. Liberty, MO: The Quality Press, Inc., 1972.

423. Holcomb, Jack B. *A History of Truett-McConnell Junior College*. Privately published, 1958.

424. James, Eleanor. *Forth From Her Portals: The First 100 Years In Belton*. Belton, TX: University of Mary Hardin-Baylor Press, 1986.

425. Jenke, James Michael. "The Growth and Development of Grand Canyon College." Ph.D. dissertation. Arizona State University, 1993.

426. Johnston, Sidney. "The Historic Stetson University Campus in DeLand, 1884-1934." *The Florida Historical Quarterly* 70, 3 (January 1992): 281-304.

    Describes the development of the campus. Based on a Bureau of Historic preservation, Florida Department of State, research project.

427. Kennedy, Larry Wells. "The Fighting Preacher of the Army of Tennessee: General Mark Perrin Lowrey." Ph.D. dissertation, Mississippi State University, 1976.

    Covers the life of the founder of Blue Mountain College from 1818 to 1885.

428. Lycan, Gilbert L. *Stetson University: The First 100 Years*. DeLand, FL: Stetson University Press, 1983.

429. Meyer, Leland W. *Georgetown College: Its Background and a Chapter in Its Early History*. Louisville: The Western Recorder, 1929.

430. Nix, Pearl. *Early History of Truett-McConnell Junior College 1944-1950*. Privately published, 1980.

431. Paschal, George Washington. *History of Wake Forest College*, 3 vols. Winston-Salem: Wake Forest College, 1935.

432. Richards, W. Wiley. *Telling the Story of Jesus: The Golden Anniversary of Florida Baptist Theological College*. Graceville, FL: Hargrave Press, 1993.

    Commissioned to honor the school's 50th anniversary, this book is the only known published account of the school's history.

433. Shaw, Bynum. *History of Wake Forest College 1943-1967*, vol. 4. Winston-Salem: Wake Forest College, 1988.

> Carries the story further, beginning where George W. Paschal's three-book account ended in 1943.

434. Snyder, Robert. *A History of Georgetown College*. Georgetown, KY: Georgetown College Press, 1979.

435. Stackhouse, A. Yvonne. *A Centennial History, Hardin-Simmons University*. Abilene, TX: Hardin-Simmons University, 1991.

> Provides a detailed history of Hardin-Simmons University in commemorating the school's 100th anniversary.

436. Startup, Kenneth Moore. *The Splendid Work: The Origins and Development of Williams Baptist College*. Walnut Ridge, AR: Williams Baptist College, 1991.

> Treats the academic and ideological history of Williams from a commentator's perspective.

437. Taylor, James H. *A Bright Shining City Set on A Hill: A Centennial History*. Williamsburg, KY: Cumberland College, 1988.

> Provides a view of Cumberland College as seen by a former student who became the school's president.

438. Tyler, Frances Landrum. "Blue Mountain College Under the Administration of Lawrence Tyndale Lowrey, 1925-1960." Ph.D. dissertation, University of Mississippi, 1974.

439. White, Fred A. *The History of Dallas Baptist University.* Dallas, TX: Dallas Baptist University, 1991.

Provides the only known written comprehensive history of Dallas Baptist University.

CHAPTER 17
Seventh-day Adventist Higher Education in the United States

George R. Knight

In 1994 the Seventh-day Adventist Church operated three universities and ten colleges in the United States, with a combined enrollment of approximately 18,000 students. These tertiary institutions are part of an international system of higher education comprised of some 85 universities and colleges.

Seventh-day Adventism grew out of the widespread interchurch interest in the second coming of Christ in the 1830s and early 1840s that centered around the work of William Miller, a Baptist preacher. The imminence of the return of Christ was the keynote of the Adventist message. By 1846 the group that later became known as Seventh-day Adventists was becoming a visible, although minute, entity.[1]

Religious groups focusing on the nearness of the end of the world have generally not felt much need for educating their children beyond the essential truths of their religious persuasion and the skills needed to earn a living. This was true of the early

Christian church, and it was true of early Seventh-day Adventists. Why send children to school, so the logic runs, if the world is soon to end and they will never grow up to use their hard-earned learning? This attitude was widespread among many Adventists.

Beginnings: 1872-1891

The earliest explorations of Seventh-day Adventists into the realm of education for its young people centered on the establishment of Sabbath schools and Sabbath-school literature in the early 1850s and schooling at the elementary level. Whereas the Sabbath school prospered, the day-school movement hopelessly floundered throughout the 1850s and 1860s. Adventists just were not ready for a parochial school system yet. That development would not take place until the 1890s.

Meanwhile, by the early 1870s the Adventist movement was nearing its quarter-century mark. Adventism was experiencing not only aging, but also growing pains. Beyond that, some of its older leaders were dying off. And if those realities weren't problematic enough, the denomination by 1874 was becoming involved in the sending of foreign missionaries. A major question looming before Adventism's leaders was where the personnel for the future were to come from. The one obvious fact was that something had to be done.

In 1872 the denomination began to consider more seriously the need for a quality school, not so much for elementary children as for older students who needed to be educated to spread the gospel message. Adventists decided to establish a school in Battle Creek, Michigan, that would be supported financially by the General Conference of Seventh-day Adventists. This school was to be for the children of those at Battle Creek and those "abroad." Its function would be to "thoroughly" acquaint its students, both young and old, "with the teaching of the Bible in reference to those great truths which pertain to this time," and to provide that general knowledge which would enable them to spread the biblical message to the world.[2]

The Battle Creek school opened on 12 June 1872 with twelve students and Goodloe Harper Bell as their teacher. It was the first "official" Adventist school. By 1873 it had added Sidney Brownsberger as principal, and by the end of 1874 the Battle Creek school had been transformed into Battle Creek College.[3]

Battle Creek College is an important institution in Adventist educational history not only because of its "firstness," but because it received a great deal of attention in terms of policy formation and goal statements. It was for this school that Ellen White, the reforming thought leader among Adventists, penned her first major statement on education, "Proper Education."

This document, which was to provide the philosophic undergirding of the proposed school, set forth an educational philosophy that was not congruent with the educational practices of the day, even though it was in tune with the ideas of contemporary reformers. It set forth an educational program emphasizing balance among the mental, physical, and spiritual aspects of students. The exposition included discussion of the differences between the training of animals and the education of human beings, discipline as self-control, the need for a thorough understanding of health, the need for the study of the Bible and the "common branches," and a strong mandate to develop manual training in connection with academic work so that both body and mind could be exercised and young people would be prepared for the practical world.

"Proper Education" played down the impractical bookish education of the times which fitted young people to be "educated dunces." On the other hand, it proclaimed:

> Ignorance will not increase the humility or spirituality of any professed followers of Christ. The truths of the divine word can be best appreciated by an intellectual Christian. Christ can be best glorified by those who serve Him intelligently. The great object of education is to

> enable us to use the powers which God has
> given us in such a manner as will best represent
> the religion of the Bible and promote the glory of
> God.[4]

In essence, "Proper Education" has proven to be a cornerstone in Adventist educational philosophy.

George I. Butler, the president of the church's General Conference, also set forth the purpose of the new school before the entire denomination. "We have," wrote Butler,

> ...no great respect for that kind of education
> which is provided in many theological schools.
> We would not spend years in pouring over
> heathen mythology and the opinions of the
> fathers and the commentators, but would rather
> come directly to the source of true knowledge,
> God's holy word. It is not so much what men
> say about it, as what God Himself says that we
> want to understand. But we want hundreds of
> our people to take three, six, twelve, eighteen,
> twenty-four months' schooling, as soon as they
> can consistently do so.[5]

The founders of Battle Creek College were explicit as to their goals. They wanted to develop a reform institution that would uplift the Bible and manual labor, prepare Christian workers in a short time, and be practical in educating young people for the everyday duties of life, rather than schooling them in the esoteric knowledge of the ancient past.

Battle Creek College, in historical perspective, turned out to be a test case for the implementation of these principles. (It should be noted that, even though it bore the name of "college," much of its work in the nineteenth century -- like many other American colleges -- was on the secondary level.) An evaluation of the institution in terms of its reform goals can be summed up in one word -- *failure*. Emmett K. Vande Vere has written that the curriculum of Battle Creek College during the 1870s was a "philosophical betrayal."[6] The school rapidly developed into a liberal arts prep school and college -- an institution that built its curriculum around the classical languages and literature, while it almost totally neglected the reform ideals that centered on the curricular primacy of religion and Scripture and the introduction of manual labor as a counterbalance to academic work.

Throughout the 1870s Battle Creek College managed to frustrate the hopes of its founders. By the end of 1881, under a newly appointed president who was not even in verbal agreement with the Adventist philosophy of education, it was headed for disaster. At a meeting in December, 1881, the college board and faculty listened to a paper entitled "Our College" which faced the problem head-on. In this paper Ellen White stated in no uncertain terms that the school had failed in meeting its purpose. The study of the arts and sciences was necessary, but "the study of the Scripture should have the first place in our system of education." She continued:

> If a worldly influence is to bear sway in our school, then sell it out to worldlings and let them take the entire control; and those who have invested their means in that institution will establish another school, to be conducted, not upon the plan of popular schools, nor according to the desires of principal and teachers, but upon the plan which God has specified.[7]

During early 1882 the situation steadily deteriorated, and in the summer officials decided to close the school indefinitely. Thus, the first official attempt at higher education by the Adventist denomination collapsed. The school reopened in the autumn of 1883 under more dedicated leadership, but it never managed to displace the centrality of the classics or to fully implement the reform curriculum during the 1880s.

The hard lessons learned at Battle Creek, however, were not lost on the denomination's budding educational mentality. The spring of 1882 saw the opening of two more church-sponsored secondary schools: Healdsburg Academy (becoming Healdsburg College in 1883 and eventually Pacific Union College) in California, and South Lancaster Academy (later to become Atlantic Union College) in Massachusetts. Even though these schools were founded by Brownsberger and Bell, respectively, the leading men in the establishment of Battle Creek College in the early 1870s, both schools made large strides toward implementing the reform curriculum through giving the Bible a larger role and by making manual labor a vital part of the school program. In some matters, however, they followed the "bad example" of the Battle Creek school.[8]

Reform: 1891-1900

A major turning point in Adventist educational development was the educational convention held at Harbor Springs, Michigan, in July and August of 1891. This six-week convention was attended by over one hundred of the denomination's foremost educators, church administrators, and thought leaders.

At the Harbor Springs convention, W.W. Prescott (since 1887 the denomination's first leader in its newly-formed department of education),[9] Ellen White, and others called for a revival in Adventist education that would place the denomination's schools on a more specifically Christian set of principles. The church's basic educational goals were restudied in the light of past failures. In particular, Harbor Springs marked the beginning of the denomination's major assault on the "heathen" classics -- an assault that absorbed much reforming energy both inside and outside Adventist education during the 1890s. This issue was seen as crucial by Adventist reformers since they were apparently beginning to realize that a curriculum cannot have two focal points. By 1891 the reform leaders sensed that the biblical perspective would never find its proper place in Adventist education as long as the classics and their world view were central. The recommendations made at Harbor Springs were, in effect, a declaration of all-out war on the traditional secondary and collegiate curriculum.

In addition, at Harbor Springs educational reform was directly linked to the renewed emphasis on the centrality of faith in Christ's righteousness which had been revitalizing the church since the 1888 meetings of its General Conference. As a result, the central place of the Bible and the role of history as seen from the biblical perspective were recommended as the foremost studies in Adventist education.[10]

The Harbor Springs convention indicates that reorientation was underway. As such, Harbor Springs should be seen as the first step in the "adventizing" of Seventh-day Adventist education.

The next step in this process began when Ellen White and her son, W.C. White, sailed for Australia in November 1891. They would remain in Australia until 1900. While there, they would have opportunity to work with some of the most responsive of the reform leaders in the Adventist church. One of the most important endeavors of the Adventists in Australia in the 1890s was the founding of the Avondale School for Christian Workers (today known as Avondale College). Australia had the advantage of being beyond the reach of the conservative Adventist leadership in the United States. In addition, it was a new mission field for Seventh-day Adventists. Thus there were no established traditions with which to contend. As a result, several innovations were piloted in Australia during the 1890s that would have been much more difficult to experiment with in the United States.

A new type of Adventist school was forged at Avondale. By the end of the century, some individuals suggested that, since this school embodied the major reform elements that were viewed as the norm for Adventist education, it should be the model for Adventist education around the world. Because the educational program and ideals of Avondale were to have a continuing impact on Adventist education at all levels in the United States, it is important to look briefly at the experimental paradigm developed there.

Milton Hook, the historian of Avondale's early years, concluded that there were two main goals underlying the Avondale School. The first goal was the conversion and character development of its students. "Higher education" was that which prepared individuals for eternal life. The second goal was the training of denominational workers for Christian service both in the local community and in worldwide mission outreach. These two goals reflect a distinct move away from the academic and classical orientation of Battle Creek College and the schools that came under its influence.

Certain strategies, noted Hook, were developed at Avondale to facilitate the achievement of these goals. Of foremost importance were the following.

(1) The selection of a rural location for the school was encouraged to provide sufficient land for agricultural pursuits, to keep young people away from the false excitement of the artificial amusements found in cities, and to place young people in contact with the beauties of nature where they could meditate upon the love of the God of nature.

(2) The placing of the Bible at the focal point of the curriculum was a definite move to teach all subjects within the framework of the biblical worldview. A corollary to the uplifting of the Bible was the removal of the classics and the classical languages from the curriculum.

(3) There was a definite initiative taken to weave missionary activities into the school program. Through missionary activity it was hoped that young people would be imbued with both the concept of service for humanity and the desire to engage in service after graduation.

(4) There was the development of a strong manual labor program in which every student would participate. Manual labor would provide the necessary balance between the mental and physical aspects of human nature and thus act as a "re-creational" and refreshing activity,

provide money for students to attend school, and furnish opportunities for young people to develop practical skills that would help them get along in undeveloped mission fields.

(5) There was a definite downplaying of the role of games and artificial amusements. The aim of the school was to bring young people face to face with the reality and needs of a world in turmoil, rather than to provide escapes from that reality. Recreation was to be found in useful employment and service to others rather than in meaningless activity.[11]

These goals, and the strategies developed to implement them, became the normative ideal of Adventist education at all levels. The Avondale experiment had almost immediate repercussions on Adventist education in America and around the world. In regard to Adventist educational development, Avondale, with its emphasis on reform, took the leadership role away from Battle Creek College.

Reform was also at the base of the explosion in the number of Adventist schools and colleges in the 1890s. The church was in the midst of a major cycle of missionary expansion, and Adventist schools came to be more and more thought of as training institutions to provide workers for this extended work both at home and abroad.[12]

The end of the century saw the curriculum of Adventist secondary and collegiate education undergoing reform as the Bible was increasingly placed at the center, while the classics were rooted out. In addition, new schools were being established on large tracts of land in rural locations after the pattern of the Avondale model. After the turn of the century this movement was extended to long-established schools. Even Battle Creek College sold its property in 1901 and moved near rural Berrien Springs in southwest Michigan where it became Emmanuel Missionary College (now Andrews University).

The experiences of the 1890s had transformed Adventist education at the secondary and collegiate levels. Not only were existing schools and colleges changed, but the decade saw the establishment of many new secondary schools and colleges with substantial preparatory departments. Beyond expansion in Adventist secondary and tertiary schools, the 1890s and the early part of the new century saw the establishment of an Adventist elementary school system and its exponential expansion.[13] That rapid increase put a strain on both the relatively small denomination (75,767 members worldwide in 1900) and its institutions of higher learning. Teacher training became a major function of Adventist colleges, while some of its academies developed "normal" departments to help cover the shortfall.

To cover the needs of a rapidly growing church and an even more rapidly expanding mission and educational work, the denomination established several colleges in the 1890s and several academies that evolved into colleges. Foremost among the new collegiate institutions were Union College (1891) in Lincoln, Nebraska, and Walla Walla College (1892) in Walla Walla, Washington. Among those academies founded in the 1890s that evolved into colleges were Graysville Academy (1892) in Tennessee (now Southern College of Seventh-day Adventists), the Keene Industrial School (1894) in Texas (now Southwestern Adventist College), and the Oakwood Industrial School (1896) in Alabama (now Oakwood College).[14]

The Oakwood school was unique among Adventist schools of the time in that it was established to train leaders in the budding North American Black work of the denomination.[15] Oakwood school was similar in many ways to Booker T. Washington's Tuskegee Institute. But, it should be noted, emphasis on useful work and practical skills in education was not restricted to Blacks among Adventists. In Adventist education the ideal was work combined with study for students of all races -- even for students preparing for professional roles. Reformed Adventist education was to be practical as well as intellectual.

A final educational development in Adventist higher education in the crucial 1890s was the establishment of the American Medical Missionary College by John Harvey Kellogg in 1895 with campuses in Battle Creek and Chicago. The purpose of the medical school was to train academically respectable physicians, nurses, and other medical workers in harmony with the health reform principles of the denomination. The graduates were to operate the rapidly expanding number of hospitals and sanitariums then being established by the denomination around the world.[16]

Consolidation and Advance: 1903-1960

The formative years for Adventist higher education were 1872 through 1903. By 1903 the direction, ideals, and patterns had been set. Developments in Adventist tertiary schooling in the new century would focus on refinements, expansion, and maturity.

The early years of the twentieth century witnessed a continuation of the reform of the 1890s. But, as is often the case, some advocates took the reforms to extremes. Such was the case of Edward Sutherland and Percy T. Magan who had removed Battle Creek College to Berrien Springs as Emmanuel Missionary College in 1901. Even though it still bore the title of college, it had been incorporated in its new location as a charitable institution rather than as an institution of higher learning. Under the new regime it no longer offered academic degrees and had no set course of study. In fact, the "college" had come to resemble more of a work farm than it did an institution of higher learning.[17] Early 1904 saw the resignation of Sutherland and Magan, who were under considerable pressure from the leading administrators of the denomination. In the wake of their resignation, those institutions that had followed Emmanuel Missionary College into extremes came back toward a middle course, which kept the best of the reforms but also aimed at academic respectability in a more traditional sense. It should be noted that most of the Adventist colleges took a much less erratic path from the traditional curriculum to a reformed curriculum than did Battle Creek/Emmanuel Missionary College.

And even that college was soon rechartered as a degree-granting institution.

By 1904 Frederick Griggs[18] and C.C. Lewis had taken over the reins of Adventist educational leadership from Sutherland and Magan. The new leadership set forth the more moderate position that was to have a lasting effect on the church's educational outlook. Lewis put forth the position of the new leaders nicely in 1906 in his address to the denomination's national educational convention:

> I do not believe that we have passed the [educational] reformation itself, and that "so-called reform," as it has been spoken of, is to be left behind and dropped out of sight. I believe that a genuine reform was begun; and, although mistakes have been made, we are profiting by those mistakes and we shall continue to profit by them…. So instead of dropping the reforms that were started a few years ago, I think we should rather be in a position where, profiting by the mistakes that have been made, we shall now go forward carrying out the true, genuine principles of reform; and we shall yet see a system of education built upon these principles that will be an honor to God and to the work of this denomination.[19]

In the meantime, Sutherland and Magan had begun a new institution of higher learning in Tennessee called the Nashville Agricultural and Normal Institute. Eventually it became Madison College. The new school initiated a new strand of Seventh-day Adventist collegiate education -- the "self-supporting" college. The idea underlying the self-supporting ideal is not that the school would be financially self-sufficient, but that it would not rely on denominational support and would thereby not be under denominational control. As a result, such schools and colleges would be freer to experiment with what some continued to object to as reformism that had gone too far.

The early decades of the twentieth century witnessed the formation of several new institutions of higher learning by the denomination and the strengthening of those already in existence.

The most important addition to Adventism's roster of tertiary institutions was the College of Medical Evangelists. The College of Medical Evangelists was founded in 1906 to take the place of the American Medical Missionary College, which was lost to the church through the apostasy of Kellogg. The denomination's new medical college would become a fully accredited medical school in the next two decades.

The subject of accreditation brings up another major topic in the development of Adventist education in the 1920s and 1930s. Caught in the fundamentalist backlash of the 1920s, many of the denomination's more advanced thinkers lost their positions in the 1920s. The new educational leadership (under such men as Warren E. Howell), while accepting professional medical accreditation and professional medical degrees, stood against both regional academic accreditation and faculty with advanced academic degrees earned in "outside" institutions. The fear in both cases was that educational philosophies foreign to that of Adventism would in one way or another be superimposed on Adventist learning.[20]

Yet even the most reactionary Adventist leaders saw the need for quality control and higher degrees. As a result, they attempted to make an end run on the problem by taking two courses of action. The first was to establish their own board of regents in 1928 to accredit Adventist colleges. The second was to create their own institution of higher learning that could offer advanced degrees. Thus the Advanced Bible School met for the first time on the campus of Pacific Union College in California in the summer of 1932.

These two attempts to avoid the "contamination of the world" failed in their primary aims. By the early 1940s most Adventist colleges in North America were either regionally accredited or in the process of being accredited. Beyond that, the denomination began a progressively more aggressive program of sponsoring its professors for doctoral study at prestigious institutions.

Those changes, however, did not spell the end of the initiatives taken in 1928 and 1932. The Adventist Board of Regents still exists. But its purpose is not to take the place of regional accreditation, but to supplement it -- partly to make sure that the distinctively Adventist goals of higher education are being met. Meanwhile, the Advanced Bible School has evolved into a university granting fully accredited Ph.D., Th.D., and Ed.D. degrees.

Maturity: 1960-1994

There is a sense in which it can be said that Adventist education began to reach maturity in 1960. Not only did an increasing number of the system's professors hold terminal degrees, but the late 1950s had seen moves toward creating two Adventist universities.

The first of those institutions had found its roots in the Advanced Bible School established in 1932. That institution became the Seventh-day Adventist Theological Seminary in 1937, and in 1957 it was merged with a newly created school of graduate studies to form Potomac University, headquartered in Washington, D.C. But "P.U.," as it was affectionately known to its students, had no physical home. That problem was solved in 1960 when the two schools of Potomac University were merged with the undergraduate school of Emmanuel Missionary College in Berrien Springs, Michigan, to form Andrews University.[21]

The next year saw the creation of Loma Linda University in California out of the various schools making up the College of Medical Evangelists. Then in 1967 La Sierra College, located about 20 miles west of Loma Linda, was pulled into Loma Linda University to add a strong liberal arts undergraduate program to the various professional programs already offered. During the next few years the La Sierra campus developed its own doctoral programs under the auspices of the university.

But the marriage between the Loma Linda and La Sierra campuses did not last. Never fully integrated, the institutions were legally separated in the late 1980s. At that time the La Sierra campus became La Sierra University.

Thus as of 1994 the Seventh-day Adventist Church operates three fully accredited doctoral-degree-granting universities in the United States. In addition, the denomination owns eight liberal arts colleges, some of which offer master's degrees.

Beyond those traditional institutions of tertiary education, the church has invested in two highly successful colleges of medical arts. Kettering College of Medical Arts (1967) in Ohio and Florida Hospital College of Health Sciences (1992) offer a variety of accredited programs in medical and para-medical fields.

The final branch of contemporary Adventist higher education represents the Madison, self-supporting strand. Whereas Madison ceased offering collegiate work in 1964, the place it held in Adventism's social structure did not remain vacant for long. The 1970s saw the rise of several self-supporting institutions dedicated to offering higher education in the Madison tradition. The most well-balanced and successful of these institutions is the Weimar Institute, located in the foothills of the Sierra Mountains in California. Weimar is quite cooperative with the denomination, graduates excellent students, and serves as a mild corrective to "mainline" Adventist higher education. Unfortunately, some of the other independent institutes do not provide the quality of Weimar.

Since 1970 the denomination's North American Division's Board of Higher Education has served as a coordinating agency for denominationally-operated colleges and universities in the United States and Canada. Part of the function of the Board is to help the institutions work together to avoid unnecessary duplication of programs. But in a situation in which the various institutions have generally had a history of autonomy and the schools are competing in a limited marketplace, the accomplishments of the Board have been less than perfect. In spite of its shortcomings, however, the Board continues to provide a moderating atmosphere as Adventist education moves toward the twenty-first century.

Endnotes

1.   For general historical information on Seventh-day Adventism, see Richard L. Schwarz, *Light Bearers to the Remnant.* Mountain View, CA: Pacific Press, 1979; George R. Knight, *Anticipating the Advent: A Brief History of Seventh-day Adventists.* Boise, ID: Pacific Press, 1993; Don F. Neufeld, ed., *Seventh-day Adventist Encyclopedia*, rev. ed., Washington, D.C.: Review and Herald, 1976.

2.   School Committee, "The Proposed School," *Review and Herald*, 7 May 1872, p. 168.

3.   The history of the Battle Creek school (later Battle Creek College, Emmanuel Missionary College, and Andrews University) is told in Emmett K. Vande Vere, *The Wisdom Seekers.* Nashville: Southern Publishing Association, 1972. Bell's influence in Seventh-day Adventist education is the topic of Allan G. Lindsay, "Goodloe Harper Bell: Pioneer Seventh-day Adventist Christian Educator," Ed.D. dissertation, Andrews University, 1982. Two helpful resources in the study of Seventh-day Adventist educational development are George R. Knight, ed., *Early Adventist Educators.* Berrien Springs, MI: Andrews University Press, 1983; and Maurice Hodgen, ed., *School Bells and Gospel Trumpets: A Documentary History of Seventh-day Adventist Education in North America.* Loma Linda, CA: Adventist Heritage Publications, 1978.

4.   Ellen G. White, *Fundamentals of Christian Education.* Nashville: Southern Publishing Association, 1923, pp. 15-46. The quotation is from pp. 44-45.

5.   George I. Butler, "What Use Shall We Make of Our School?," *Review and Herald*, 1 April 1873, p. 124.

6.   Vande Vere, *The Wisdom Seekers*, p. 23.

7.   Ellen G. White, *Testimonies for the Church.* 9 vols. Mountain View, CA: Pacific Press, 1948, Vol. 5, pp. 25-26.

8. For the history of the Healdsburg school, see Walter C. Utt, *A Mountain, A Pickax, A College.* Angwin, CA: The Alumni Association of Pacific Union College, 1969. For the history of the South Lancaster school, see Myron F. Wehtje, *And There Was Light.* South Lancaster, MA: The Atlantic Press, 1982.

9. For an informative treatment of Prescott's contributions, see Gilbert Murray Valentine, "William Warren Prescott: Seventh-day Adventist Educator," 2 vols., Ph.D. dissertation, Andrews University, 1982. A less extensive form of Valentine's study has been published as *The Shaping of Adventism: The Case of W.W. Prescott.* Berrien Springs, MI: Andrews University Press, 1992.

10. For the most complete account of this convention, see Craig S. Willis, "Harbor Springs Institute of 1891: A Turning Point in Our Educational Conceptions," Ellen G. White Research Center, Andrews University, 1979. See also W.W. Prescott, "Report of the Educational Secretary," *General Conference Bulletin,* 23 February 1893, p. 350; and Percy T. Magan, "The Educational Conference and the Education Reform," *Review and Harald,* 6 August 1901, p. 508.

11. For the most complete account of the Adventist educational experience in Australia and the impact of that experience on Adventist education in the United States, see Milton R. Hook, "The Avondale School and Adventist Educational Goals, 1894-1900," Ed.D. dissertation, Andrews University, 1978; and Allan G. Lindsay, "The Influence of Ellen White upon the Development of the Seventh-day Adventist School System in Australia, 1891-1900," M.Ed. thesis, University of Newcastle, 1978.

12. See George R. Knight, "The Dynamics of Educational Expansion: A Lesson from Adventist History," *Journal of Adventist Education* 52 (April-May 1990): 13-19, 44-45.

13. For a sketch of the development of Seventh-Day Adventist schooling, see George R. Knight, "Seventh-day Adventist Schooling in the United States," in Thomas C. Hunt

and James C. Carper, eds., *Religious Schools in the United States, K-12: A Source Book*. New York: Garland Publishing, 1993.

14.   Walla Walla and Union Colleges each have excellent published histories. See Terrie Dopp Aamodt, *Bold Venture: A History of Walla Walla College*. Walla Walla, WA: Walla Walla College Press, 1992; and Evertt Dick, *Union College of the Golden Cords*. Lincoln, NE: Union College Press, 1967.

15.   For the origin of Adventist educational work among American Blacks in the South, see Ronald D. Graybill, *Mission to Black America*. Mountain View, CA: Pacific Press, 1971; Louis B. Reynolds, *We Have Tomorrow: The Story of American Seventh-day Adventists with an African Heritage*. Washington, D.C.: Review and Herald, 1984, pp. 46-107, 190-211; and Alta Robinson, "James Edson White: Innovator," in Knight, *Early Adventist Educators*, pp. 137-58.

16.   For the best history dealing with Kellogg and his contribution to the American Medical Missionary College, see Richard W. Schwarz, *John Harvey Kellogg, M.D.* Nashville: Southern Publishing Association, 1970. See also Dores Eugene Robinson, *The Story of Our Health Message: The Origin, Character, and Development of Health Education in the Seventh-day Adventist Church*. 3rd ed., Nashville, Southern Publishing Association, 1965.

17.   For the most adequate treatments of Sutherland and Magan, see Warren S. Ashworth, "Edward Alexander Sutherland and Seventh-day Adventist Educational Reform: The Denominational Years, 1890-1904," Ph.D. dissertation, Andrews University, 1986; and Merlin L. Neff, *For God and C.M.E.: A Biography of Percy Tilson Magan upon the Historical Background of the Educational and Medical Work of Seventh-day Adventists*. Mountain View, CA: Pacific Press, 1964.

18.   Griggs' contributions to Seventh-day Adventist education are the topic of Arnold Colin Reye, "Frederick Griggs: Seventh-day Adventist Educator and Administrator," Ph.D. dissertation, Andrews University, 1984.

19.   "Story of the Convention," *Central Union Conference Bulletin* (October 1906): 74-75.

20. See William G. White, "Flirting with the World: How Seventh-day Adventist Colleges in North America Got Accredited," *Adventist Heritage* 8 (Spring 1983):40-51. For the best biography of Howell, see John F. Waters, "Warren Eugene Howell: Seventh-day Adventist Educational Administrator," Ed.D. dissertation, Andrews University, 1988.

21. See Vande Vere, *The Wisdom Seekers*, pp. 243-66.

Bibliographic Entries

440. Aamodt, Terrie Dopp. *Bold Venture: A History of Walla Walla College.* Walla Walla, WA: Walla Walla College Press, 1992.

Presents a well-documented history of one of Adventism's strongest colleges. This is the first history of Walla Walla College to be published since 1952.

441. Benson, Peter L. and Michael J. Donahue. *Valuegenesis: Report 1, A Study of the Influence of Family, Church and School on the Faith, Values and Commitment of Adventist Youth.* Silver Spring, MD: North American Division of Seventh-day Adventists, 1990.

Represents the first published release of Valuegenesis data. Based upon 14,748 usable questionnaires from youth, parents, teachers, Adventist school principals, and pastors of supporting churches, this massive study is doing much to shed light on the strengths and weaknesses of Adventist education in the school, the home, and the congregation. Its implications are many for Adventist higher education.

442. Benson, Peter L. and Michael J. Donahue. *Valuegenesis: Report 2, A Study of the Influence of Family, Church and*

School on the Faith, Values and Commitment of Adventist Youth. Silver Spring, MD: North American Division of Seventh-day Adventists, 1991.

Applies the data of the Valuegenesis study to each of the eight union conferences in the United States and the one in Canada. Thus *Report 2* is in actuality nine separately-bound reports with one title.

443.   Benson, Peter L. and Michael J. Donahue. *Valuegenesis: Report 3, A Study of the Influence of Family, Church and School on the Faith, Values and Commitment of Adventist Youth.* Silver Spring, MD: North American Division of Seventh-day Adventists, 1991.

Summarizes information on school quality gleaned from an in-depth study of 204 Adventist elementary and secondary schools. Recommendations for Adventist schools are made in the final chapter.

444.   Brantley, Paul S. and Shirley A. Freed. "Do Adventist Teachers Feel Valued? Research on Faculty in SDA Colleges and Universities." *Journal of Adventist Education* 52 (April-May 1990): 9-12.

Reports the findings of the Professional Recognition of Adventist Educators Survey in North America. Also discusses the implications of the survey's findings.

445.   Coy, Gerald Wayne. "Manual Training: Its Role in the Development of the Seventh-day Adventist Educational System." Doctor of Industrial Technology dissertation, University of Northern Iowa, 1987.

Develops the history of manual training in Adventist schools and provides correlations with developments in the public system.

446. Dudley, Roger L. "Faith Maturity and Social Concern in College-age Youth: Does Christian Education Make a Difference?" *Journal of Research on Christian Education* 3 (Spring 1994): 35-49.

Reports on a study of faith maturity among Adventist youth that utilizes a different instrument from the Valuegenesis study. This study suggests that corrections of some of the initial Valuegenesis interpretations are needed in the area of faith maturity.

447. Dudley, Roger L. and Janet Leigh Kangas. *The World of the Adventist Teenager*. Washington, D.C.: Review and Herald, 1990.

Explores (on the basis of more than 1,500 surveys completed by baptized Seventh-day Adventist teenagers) the attitudes, backgrounds, and behaviors of Adventist youth. The study is especially concerned with the large percentage leaving the denomination. It also provides strategies for alleviating the problem.

448. Dudley, Roger L. with V. Bailey Gillespie. *Valuegenesis: Faith in the Balance*. Riverside, CA: La Sierra University Press, 1992.

Reports on many of the implications gathered from over 12,000 youth in the Valuegenesis study sponsored by Adventism in the late 1980s. The first in a series of books, *Faith in the Balance* presents a large amount of descriptive data regarding the effects of religious education in Adventist schools, homes, and congregations. The book closes with a chapter on recommendations.

449. Gillespie, V. Bailey, ed. *Perspectives on Values*. La Sierra, CA: La Sierra University Press, 1993.

Growing out of the Project Affirmation/Valuegenesis study, *Perspectives on Values* treats the topic of values all the way from the Old Testament roots of the topic up to present-day application. The volume's eleven chapters are written by one non-Adventist and ten Adventist scholars.

450. Guy, Fritz. "The Future of Adventist Higher Education: A Look at the Options." *Journal of Adventist Education* 56 (April/May 1994): 14-19.

Presents a provocative taxonomy of seven possible futures for Seventh-day Adventist higher education that includes liquidation, consolidation, simplification, privatization, specialization, centralization, and continuation.

451. Hammill, Richard L. *Pilgrimage: Memoirs of an Adventist Administrator*. Berrien Springs, MI: Andrews University Press, 1992.

Presents an insider's view on the development of Adventist universities in the 1960s by the second president of Andrews University and a member of the Department of Education of the General Conference of Seventh-day Adventists during the formative period for developing Loma Linda and Andrews Universities.

452. Kangas, Janet Leigh. "A Study of the Religious Attitudes and Behaviors of Seventh-day Adventist Adolescents in

North America Related to Their Family, Educational, and Church Backgrounds." Ph.D. dissertation, Andrews University, 1988.

Examines the reasons why Adventist youth leave the church. This work is the first report of a 10-year longitudinal research project. It sought to identify attitudes and behaviors of Adventist adolescents and examine possible correlations with the religious backgrounds and influences of their homes, churches, and schools.

453. Knight, George R. "The Dynamics of Educational Expansion: A Lesson from Adventist History." *Journal of Adventist Education* 52 (April-May 1990):13-19, 44-45.

Examines the educational "explosion" that took place in Seventh-day Adventist elementary and secondary education in the late 1890s and notes the relationship of that development to spiritual renaissance and interest in Christian missions. The article treats those relationships within the context of a similar revival taking place in the Bible school movement and Protestant missions.

454. Larson, Roland and Doris Larson. *Teaching Values*. La Sierra, CA: La Sierra University Press, 1992.

Growing out of the Project Affirmation/Valuegenesis study, *Teaching Values* develops models for teaching values to all levels of Seventh-day Adventist youth.

455. Rasi, Humberto M., comp. *Christ in the Classroom: Adventist Approaches to the Integration of Faith and Learning*. 10 vols. Silver Spring, MD: Institute for Christian Teaching, 1991-1994.

Presents papers and articles by Adventist college and university teachers and administrators on various aspects of curricular integration. Many of these papers were originally presented to the International Faith and Learning Seminar sponsored by the Institute for Christian Teaching. Many of the articles were previously published in Adventist periodicals.

456. Rasi, Humberto M. and Victor Korniejczuk. *Christ in the Classroom: A Select Bibliography on the Integration of Faith and Learning*. Silver Spring, MD: Institute for Christian Teaching, 1993.

Presents what attempts to be an exhaustive bibliography on the integration of faith and learning in both its general sense and for each academic area.

457. Rice, Gail. *Valuegenesis: Report 4, A Study of the Influence of Family, Church and School on the Faith, Values and Commitment of Adventist Youth*. Loma Linda, CA: Loma Linda University, 1993.

Provides a profile of Adventist teachers in North America, including such areas as demographic data, education, satisfaction, and attitudes to students.

458. Rice, Gail and V. Bailey Gillespie. "Valuegenesis: A Megastudy of Faith Maturity and Its Relationship to Variables Within the Home, School, and Church." *Journal of Research on Christian Education* 1 (Autumn 1992): 49-67.

Presents a survey of the main strategies and findings in the Valuegenesis study of faith maturity.

459. *Risk and Promise: A Report of the Project Affirmation Taskforces.* Silver Spring, MD: North American Division of Seventh-day Adventists, 1990.

Summarizes the major findings of the Project Affirmation task forces (Academic and teacher quality; faith, value, and commitment; Marketing; and Financial) as they were presented to the delegates to the North American Division Year-End Meeting in October 1990. The initial reports of all four task forces make up the bulk of the volume. Project Affirmation was a massive study of the present condition of Adventist education linked to recommendations for future health.

460. Schwab, Robert C. and Allan F. Stembridge. "Adventist Professor Remuneration: What's Happened in 20 Years?" *Journal of Adventist Education* 56 (April/May 1994): 26-31.

Empirically presents an analysis of the eroding benefit package of Seventh-day Adventist professors and makes suggestions on how to remedy the situation.

461. Seltzer Daley Companies. "Seventh-day Adventist Education, Planning Research: Preliminary Findings." Research report, Princeton, NJ, 1987.

Highlights the challenges facing Adventist education in the late 1980s. This important study stimulated the massive Project Affirmation study.

462. Smith, Tom. "The Fire This Time: Enrollment Drops Threaten North American Academies and Colleges." *Spectrum* 18 (December 1987): 44-49.

Graphically presents the crisis in the enrollment of Seventh-day Adventist secondary schools and colleges that had been underway since 1981. Also provides some recommendations.

463.   Thayer, Jerome D. "Measuring Faith Maturity: Reassessing Value-genesis and Development of a Denomination-specific Scale." *Journal of Research in Christian Education* 2 (Spring 1993): 93-113.

Argues that some of the scales utilized for the Valuegenesis study were inappropriate. Proposes the development of faith-maturity scales specifically aimed at Seventh-day Adventists.

464.   Valentine, Gilbert M. *The Shaping of Adventism: The Case of W.W. Prescott.* Berrien Springs, MI: Andrews University Press, 1992.

Discusses the role of Adventism's leading educator in the 1880s and early 1890s. Analyzes Prescott's significant contribution to Adventist education during its formative period.

465.   Waters, John F. "Warren Eugene Howell: Seventh-day Adventist Educational Administrator." Ed.D. dissertation, Andrews University, 1988.

Analyzes the life and work of the leader of the General Conference Department of Education during the 1920s. Of special interest is Howell's relationship to the accreditation crisis that proved stressful to Adventists in the 1920s.

CHAPTER 18
Jewish Seminaries and Colleges

Harold S. Wechsler

Nineteenth-century American Jewry established many religious and social institutions, but faced serious obstacles founding a Jewish seminary or college. Jewish partisans of higher education were divided -- was the goal the higher education of Jews or Jewish higher education; that is, should an institution sponsored by Jews educate a knowledgeable lay community, or should it prepare rabbis and teachers? Some opponents objected to envisioned secular education components; others argued that American Jews could indefinitely rely upon immigrant rabbis.

Despite the eloquence of proponents, and verbal competition between cities that might house a Jewish institution of higher learning, success awaited the last quarter of the nineteenth century. These institutions were rabbinical seminaries -- not general colleges -- a response to a growing consensus in favor of an American-educated rabbinate. Even in the twentieth century, save for a handful of small, specialized institutions, Jews lacked the equivalent of the denominationally-sponsored liberal arts colleges available for Protestants and Catholics, or of the colleges for women and African-Americans.

The turn-of-the century East European Jewish migrations to America resulted in an influx of Jewish students, first into urban public school systems, and then into American universities and public colleges in urban centers. By World War I, for example, Jews dominated the student population at the College of the City of New York, and had created a "problem" for Columbia, Harvard, and other east coast universities.[1] The ensuing admissions restrictions channeled Jewish students away from the Ivies to public colleges or to independent institutions with a liberal social outlook or with budgetary red ink. Colleges sponsored by Jews -- save for Brandeis University after World War II -- were not built as a response to discrimination. With the exceptions noted below, postwar growth among Jewish postsecondary institutions centered in the seminaries, which assumed multiple functions. Today, a large majority of Jewish youth attends college, but the *types* of institutions preferred by these students have remained largely the same since the turn of the century.

Most nineteenth-century attempts at creating a Jewish higher education institution failed, usually for lack of funds; sometimes for a lack of students. Moses Levy, for example, proposed, but did not establish, a Jewish college in 1821 in connection with his attempt to found a major Jewish settlement in Florida.[2] In the 1840s, Isaac Leeser, the first American to translate the Jewish Bible into English, promoted a seminary with both Jewish and secular curricula to remedy the shortage of American rabbis and teachers. Inadequate funds thwarted the project, though the Pennsylvania legislature chartered the seminary in 1849. A similar New York effort failed in 1852; so did Isaac Mayer Wise's Cincinnati-based Zion Collegiate Association in the mid-1850s, an 1864 attempt by younger Jews to establish a National Hebrew College based upon existing Hebrew literary societies, an 1866 endeavor by Benjamin Franklin Peixotto of the Order of B'nai B'rith to establish an American Jewish university, an initiative by New York's Temple Emanu-El congregation to establish a seminary for Reform rabbis, and Maimonides College (1867), a short-lived Philadelphia institution for the preparation of rabbis.[3]

Lack of funds, scholars, or enthusiasm continued to thwart all efforts until Isaac Mayer Wise successfully established Hebrew Union College (HUC) in Cincinnati in 1875, a rabbinical seminary intended to provide English-speaking rabbis with both secular and Jewish higher education.[4] The seminary initially attracted widespread support, even from rabbis who personally disagreed with Wise's brand of Jewish liberalism. These rabbis, knowing the history of similar failed attempts, concluded that HUC, added to the presence of seminaries in Breslau, Berlin, Vienna, Budapest, and England, would siphon off resources aimed at institutions of Jewish learning -- as well as students. HUC, under Wise, became the "fountainhead" of Reform Judaism, a retreat from its original goal of educating rabbis for all of American Jewry.

"Traditional" Jews strenuously objected to Wise's liberalism, the symbolism of the Treifa Banquet, when nonkosher food was served at the dinner for HUC's first graduating class (1883), and the challenge to *halachic* Judaism posed by the 1885 Pittsburgh Platform, which Wise accepted. Exclusive reliance on HUC for rabbis, these traditionalists concluded, meant the end of *halachic* Judaism in America. The traditionalists resolved to open a new seminary in New York, the location of the nation's largest Jewish population. Their creation, the Jewish Theological Seminary (JTS), led a marginal existence for the first 15 years after its founding in 1886. Underfinanced, burdened by an unwieldy governance system, and reliant for instruction on rabbis who faced competing demands for their time, the Seminary graduated only 17 students before 1902.

The passing of the Seminary's first generation of stalwarts, including president Sabato Morais (1886-1897), and the lack of a sound financial footing led to a reorganization in 1902. The reorganizers subsidized the Seminary's budget -- rabbinical students paid no tuition until the 1970s -- and facilitated the emergence of a full-time faculty rewarded for its scholarship.

Reform Jews, prominent among the reorganizers, were motivated by a desire to provide Americanized, if traditional, rabbis for the growing immigrant populations and by a desire to recruit Cambridge University professor Solomon Schechter -- world famous for his discovery of the Cairo *genizah*, a storehouse of Jewish texts -- for the Seminary's presidency (1902-1915). The Seminary soon followed Columbia University's move from midtown Manhattan to the more "academic" atmosphere of the Morningside Heights section. In 1930, the Seminary moved to its current home on Broadway at 122nd Street.

Cyrus Adler, who received the first American Ph.D. in Semitics from Johns Hopkins and had taught at JTS beginning in 1886, became chair of the Seminary's trustees, succeeded Schechter after his death in 1915, and led the Seminary for the next quarter century, while simultaneously presiding over Dropsie College for Hebrew and Cognate Studies in Philadelphia, a research institution founded in 1906.

The rabbinical program was elevated to the graduate level under Schechter. JTS subsequently established a Teacher's Institute (1909) and an undergraduate track (1915). Adler reorganized the collegiate unit, which became the Seminary College of Jewish Studies, in 1931 (now the Albert A. List College of Jewish Studies). Adler became involved, and in turn involved faculty members at the Seminary and other Jewish seminaries and colleges, in many projects that promoted Jewish scholarship including the American Jewish Historical Society (located at JTS until a move to the Brandeis University campus in the 1960s) and the American Academy for Jewish Research.

The East European Jewish migrations resulted in the opening of Yeshiva Etz Chaim in 1886 and of the Rabbi Isaac Elchanan Theological Seminary (RIETS) on New York's Lower East Side in 1896. These schools combined in 1915, and the resulting seminary became Yeshiva College, a central institution for the education of Orthodox rabbis. During Bernard Revel's presidency (1915-1940), an affiliated Jewish high school opened, the Teachers Institute, founded by the Mizrachi Organization of America. In

1917, it merged with RIETS. Yeshiva College offered the baccalaureate degree (1928), and the merged institution moved to its current home in upper Manhattan (1929). In 1908, RIETS students went on strike to protest the exclusion of secular studies, and Revel's 1915 incorporation of secular subjects into the RIETS curriculum demonstrated a partial surmounting of this fear of the Enlightenment. Yeshiva endured attacks on its policy of *Torah U-mada* [Torah and secular studies], and the expansion of functions that it justified, from Orthodox Jews who argued for the curricular exclusivity of Torah studies.[5]

Reform, Conservative, and later Reconstructionist Judaism each relied mainly upon one seminary for the education of their rabbis.[6] This centralization counterbalanced the centripetal tendencies inherent in an American Judaism based on congregations. JTS had no direct Conservative challenger until 1989, but Reform Jews established the Jewish Institute of Religion (JIR), presided over by Steven S. Wise, rabbi of the Free Synagogue of New York, the Institute's home.[7] JIR conducted all instruction in Hebrew, opposed the anti-Zionism of HUC under Kaufmann Kohler (1903-1921), the orthodoxy of RIETS, and the traditionalism of JTS under Cyrus Adler.[8] HUC had, meanwhile, established its own presence in New York City by opening a School for Teachers in 1923. The school, which closed during the Depression and reopened in 1947, offered a master's degree in Jewish education. HUC also opened a School of Sacred Music in New York in 1948.

Secure as long as Wise remained president, though in constant financial difficulty, JIR began merger discussions with HUC after World War II. HUC's anti-Zionism faded after adoption of the 1937 Columbus Platform, which embraced the concept of Jewish peoplehood. Nelson Glueck became head of HUC in 1947, succeeding Julian Morgenstern (1921-1947). He succeeded Wise as head of JIR the following year. The institutions merged in 1950.

Orthodox Judaism, though reliant upon RIETS at Yeshiva College for rabbis, also drew upon other postsecondary *yeshivot* that opened before World War II. Hebrew Theological College (HTC) (1922), for example, had several Chicago homes before relocating to Skokie, Illinois, in 1958. HTC also opened a Teachers Institute for Women (1922), cosponsored the Chicago Jewish Academy (1942), an all-day Jewish high school, and started a liberal arts division, the Jewish University of America, in 1959. Ner Israel Rabbinical College in Baltimore (1933) offered baccalaureate and advanced degrees in Talmudic law, and operated a teacher's institute and a high school. Beth Medrash Govohoa (1943), a school of Talmudic learning in Lakewood, New Jersey, established ten collegiate schools of pre-rabbinic studies between 1952 and 1976. Successful students could transfer to the Lakewood campus.

Seminaries, the most prominent Jewish higher education institutions, coexisted with several small collegiate institutions founded before World War II. When Hyman Gratz's bequest for the education of Philadelphia Jewry became available in the 1890s, leaders of the Philadelphia Jewish community, including some founders of JTS, contemplated alternatives. Some desired a Jewish university; others, recalling the failed attempt to sustain Maimonides in Philadelphia, called for a teacher-education school -- JTS did not open its own Teachers Institute until 1909 -- that would also prepare students at the secondary school level for rabbinical study at JTS. Gratz College, embodying the latter vision, opened in 1897, and required study of Jewish history, law, and literature and of Hebrew language. Henry Speaker, its first president, was a JTS graduate. Reorganized in 1928 by merging with the Hebrew Education Society of Philadelphia, Gratz added baccalaureate education to its normal school and Hebrew high school in 1952, and master's degrees in 1973.[9]

A bequest from attorney Moses Aaron Dropsie, another Philadelphian, led to the 1909 opening of Dropsie College for Hebrew and Cognate Learning (Dropsie University in 1969). A nonsectarian, non-theological institution, Dropsie offered graduate-level instruction in Hebrew and other Semitic languages, and in Biblical and Middle Eastern studies. In the

1980s, Dropsie, renamed the Annenberg Institute for Advanced Research, solved long-standing financial difficulties by becoming a research unit at the University of Pennsylvania.[10]

Several other research institutes specialized in Judaica. The Yiddish Scientific Institute -- YIVO, the *Yidisher Visenschaftlikher Institut* -- was founded in Vilna (1925); Berlin, Warsaw, and New York branches followed. YIVO mainstay Max Weinreich and his family found themselves in Denmark at the outbreak of World War II, thereby avoiding the fate of most European Jews. Upon migrating to New York, Weinreich transformed the New York branch into an autonomous research center on the culture, language, literature, and folklore of East European Jewry (1940). After World War II, YIVO acquired many documents and books stolen from European Jews by the Nazis.[11] The Leo Baeck Institute, founded in 1955 by the Council for Jews from Germany, specializes in the history of German-speaking Jews. The New York branch includes a major archive and library; the Institute also has Jerusalem and London branches. Both institutes publish research yearbooks.

Several non-theological Jewish colleges opened after World War I, including the Chicago College of Jewish Studies (1925; Spertus College of Judaica, 1970; Spertus Institute of Jewish Studies, 1993), the Jewish Teachers Institute of Cleveland (1920s, Cleveland College of Jewish Studies, after a 1947 merger with the Hebrew Teacher Training School), Hebrew Teachers College in Boston (1921; Hebrew College, 1969), and the Baltimore Hebrew College (1919).[12] These colleges, some initially controlled by local bureaus of Jewish education, prepared teachers for local day and after-school programs of Jewish education, offered adult education classes, operated summer camps, and maintained significant Judaica libraries.

The Holocaust spurred the opening of other institutions formerly located in Eastern Europe. The Rabbinical College of Telshe moved from Lithuania to Cleveland in 1941, and within a decade opened men's and women's preparatory divisions, high schools, and teachers institutes. Jewish colleges and seminaries became a haven for European Jewish refugee intellectuals. Several institutions jointly sponsored historian Ismar Elbogan, a mainstay at Berlin's Hochschule für die Wissenschaft des Judentums. Theologian Abraham Joshua Heschel moved from Germany, via Poland and England, to HUC (1940). He joined the JTS faculty in 1945.

Reconstructionism, the "fourth" movement in American Judaism, originated in the theology of Mordecai Kaplan, who taught at JTS from 1909 to 1963 -- his entire career.[13] Kaplan had turned down Steven Wise's invitation to co-found JIR in 1922, the same year in which he founded the Society for the Advancement of Judaism. Reconstructionists, like members of other Jewish movements, established a rabbinical association (Reconstructionist Rabbinical Fellowship, 1950), a congregational association (Fellowship of Reconstructionist Congregations, 1958), and a seminary (Reconstructionist Rabbinical College [RRC], Philadelphia, 1968). RRC asked its rabbinical candidates to study simultaneously for the doctorate in religion at Temple University or another Philadelphia university.[14]

Shaky finances thwarted growth of Jewish seminaries and colleges during the interwar years. But the destruction of European Jewry and Jewish educational institutions in Europe, and the uncertainties of the post-independence situation in Israel, implied an expanded international role for American Jewish seminaries. The post-war baby boom also led to significant domestic congregational and institutional growth. The seminaries responded with ambitious expansion plans. Yeshiva, under presidents Samuel Belkin (1943-1976) and Norman Lamm (1976-present), became a university in 1945, adding many professional schools and graduate divisions, including medicine (1955), and law (1976). Stern College, an undergraduate women's college, located in midtown Manhattan, opened in 1954.

Under Louis Finkelstein (president, 1940-1951; chancellor, 1951-1972), JTS added several research institutes, including the Herbert H. Lehman Institute for Judaica research (1951), the American Jewish History Center (1953), and the Melton Research

Center for Jewish Education (1960). The Seminary also opened the Cantors Institute-Seminary College of Jewish Music (1952) -- a response to HUC's 1948 initiative -- and a Graduate School. JTS expanded its teacher education, and adult and continuing education activities (including regularly scheduled radio and television programming), ventured into interfaith activities (including the Institute for Religious and Social Studies and the Conference on Science, Philosophy, and Religion), and developed an educational feeder system (including the Ramah summer camps and high school level activities). Later, JTS and Columbia University began joint programs in undergraduate education and social work.

HUC opened the American Jewish Archives (AJA), directed successively by Jacob Rader Marcus and Abraham Peck, in 1948. AJA and the American Jewish Historical Society became prime repositories for manuscripts relating to American Jewish history. HUC also opened a graduate school, and the New York campus moved to Washington Square, next to New York University, in 1969. Alfred Gottschalk succeeded Glueck as HUC-JIR president in 1971, and became chancellor in 1994.[15]

All three seminaries opened West Coast branches to accommodate the needs of a rapidly dispersing Jewish community, and Jerusalem branches to establish a presence in Israel. The University of Judaism, the Los Angeles branch of JTS, opened in 1947, and expanded throughout the 1970s to include undergraduate and graduate instruction, adult and continuing education, as well as rabbinical instruction. HUC's Los Angeles campus (1947), initially offering teacher training and adult learning, added the first two years of rabbinic education, undergraduate and graduate instruction, and a School of Jewish Communal Service (1968). Yeshiva reorganized its west-coast teachers college as Yeshiva University of Los Angeles (1977).

Under Nelson Glueck, who had conducted archaeological excavations in Palestine for many years, HUC established a presence in Jerusalem during the 1950s, opened a permanent building in Jerusalem in 1963, and expanded its Jerusalem campus during the 1980s to include the Nelson Glueck School of Biblical Archaeology and the School of Jewish Studies. JTS did not move to Israel, as requested by Prime Minister Ben Gurion, but it built an American Student Center (1962), and later required a year's residence at the center for all rabbinical students. Yeshiva University similarly offered a year's study in Jerusalem at the Gruss Institute (1977) for men and the Gold College for Women.

The post-war years also witnessed the opening of Brandeis University, in Waltham, Massachusetts (1948), in part a response to the denial of admission to Jewish students at nominally secular colleges and universities. Led by Abram Sachar (1948-1968), Brandeis matured into a university not unlike the Ivies, but with significant numbers of Jewish students, trustees, faculty members, and administrators.[16] An ongoing debate about its "Jewishness" came to a head during Evelyn Handler's presidency in the late 1980s. In an echo of the 1885 Treifa Banquet, the Brandeis community split over the introduction of shellfish and pork to the cafeteria -- part of a scheme to make the university more attractive to non-Jews. The incident contributed to Handler's subsequent departure.[17]

The Jewish teachers colleges also redefined and expanded their roles after the war. The renamed Spertus College of Judaica became the Jewish studies department of over a dozen local Chicago colleges and universities -- public, independent-secular, and Catholic -- and added a museum to its Judaica library. Other colleges entered into similar cooperative agreements, or established joint degree or reciprocal privileges programs. Relatively small enrollments made financial conditions precarious, and several colleges reorganized during the past decade.

Jewish seminaries in recent decades faced issues that also confronted American Christian seminaries, including the balancing of academic and professional-relational skills in the curriculum,[18] the relative importance of the clerical division within the expanded role of these seminaries, relations with colleges and universities -- the seminaries provided faculty members for the growing number of Jewish studies courses and departments in secular colleges and universities while competing with the same departments for the resources available for Jewish learning[19] -- and the admission and ordination of women.

HUC and RRC began to ordain women rabbinical-course graduates in the 1970s; a controversial decision by JTS to follow suit during the administration of Gerson Cohen (1972-1986) contributed to the establishment of the Union for Traditional Conservative Judaism (1984, now the Union for Traditional Judaism), and the Institute of Traditional Judaism in Mt. Vernon, New York (1989, David Weiss Halvini, rector). The Institute had a stated goal of "strengthening open-minded observant Judaism." Orthodox Judaism -- and therefore Yeshiva University and the other Orthodox seminaries and *yeshivot* -- rejects the ordination of women.[20]

Externally, Jewish seminaries and colleges claim major roles in assuring the "survival" of Judaism in America -- a theme of much writing about these seminaries -- not unsurprising in a faith that places study high among its *mitzvot*.

Endnotes

1. See Harold S. Wechsler, *The Qualified Student: A History of Selective College Admission in America, 1870-1970*. New York, NY: Wiley-Interscience, 1977.

2. Levy's contemporary, Mordechai Noah, seconded the idea. See Moshe Davis, *The Emergence of Conservative Judaism: The Historical School in 19th Century America*. Philadelphia, PA: The Jewish Publication Society of America, 1963, p. 54; and Jonathan D. Sarna, *Jacksonian Jew: The Two Worlds of Mordechai Noah*. New York, NY: Holmes and Meier, 1981, pp. 127-28.

3. Davis, *The Emergence of Conservative Judaism*, pp. 53-59; Diane A. King, "Jewish Education in Philadelphia," in Murray Friedman, ed., *Jewish Life in Philadelphia, 1830-1940*. Philadelphia,

PA: Institute for the Study of Human Issues, 1983, pp. 242-44; and Bertram Wallace Korn, *Eventful Years and Experiences: Studies in Nineteenth Century American Jewish History*. Cincinnati, OH: The American Jewish Archives, 1954, p. 181.

4. See David Philipson, *The Reform Movement in Judaism*. New York, NY: The Macmillan Company, 1931, pp. 377-99; Michael A. Meyer, "A Centennial History," in Samuel Karff, ed., *The Hebrew Union College -- Jewish Institute of Religion at 100 Years*. Cincinnati, OH: Hebrew Union College Press, 1976, pp. 7-47; James G. Heller, *Isaac Mayer Wise: His Life, Work and Thought*. New York, NY: Union of American Hebrew Congregations, 1965; Andrew F. Key, *The Theology of Isaac Mayer Wise*. Cincinnati, OH: American Jewish Archives, 1962; Israel Knox, *Rabbi in America: The Story of Isaac M. Wise*. Boston, MA: Little Brown, 1957; Max Benjamin May, *Isaac Mayer Wise: The Founder of American Judaism*. New York, NY and London, UK: G.P. Putnam's Sons, 1916; and Sefton D. Temkin, *Isaac Mayer Wise: Shaping American Judaism*. New York, NY: Oxford University Press, 1992.

5. See Jeffrey S. Gurock, *The Men and Women of Yeshiva: Higher Education, Orthodoxy, and American Judaism*. New York, NY: Columbia University Press, 1988; Gilbert Klapperman, *The Story of Yeshiva University: The First Jewish University in America*. New York, NY: The Macmillan Co., 1969; Deborah Dash Moore, *At Home in America: Second Generation New York Jews*. New York, NY: Columbia University Press, 1981, chapter 7; and Aaron Rothkoff, *Bernard Revel: Builder of American Jewish Orthodoxy*. Philadelphia, PA : Jewish Publication Society of America, 1972.

6. The two exceptions, mentioned below, are the Jewish Institute of Religion and the Institute of Traditional Judaism.

7. See Hyman J. Fliegel, "The Creation of the Jewish Institute of Religion," *American Jewish Historical Quarterly* 58 (December 1968): 260-70.

8. On Adler, see Ira Robinson, ed., *Cyrus Adler: Selected Letters*. 2 vols. Philadelphia and New York: Jewish Publication Society, 1985.

9. King, "Jewish Education in Philadelphia," pp. 245-48; and King, "A History of Gratz College, 1893-1928." Ph.D. dissertation, Dropsie University, 1979.

10. See Meir Ben-Horin, "Scholars' 'Opinions': Documents in the History of Dropsie University," in *Salo Wittmayer Baron Jubilee Volume on the Occasion of His Eightieth Birthday, English Section*. Jerusalem: American Academy for Jewish Research, 1974, I, pp. 195-96; King, "Jewish Education in Philadelphia," pp. 251-52; Herbert Parzen, "New Data on the Formation of Dropsie College," *Jewish Social Studies* 28 (1966): 131-47; and Frank J. Rubenstein, *The Early Years 1908 to 1919: The Dropsie College for Hebrew and Cognate Learning*. Philadelphia, PA: Dropsie University, 1977.

11. See Dan Miron, "Between Science and Faith: Sixty Years of the YIVO Institute," *YIVO Annual of Jewish Social Science*, 19 (1990), pp. 1-15; Solomon Liptzin, *The Maturing of Yiddish Literature*. New York, NY: Jonathan David, 1970, 218-24; idem, *YIVO in America*. New York, NY: YIVO, 1945; Liptzin, *YIVO's Way*. New York, NY: YIVO, 1943; David Rosenthal, "In the Springtime of the Modern Jewish Spirit," *Jewish Frontier* 42 (December 1975): 7-12; and Arnold Shankman, "YIVO Institute for Jewish Research," in Michael N. Dobkowski, ed., *Jewish-American Voluntary Organizations*. New York, NY, Westport, CT, and London, UK: Greenwood Press, 1986, pp. 502-05.

12. See Morris Jacob Loren, "Hebrew Higher Educational Institutions in the United States." Ph.D. dissertation: Wayne State University, 1976; and Byron L. Sherwin, *Contexts and Content: Higher Jewish Education in the United States: Spertus College of Judaica-A Case Study*. Chicago, IL: Spertus College of Judaica Press, 1987.

13. See Charles S. Liebman, "The Training of American Rabbis," *American Jewish Yearbook* 66 (1965), pp. 21-97; Jacob Rader Marcus, and Abraham J. Peck., eds., with contributions by Jeffrey S. Gurock, et al., *The American Rabbinate: A Century of Continuity and Change, 1883-1983*. Hoboken, NJ: Ktav Publishing House, 1985; and Marc Lee Raphael, *Profiles in American Judaism:*

The Reform, Conservative, Orthodox, and Reconstructionist Traditions in Historical Perspective. San Francisco, CA: Harper and Row, 1984.

14.   On Kaplan, see Emanuel S. Goldsmith, Mel Scult, and Robert M. Seltzer, eds., *The American Judaism of Mordecai M. Kaplan*. New York, NY: New York University Press, 1990; Richard Libowitz, *Mordecai Kaplan and the Development of Reconstructionism*. Lewiston, NY and Toronto, ONT: Edward Mellen Press, 1983; and Mel Scult, *Judaism Faces the Twentieth Century: A Biography of Mordecai Kaplan*. Detroit, MI: Wayne State University Press, 1993.

15.   See Ezra Goldstein, *Alfred Gottshalk's 20 Years at HUC-JIR*. New York, NY: Empire Publishing Co., 1991.

16.   See Abram L. Sachar, *A Host at Last*. Boston, MA: Little Brown, 1976.

17.   Marvin Fox, "Jewishness and Judaism at Brandeis University," *Cross Currents* 43 (Winter 1993): 464; John H. Gliedman, "Brandeis University: Reflections at Middle Age," *American Jewish History* 78 (June 1989), pp. 513-26; Louis A. Gordon, "Judaism and Jewishness at Brandeis University," *The Jewish Spectator* 57 (4) (Spring 1993): 16; and Edward S. Shapiro, *A Time for Healing: American Jewry Since World War II*. Baltimore, MD: Johns Hopkins University Press, 1992, pp. 73-76.

18.   On other JTS faculty members, see Herman Dicker, ed., *The Mayer Sulzberger-Alexander Marx Correspondence, 1904-1923*. New York, NY: Sepher-Hermon Press, 1990; Eli Ginzberg, *Keeper of the Law: Louis Ginzberg*. Philadelphia, PA: Jewish Publication Society of America, 1966; Herbert Parzen, *Architects of Conservative Judaism*. New York, NY: Jonathan David, 1964; and Baila R. Shargel, *Practical Dreamer: Israel Friedlaender and the Shaping of American Judaism*. New York, NY: The Jewish Theological Seminary of America, 1985.

19.   See Paul Ritterband and Harold S. Wechsler, *Jewish Learning in American Universities -- The First Century*. Bloomington and Indianapolis: IN: Indiana University Press, 1994.

20. See Simon Greenberg, ed., *The Ordination of Women as Rabbis: Studies and Responsa*. New York, NY: Jewish Theological Seminary of America, 1988.

Bibliographic Entries

466. Cardin, Nina Beth, and David Wolf Silverman, eds. *The Seminary at 100: Reflections on the Jewish Theological Seminary and the Conservative Movement*. New York, NY: The Rabbinical Assembly and The Jewish Theological Seminary of America, 1987.

Anthologizes responses to three key issues for members of the Conservative movement during the 1980s. First, what is the ideal relationship between JTS, the Conservative movement, and its other institutional components? Second, how do Seminary faculty members reconcile their faith with the demands of critical scholarship? Third, what visions do the current generation of leaders and observers offer for the future of Conservative Judaism?

467. Fierstein, Robert E. *A Different Spirit: The Jewish Theological Seminary of America, 1886-1902*. New York, NY: The Jewish Theological Seminary of America, 1990.

Traces the history of JTS from its 1886 founding through the 1902 reorganization, emphasizing its daily functioning. Argues that the Seminary was intellectually vigorous, if not financially robust, and that its graduates, if not numerous, played a significant role in the intellectual and institutional development of American Judaism in the twentieth century. An expansion of the argument made in item 778, in T. Hunt and J. Carper, eds., *Religious Seminaries in America: A Selected Bibliography*, 1989, p. 130.

468. Finegold, Henry. *A Time for Searching: Entering the Mainstream, 1920-1945.* Baltimore, MD: Johns Hopkins University Press, 1992.

Emphasizes the development of the key movements in American Judaism and their rabbinical seminaries during the interwar period. Shows the institutional manifestation of doctrinal and political conflicts within the movements -- the challenge to the inclusion of secular studies at Yeshiva College, the fissures within JTS brought about by the teachings of Mordecai Kaplan, the gradual reconciliation of Reform Judaism and Zionism. Explores implications of Kaplan's attempt to "refashion Judaism along communal lines."

469. Friedenberg, Robert V. "The Status of Homiletic Training in America's Rabbinical Seminaries." *Journal of Communication and Religion* 10 (March 1987): 26-33.

Describes, compares, and evaluates homiletic programs offered by American rabbinical seminaries. The extensive programs at HUC and JTS reflect the emphasis on preaching in Reform and Conservative Judaism. HUC teaches students to organize and critique their own work by exposing them to homiletic thought and rhetorical theory and then providing preaching experience. Faculty members, lamenting the lack of oratorical preparation in entering students, argued for more homiletical instruction, especially exposure to accomplished orators. The JTS program, emphasizing text interpretation and language skills, must compensate for student weaknesses in written English. RIETS students can avoid homiletical training altogether; RRC offers one relevant course. Jewish homiletic instruction usually emphasizes links between traditional Jewish sources and current events, life cycle events, and holidays. Effective preaching is high among a Reform or Conservative congregation's desiderata when seeking a new rabbi.

470. Gillman, Neil. *Conservative Judaism: The New Century.* West Orange, NJ: Behrman House, 1993.

Outlines the history of Conservative Judaism and of the role of JTS in its nurture. Discusses reasons for the movement's growth, but questions its strength, noting the absence of significant numbers of observant American Jews, the enduring difficulties in articulating positive content for the movement, and the need to maintain consensus within the movement while navigating between Orthodox and Reform Judaism. Traces these problems to decisions made in formulating the direction of the Seminary.

471. Gillman, Neil. "Inside or Outside? Emancipation and the Dilemmas of Conservative Judaism." *Judaism* 38 (Fall, 1989): 408-26.

Argues that many problems faced by Conservative Judaism arose from faculty commitment to the tenets of *Wissenschaft des Judentums*, the movement for the scientific study of Judaism that arose in the early nineteenth century. JTS, by valuing "objectivity" in Jewish scholarship over religiosity, created ambiguities for the rabbis it graduated. Sees the creation of the Graduate School in 1970 as freeing rabbinical students to confront key theological and philosophical issues previously avoided, and thereby permitting JTS to become the true fountainhead for Conservative Judaism.

472. Gillman, Neil. "Judaism's Fragile Center." *Christianity and Crisis*, 10 June 1991, pp. 198-202.

Explains that Conservative Judaism originated in JTS, an academy committed to *Wissenschaft des Judentums*, the scientific study of Judaism. This beginning accounts for the movement's "academic, clerical, and elitist" cast. Incongruities within the movement remained unaddressed until the 1980s, when the ordination of women forced JTS to confront the relative importance of tradition and modernity. In 1988, the Conservative movement issued its first statement of principles. A year later, the Seminary introduced a new Rabbinical School curriculum that emphasizes theological and religious integration.

473.   Gliedman, John A. "Brandeis University: Reflections at Middle Age." *American Jewish History* 78 (June, 1989): 513-26.

Traces the ambiguities in current discussion of the "Jewishness" of Brandeis University to its founders, who attempted to distinguish a Jewish-supported university (a "host") from a university for Jewish students. Adopting a universalist rhetoric -- Brandeis admitted all students on merit -- allowed its administrators to implement identifiably Judaic and Jewish initiatives. The ambiguity went unresolved through the 1980s, and a controversial decision to introduce non-kosher foods into the Brandeis cafeteria precipitated a campus-wide debate on the issue.

474.   Lerner, Stephen C. "Conservative Judaism's Academy." *Christianity and Crisis*, 10 June 1991, pp. 195-98.

Discusses the shift in the Seminary during the past quarter century from its mid-century role as a center of Jewish scholarship, only remotely connected to

Conservative Judaism, to its greater participation in the movement. Notes the religious commitment of the rabbinical students, who often come to the Seminary after a first career elsewhere, but adds that many students have little background in Jewish scholarship. Describes the price paid for greater curricular attention to preparing congregational rabbis, rather than scholars, including classroom uneasiness among some faculty members, and the uneven implementation of the new Rabbinical School Seminar.

475. Marcus, Jacob Rader. *United States Jewry, 1776-1985.* 4 vols. Detroit: Wayne State University Press, 1989-1993.

Describes antebellum attempts at creating a higher education institution under Jewish auspices (vol. 2, chap. 11), and the rise and development of American Jewish seminaries in the late nineteenth century (vol. 3, chap. 5). The *magnum opus* of America's most famous historian of the Jews, the set also traces the contributions of American Jewish scholars to the fields that make up Jewish scholarship, including Bible, Rabbinics, Semitics, history, and philosophy (vol. 3, chap. 20). Volume 4 analyzes developments after 1920.

476. Nadell, Pamela S. "The Fountainhead of a Movement: The Jewish Theological Seminary of America." in *Conservative Judaism in America: A Biographical Dictionary and Sourcebook*, pp. 263-94. New York, NY, Westport, CT, and London, UK: Greenwood Press, 1988.

Outlines the Seminary's history, emphasizing tension between scholarship and movement leader. Delineates Solomon Schechter's nurture of Jewish scholarship, the rabbinical and teachers programs, and the library. Notes tensions between Cyrus Adler and the Seminary faculty over faculty appointments and attitudes towards Zionism; the Seminary's precarious financial position, perhaps exacerbated by Adler's protection of dissident faculty member Mordecai Kaplan; and the curricular tension between the Seminary's emphasis on Jewish scholarship and the needs of pulpit rabbis. Shows how Louis Finkelstein expanded the Seminary's base of financial support, its functions, and its influence, and how it adjusted to its position as head of Conservative Judaism. Traces the attempts by Gerson Cohen to resolve inherent tensions, and his role in securing the ordination of women rabbis.

477. Olitzky, Kerry M., Lance Jonathan Sussman, and Malcolm H. Stern. "Hebrew Union College-Jewish Institute of Religion," in *Reform Judaism in America: A Biographical Dictionary and Sourcebook*, pp. 247-62. Westport, CT: Greenwood Press, 1993.

Juxtaposes the envisioned roles for HUC and JIR delineated by Isaac Mayer Wise and Stephen S. Wise, their respective founders, with the institutional realization. Finds that the combined institution, with its four campuses, multiple programs that complement the core rabbinical curriculum, and numerous graduates in pulpits, academic, and communal positions, exceeds the envisioned scope and influence.

478. Robinson, Ira. "Cyrus Adler and the Jewish Theological Seminary of America: Image and Reality." *American Jewish History* 78 (March 1989): 363-81.

Challenges the "received" image of Adler as a "sterile bureaucrat," rather than as a scholar, theologian, or leader by tracing his career at JTS. Adler had taught at the Seminary during the tenure of Sabato Morais, and continued as the chief administrative officer and a trustee after its 1902 reorganization. Among the factors that complicate the "received" image: Adler's correct but impersonal relationship with the JTS faculty (made more difficult after his selection first as president of Dropsie College, and later JTS -- positions to which JTS faculty members aspired), his academic specialization in Bible, a subject not emphasized in the JTS rabbinical curriculum, and his preference for creating coalitions behind the scenes.

479.   Sarna, Jonathan D. "Cyrus Adler and The Development of American Jewish Culture: The 'Scholar-Doer' as a Jewish Communal Leader." *American Jewish History* 78 (March 1989): 382-98.

Shows Adler's centrality in the Americanization and professionalization of Jewish scholarship. Rather than pursue a scholarly career, Adler, who received the first Ph.D. in Semitics awarded by an American university, opted to nurture academic institutions. American Jewish scholarship thereby flourished, but the field also changed [Americanized] in response to its new setting. Adds that Adler represents a heretofore unrecognized type of Jewish communal leader, "the scholar-doer," who could influence others because his arguments appeared "authoritative" and "non-partisan."

480.   Scult, Mel. "The World As Classroom: The Jewish Theological Seminary," in Scult, *Judaism Faces the Twentieth Century: A Biography of Mordecai M. Kaplan.* Detroit, MI: Wayne State University Press, 1993.

Discusses the ambivalent relationships between Cyrus Adler, other JTS officials, and faculty member Mordecai Kaplan, the architect of the Reconstructionist movement. Suggests that Kaplan's decision to remain among hostile faculty colleagues arose from inertia, but that his continued presence made salient his ideological radicalism. Includes a discussion of overtures to Kaplan from JIR and from HUC (pp. 268-79).

481.   Shapiro, Edward. *A Time for Healing: American Jewry Since World War II*. Baltimore, MD: Johns Hopkins University Press, 1992.

Analyzes the place of Jewish seminaries among the institutions that sponsor teaching and research in Jewish learning in America. Singles out the response of the seminaries to the rise of Jewish studies programs in secular colleges and universities, and to attacks on seminary-based scholarship by partisans of these programs. Traces the debate over the "Jewishness" of Brandeis University, especially the attitudes of the presidents, and ways that the institution attempted to retain Jewish identity while adhering to the norms accepted at secular universities.

482.   Sherwin, Byron L. *Contexts and Content: Higher Jewish Education in the United States: Spertus College of Judaica -- A Case Study*. Chicago, IL: Spertus College of Judaica Press, 1987.

Traces the evolution of the college from its inception as the Chicago College of Jewish Studies, a teacher-training college, through its years as the Jewish studies department for many Chicago-area institutions. Advocates a contraction of the consortial function, an expansion of adult learning, a single standard for credit and non-credit education, and greater educative roles for the museum and the library. The published version of item 1450 in T. Hunt and J. Carper, eds., *Religious*

Colleges and Universities in America: A Selected Bibliography (1988), p. 221.

483. Sorin, Gerald. *A Time for Building: The Third Migration, 1880-1920.* Baltimore, MD and London, UK: Johns Hopkins University Press, 1992.

Places the emergence of the three major Jewish seminaries in the context of the emerging movements within American Judaism and the creation of the institutional supports for these movements. Emphasizes the rabbi's role in helping turn of the century Jews to reconcile their American and Jewish identities.

484. Temkin, Sefton D. *Isaac Mayer Wise: Shaping American Judaism.* New York, NY: Oxford University Press, 1992.

Notes the influence of Enlightenment and American thought on Wise, and his resultant determination to create a unified American Jewry -- minor adaptations of European Judaism would not assure the survival of Judaism in America. Discusses his presidency of HUC as an attempt to shape a rabbinate for American Judaism -- not for one movement. Adds that Wise's impetuosity lost him battles, while his persistence provided him with victories.

485. Wilkes, Paul. "The Hands That Would Shape Our Souls: The Changing and Often Deeply Troubling World of America's Protestant, Catholic, and Jewish Seminaries," *The Atlantic,* 266, December 1990, pp. 59-78.

Suggests that many seminaries suffer academic decline because, pressed for students, they accept nearly all applicants with either the tuition or a recommendation from a prominent cleric. For some denominations, increases in women's attendance reduced the academic price paid for the reduction in selectivity. Quotes JTS dean Neil Gillman on the need for authenticity and spirituality, as opposed to academic knowledge, in the current generation of Jewish seminarians. Adds that JTS blends the classical, the practical, and the theoretical. Concludes that academic specialization and seminarian desires -- not necessarily congregational needs -- determine the typical seminary curriculum.

CHAPTER 19
American Bible Colleges

Virginia Lieson Brereton

The earliest American Bible schools that survive today are the Missionary Training School, founded by A.B. Simpson in New York City in 1882 (now Nyack College); Moody Bible Institute, established by Dwight L. Moody in 1886 in Chicago; and A.J. Gordon's Boston Missionary Training School (now Gordon College and Gordon-Conwell Seminary), 1889. Other existing American Bible schools are Toronto Bible College (1894), W.B. Riley's Northwestern Bible Schools in Minneapolis (1904), Bible Institute of Los Angeles (1908), and two Philadelphia schools that were later to merge, Bible Institute of Pennsylvania (1913) and Philadelphia School of the Bible (1914). The founders of the early American Bible schools traced the lineage of their institutions to a collection of nineteenth-century European missionary training schools, most notably Kaiserswerth in Germany (1836), a Lutheran deaconess training institution; Mildmay, near London and dating from the mid-nineteenth century; and the H. Grattan Guinness East London Institute for Home and Foreign Missions (1872).[1]

In their early years the American Bible schools had a number of close family relatives: a number of missionary training schools for women (the first we know of was the Baptist Missionary Training School in Chicago, 1881); and a collection of schools for the training of deaconesses, YMCA and YWCA secretaries, and Salvation Army workers. In fact, there were no strict lines separating these types of schools from each other; the clearest thing that could be said about them was that none of these institutions was a college or theological seminary. None of them granted a recognized bachelor's degree, though some offered a certificate for the completion of a stated course of training, usually one or two years. The schools that would later participate in a "Bible school movement" were almost indistinguishable from the rest: all the schools made study of the English Bible central to their curricula, emphasized practical experience to supplement classroom learning, welcomed almost all comers, and touted the virtues of a relatively brief but effective period of training. For future Bible schools the chief identifying characteristic was often their premillennialist, often dispensationalist theology.

The religious training schools had roots in the missionary training schools of Europe, but they must also be understood as arising out of American circumstances. One set of circumstances was religious. For American Protestantism, the nineteenth century was a period of repeated swellings of missionary, evangelistic waves. Late in the century Protestants experienced a renascence of their perennial interest in the Bible; they were also motivated by a strong conviction that numerous places on earth needed "Christianizing": the continents of Asia, Africa, and Latin America; the American frontier; and, increasingly, American cities, where growing numbers of immigrants had gathered, many of them Catholic. If the unevangelized areas of the world were to feel the influence of Protestantism, the churches would have to launch myriads of workers, lay as well as ordained, women as well as men -- a virtual army of evangelists and missionaries.[2]

But these workers would have to be trained, and here the second set of circumstances intersects with the first. If America was in the grips of a recurrent religious revival, it was also enmeshed in a more or less constant educational revival. Perhaps it would be more accurate to call it a revival of *schooling*. The last half of the nineteenth century saw the rise of the universities, including the public universities; the spread of higher education for women; the reform of education in law, medicine, and the ministry, and the emergence of new forms of professional education, in business, social work, engineering, and teaching; the growth of public high schools; and the creation of correspondence schools, extension education, and evening schools for students who could not come to campus. Given this mushrooming of schools, it is not surprising that religious leaders, too, waxed enthusiastic about founding new educational institutions.

The early Bible schools were small and informal. In the beginning, they seldom possessed special buildings but rather found lodging in a church basement or vestry, in an old house, or even on the floor over a commercial establishment. Their student bodies, often predominantly female, were small, sometimes a mere handful of students -- though, as time went on and if a school became better known, it might attract as many as twenty or thirty students in a class. (Student bodies in denominational schools tended to remain small, especially if the denomination itself was small and new.) The faculty was usually part-time, with only the founder and maybe one other full-time teacher. Students attended as duties and other circumstances dictated, sometimes even starting in the middle of a school year or leaving in the middle. The schools charged no tuition (following then-current tradition of the theological seminary). But students often had to work to pay for their living expenses. Occasionally a Bible school had a manual training component to defray its expenses (e.g., Johnson Bible School in Tennessee). Many Bible schools began as evening or as correspondence schools and only developed day schools later on. The American

Home Bible Institute started out in 1921 as a correspondence school, for instance.

The curriculum varied according to the particular convictions of the founder or founders, and what teaching personnel were available. But courses in the English Bible were a constant, as was some sort of practical work in the surrounding community, teaching Bible or Sunday school classes, leading choirs, visiting from door to door, or holding street services. In 1912, for instance, Missionary Training Institute students at Nyack, New York, were visiting prisons and hospitals, organizing a Christian Endeavor Society in a "colored" Methodist church, teaching a class for Italian immigrants in Nyack, and exhorting drinkers in the saloons of Nyack, Sparkill, and Piermont to adjourn to the Nyack Gospel Mission.[3] Beyond that, there might be courses in missions, pedagogy, doctrine, music, and an early form of sociology. If the educational level of the students was particularly low (as in the early pentecostal schools), there might be offerings as basic as arithmetic or penmanship. The devotional life -- worship, prayer groups, hymn singing -- was at least as important as the academic.

Early students tended to be older than later students in Bible schools; they were often in their early twenties and had already held a job as clerk, secretary, or teacher. Typically they lived at home or in rooming houses. Owing to their relative maturity and the fact that much of their time was spent away from school, their private lives were not closely supervised.

It is a little anachronistic to talk about the academic level of these institutions, at a time when colleges might have preparatory departments larger than the college proper, or secondary schools might boast small college departments. The educational boundaries blurred almost everywhere, and nowhere was this truer than in religious training schools. The student body might well include a college graduate or two and certainly a few students who had attended college briefly, some high school graduates, and probably a large number of people with a grammar school education.

Bible school or religious training school leaders saw their endeavors as supplementing rather than replacing the more conventional education of four-year college and three-year seminary. Their schools, they argued, served a different student body, one more female, generally less educated, and often lower middle-class. The training schools were not educating the pastors, the "generals" for the Christian army; rather, they were training the laity -- the "foot soldiers" in that army. In their modesty, however, they were sometimes ingenuous, for they implicitly criticized the exclusiveness of the seminaries by advertising the inclusiveness of their own student bodies and were known to describe the classical curriculum of the seminaries with its emphasis on Hebrew and Greek as tedious, stultifying, and impractical. Certainly the supporters of seminaries perceived the training schools as competitors and as intentional reproaches to their way of doing things; they sometimes disparaged the training schools for being "short-cut" institutions.

It is true that most early Bible schools did not set out to train pastors (one exception was the Advent Christian Boston Bible School, founded 1897). But some male students from denominations that did not require graduation from college and a theological seminary as prerequisites for the ministry used the school as a springboard into the pastorate. It was quite common for Baptist students, for instance, to go from Moody Bible Institute into the ministry.[4] In the early 1900s, accordingly, some of the schools started formalizing this *de facto* preparation for the ministry by introducing a two- or three-year pastoral course in addition to the courses that already existed.

With the emergence of the fundamentalist movement in the early 1900s, Bible schools took on a more distinctive identity as the standard bearers of the movement. Moody Bible Institute in particular became known as the "West Point of Fundamentalism."[5] Increasingly the Bible schools became identified with a certain group of conservative doctrines such as the inerrancy of Scripture, the second coming of Christ, the substitutionary atonement, the bodily resurrection of Christ, and the authenticity of the biblical miracles. It became more usual for the oldest of the schools to erect the buildings for a modest campus. For a while the Bible schools had the field in conservative evangelical education largely to themselves; most Protestant colleges and seminaries had come under the control of the more progressive elements in the denominations and turned unacceptably liberal. Another circumstance that increased the distinctiveness of Bible schools was the virtual disappearance of their sister religious training schools as a discernible category. In the late 1920s or early 1930s, most of those schools closed, merged with an already existing college or seminary, or were upgraded into colleges or seminaries.[6]

Though a formal organization of Bible schools awaited the late 1940s, an informal network of Bible school workers and students existed from the 1920s (if not earlier). Teachers and administrators visited and lectured at each other's schools; faculty and students often spent time in more than one Bible school; and organizers of new schools studied the older schools, particularly Moody Bible Institute, which became a model for its sister institutions. Partly owing to the influence of Moody, the Bible school curriculum became regularized in the 1910s and 1920s: typically students could select the General Bible, Missions, Bible Teachers, Pastors, or Music courses. As some of the schools got larger, students chose more specialized classes -- in Jewish evangelism, for instance, missionary aviation, or work with children. Practical work continued as in the early schools, but was more likely to be formally supervised, perhaps by a full-time director.[7] Student bodies got younger and were more frequently housed in dormitories. A stricter regimen was imposed on their lives outside classes.

Bible schools played important roles in the formation and organization of the evangelical world. At a time when conservative evangelicals were short on money and also nervous about the potential of education to destroy the faith of young people, the Bible schools were inexpensive to run and were regarded as religiously and morally "safe." For denominations (e.g., Advent Christians) or denomination-like entities (the Christian and Missionary Alliance), they served as headquarters and organizing centers and sources of leadership. They also acted as the educational and launching centers for regional organizations -- for instance, conservative Baptists in Minnesota or independent Bible churches surrounding the Birmingham Bible College in central Alabama.[8] Outside of denominations, Bible schools -- especially the nondenominational ones -- have fulfilled the function of informal headquarters for groups of like-minded Protestants. They have become parachurch organizations. This is particularly true of Moody Bible Institute (MBI); generations of Christians have identified themselves with the teachings and teachers of MBI and its various outreach programs, such as its radio, its films, and extension department -- more than they have identified themselves with a particular denomination.

The 1930s, a rough period in education generally, dealt its share of difficulties to the Bible schools, especially to those that had achieved some prosperity (and with it some debt) in the 1920s. However, the majority of Bible schools benefited from the fact that they had always been low-budget operations and could cut expenses without greatly altering their goals and identities.

The late 1940s mark a point of departure for the Bible school movement. Several factors came together to greatly alter the movement. First, conservative evangelicals began their most serious organization to date, the National Association of Evangelicals, established in 1942. The new association formed several committees to deal with such areas as publishing, missions, and education, indicating the beginnings of efforts to regularize these activities. Second, a sizeable portion of the Bible school constituency was achieving upward mobility, which meant among other things that they wanted their higher education (or that of their children) to yield respectable certification, which in turn meant that the Bible schools needed to be accredited in some form so that they could award bachelor's degrees that would be recognized at the graduate level. But for the Bible schools accreditation was not a simple matter of securing the finances; even where sufficient funds were forthcoming, there was a persisting tension. Bible school leaders had traditionally prided themselves on rejecting "worldly" educational standards. One requirement that they pointedly spurned was the educational endowment so much emphasized by college-accrediting associations; Bible school leaders who were convinced that the Lord would come any minute regarded it as futile and faithless to "lay up treasure" for the future.

For a while Bible school arrangements had worked quite well; lower middle-class students trained there and then found vocations in a conservative evangelical opportunity structure. For conservative evangelicals more self-conscious about educational credentials, there were a few "safe" Christian liberal arts colleges (Wheaton, Houghton, Gordon by the 1920s) and seminaries (Northern and Eastern Baptist Theological Seminary; Evangelical Theological College/Dallas Seminary).

But as the rest of education came to be increasingly accreditation-conscious and well-defined (institutions had to be either four-year colleges offering a B.A. or B.S. or post-graduate schools offering a master's or doctorate), Bible school leaders had to rethink their positions. In addition, after World War II the federal government poured a great deal of money into higher education through its support of returning GIs; the Bible schools needed to attract their share of these older students. In the late 1940s the leaders of the most prominent Bible schools began to organize an accrediting association, with the result that the Accrediting Association of Bible Institutes and Bible Colleges came into being in 1947 (the name later became American Association of Bible Colleges [AABC]). As a result of accreditation there came to be more emphasis on the liberal arts, endowments and financial stability generally, faculty with advanced degrees in certain academic specialties (versus the experience in evangelism that had previously been privileged); libraries had to be upgraded, science labs and athletic facilities to be added, and more support personnel had to be hired. Many Bible schools that had begun primarily as evening schools and correspondence departments switched to almost exclusive concentration on regularly matriculated day students.

Increasingly, then, Bible schools became Bible colleges, and in recent years they have increasingly sought accreditation from regional associations (those that accredit secondary schools and colleges) as well as from the AABC. Regional accreditation has represented accommodation on both sides, from the side of Bible colleges and from the regional associations, which have gotten somewhat more broad-minded about the diversity of educational purposes and methods.[9] At the same time, unaccredited, unaccreditable institutions, mostly for lay people who often attend part-time and at night, continue to be organized, often in connection with a particular church. As in the beginning, this simplest form of the Bible school, inexpensive and flexible, has proven to be useful for groups that lack funds and educational resources: African Americans, Latinos, and working-class whites.

Until recently Southern Bible schools have not received much attention from scholars. They are a later development on the educational scene than the schools in the North. Except for the Toccoa Falls Institute (Christian and Missionary Alliance) which dates from 1913, the oldest and most prominent schools date from the 1920s, 1930s and 1940s (Columbia Bible College, 1923, and Birmingham Bible College, 1942). They resembled their Northern counterparts in many respects; in fact, the formation of many had been influenced by Northern Bible conference teachers and they took many of their cues from Moody Bible Institute and other prominent Northern schools. But they had to adapt to particular conditions in the South, such as the region's pronounced denominationalism. The Southern schools also drew particularly heavily for faculty and administration on the Dallas Seminary.[10]

Endnotes

1. "Missionary Training Colleges," *Christian Alliance* 1 (May 1888): 76; "Missionary Training Schools -- Do Baptists Need Them? A Discussion," *Baptist Quarterly Review* 12 (January 1890): 77; and C.F. Schlienz, *The Pilgrim Institution of Chrischona, of Basle, in Switzerland*. London: John Farquhar Shaw, 1850.

2. A.T. Pierson, *The Crisis of Missions: Or, the Voice Out of the Cloud*. New York: Robert Carter and Bros., 1886.

3. G. Jennings, "Students' Evangelistic Work," *Alliance Weekly*, 29 June 1912, p. 204.

4. Virginia Lieson Brereton, *Training God's Army: The American Bible School, 1880-1940*. Bloomington: Indiana University Press, 1990, p. 67.

5. E.g., William Cobb, "The West Point of Fundamentalism," *American Mercury* 16 (1929): 104-12.

6. Virginia Lieson Brereton, "Preparing Women For the Lord's Work," in Hilah F. Thomas and Rosemary Skinner Keller, eds. *Women in New Worlds: Historical Perspectives on the Wesleyan Tradition*. Nashville, TN: Abingdon, 1981.

7. Brereton, *Training God's Army*, p. 111.

8. William V. Trollinger, Jr. *God's Empire: William Bell Riley and Midwestern Fundamentalism*. Madison: University of Wisconsin Press, 1990; Dwain Waldrep, "Fundamentalism, Interdenominationalism, and The Birmingham School of the Bible," *Alabama Review*, forthcoming.

9. Cocking, Herbert, "Bible School Accreditation by the North Central Association: 1970-1970." Ph.D. dissertation. University of Michigan, 1982.

10. Glass, William Robert, "The Development of Northern Patterns of Fundamentalism in the South, 1900-1950." Ph.D. dissertation, Emory University, 1991. Dwain Waldrep, a doctoral student at Auburn University, is exploring the issue of Southern Bible schools with Birmingham Bible College as his focus.

Bibliographic Entries

486. American Association of Bible Colleges. *Directory*. Wheaton, IL.: American Association of Bible Colleges.

     Lists the colleges that are currently members of the accrediting association of Bible colleges.

487. Balmer, Randall. "We Do Bible Better." *Christianity Today*, 35, 16 September 1991, pp. 22-26.

     Examines the history and role of the Bible school, using interviews and visits at the Multnomah School of the Bible, Portland, Oregon, as the focus.

488. Barcalow, Douglas Allen. "Continuing Education in the Bible School Movement: A Historical Study of Five Institutions (Evening Schools, Correspondence, Extension)." Ed.D. dissertation. Northern Illinois University, 1986.

     Examines the non-day-school programs at Columbia Bible College, Moody Bible Institute, Philadelphia College of the Bible, Washington Bible College, and William Tyndale College. These and other institutions began with strong offerings for untraditional students, but have switched in the past few decades, partly under the pressures of accreditation, to emphasis on regular day programs.

489. Brereton, Virginia Lieson. *Training God's Army: The American Bible School, 1880-1940*. Bloomington, IN: Indiana University Press, 1990.

     A revision of the writer's dissertation, with Biola College added as a focus.

490. Cocking, Herbert. "Bible School Accreditation by the North Central Association: 1970-1980." Ph.D. dissertation. University of Michigan, 1982.

    Examines the changes that took place in the North Central Association's accrediting criteria toward a more inclusive definition of higher education; compares Ft. Wayne Bible College's unsuccessful bid for North Central Association accreditation in 1969 and St. Paul Bible College's successful application in 1980.

491. Crosby, James Ray. "Factors in Student Retention Among Selected Member Institutions of the American Association of Bible Colleges." Ed.D. dissertation. Michigan State University, 1985.

    Locates the factors that predict a student will stay in Bible college: she is female, has graduated from a Christian high school, has a definite vocation in mind, and gets good grades.

492. Evearitt, Daniel J. *Body and Soul: Evangelism and the Social Concern of A.B. Simpson.* Camp Hill, PA: Christian Publications, 1994.

    Examines an underemphasized dimension of the life and work of the founder of the Missionary Training Institute.

493. Gardner, H. Lynn. "Ozark Christian College: 1942-1990." Ed.D. dissertation. University of Arkansas, 1991.

    Traces the history of a Christian churches and Churches of Christ institution that was founded as Ozark Bible College.

494. Glass, William Robert. "The Development of Northern Patterns of Fundamentalism in the South, 1900-1950." Ph.D. dissertation. Emory University, 1991.

Describes the rise of a "Southern" variety of fundamentalism, stimulated by Bible teachers from the North, especially in the years after 1920 and 1930; prepares the ground for future studies of Southern Bible schools; discusses the histories of Columbia Bible College, Toccoa Falls Institute, John Brown College, and Evangelical Bible College (later Dallas Seminary).

495. Hannah, John David. "The Social and Intellectual History of the Origins of the Evangelical Theological College." Ph.D. dissertation. University of Texas at Dallas, 1988.

Explores thoroughly the early history of an institution that was to educate the faculty and leadership for many Southern Bible schools.

496. Jacobs, Paul David. "The History and Development of the Criswell College, 1971-1990." Ph.D. dissertation. University of North Texas, 1992.

Gives a history of Criswell College, founded in 1971 by W.A. Criswell, a prominent Dallas Baptist pastor.

497. Jenkins, Jerry B. *Generous Impulse: the Story of George Sweeting*. Chicago: Moody Press, 1987.

Recounts the life of the president of Moody Bible Institute between 1971 and 1986; Sweeting was also an alumnus of the school.

498. Kallgren, Robert C. "Bible Colleges: Their Present Health and Possible Futures." Ed.D. dissertation. University of South Carolina, 1988.

   Finds that the future of Bible colleges is uncertain. Bible college enrollments had declined in the eight years before 1987, whereas the enrollments of other Protestant evangelical liberal arts colleges and seminaries had risen.

499. Kallgren, Robert C. "The Invisible Colleges." *Christianity Today*, 35, 16 September 1991, pp. 27-28.

   Offers a digest of the author's doctoral dissertation.

500. Martin, John, Alfred. "The Last Years of Dallas Bible College (1983-1985)." Ph.D. dissertation. University of North Texas, 1991.

   Examines the circumstances of the closing of Dallas Bible College, founded in 1940.

501. Mathisen, James Albert. "The Moody Bible Institute: A Case Study in the Dilemmas of Institutionalization." Ph.D. dissertation. Northwestern University, 1979.

   Explores the organizational difficulties experienced by Moody Bible Institute, partly as a result of its rapid expansion, at various points in its history.

502. McKinney, Larry James. "The Fundamentalist Bible Schools as an Outgrowth of the Changing Patterns of Protestant Revivalism, 1882-1920." *Religious Education* 84 (Winter 1989): 589-605.

   Gives the gist of the writer's dissertation.

503.   McKinney, Larry James. "An Historical Analysis of the Bible College Movement During Its Formative Years." Ph.D. dissertation. Temple University, 1986.

Examines the emergence of the Bible school movement out of the late nineteenth-century revival; explores the commonalities among four Bible schools: Gordon College, Nyack College, Moody Bible Institute, and Philadelphia College of the Bible.

504.   Moncher, Gary Richard. "The Bible College and American Moral Culture." Ph.D. dissertation. University of California, Berkeley, 1987.

Examines the "culture" of the Bible college through participant observation and interviews at seven Bible colleges.

505.   Moothart, Lorene. *Achieving the Impossible ...with God: the Life Story of Dr. R.A. Forrest.* Toccoa Falls, GA: Toccoa Falls Institute, 1956.

Gives a biography of the Christian and Missionary Alliance leaders and founder of Toccoa Falls Institute.

506.   Trollinger, William Vance, Jr. *God's Empire: William Bell Riley and Midwestern Fundamentalism.* Madison, WI: University of Wisconsin Press, 1990.

Provides a scholarly history of the Northwestern Bible School, founded by a foremost leader of 1920s and 1930s fundamentalism. Shows how the school developed as a spearhead for the fundamentalist organizations in Minneapolis and the state of Minnesota.

507.   Wiles, David E. "Miami Christian College: Thirty Years of History, 1939-1979." *Communicare*, Fall, 1979, pp. 8-9.

508.   Winters, Richard William. "Metamorphosis of a Dream: the History of Appalachian Bible College (1950-1983)." Ed.D. dissertation. Virginia Polytechnic Institute and State University, 1985.

Documents how the Appalachian Bible College developed from an institution resembling a home missionary organization to a more conventional educational establishment.

CHAPTER 20
Higher Education in the United Methodist Church

L. Glenn Tyndall

I. Introduction

Among the many contributions made by the founder of Methodism to his American followers was a concern for nourishment of the whole person, in mind as well as in body and spirit. John Wesley is reported to have said: "Let us unite the two so long divided: knowledge and vital piety." Wesley bequeathed an interest in education that was never to be seen in a narrow sense only as religious education. While the Sunday School movement became a vital part of the Methodist development in education, general education of all people was also a major concern of the early Methodists.

As the educational level of the general population continued to rise, it was inevitable that the focus of the infant denomination would eventually turn to higher education. In the just over 200 years since Methodism's early abortive attempt to establish a college, the denomination has continued to grow in its focus on higher education, becoming a leader within the field in the United States. At present, the United Methodist Church has an established relationship with 123 schools, colleges, universities, and theological seminaries, representing a total student enrollment of approximately a quarter of a million students.[1] Methodist educational institutions have been started in 44 of the 50 states.

Our consideration turns now to the historical development of the unique features of United Methodist higher education in order to track how it parallels the history of the denomination. The current counterpart of the early Methodist movement is now a major Protestant denomination in the last decade of the twentieth century, bearing a new name, the United Methodist Church. It is therefore necessary to look at the progression of splits and mergers that led to the church we know today.

In order to talk about United Methodist higher education, we must consider such topics as the split between the Methodist Episcopal Church and the Methodist Episcopal Church, South; the Methodist Protestant Church; the Evangelical United Brethren and its predecessor denominations; and the education of African Americans. We will look first at the parts that came together to make up the Methodist Church in 1939 (merger of the Methodist Episcopal Church, the Methodist Episcopal Church, South, and the Methodist Protestant Church); then turn to the mergers resulting in the Evangelical United Brethren in 1946 (the Evangelical Church and the United Brethren in Christ); and finally describe the important role played by the people called Methodist in the education of African Americans. In addition, some attention will be focused on the development of United Methodist theological education within each of these traditions of Methodism.

II. Methodists and Higher Education

The first attempt at starting an educational institution was the opening of Cokesbury College in 1787 with 70 students in Abingdon, Maryland, under the guidance of the early Methodist leader, Francis Asbury. Actually the famous 1784 Christmas Conference in Baltimore, which created the Methodist Episcopal Church, also developed plans for Cokesbury College. Asbury was not sure of the value of education, but went along with the enterprise because of the experience of his mentor, John Wesley, in England. Although it was called a "college," it really resembled what we would call a preparatory school. It was a courageous but ill-fated venture. When the facilities burned down in 1795 after eight years of moderately successful operation, Asbury thought that it might be a sign from God that the Methodists were not intended to build colleges.[2] A second feeble attempt was made to move Cokesbury into a building in Baltimore in 1795, but it too burned down the following year. A third try was made in Baltimore with Asbury College, chartered in 1818, but it died "for want of money and of a mongrel religion," a reference to the fact that quite a few of the original teachers were not Methodist.[3]

As a result of this failed attempt, the development of higher education by the Methodists was relatively dormant until the second quarter of the nineteenth century (1830). Although they later became leaders in the higher-education movement, the Methodists were latecomers when compared with their peers in the United States. The chartering of Randolph-Macon College in 1830 was the establishment of the oldest permanent institution of higher learning by American Methodists. This monumental event came 65 years after the first Baptist institution, 84 years after the first Presbyterian, 137 years after the first Protestant Episcopal college, and 194 years after the first Congregational college.[4] The founding of Emory College in Oxford, Georgia, followed soon after.

Wesleyan University in Connecticut was chartered one year later than Randolph-Macon College (1831), and opened the same year, one year before Randolph-Macon actually opened its doors. Also in that decade, the Methodist Episcopal Church started Dickinson College and Allegheny College in Pennsylvania, McKendree College in Illinois, and Indiana Asbury College (later Depauw University). Dickinson College actually dates back to 1783, but it was under Presbyterian influence until 1832, when its control was transferred to the Baltimore Conference and the Philadelphia Conference of the Methodist Episcopal Church. Likewise, Allegheny College started out with the Presbyterians, but lost out to Presbyterian competitors in Pennsylvania, closing its doors in 1831, and opening as a Methodist institution the following year.[5]

It is also interesting to note that the Methodists were cognizant of the educational needs of women, needs that began to be addressed during this same period. The oldest college for women in the world is Wesleyan College in Macon, Georgia, which was started in 1836, and became a college of the Methodist Episcopal Church in 1839.[6] Another Methodist college for women was established in Greensboro, North Carolina, with classes beginning in 1846. Both of these institutions are still in operation, although Greensboro College has been co-educational since 1954.[7]

The small church college has, for the most part, been essentially a frontier institution. The reason that small church colleges multiplied the way that they did in newly settled areas is clear when we examine the general situation presented by the American frontier. People who lived in these areas were uniformly poor, and sending their sons to elite eastern institutions was financially out of the question. Therefore, education was brought to the frontier as the only means for frontier youth to receive training. With the closing of the frontier, the founding of small church colleges came to a virtual standstill. The educational effort of the Methodists in later years, like other major churches, has been in the direction of amalgamating small colleges and strengthening existing institutions.[8]

As the church moved west, institutions of higher education were soon to follow. The Methodist Episcopal Church founded Iowa Wesleyan College, one of Iowa's first colleges, in 1842. Baker University in Kansas was founded in 1858. Likewise, Hamline University in Minnesota, and Lawrence College in Wisconsin, were established in 1847. The University of Denver was founded in 1864 in Colorado, and Willamette University in Oregon began in 1842. In every case, these colleges were established even before their respective territories became a state. In 1851, California Wesleyan College (later College of the Pacific and now University of the Pacific) was established prior to California becoming a state, and eighteen years before California had a state university. This was the first college of liberal arts and the first medical school in California.[9]

Institutions of higher education were also begun by the Methodist Episcopal Church in border states, and after the split in the denomination in 1844 creating the Methodist Episcopal Church, South, these schools remained with the northern church. The University of Chattanooga, and Tennessee Wesleyan College, plus Union College in Kentucky, were all established by 1839.[10] Other colleges were founded in the decades just before the Civil War: Ohio Wesleyan and Northwestern in the North, and Trinity (later Duke), Wofford (in South Carolina), and Central (in Missouri) in the South. Drew, founded in 1867, was a theological seminary only at first, but later expanded to become a university. Soon after, Syracuse and Boston Universities opened in the northeast.[11]

Although a number of other collegiate institutions had been established in the South, there were no universities as such. Vanderbilt University, opened in 1875 in Nashville, was funded with a major gift from Cornelius Vanderbilt. Vanderbilt quickly became recognized as one of the quality private institutions in the South. It was created under the auspices of several Annual Conferences, and soon was controlled by the General Conference of the southern church. In 1905, however, a complicated legal struggle ensued when the chancellor and trustees tried to wrest control from the ecclesiastical body, the Methodist Episcopal Church, South.[12] The case was finally settled in favor of the university, which continued to flourish through additional substantial gifts.

Primarily because of the loss of Vanderbilt University, the southern church felt the need to create two new universities in the South, Southern Methodist University in Dallas in 1911, and Emory University in Atlanta (Emory College in Oxford, Georgia was much older, and remained there after the University was established to join the Candler School of Theology in 1914).[13]

In 1924, brothers James B. and Benjamin N. Duke, heirs of the Duke tobacco fortune, proposed a plan for a new Christian university in the South. Dangling their tobacco millions as bait, the Duke brothers traveled around the South, hoping to find an existing institution that would serve as the foundation for their new university. The institution that was chosen and moved to Durham, North Carolina, was Trinity College, then located in the small town of Trinity, North Carolina.[14] At the time, Trinity College was thought to be the strongest liberal arts college in the South, with property and endowment of $6,000,000. The Duke family had long been strong benefactors of Trinity College, but their gift of $40,000,000 for the support of the new Duke University was at the time the largest ever made for the furtherance of Christian education in the United States.[15]

In the early nineteenth century, some African Americans withdrew from the parent denomination to form their own Methodist groups. But the first major schism that developed in the Methodist Episcopal Church came about in 1830, resulting in the formation of the Methodist Protestant Church. This schism has been widely seen as an attempted reform movement within the Methodist Episcopal Church which failed. The primary reasons for the schism were focused on polity and practice, a reform directed against the inherited Methodist governance.[16] The protests of the reformers, in part, insisted on the further

Americanization of the Methodist movement, but those who wanted to retain the English flavor won out, and the reformers left to form their own church. This schism, along with the subsequent division between the northern church and the southern church over slavery, was to divide the Methodist denomination for more than a century.

While the Methodist Protestant Church was in existence as a denomination, it continued to expand in the area of higher education in much the same way as its former partners. Adrian College in Michigan was founded in 1859 by Methodist Protestants (actually at the beginning it was a part of the Wesleyan Methodist Church but ended up with the Methodist Protestants). The school with the largest resources within the Methodist Protestant Church was Western Maryland College, founded in 1867 in Westminster, Maryland. In a unique relationship with the state of Maryland, the school provides state-supported teacher scholarships that are available even today.[17] A third college was begun in North Carolina, High Point University, in 1924. When the three major strands of Methodist groups reunited in 1939, the Methodist Protestant Church brought with it five institutions: one seminary (which later became Wesley Theological Seminary in Washington, DC), three senior colleges, and one junior college.[18]

III. Evangelical United Brethren and Higher Education

Just as three strands of Methodist folk found themselves coming together in 1939 to reunite and form the Methodist Church, there were four predecessor bodies which in 1946 joined to form the Evangelical United Brethren. Less than a generation later, the Methodist Church and the Evangelical United Brethren would meet in historic session in 1968 to bring to birth a totally new creation, the United Methodist Church. In order to more fully understand and appreciate the development of higher education for United Methodists, it is necessary now to turn to specific consideration of higher education in the Evangelical United Brethren Church.

The predecessors of the Evangelical United Brethren Church were the following: the Church of the United Brethren in Christ, the Evangelical Association, the United Evangelical Church, and the Evangelical Church. The Church of the United Brethren in Christ was founded in 1800, but its roots may go back even a half-century earlier.[19] It was formed primarily as a revolt against the lack of deeply personal pietistic religion among the established churches of eighteenth-century America. Philip William Otterbein became pastor of the Reformed Church in Lancaster, Pennsylvania, having had a personal experience resulting in his assurance of salvation. This was an important doctrine for him, and led him into a conflict with his Reformed brethren and into a new denomination.[20]

There was a lack of interest at first regarding the starting of formal educational institutions. But in 1845, an important figure, The Reverend Lewis Davis in Ohio, emerged as an advocate for higher education, and his leadership resulted in the founding of Otterbein University in Westerville, Ohio, in 1847.[21] Mt. Pleasant College in Pennsylvania opened the next year, but its assets were transferred to Otterbein ten years later.

Following 1848, schools and colleges associated with the United Brethren in Christ Church proliferated. Between 1847 and 1913, thirty institutions emerged, including four universities, twelve colleges, seven seminaries, six academies, and one institute.[22] The early colleges in this denomination intentionally avoided the label of "preacher factories," for they were meant to provide an education for all the sons and daughters within their fellowship; formal ministerial education, as with the Methodists, would come later.

The Evangelical Association grew out of the influence of the Great Revival and the spiritual enthusiasm it engendered. The denomination was founded in 1800 by Jacob Albright and his followers among the Germans of Pennsylvania.[23] They shared the suspicion of formal education of the United Brethren in Christ, but their Manifesto of 1843 professed support for higher education and theological education, though it qualified that support by stressing that such education must be under the supervision of "Divine unction and grace."[24] They felt that institutions under their control could avoid the "cold hearts and evil minds" that they witnessed in other colleges in general.

The Evangelical Association's higher education focus merged with its concern for ministerial education as it brought into being the Albright Seminary in New Berlin, Pennsylvania, in 1853, and Union Biblical Institute in Naperville, Illinois, in 1872.[25] This institute, which was similar to biblical institutes begun by other denominations, later became Evangelical Theological Seminary; after the union with the Methodist Church in 1968, it was combined with Garrett Biblical Institute in Evanston, Illinois, becoming Garrett-Evangelical Theological Seminary.

Relationships within the Evangelical Association became problematic, however, and a schism was inevitable. Thus the United Evangelical Church was founded at Naperville, Illinois, on November 30, 1894, forming the third of the predecessors of the Evangelical United Brethren Church.[26] Union Seminary in Pennsylvania had been founded by the Evangelical Association. The property belonged to the Evangelical Association, but the majority of faculty and students were sympathetic to the United Evangelical Church. The United Evangelical Church purchased the college in 1894. It stayed at New Berlin until 1902, when it merged with Albright College and moved to Myerstown, Pennsylvania. An Evangelical Association college at Naperville, North-Western College, began to experience schismatic tendencies, and so a disgruntled minority moved to establish a new institution of The United Evangelical Church at LeMars, Iowa, in 1900, Western Union College (later Westmar).[27]

The schism was overcome in 1922 when the Evangelical Association and the United Evangelical Church reunited after an extended process that had begun in 1911. This resulted in the formation of the Evangelical Church.[28] Schuylkill Seminary, an Evangelical Association school, became a college and merged with the United Evangelical Albright College in 1922. After the new Evangelical Church was formed in 1922, the college moved to Reading, Pennsylvania, and the name was changed in 1928 to Albright College of The Evangelical Church.

In November 1946, seven years after the three-fold reunion of the Methodist Church, the first General Conference of the Evangelical United Brethren Church was held to celebrate the union of the United Brethren in Christ and the Evangelical Church.[29] In spite of what were at times emotional differences, the two traditions were remarkably similar, and their eventual union was perhaps inevitable. Both partners of the union had originally preached to German-speaking people in German. Both were from the same geographical areas. Both called all to a fundamental, Protestant, evangelical faith. Both were influenced by the polity and doctrine of the Methodists. And both were markedly similar in their approach to higher education: hesitancy and suspicion at first, but eventual acceptance of the mission of higher education with faith and devotion.[30]

The 1946 General Conference also established a Study of Higher Education, which was set in motion by the Board of Christian Education one year later. The Board's goals were to establish an additional Bible school, establish standards for accreditation, set educational and spiritual objectives, determine a geographical allocation of territory for its respective institutions, and place all three theological schools of the new Evangelical United Brethren Church under a single Board of Trustees.[31] This study was conducted by an employed consultant, whose name was attached to the final report, the Gage report. Looking at the extant eight colleges and three theological seminaries in 1947, the report concluded that the higher education enterprise was a necessary part of the mainstream of the new Church, and the Church must affirm that enterprise proudly and unapologetically.[32]

The 1950s witnessed further developments in the Evangelical United Brethren Church. At LeMars, Iowa, Westmar College and York College merged under Westmar's name in 1955.

Shenandoah College moved from Dayton, Virginia, to Winchester, Virginia, and changed its name to Shenandoah Junior College and Conservatory of Music. In the late 1980s this school became Shenandoah University. In 1954 Evangelical Theological Seminary in Reading, Pennsylvania, and Bonebrake Theological Seminary in Dayton, Ohio, merged under the name United Theological Seminary in Dayton. Evangelical Theological Seminary continued on its own in Naperville, Illinois. A $4 million campaign in behalf of the educational institutions was developed and successfully conducted during the quadrennium 1955-1959.[33]

Quentin Charles Lansman, in his exhaustive history of higher education in the Evangelical United Brethren Church published in 1972, reached the following conclusions. In the first place, the Church, along with its predecessors, was one of the many Protestant denominations clearly identified with and concerned about the establishment of and support of higher education. Second, and more from a negative point of view, he concluded that a carefully articulated philosophy of higher education was never stated at any point by the Evangelical United Brethren Church. Third, the original attitude of the church on higher education was negative. This position was reversed when the purpose of higher education was discovered to be more in keeping with the mission of the Church, a movement which peaked in 1920.[34] Fourth, Evangelical United Brethren colleges held a unique place in history, with the principle of co-education the norm in all but one of their institutions from the very beginning; likewise, instructional staff included women from the first. Restrictive admission practices were never present. Fifth, none of the institutions ever severed ties with the parent church bodies or the resulting denomination; some died, but none of them defected. Sixth, these schools were marked by an emphasis on vocational education. And finally, Lansman concluded, there was growing uncertainty about the future.[35]

In view of the Evangelical United Brethren's proud heritage as a denomination, and its role as a champion of higher education, there was a natural fear of its being overshadowed by its new partner in the United Methodist Church. For as of the 1968 General Conference, or Uniting Conference, a new church was born, the United Methodist Church. The new church was made up of a cautious blend of the Evangelical United Brethren Church and the Methodist Church. At the same time, the new church would attempt to redress ancient wrongs in its history with regard to the education of African Americans in the Methodist tradition.

IV. Methodists and the Education of African Americans

Looking all the way back to the inception of the Methodist Episcopal Church in 1784, one can see that the denomination has had an uneven record in dealing with African Americans in its family of believers. On the one hand, Methodists historically took the lead among religious folk in the education of freed slaves (referred to as freedmen) following the Civil War. At the same time, schools and colleges that were started for the freedmen after the war remained educational institutions only for African Americans for the most part until well past the mid-twentieth century. This separation resulted from a church not knowing how fully to relate its faith to the issue since the church split over slavery in 1844.

African Americans had been a part of Methodist fellowships in America almost from the beginning. The first notable trouble came in 1787 in St. George's Methodist Episcopal Church in Philadelphia. A series of issues arose in the life of the congregation involving discrimination, including segregation in the gallery. When ushers disturbed two African-American worshippers who were in the midst of praying and asked them to move, Richard Allen, a former slave who had purchased his freedom and become a successful preacher, led his followers out of the church, never to return. They worshipped for a time in separate Methodist facilities, but in 1816 African-American leaders came together in Philadelphia to form the African Methodist Episcopal Church, with Richard Allen as the first bishop.[36] Other African Americans continued within the Methodist Episcopal Church. A faction that arose within Allen's church led to the formation of the African Methodist Episcopal Church, Zion, in 1826, in New York.[37]

An even more significant schism that was to have a dramatic effect on the future of Methodism in America occurred in 1844. Like the Presbyterians and the Baptists, the Methodist Episcopal Church as a national, rather than a regional church, was racked by emotional debate over slavery. As the controversy raged in church and society, the Methodist Episcopal Church devised a plan whereby colleges, agencies, and churches of the respective regions would be divided in the event of a split. The split did come about in the General Conference of 1844, resulting in the creation of the Methodist Episcopal Church, South, a schism that remained for ninety-five years until the reunion in 1939 of the two regional factions, plus the Methodist Protestant Church.[38]

The union of 1939 was widely regarded as a progressive step for the Methodist movement, overcoming regional factionalism long before the Presbyterians and Baptists. Yet as far as African Americans were concerned, it was not nearly progressive enough. The new Methodist Church in 1939 would be arranged into geographical regions, or jurisdictions. But all African-American churches and members who were Methodist would be segregated into a non-geographical, Central Jurisdiction. While many African-American Methodists went along with this plan, the African Methodist Episcopal Church and the African Methodist Episcopal Church, Zion, would have nothing to do with this arrangement. So they opted to remain independent, outside the main Methodist fold. This segregated arrangement continued until 1968, ending only when the Uniting Conference of 1968 brought together the Methodist Church and the Evangelical United Brethren Church, and also abolished the Central Jurisdiction.

Shortly after the Civil War, a number of commissions at the national level were created to deal with the education of free slaves. In 1866, the Methodist Episcopal Church withdrew from these commissions and formed its own organization, the Freedmen's Aid Society of the Methodist Episcopal Church.[39] The Society attempted to address many needs; education was principal among them. Under the leadership of the Freedmen's Aid Society, the northern church made great strides in educating the freed slaves and their children. At first, education was at such a low level that the first Methodist schools for this purpose were little more than elementary schools. But as the educational attainment of freedmen increased, the need for secondary schools and then institutions of higher education became apparent.

The story of the founding of colleges for African Americans in the United Methodist Church is a story of sacrifice, courage, love, heroism, and hope. Begun at a time when the doors of almost all institutions of higher education were closed to the recently freed slaves, and when the white majority's prevailing philosophy was that African Americans either did not need and/or were not capable of higher education, these colleges withstood the pressures and the sentiment against them to become vital centers of education, nurture, and survival, both spiritually and culturally.[40] And so it was that, from their inception, various constituencies understood that these colleges would be closely associated with the church to provide culture for service and socialization, symbols of hope and self-esteem, and the embodiment of the collective aspirations of Methodist African Americans and others under their influence.[41]

Within the first fifty years of the life of the Freedmen's Aid Society, the following institutions for African Americans were founded and supported through its work:

Bennett College, Greensboro, North Carolina

Central Tennessee College, Nashville, Tennessee (later Walden)

Claflin University, Orangeburg, South Carolina

Clark College, Atlanta, Georgia

Samuel Huston College, Austin, Texas

Morristown College, Morristown, Tennessee

Morgan College, Baltimore, Maryland

New Orleans University

Shaw University, Holly Springs, Mississippi (later Rust College)

Philander Smith College, Little Rock, Arkansas

George R. Smith College, Sedalia, Missouri

Wiley University, Marshall, Texas

It should be noted that, of these twelve institutions, eight of them are still actively related to the United Methodist Church, although some have different names today.

Also within the time frame of fifty years, the Freedmen's Aid Society was responsible for the establishment of twenty academies. One theological school was started in Atlanta, Georgia, as the Gammon Theological Seminary, and one medical school, Meharry Medical School, was begun in Nashville, Tennessee. During the same period, the Methodist Episcopal Church established only three new colleges or universities and 19 academies for whites.[43]

Other developments were to follow after the close of the aforementioned fifty-year period. In 1922 the Cookman Institute at Jacksonville, Florida, merged with Daytona Normal and Industrial Institute for Negro Girls to form Bethune-Cookman College in Daytona Beach. Bennett College, which had been co-educational, became Bennett College for Women in 1926. In 1935 Walden College in Nashville, Tennessee, closed its doors, and New Orleans University merged with the Congregational school, Straight College, to form Dillard University in New Orleans. Morgan College was taken over by the state of Maryland in 1937. Paine College, which was started in 1882 by the Colored Methodist Episcopal Church, came under the auspices of the new Methodist Church in 1940. Clark College became a part of the Atlanta University Center in 1941, and Samuel Huston College and Tillotson College (Congregational) were merged in 1952 to form Huston- Tillotson College.[44]

A special word should be said about one of the unique United Methodist institutions for African Americans. Meharry Medical College, in Nashville, Tennessee, founded in 1876, is the largest private, comprehensive institution for educating African-American health professionals in the United States.[45] Meharry graduates constitute nearly 40 percent of the African-American faculty in medical schools and 15 percent of the African-American faculty in dental schools across the nation. Three-fourths of Meharry graduates practice in medically underserved inner-city and rural areas where the nation's immense unmet health needs are concentrated.[46] The college was established as the Meharry Medical Department of Central Tennessee College, which became Walden University in 1900; thus it became Meharry Medical College of Walden University. In 1905 Meharry Medical College was established as a separate nonprofit institution.[47]

The unification of the three branches of Methodism in 1939 closed an era. The Methodist Episcopal Church, under whose auspices the African-American institutions were founded and sponsored for more than seven decades, reunited and brought back together the factions that split over slavery and remained separate in part because of race relations. In the reunion, the Methodist Episcopal Church became a major part of the Methodist Church. In the Methodist Church, the colleges historically serving African Americans came into new relationships, with opportunities for increased support and new outreaches in race relations, a situation which continued into the second half of the twentieth century for the United Methodist Church.

The question now remains for United Methodists: Is there any reason to maintain institutions historically serving African Americans? The integration of higher education at large presented new problems for United Methodist institutions for African Americans. Predominantly white schools began to recruit African-American students, faculty, and financial resources, all of which put great strain on these institutions. United

Methodists, whose ancestors would have nothing to do with the education of African Americans, now complain because of special funding requests by the church at large for the maintenance and further support of these institutions. James P. Brawley gives careful, thoughtful attention to this question in his 1974 volume on Methodist concern for African-American education.

> There is no defensible rationale for a Black college to remain exclusively so on a discriminatory basis just for the sake of being Black. Black colleges founded by the Freedmen's Aid Society have not been and are not now discriminating institutions to the exclusion of other racial groups. They are Black colleges because of discrimination against them. They have been Black colleges historically not by choice but by rejection.[48]

Brawley then turns his attention to reasons why there should continue to be African-American colleges in the United Methodist Church. The first and foremost is the quality of the institutions. They responded to a need to dispel the myth of white superiority. Brawley contends that except at the very top, these colleges and universities are comparable to predominantly white institutions at every level.[49] In addition, historically African-American institutions can best deal with the problems of educational and cultural deficiencies of African-American students in a positive environment, and increase African-American identity and self-esteem. And finally, these institutions are the best resources and instruments available for the creation, development, and preservation of African-American culture.[50]

V. Theological Education

We have seen how disparate groups within the Methodist tradition finally came together in 1968 in order to form a new church that continues to this day. We have seen how each strand of United Methodism has had a critical stake in the development of higher education in the United States. Even though the description thus far has made passing reference to formal theological education in each of the traditions, it is necessary now to take a closer look at this subject.

From the time the Methodist Episcopal Church was begun in the United States in 1784 until the end of the first quarter of the nineteenth century, the development of formal theological education was either deemed unimportant or opposed outright. Most early Methodist lay folk were untrained and unlettered, and it was deemed appropriate by most that formal education for the ministry was either a waste of time or an enterprise which would sap the ministry of its zeal and spiritual foundation. Whether dealing with Methodists, Evangelicals, or United Brethren, fear of an intellectually top-heavy clergy was a prime source of opposition to the establishment of any church-related school. Some believed that formal ministerial education might drive a wedge between educated and non-educated clergy, while others argued that time in school was critical time away from active ministry. On the other hand, as the church moved into the nineteenth century, the rising level of education among church people called new attention to the needs for an educated ministry.

While early colleges in the denomination would provide some education for ministers and their children, the primary source of education for the ministry was what came to be known as the Course of Study. This was first put into effect by the 1816 General Conference.[51] The Course of Study was a prescribed listing of required reading of academic works on which clergy would be examined. This Course of Study was first published in the Discipline in 1848 in the North and 1855 in the South.[52]

Although a college and seminary education are the primary qualification for ordination today, the Course of Study does continue down to the present time.

The General Conference of the Methodist Episcopal Church of 1816 was the first to consider seriously the specific educational qualifications of Methodism's preachers. Gerald O. McCulloh, who has written a comprehensive history of ministerial education in the United Methodist Church, quotes Nathan Bangs, an early Methodist publisher, and a member of that Conference, on the subject:

> Although a collegiate education is not, by your Committee, deemed essential to a gospel ministry, yet it appears absolutely necessary for every minister of the gospel to study to show himself approved unto God, a workman that needeth not be ashamed. Everyone, therefore, who would be useful as a minister in the church ... should strive by every lawful means to imbue his mind with every science which is intimately connected with the doctrine of salvation by Jesus Christ, and which will enable him to understand and illustrate the sacred scriptures.[53]

Not long after the General Conference, a movement commenced to establish a theological school for Methodist ministers.

The date usually given for the founding of the first Methodist theological school in the United States is 1829, when the Newbury Biblical Institute was begun in Newbury, Vermont.[54] The school later moved to Concord, New Hampshire, then to Boston, where it ultimately became the School of Theology of Boston University and one of United Methodism's premier theological institutions. A second school, Garrett Biblical Institute, was founded in 1853 in Evanston, Illinois.[55] The use of the designation "biblical institute" was in response to those who opposed formal theological training, stressing that the primary purpose of theological education at that time was biblical studies.

One name that ties these two schools together is that of John Dempster, who is regarded as the father of Methodist theological education. He had been instrumental in helping the church realize the need for its first theological school at Newbury, becoming its president when it moved to Concord, New Hampshire. Dempster then moved from the presidency of the school in Concord to serve as Garrett's first president until 1863, when he left for the Far West and an attempt to found another theological school there, an attempt that was deterred by his death.[56]

The first theological school begun by the United Brethren was in Dayton, Ohio, in 1871, when Union Biblical Seminary was formed. This institution later changed its name to Bonebrake Theological Seminary, and following union with the Methodist Church in 1968, its name was changed once more to United Theological Seminary.[57] Likewise the Evangelical Association opened its Union Biblical Institute in 1877 in Naperville, Illinois, which later became Evangelical Theological Seminary. Following union in 1968, since both schools were in the Chicago area, Evangelical was merged with Garrett to form the Garrett-Evangelical Theological Seminary.[58]

The Methodist Protestant Church, one of the three partners in the 1939 merger, overcame widespread objection to theological education by establishing a school at Westminster, Maryland. Instruction began there in 1882 at Western Maryland College, and Westminster Theological Seminary was established two years later. Eventually, Westminster would move to the nation's capital in 1955 and become Wesley Theological Seminary adjacent to American University.[59]

In 1866, the celebration of the Methodist Centenary took place, recognizing the birth of the Methodist movement in the United States (although the Methodist· Episcopal Church was established eighteen years later in 1784). The Centenary effort, generously helped by a gift from millionaire Daniel Drew, made possible the founding of Drew Theological Seminary in 1867, in Madison, New Jersey.[60] Drew's gift of $500,000 was the largest of its kind up to that point. The first thought was to place the school in Carmel, New York, Drew's hometown, but this site was rejected as too rural, and Madison was chosen.[61] Drew University was established in 1928 with the theological school as its major professional school. On the occasion of the Centenary, it was noted that "experience with its first theological schools had shown that many of the fears regarding an educated ministry were ungrounded."[62]

The Methodist Episcopal Church, South, entered the arena of theological education with the initiation in 1894 of a training school for ministers at Oxford, Georgia, named Emory College. The college moved to Atlanta in the early twentieth century and eventually became Emory University and the Candler School of Theology, aided by a one-million-dollar grant in 1914.[63] This move and the development of the theological school were a direct result of the case in Tennessee involving Vanderbilt University and its Divinity School. When Vanderbilt became independent of the southern church, the church no longer had its own seminary. Emory College was left behind in Oxford to serve as a junior college, which it has continued to do until the present.

In 1908, Edwin D. Mouzon joined the faculty of Southwestern University in Georgetown, Texas, as the dean of its theological faculty. Mouzon moved to Dallas to organize the faculty of the School of Theology at Southern Methodist University, which opened in 1915, also as a result of the loss of Vanderbilt.[64] Finally, Duke University, moving from Trinity College in Trinity, North Carolina, to Durham in 1924, established a School of Religion as a part of the new university, and the name was changed to The Divinity School of Duke University in 1941.[65]

As was already noted, Gammon Theological Seminary was an institution created by the Methodist Episcopal Church, South, to address the needs of African-American candidates for the ministry. This school was made possible through gifts from the Reverend Elijah Gammon and his wife. At first it was the theology department of Clark University in Atlanta, but in 1882 it was formed as Gammon Theological Seminary with further gifts from the Gammons.[66] Gammon became a part of the Interdenominational Theological Center, a consortium of six seminaries in Atlanta.

Using a gift of $100,000 from John Wesley Iliff, a new seminary was begun in Denver in 1892, bearing the name of its benefactor, Iliff School of Theology. The seminary was associated with the University of Denver. At about the same time, a theological enterprise was being started on the west coast. Two brothers, Charles Maclay, who served as a United States Senator, and Robert Maclay, who was a missionary to China, were instrumental in establishing the Maclay College of Theology at San Fernando, California, in 1885. The college was actually a part of the California state system. In 1910, it was transferred to the University of Southern California campus in Los Angeles as the Graduate School of Religion. In 1956 its title was transferred to the Southern California-Arizona Conference and it became the Southern California School of Theology, and later the Claremont School of Theology, located at Claremont.[67]

The ministerial education needs of the Pacific Northwest were addressed at first by the Methodist school in Oregon, Willamette University, where a college of theology was attempted in 1905. But it was closed by its trustees in 1930, with the suggestion that the Methodists in the region work out a cooperative arrangement with the interdenominational Pacific School of Religion.[68]

Only two Methodist seminaries were established following the union in 1939, Saint Paul School of Theology, in Kansas City, Missouri, and the Methodist Theological School in Ohio, which was founded in 1960 at Delaware, Ohio. Saint Paul opened in 1958 on the campus of National College, a school for diaconal ministers owned by the Woman's Division of the Board of Missions. Eventually the college closed and the property was given to the seminary. Two additional seminaries were added to the roster after the union with the Evangelical United Brethren Church in 1968. The Evangelical Church had its own seminary at Naperville, Illinois, and the United Brethren in Christ had a seminary at Dayton, Ohio, United Theological Seminary. Since the Methodists had only recently started a seminary in Ohio, some expressed concern at the time of union about a proliferation of seminaries in the same geographical region.

At the same time, care was given not to have the Evangelical United Brethren schools merely absorbed by the largest Methodist contingent. The school at Naperville was so close to Garrett in Evanston that a merger of these two was inevitable, forming Garrett-Evangelical Theological Seminary on the Evanston campus. Some thought that a merger of the two Ohio schools would occur as well, but after considerable debate both schools were retained as United Methodist seminaries.

As we bring to a close this consideration of United Methodist theological education, it is important to note several unique characteristics that center on the manner in which theological education in this denomination has related to the society at large around the church and its educational enterprise. In his definitive work on Methodist ministerial education, McCulloh notes that it was out of a concern for the church at the urban crossroads of the nation that most of the United Methodist seminaries were located in urban areas, where the needs of the larger society were readily apparent.[69] Without a doubt, this strategic location has tempered United Methodist theological education with a sense of social justice and concern for society.

In addition, in almost every case, United Methodist seminaries are located on the campus of, or very close to, a major university with a Methodist heritage. This has undergirded the denomination's attempt to provide for an educated clergy with a degree of quality and high standards for academic integrity that is likely without peer in the country. One need only list the universities involved, such as Boston, Duke, American, Emory, Northwestern, Southern Methodist, to recognize that United Methodist theological education has clearly been marked by a dedication to academic excellence as well as service to the church. United Methodist seminaries have been leaders in offering theological education for women, with approximately one third of current enrollment made up of women. This juxtaposition with urban centers and academic institutions has also aided these seminaries in taking the lead in issues such as race relations, sexism, concern for global issues such as peace and hunger, and environmental concerns.

V. Conclusion

Having survived an early history that was marked by anti-intellectualism and outright opposition to formal education for clergy, United Methodists and their historical antecedents have neared the close of the twentieth century with a long and distinguished history in higher education. This history has demonstrated without a doubt that most of these early fears were unfounded. United Methodist higher education has, through the more than 200 years since its inception, remained faithful to the task of making education available to the widest possible range of persons within both church and society.

Due to the influence of the Evangelical United Brethren, United Methodists stressed coeducation earlier than most, and have an outstanding record in making quality education available to women. Due to the work of the Methodist Episcopal Church through the Freedmen's Aid Society following the Civil War, the United Methodist Church can point with pride to a record of providing education at all levels for African Americans that is without peer in the United States. Due to the creation of a network of preparatory schools and junior colleges, the United Methodist Church has been able to provide a bridge for those persons who were perhaps not yet able to reach the senior college level, for either financial or academic reasons. And due to the creation, support, and maintenance of thirteen quality theological schools, the United Methodist Church has established strong academic preparation and professional training for thousands of candidates for the ministry every year.

In conclusion, there are lessons that can be learned from the United Methodist involvement in the development of higher education in the country. In the first place, the United Methodist Church and its forebears have a magnificent history in the support of higher education. Its continued success in the field is in effect out of proportion to its percentage of the population of the country. When you add to the list of United Methodist institutions those schools like Vanderbilt University and others that were started by the church but later became independent, it is clear that this denomination has made an indelible mark on the quality and development of higher education in the United States.

A second lesson to be learned is that these institutions were supported for their educational value, not for the purpose of religious indoctrination. In the history of religious higher education in the United States, this has not always been the case. In fact, even today there are religious colleges and universities that appear to see religious indoctrination as one of their primary purposes. United Methodists have always had a broader concept of higher education than that -- blending spiritual values with a concern for the whole person, and seeing higher education from the earliest times as much more than educating clergy.

A third lesson that comes from United Methodist history is the awareness that the development of United Methodist institutions paralleled that of the historical development of the country. What is primarily meant by this statement is that the United Methodist Church was a frontier church at first, following its people as the young country moved West. Because of this, the church reflected the American ideals of democracy and educational opportunities for all. Following the move from an agrarian to an industrialized economy, the United Methodist Church moved to the urban crossroads, where many of its outstanding universities and theological schools were founded and remain until this day.

Finally, the United Methodist system of higher education was dynamic. It was never frozen into an artificial equilibrium, but always responded to the changing society it served. This aspect of United Methodist schools has already been mentioned in a previous paragraph, but it is important to note it in this context as well. The flexibility of the system was a major reason for its success. As it became apparent that a school in question was struggling financially, or perhaps in an obviously bad location, the church was willing to give it up and apply its resources in places with a better chance of success. In some cases, schools grew to a point when independence from the parent church was advisable and they freely achieved their independence from the church. In other cases, mergers of existing institutions in order to preserve resources and enhance the chances of success were made with little resistance. In short, the success of the denomination in higher education was in large part assured by the flexibility that was at the heart of its focus.

Methodists, ever since the days of John and Charles Wesley and their associates at Oxford University in England, have been known as Christians with warm hearts, zealous in good works. They have also placed great stress upon educational activities both at home and abroad. These activities have borne rich fruit in the quality of leadership in the ministry and in the church and society at large. Arlo Ayres Brown, a former President of Drew University, concluded an article in 1947 on Methodism's educational activities with the following words, which also provide a fitting end to our look at United Methodist higher education:

> A new day is dawning which will put a still heavier strain upon our churches and schools to produce men and women who can think in global terms and adjust themselves to change. The new world order will become either more Christian or more secular. The kind of persons produced by Christian education will largely determine the future. Christians and people with like ideals have resources enough, human and divine. The world has a right to expect us to make the most of them.[70]

Endnotes

1. *Handbook of United Methodist-Related Schools, Colleges, Universities, and Theological Schools*. Nashville, TN: General Board of Higher Education and Ministry, The United Methodist Church, 1922, p. 5.

2. Arlo Ayres Brown, "Methodism's Educational Activities," in William K. Anderson, ed., *Methodism*. Nashville, TN: The Methodist Publishing House, 1947, p. 179.

3. William Warren Sweet, *Methodism in American History*. New York: Abingdon Press, 1954, p. 210.

4. Emory Stevens Bucke, *et al.*, eds., *The History of American Methodism in Three Volumes*. New York, NY: Abingdon Press, 1964, vol. I, pp. 549, 555.

5. Sweet, *Methodism in American History*, pp. 217-18.

6. Frederick A. Norwood, *The Story of American Methodism: A History of the United Methodists and Their Relations*. Nashville, TN: Abingdon Press, 1974, p. 219.

7. *Ibid.*

8. *Ibid.*, p. 207.

9. Bucke, *The History of American Methodism*, vol. III, p. 213.

10. *Ibid.*, p. 214.

11. Norwood, *The Story of American Methodism*, p. 303.

12. *Ibid.*

13. *Ibid.*

14. Bucke, *The History of American Methodism*, vol. III, p. 233.

15. *Ibid.*

16. Brown, *Methodism*, pp. 53-54.

17. Bucke, *The History of American Methodism*, vol. III, p. 240.

18. *Ibid.*

19. Quentin Charles Lansman, *Higher Education in The Evangelical United Brethren Church*. Nashville, TN: Division of Higher Education, The United Methodist Church, 1972, p. 1.

20.   *Ibid.*, p. 2.

21.   *Ibid.*, p. 7.

22.   *Ibid.*, pp. 173-74.

23.   *Ibid.*, p. 61.

24.   *Ibid.*

25.   *Ibid.*, p. 62.

26.   Albright, Raymond W. *History of the Evangelical Church.* Harrisburg, PA: The Evangelical Press, 1942, p. 326.

27.   Lansman, *Higher Education in The Evangelical United Brethren Church*, p. 65.

28.   *Ibid.*, p. 66.

29.   *Ibid.*, p. 73.

30.   *Ibid.*, pp. 73-74.

31.   *Ibid.*, pp. 74-75.

32.   *Ibid.*, p. 78.

33.   *Ibid.*, pp. 81-82.

34.   *Ibid.*, p. 159.

35.   *Ibid.*, p. 160.

36.   Norwood, *The Story of American Methodism*, pp. 170-71.

37.   *Ibid.*, p. 174.

38.   *Ibid.*, p. 199.

39.   James P. Brawley, *Two Centuries of Methodist Concern: Bondage, Freedom, and the Education of Black People.* New York: Vantage Press, 1974, p. 56.

40.   William B. McClain, *Black People in the Methodist Church: Whither Thou Goest?* Nashville, TN: Abingdon Press, 1984, pp. 68-69.

41.   *Ibid.*, p. 69.

42.   Brawley, *Two Centuries of Methodist Concern*, p. 84.

43.   *Ibid.*, p. 85.

44.   *Ibid.*, p. 150.

45.   *Handbook of United Methodist-Related Schools, Colleges, Universities, and Theological Schools*, p. 225.

46.   *Ibid.*

47.   *Ibid.*

48.   *Ibid.*, p. 560.

49. *Ibid.*, pp. 560-61.

50. *Ibid.*, pp. 562-64.

51. Norwood, *The Story of American Methodism*, p. 306.

52. Gerald O. McCulloh, *Ministerial Education in the American Methodist Movement*. Nashville, TN: United Methodist Board of Higher Education and Ministry, Division of Ordained Ministry, 1980, p. 12.

53. *Ibid.*, p. 10.

54. *Ibid.*, p. 19.

55. Myron F. Wicke, *The Methodist Church and Higher Education 1939-1964*. Nashville, TN: Division of Higher Education, Board of Education, The Methodist Church, 1965, p. 45.

56. Norwood, *The Story of American Methodism*, p. 307.

57. McCulloh, *Ministerial Education in the American Methodist Movement*, p. 24.

58. *Ibid.*

59. *Ibid.*

60. Norwood, *The Story of American Methodism*, p. 309.

61. McCulloh, *Ministerial Education in the American Methodist Movement*, p. 34.

62. *Ibid.*, p. 33.

63. *Ibid.*, pp. 25, 47.

64. *Ibid.*

65. Robert F. Durden, *The Launching of Duke University, 1924-1949*. Durham, NC: Duke University Press, 1993, p. 333.

66. *Ibid.*, pp. 38-39.

67. *Ibid.*, pp. 40-42.

68. *Ibid.*, pp. 43-44.

69. *Ibid.*, p. 82.

70. Brown, *Methodism*, p. 191.

Bibliographic Entries

509.   Barth, Eugene Howard. *Discovery and Promise: a History of Albright College, 1856-1981*. Reading, PA: Albright College, 1989.

Updates the 1956 history (Gingrich and Barth, *A History of Albright College*). Includes some new material for earlier years of Albright and the colleges with which it merged.

510.   Beddow, James B. "College of the Prairie," In *Idea to Institution: Higher Education in South Dakota*. Edited by Ruth Ann Alexander. Vermillion, SD: University of South Dakota Press, 1989, pp. 181-91.

511.   Breck, Allen D. *From the Rockies to the World*. Denver, CO: University of Denver Division of Arts and Humanities, 1989.

Gives a general university history, focusing on individuals and significant programs, and how they developed.

512.   Brooks, Frances M. *The Hiwassee I Remember: A Pictorial History*. Nashville, TN: United Methodist Publishing House, 1987.

Provides a history of Hiwassee College, told in photographs and anecdotes.

513.   Burtchaell, James Tunstead. "The Alienation of Christian Higher Education in America: Diagnosis and Prognosis," In *Schooling Christians: 'Holy Experiments' in Higher Education*. Edited by Stanley Hauerwas and John H.

Westerhoff, pp. 129-83. Grand Rapids, MI: William B. Eerdmans Publishing Co., 1992.

Chronicles the controversy between Vanderbilt University and the Methodist Episcopal Church, South, resulting in Vanderbilt's independence from the denomination. Stresses that Christian commitment to higher education must be supported by a substantive Christian vision.

514. Cartwright, Michael G. "Looking Both Ways: A 'Holy Experiment' in American Higher Education," In *Schooling Christians: 'Holy Experiments' in Higher Education*, pp. 184-213. Edited by Stanley Hauerwas and John H. Westerhoff, Grand Rapids, MI: William B. Eerdmans Publishing Co., 1992.

Offers discussion of the relationship between Allegheny College and the Western Pennsylvania Conference of the United Methodist Church, plus a proposal for how to "reconstruct" the church-college relationship.

515. Chamberlain, Marigene. "Covenant Discipleship and Higher Education." *Covenant Discipleship Quarterly* 9 (Spring 1994): 8-9,12.

Reports on the ways in which Wesley Theological Seminary uses covenantal discipleship groups as a way to ground the practice of ministry in the local congregation and to model how clergy and laity share pastoral power.

516. Cunningham, John T. *University in the Forest: the Story of Drew University.* 2nd Ed. Florham Park, NJ: Afton Publishing Co., 1990.

517.   Dew, Lee A. *In Pursuit of the Dream: A History of Kentucky Wesleyan College.* Owensboro, KY: Kentucky Wesleyan College Press, 1992.

Covers the history of Kentucky Wesleyan College from its beginnings in the mid-nineteenth century to 1992.

518.   Division of Higher Education, The United Methodist Church. *Handbook of United Methodist-Related Schools, Colleges, Universities and Theological Schools.* Nashville, TN: General Board of Higher Education and Ministry, 1992.

Provides a comprehensive overview of the 123 institutions related to the United Methodist Church, including theological schools, universities, colleges, and preparatory schools. Offers a capsule look at each of the institutions with information about enrollment, curriculum, and philosophy, plus a photographic page on each one.

519.   Durden, Robert F. *The Launching of Duke University, 1924-1949.* Durham, NC: Duke University Press, 1993.

Tells the story of the formation of Duke University, beginning with its creation as a new institution organized around Trinity College. Focusing on the early accomplishments of President William Preston Few, the distinguished Duke historian Durden commemorates Few's remarkable successes while recognizing the painful realities and uncertainties of a young institution especially during its first quarter of a century.

520.   Early, James. *On the Frontier of Leadership 1888-1988.* Tacoma, WA: University of Puget Sound, 1988.

Provides a review of the first 100 years of the university with sections devoted to each president's successes and changes. Includes historical data with prominent mention of United Methodist tradition on campus.

521. Eckley, Robert S. *Pictures at an Exhibition: Illinois Wesleyan University, 1968-1986, An Academic Memoir.* Bloomington, IL: Illinois Wesleyan University, 1992.

Contains the memoirs of Dr. Eckley, who was President of the university from 1968 to 1986. Has separate chapters on the students, faculty and staff, curriculum, the campus, the finance of the university, and volunteers, plus appendices listing faculty, staff and trustees during the years and a vita of the author.

522. Erickson, Lori. "Simpson College." *The Iowan.* 41, Fall, 1992, pp. 34-41.

Provides a pictorial essay on the college as it is today. Relates its founding in 1860 as the Indianola Seminary. Cites Simpson as one of the up-and-coming liberal arts colleges in the Midwest.

523. Gerling, Edwin G. *The One Hundred Seventeenth Illinois Infantry Volunteers: the McKendree Regiment, 1862-1865.* Highland, IL: E.C. Gerling, 1992.

Contains information on the history of McKendree College and the involvement of its people in the Civil War, although the main focus is on the history of the one hundred seventeenth regiment of the U.S. Army.

524. Godsey, John D., comp. *Brief Autobiographies and Reflections of the Faculty, Deans and Presidents of Wesley*

Theological Seminary, 1890-1991. Privately printed, 1991. Typescript.

Views Wesley Theological Seminary through the personal reflections of key figures in its past history to 1991.

525. Godsey, John D., comp. *Brief Autobiographies and Reflections of the Faculty, Deans and Presidents of Wesley Theological Seminary, Supplement.* Privately printed, 1993.

Supplements the work by the same compiler in 1991.

526. Greene, Amy. "Candler Seminary: Transforming Mission (the Metamorphosis of a Methodist Seminary)." *Christianity and Crisis* 51, 8 April 1991, p. 112.

Gives an account of the way in which the mission of Candler School of Theology has changed through the years.

527. Grimes, Lewis Howard. *A History of Perkins School of Theology.* ed. by Roger Loyd. Dallas, TX: Southern Methodist University Press, 1993.

Sets forth the close relationship between Perkins School of Theology and the United Methodist Church and the need for each other. Traces the story of one continuum: Perkins' special provision from its inception in 1915 to the present for the graduate professional training of Christian ministers.

528. Haselmayer, Louis A. *A Sesquicentennial History of Iowa Wesleyan College (1842-1992).* Iowa Wesleyan College: Mt. Pleasant, IA, 1992.

Provides an 82-page history of Iowa Wesleyan College written by the college archivist and long-time past President. Contains numerous black-and-white plates, plus information about the Mount Pleasant Gerona College. Lists by means of appendices the past presidents, trustees, faculty chairs, and honorary-degree recipients.

529. Jones, Bartlett C. and Dodson, Joy, eds., *Central Methodist College, 1961-1986*. Nashville, TN: Abingdon Press, 1987.

Covers the administrative, academic, and student life of Central Methodist College in Fayette, Missouri, from 1961 until 1986. Includes lists of faculty and administrators; also includes photographs.

530. Knight, Douglas M. *Street of Dreams: The Nature and Legacy of the 1960s*. Durham, NC: Duke University Press, 1989.

Gives an honest account of Duke University's experience during the 1960s clash on that campus between and among students, faculty, administrators, and trustees. Draws parallels to the situation on other campuses and seeks to comprehend the time and its enduring influence. Offers a first-hand account by the individual who was Duke University's president at the time.

531. Larson, Ellis L. *A Profile of Contemporary Seminarians: Comparison of M. Div. Students Enrolled in 1986 and 1991 (for Methodist Theological School in Ohio)*. Washington, D.C.: Wesley Theological Seminary, 1992.

Focuses through a research study on a description of the phenomenon of older and second-career seminarians.

Master of Divinity students were included in a stratified random sample of 549 accredited seminaries in the United States. Each seminary received a report of its own enrollees, compared with those in seminaries in its own denominational family and all Protestant schools.

532.   Mack, Thomas B. *History of the Citrus Institute, Florida Southern College 1947-1993.* Lakeland, FL: Florida Southern College Citrus Institute, 1993.

Focuses on the development and growth of the Citrus Institute at Florida Southern College. Includes some general history on the College. Illustrated.

533.   MacKaye, William R. and Barbara E. Taylor. "How Wesley Counts: Judging Seminary Performance by the Numbers." *Trust* 4 (Autumn 1992): 5-13.

534.   MacNaughton, A. Douglas. *A History of Adrian College.* Adrian, MI: publisher to be determined, 1994.

This 947-page book is a chronology of the people and events of Adrian College from its founding in the 1850s to 1988.

535.   McCabe, Mike, ed. "A Proud and Tenacious History: Brevard College Historic Time-Line." *Brevard Magazine* (Winter 1994): 7-18.

Covers the period 1853-1993 and chronicles the merger of Rutherford College, Weaver College, and Brevard Institute to form Brevard College in 1934. Highlights some of the leaders and events that guided Brevard College to meet 140 years of educational needs in the mountains of western North Carolina.

536. McClish, Glen Arthur. *Southwestern University: The Student's Perspective*. Georgetown, TX: Southwestern University, 1993.

Contains papers written by students in an advanced composition class in the spring of 1993. Includes topics such as personal narratives, student organizations, women at Southwestern, minority presence, folklore, and visions for the future.

537. Mickey, David H. *Of Sunflowers, Coyotes, and Plainsmen*. 3 Vols. Lincoln, NE: Nebraska Wesleyan University, 1992.

Provides a detailed history of Nebraska Wesleyan University -- written by an emeritus professor of History whose family has been involved with the university since its founding in 1888. Volumes I and II are complete; Volume III is currently in progress. First two volumes are profusely illustrated.

538. Murchland, Bernard, ed. *Noble Achievements: The History of Ohio Wesleyan University from 1842 to 1992*. Ohio Wesleyan University, Delaware, Ohio, 1992.

Provides a documented history supplementing an earlier history of the institution (Hubbart), with chapters researched and written by Ohio Wesleyan authorities. Includes chapters on: the presidents, student life, alumni, curriculum, religious life, assets of the college, plus interview with the sesquicentennial president.

539. Orwig, Timothy. *Morningside College: A Centennial History*. Sioux City, IA: Morningside College, 1994.

Presents through words and pictures the history of Morningside College and its predecessors: University of the Northwest, The German-English School of Galena, Illinois, and Charles City College.

540. "Philander Smith College: To Make a Living, To Build a Life." *Black Excellence*. Washington, DC: NAEFO Excellence, Inc., 1992, pp. 60-61.

Profiles Philander Smith College in Little Rock, Arkansas. Covers the proud past and the bright future of the college, along with a description of the college's mission and philosophy.

541. Phillips, Clifton J. and John J. Baughman. *Depauw: A Pictorial History*. Greencastle, IN: Depauw University, 1987.

Provides an excellent resource to supplement but not supersede the 1962 Manhart history (*Depauw Through the Years*). Makes use of the voluminous photograph collection in the Depauw Archives and contains some new information from recent research.

542. Pogue, Jan. *More Valuable Than Gold: The Reinhardt College Story*. Atlanta, GA: Corporate Stories, 1994.

Gives an overview of Reinhardt College in Waleska, Georgia, from its founding in 1883 to today, as told through the stories of its people -- faculty, staff, students, alumni, friends, and donors. Contains 111 pages and is richly illustrated with photographs from the early years up to the present.

543. Robert, Dana. "Mission Study at the University-related Seminary: The Boston University School of Theology As a Case Study." *Missiology* 17 (April 1989): 193-202.

Marks the rise and decline of mission study at the Boston University School of Theology. Notes that the situation there parallels that of other mainline ecumenically-oriented and university-related seminaries. Questions whether "globalization" is the new paradigm for mission education at such schools.

544. Scheffler, Steve. "Back From Broke: Lindsey Wilson College Goes on a Quality Quest." *A Continuous Journey* (June-July 1993): 8-17.

Describes how the college came back from financial difficulties through the medium of a magazine dedicated to success stories in the field of higher education.

545. Small, Laura T., ed. *Religion In Montana, Pathway To the Present, Vol. I-II*. Billup, MT: Rocky Mountain College, 1994.

Contains chapters on Methodism, Presbyterianism, and Congregationalism, including information about Rocky Mountain College and its predecessor institutions, i.e., College of Montana (Presbyterian), Montana Wesleyan (Methodist), Intermountain Union (Methodist-Presbyterian), and Billup Presbyterian Institute (Congregational).

546. Sweet, Pearl. *Methodist Higher Education Institutions in the California-Nevada Conference*. Master's Thesis, California State University at Long Beach, 1994.

Provides historical sketches in some detail of the institutions of higher education that the United Methodist Church supports through the California-Nevada Annual Conference.

547. Templin, J. Alton, ed. *An Intellectual History of the Iliff School of Theology: A Centennial Tribute, 1892-1992.* Denver, CO: The Iliff School of Theology, 1992.

Offers a collection of knowledge, impressions, and printed records of many of the intellectual leaders at Iliff. Includes some biographical or other personal details along with an analysis of the strictly intellectual contributions. Includes only those faculty members or presidents whose careers are completed.

548. Tull, Barbara Mitchell. *150 Years of Excellence: A Pictorial View of Ohio Wesleyan University.* Delaware, OH: Ohio Wesleyan University, 1991.

Contains a pictorial history of Ohio Wesleyan in celebration of 150 years of existence. Includes a substantial text accompanying the photographs, giving a flavor of the university.

549. Walt, Joseph W. *Beneath the Whispering Maples: The Story of Simpson College.* Indianola, IA: Simpson College Press, 1995.

Contains a comprehensive history of a Midwestern college. Chronicles the development of the institution from its beginnings in 1860 as the "Indianola Male and Female Seminary" to the liberal arts college of the present. Sets the story of Simpson in the context of its times, relating the events of its past to the development of education in Iowa and the nation.

550. Ward, Richard F. "Finding Common Ground: Drama, Liturgy, and Preaching Intersect at Candler School of Theology." *Journal of Communication and Religion* 12 (September 1989): 34-37.

   Describes how the emphasis on preaching at Candler has broadened to embrace drama, and how the two are connected in the worship experience.

551. Willard, George-Anne. *Louisburg College Echoes: Voices from the Formative Years, 1787-1917; With a Summary of the Expansion Years, 1917-1987.* Louisburg, NC: Louisburg College, 1988.

   Provides an important history of Louisburg from its inception down to the present.

CHAPTER 21
Mennonite Institutions of Higher Education

Donovan D. Steiner and Judy H. Mullet

Introduction

The story of Mennonite higher education in the United States over the past 150 years reveals an authentic search by capable church leaders and enterprising individuals to either preserve or shape community life and the mission of the church through higher education. In this essay the historical and contemporary contexts of Mennonite seminaries, colleges, and Bible institutes in the United States are described. The chronology reflects generational transitions molded by the forces of theological, political, and sociological change. Mennonite institutions of higher education in the United States include eight affiliated colleges, three seminaries, and two Bible institutes, each of which identifies with a specific Mennonite Church conference.

Eight U.S. Mennonite colleges participate in the Council of Mennonite Colleges, a coordinating council founded in 1946.

These colleges are Bethel College, Newton, Kansas (1887); Bluffton College, Bluffton, Ohio (1899); Eastern Mennonite University, Harrisonburg, Virginia (1917); Fresno Pacific College, Fresno, California (1944); Goshen College, Goshen, Indiana (1894); Hesston College, Hesston, Kansas (1909); Messiah College, Grantham, Pennsylvania (1909); and Tabor College, Hillsboro, Kansas (1908). The Council of Mennonite Seminaries, an organization that sponsors conjoint projects, is comprised of Associated Mennonite Biblical Seminaries, Elkhart, Indiana (1958); Eastern Mennonite Seminary, Harrisonburg, Virginia (1965); and Mennonite Brethren Biblical Seminary, Fresno, California (1955). Two Bible institutes sponsored by Conservative Mennonite Church Conferences include Rosedale Bible Institute, Irwin, Ohio (1952) and Sharon Mennonite Bible Institute located in Harrisonville, Pennsylvania (1977).[1]

Context of Mennonite Higher Education

Mennonite institutions of higher education began as preparatory schools or Bible schools that emphasized Biblical studies, general studies, and vocational preparation. They adopted liberal arts curriculums and upgraded their programs by seeking accreditation from secular agencies while maintaining their distinctive conference affiliations. Of the eight U.S. colleges in the Council of Mennonite Colleges, seven were established within a twenty-five-year period between 1893 and 1917.

As employment opportunities increased in urban settings in the early 1900s, the vocational aspirations of Mennonite young people rose accordingly. In addition, revivalism and the religious awakening that swept the country at the turn of the twentieth century stimulated new interest among young Mennonites to enter missions and church work. New church publications like *Mennonite Weekly Review*, an inter-Mennonite newspaper published weekly since 1923, permitted denominational conversation across church conferences. Higher education, once viewed with skepticism by Mennonites, gained an increased measure of acceptance.[2]

Early Development of Mennonite Colleges and Seminaries

The German-speaking Dutch-Russian Mennonites, who founded Bethel and Tabor Colleges, educated to preserve German culture, enhance community life, and develop spiritual discipline. For Bluffton, Goshen, and Hesston Colleges, the objectives centered on the transmission of culture, Biblical studies, and vocational and general knowledge preparation. Mennonite colleges also sought to retain Mennonite youth in the church, reconcile traditional religious values with modernism, and prepare young people for leadership positions in the church and community.[3]

Not all efforts to establish higher-education institutions were successful. While Mennonite Church higher education gained momentum at the close of the nineteenth century, earlier efforts to establish post-elementary schools were not sustained, primarily due to financial hardships or theological controversies. The Joseph Funk Music Schools, Singers Glen, Virginia (1825-1862); Freeland Seminary, Collegeville, Pennsylvania (1848-1869); and the Christian Education Institute of the Mennonite Denomination, Wadsworth, Ohio (1868-1878), closed by 1878.[4] Upland College in Upland, California, and Freeman Junior College in Freeman, South Dakota, closed in 1965 and 1985, respectively.[5]

From 1893 to 1917 when most of the Mennonite colleges were founded, college faculty and church constituencies were caught in a web of controversy surrounding theological fundamentalism and liberalism. Revivalism, societal change, World War I, and a first generation of leaders who had travel experience and college educations fueled dissension. Goshen College was closed in 1923 by the Mennonite Board of Education due chiefly to its alleged liberal theology. Hesston College and Eastern Mennonite College, now Eastern Mennonite University, were founded as alternatives to Goshen.[6]

To understand more fully the development of Mennonite ministerial training, it is necessary to review the origin of the Mennonite Church. During the Reformation of the sixteenth century, Anabaptists led by Dutch theologian Menno Simons sought to uphold biblical teachings of the New Testament. They rejected infant baptism, use of the sword, and the state-church patterns of organization. For these beliefs, Anabaptists were severely persecuted by state and established religious authorities. In an attempt to be true to the gospel, they organized themselves into small communities and relied on lay leaders to provide spiritual care. This pattern of church organization continued as Mennonites immigrated from Europe to the United States beginning in the mid-seventeenth century. Mennonite leaders were selected by conferences and local congregations. Formal seminary training was considered to be unimportant. In fact, there was much skepticism of trained clergy due to the persecution experienced by their Anabaptist forefathers in Europe. As Mennonites became more urbanized and foreign missions developed, however, ministerial training became more important.[7]

The first Mennonite seminary was established at Wadsworth, Ohio, in 1868 and functioned for ten years before it closed.[8] Although the seminary at Wadsworth remained open for only a decade, a number of early Mennonite church leaders received their training there. Further development of Mennonite ministerial training is recorded in S. F. Pannabecker's *Ventures of Faith*, written to celebrate the 30th anniversary of the Associated Mennonite Biblical Seminaries of Elkhart, Indiana, the largest center for Mennonite theological preparation.[9]

Descriptions of Mennonite Institutions of Higher Education

In 1994 approximately 8,000 students are enrolled in Mennonite-related colleges, seminaries, and Bible institutes.[10] Curricular offerings and special study centers emphasize cross-cultural studies and peacemaking. Liberal Arts studies connect Christian faith with learning and service. Highest enrollments are found in teacher education, nursing, social work, and business.[11] Fresno Pacific College has offered graduate studies in education since 1972[12] and Eastern Mennonite University has recently initiated graduate programs in education, counseling, and conflict analysis and transformation.[13] A brief historical narrative for each institution follows by conference or church affiliation.

General Conference Mennonite Church Colleges

Bethel College (Newton, Kansas)

As the first Mennonite institution of higher education in North America, Bethel was founded in 1887 to uphold the principles of the church, preserve its historical traditions, and promote the liberal arts. Religious leaders from the 1874 immigration of Mennonites to Kansas from Russia, Switzerland, and South Germany brought with them both a vision for and experience in higher education.[14] Historically, emphasis has been placed on campus community, religious life, leadership development, and academic studies.[15] Bethel College continues to offer a strong liberal arts program to approximately 650 students of whom five percent eventually complete the doctorate.[16]

Bluffton College (Bluffton, Ohio)

Founded in 1899 as Central Mennonite College, the purpose of the school was to prepare young people of the Middle District of the General Conference Mennonite Church for missions and vocations. Central Mennonite College was renamed Bluffton College and Mennonite Seminary in 1914. By 1921, the seminary had separated from Bluffton College to became Witmarsum Theological Seminary, an institution that functioned from 1921 to 1931.[17]

Informed by historic peace-church traditions, Bluffton College "seeks to prepare students of all backgrounds for life as well as vocation, for responsible citizenship, for service to all peoples, and ultimately for the purposes of God's universal kingdom." Today Bluffton college enrolls approximately 900 students.[18]

A Joint Seminary of the General Mennonite and Mennonite Church Conferences

The Associated Mennonite Biblical Seminaries (Ekhart, Indiana)

The Associated Mennonite Biblical Seminaries (AMBS) is an inter-Mennonite cooperative program of the Mennonite and General Conference Churches. Established in 1958, Goshen College Biblical Seminary and the Mennonite Biblical Seminary joined forces in creating a program "committed to the Anabaptist heritage and the Christian Church's global mission." In 1970, the two member programs moved to Elkhart to share a joint campus. Accredited by the Association of Theological Schools and the North Central Association of Colleges and Schools, AMBS presently offers a Master of Divinity, Master of Arts in Peace Studies, and a Master of Arts in Theological Studies.[19]

The People of God, a treatise on a Mennonite interpretation of the Free Church tradition by Ross T. Bender, is considered to be one of the most substantial books on Mennonite theological education. The concepts set forth by Bender served as a model for theological education as currently practiced at Associated Mennonite Biblical Seminaries.[20]

Mennonite Church Conference Seminary and Colleges

Eastern Mennonite Seminary (Harrisonburg, Virginia)

Advanced Bible courses were offered at Eastern Mennonite School as early as 1918, one year after the school opened in Harrisonburg, Virginia. Although the founding vision for Easter Mennonite School did not include a seminary, college biblical offerings increased steadily until, by 1937, a four-year Bible course was created. The program became a distinct entity in 1965 when it officially became Eastern Mennonite Seminary (EMS). Housed in a new (1993) complex at Eastern Mennonite University, EMS offers a Master of Divinity, Master of Arts in Church Leadership, Master of Arts in Religion, and a Certificate in Pastoral Studies or Biblical Studies. All Master of Divinity seminarians gain cross-cultural experience through field experiences or seminars. Accredited by the Association of Theological Schools and the Southern Association of Colleges and Schools, EMS is rooted in an Anabaptist believers' church tradition, but opens its doors to other denominations.[21]

Eastern Mennonite University (Harrisonburg, Virginia)

In 1917 Virginia Mennonites initiated a "Bible School" that evolved into Eastern Mennonite School in Harrisonburg, Virginia. Supported from its inception by Mennonite conferences primarily in Virginia, Pennsylvania, and Maryland, Eastern

Mennonite School was founded as a "fortress to defend the conservative faith."[22]

Originally an academy for Biblical, academic, and vocational studies, Eastern Mennonite became an accredited four-year liberal arts institution in 1944. Eastern Mennonite High School officially separated from College control in 1981. On August 22, 1994, Eastern Mennonite College was renamed Eastern Mennonite University to unify undergraduate, graduate, and seminary programs.[23]

In 1968, Eastern Mennonite pioneered an interdisciplinary team taught core curriculum that developed into the present "Global Village Curriculum." All students are required to study abroad or in a stateside cross-cultural setting. The College proposes to challenge students to service and peacemaking in a "campus village" that is "conscious of its own heritage, but open to and connecting with the vitality of great world cultures." Emphasis on intellectual development, personal growth, social responsibility, and church accountability flows from Anabaptist-Mennonite principles honoring Christian discipleship, community, peacemaking, service, simple living, and evangelism.[24]

Goshen College (Goshen, Indiana)

In 1894 Mennonites from Elkhart, Indiana, including church leader John F. Funk, encouraged Mennonite physician and educator Dr. Henry A. Mumaw to privately establish the Elkhart Institute of Sciences, Industry and the Arts.[25] For several years the institute operated primarily as an academy and junior college. With the need for expansion, the school moved in 1903 from Elkhart to Goshen, Indiana, and became an official institution of the Mennonite church two years later. In an agreement with church and city officials the institute was renamed Goshen College. With a new identity and in a new location, Goshen College continued under the leadership of Mennonite educator Noah E. Byers, who served as president during the transition years 1898-1913. During Byers' administration and in the next decade, tension developed between Goshen College and the Mennonite Church constituency over Fundamentalist-Modernist issues. In 1923 the college was closed by the Mennonite Board of Education for one year. Under the leadership of Stanford C. Yoder, Goshen College reopened in 1924 with a new curriculum combining the liberal arts with theological studies.[26]

Today the motto "Culture for Service" exemplifies Goshen College, an academic community dedicated to developing "informed, articulate, sensitive and responsible Christians" for servant leader roles in church and international arenas.[27] Recognized historically as progressive, Goshen pioneered an international Study Service Term in 1968 that continues to gain national and international attention.[28] The College serves approximately 1,100 students.

Hesston College (Hesston, Kansas)

In 1909 Kansas Mennonites founded Hesston Academy and Bible School offering "Bible, normal and academic" coursework. Hesston was established as an alternative for Mennonite higher education in the Midwest. A strong vocal music emphasis, long associated with Mennonites, complemented a "learning by doing" philosophy by which students aspired "to live in perfect harmony with the will of God."[29]

Today Hesston College is the only two-year liberal-arts-and-career-program college offered by the Mennonite church. With 500 students from 32 states and 30 countries, Hesston College provides an Associate of Arts degree in agriculture, automotive technology, electronics, aviation, liberal arts, Bible, business, nursing, and pastoral ministries. Twenty percent of Hesston's students claim a nursing major. Committed to a self-described style that is "radically person-centered," Hesston College "seeks to understand, create and communicate Christian community." Cooperative agreements with Goshen College and Eastern

Mennonite University provide efficient transfer of credit. Hesston's Pastoral Ministries program was initiated during a time of shifting enrollments, attracting older, nontraditional students to the college. The Peace Scholarship Program, begun in 1991, brings students from Central America and the Caribbean to study computers and electronics and continues to add to campus diversity within the mission of Hesston College.[30]

Mennonite Brethren Church Seminary and Colleges

Mennonite Brethren Biblical Seminary (Fresno, California)

Mennonite Brethren Biblical Seminary (MBBS) was founded in 1955, fulfilling a vision of the 1948 convention of the North American Mennonite Brethren church. The seminary offers three degree programs including a Master of Divinity, Master of Arts in Theology, and Master of Arts in Marriage and Family Counseling. The seminary seeks to personalize instruction and build a strong sense of community consistent with a theological tradition "committed to nurturing personal, spiritual and intellectual growth." MBBS is an evangelical education institution serving over 360 churches in the U.S. and Canada. The seminary is accredited by the Association of Theological Schools and by the Western Association of Schools and Colleges.[31]

Fresno Pacific College (Fresno, California)

Fresno Pacific College is located on a forty-acre campus. Started as Pacific Bible Institute in 1944, Fresno Pacific College grew from a transitional junior college to a fully accredited four-year liberal arts college in 1965.[32] The College seeks to combine personal fulfillment, spiritual growth, interpersonal competence, and social responsibility to help students develop a mature relationship with God through Jesus Christ. With growing departments in business, religious studies, and teacher education, Fresno Pacific College emphasizes cross-cultural study programs and conflict and peacemaking studies. The Activities Integrating Math and Science (AIMS) Foundation, a mathematics and science curriculum for elementary teachers, has achieved national acclaim for its focus on inquiry methods. Graduate programs in education begun in the 1970s have been successful in serving teachers and administrators of the Fresno region.[33]

Tabor College (Hillsboro, Kansas)

Sensing the need for a Mennonite Brethren College in Kansas, visionaries Henry W. Lohrenz and J.K. Hiebert gained the support in 1907 of the Mennonite Brethren Conference to begin a college that would "glorify God and serve the church." Tabor College, named after the biblical Mt. Tabor, purposed to be "a place where young people might encounter Christ and be transformed into servants of God and people." Opened in 1908 the first curriculum offered commercial subjects, vocal music, organ, German, and Biblical studies.[34]

The economic challenges brought on by the stock-market collapse and dust bowl of the 1930s were life-threatening to Tabor College. Creative leadership, however, was able to keep the college afloat. During the 1940s Tabor experienced enrollment increases and greater visibility when it became accredited by the North Central Association of Colleges and Secondary Schools. In the 1950s the College of Theology located at Tabor College was relocated at Fresno Pacific College. By 1979 control of Tabor College and Fresno Pacific College was shifted to district conferences.[35] Today Tabor College enrolls approximately 500 students and promotes Christ-centered education as a hallmark of its liberal arts program.[36]

A Brethren in Christ Church College

Messiah College (Grantham, Pennsylvania)

Messiah College is linked to Mennonite colleges by virtue of its Brethren in Christ Anabaptist heritage and its participation in the Council of Mennonite Colleges. First established in Harrisburg, Pennsylvania, in 1909, and known as Messiah Bible School and Missionary Training Home, Messiah College emerged as an institution from the revivalism and the religious awakening of the late nineteenth century. The college was chartered "to educate men and women for home and foreign mission or evangelistic work ... and to give men and women an opportunity of preparing themselves in secular studies for future occupations, especially for religious work."[37] Messiah College enrolls approximately 2,300 students who study on campus or satellite campuses in Philadelphia and Nairobi, Kenya.

Bible Institutes of the Conservative Mennonite Conferences

Rosedale Bible Institute (Irwin, Ohio)

Founded in 1952, Rosedale Bible Institute operates under the direction of the Conservative Mennonite Conference. Core curriculum of Bible, theology, leadership, and missions courses are offered in five six-week terms from September through May. As an Anabaptist Mennonite Bible Institute, Rosedale seeks to prepare persons as leaders in missions, pastoral ministry, and community service.[38] A comprehensive history is included in *We Beheld His Glory: 1952-1992* edited by Yoder and Showalter.[39] Rosedale serves approximately 200 students.

Sharon Bible Institute (Harrisonville, Pennsylvania)

Sharon Bible Institute operates under the auspices of a 16-member board of associates representing Keystone Mennonite, Mid-Atlantic Mennonite, and Southeast Virginia Mennonite conferences. Approximately 50 students are enrolled for each of three six-week terms. The curriculum consists of Bible studies, mission courses, and choral music classes. The Institute invites students to do systematic Bible study, develop enthusiastic loyalty to Christ, and prepare for intelligent and dedicated leadership in evangelism and church life.[40]

Conclusion

Mennonite institutions of higher education, in continuity with the Anabaptist-Mennonite tradition, identify Christian faith and praxis as foundational to their purposes. They engage students in peace and justice studies and cross-cultural experiences around the world. Mennonite colleges offer a solid core of liberal studies and promote professional programs related to careers in teaching, social work, business, and health professions. These institutions as a rule maintain strong denominational ties with their respective conference or supporting church and have resisted secularization in favor of identification with the church.

Endnotes

1. James E. Horsch, ed., *Mennonite Yearbook and Directory, 1993.* Scottdale, PA: Mennonite Publishing House, 1993, pp. 132-34.
2. Calvin W. Redekop, *Mennonite Society.* Baltimore, MD: The Johns Hopkins University Press, 1989, p. 182.
3. James C. Juhnke, *Vision, Doctrine, War: Mennonite Identity and Organization in America 1890-1930.* The Mennonite

Experience in America Series. Scottdale, PA: Herald Press, 1989, pp. 173-77.

4.　Ira Ebersole Miller, "The Development and the Present Status of Mennonite Secondary and Higher Education in the United States and Canada," Ed.D. dissertation, Temple University, 1953, pp. 79-96.

5.　Cornelius J. Dyck and Dennis Martin, eds., *The Mennonite Encyclopedia. A Comprehensive Reference Work on the Anabaptist-Mennonite Movement, Volumes A-Z*. Scottdale, PA: Herald Press, 1990, s.v. "Education," by Adolph Ens.

6.　Hubert R. Pellman, *Eastern Mennonite College, 1917-1967: A History*. Harrisonburg, VA: Eastern Mennonite College, 1967, p. 43.

7.　Harold Ernest Bauman, "The Believers' Church and the Church College," Ed.D. dissertation, Teachers College, Columbia University, 1972, p. 83.

8.　Theron F. Schlabach, *Peace, Faith, Nation: Mennonites and Amish in Nineteenth-Century America*. The Mennonite Experience in America Series. Scottdale, PA: Herald Press, 1988, pp. 132-34.

9.　Samuel Floyd Pannebecker, *Ventures of Faith: The Story of Mennonite Biblical Seminary*. Elkhard, IN: Mennonite Biblical Seminary, 1975, pp. 5-11.

10.　Rich Preheim, "College, Seminary Enrollment Up Slightly," *Mennonite Weekly Review*, 3 November 1994, p. 3. (This article does not include enrollment at Messiah College.)

11.　Cornelius J. Dyck and Dennis Martin, eds., *The Mennonite Encyclopedia. A Comprehensive Reference Work on the Anabaptist-Mennonite Movement, Volumes A-Z*. Scottdale, PA: Herald Press, 1990, s.v. "Education," by Adolph Ens.

12.　Charles Larson, ed., "In-Service Education," *Pacific Magazine*, Spring 1990, pp. 4-5.

13.　Joseph L. Lapp, letter to Board of Trustees of Eastern Mennonite College and Seminary, 8 July 1993.

14.　Peter J. Wedel, *The Story of Bethel College*. North Newton, KS: Bethel College, 1954, pp. 50-63.

15. David A. Haury, ed., "A Bethel Sampler, 1887-1987." *Mennonite Life* 42 (March 1987): 1-47.

16. *Bethel College 1993-1995 Catalog*. North Newton, KS: 1993, p. 6.

17. C. Henry Smith and E.J. Hirschler, eds., *The Story of Bluffton College*. Bluffton, OH: Bluffton College, 1925, pp. 125-27, 143.

18. *Bluffton College 1994-95 Catalog*. Bluffton, OH: 1994, p. 4.

19. *Associate Mennonite Biblical Seminary Catalog 1994-1996*. Elkhart, IN: 1994, p. 1.

20. George R. Brunk III to Donovan D. Steiner, 14 September 1994, Memorandum.

21. *Eastern Mennonite Seminary Catalog*. Harrisonburg, VA: 1993, pp. 6-9.

22. Hubert R. Pellman, *Eastern Mennonite College, 1917-1967: A History*. Harrisonburg, VA: Eastern Mennonite College, 1967, pp. 15-43.

23. Steve Shenk, "Eastern Mennonite to Become 'University' in August," Eastern Mennonite College and Seminary Communications Department News Release, 23 March 1994.

24. *Eastern Mennonite College Catalog 1993-1995*. Harrisonburg, VA: 1993, p. 10.

25. Bryan Kehr, "John F. Funk and Elkhart Institute," *Mennonite Historical Bulletin* 46 (October 1985): 1-7.

26. Susan Fisher Miller, *Culture for Service: A History of Goshen College, 1894-1994*. Goshen, IN: Goshen College, 1994, p. 87.

27. *Goshen College Catalog 1994-95*. Goshen, IN: pp. 6-8, 126.

28. Scott Heller, "52 Private Colleges Said to Assume Major International Affairs Role," *Chronicle of Higher Education*, 26 June 1991, p. A14.

29. Mary Miller, *A Pillar of Cloud: The Story of Hesston College*. North Newton, KS: Mennonite Press, 1959, pp. 7-26, 233.

30. *Hesston College Catalog 1993-95*. Hesston, KS: 1994, pp. 2, 16-17, 70.

31. *Mennonite Brethren Biblical Seminary Catalog 1993-1995*. Fresno, CA: 1994, pp. 8, 23.

32. *Fresno Pacific College Catalog 1993-94*. Fresno, CA: 1993, p. 4.

33. Richard Kriegbaum, "Hungry, Thirsty Professionals," *Fresno Pacific College Magazine*, Winter 1988, p. 2.

34. Wesley, J. Prieb and Don Ratzlaff, *To a Higher Plane of Vision*. Hillsboro, KS: Tabor College, 1983, pp. 5, 14.

35. Carol Harrison, "A Decade Apart: Regionalization Revisited," *The Christian Leader* 19 December 1989, pp. 14-18.

36. Sheree Nikkel, "Vision of Purpose," *Tabor College Magazine*, Fall 1992, p. 4.

37. E. Morris Sider, *Messiah College: A History*. Nappanee, IN: Evangel Press, 1984, p. 33.

38. *Rosedale Bible Catalog 1994-95*. Irwin, OH: 1994, pp. 2-4.

39. Elmer S. Yoder and Jewel Showalter, *We Beheld His Glory: Rosedale Bible Institute, The First Forty Years, 1952-1992*. Irwin, OH: Rosedale Bible Institute, 1992.

40. *Sharon Mennonite Bible Institute Catalog 1994-95*. McConnellsburg, PA: 1994, p. 3.

Bibliographic Entries

552. Ainlay, Stephen C. "The 1920 Seminary Movement: A Failed Attempt at Formal Theological Education in the Mennonite Church." *Mennonite Quarterly Review* 64 (October 1990): 325-51.

Recounts a failed attempt by key leaders in the Mennonite Church to establish seminary education. Informs readers of the modernist/fundamentalist debates and reasons for the demise of the effort.

553. Bontrager, Robert M. "Enrollment Strategies for Three Mennonite Colleges." Ed.D. dissertation. Arizona State University, 1987.

Examines enrollment problems evidenced in three colleges of the Mennonite Church. Suggests that the Mennonite Colleges should focus marketing efforts on enhancing professional programs, developing adult degree programs, identifying non-Mennonite markets, and promoting cooperation with the church constituency.

554. Brubaker, Beryl H. and Roman J. Miller. *Bioethics and the Beginning of Life: An Anabaptist Perspective.* Scottdale, PA: Herald Press, 1990.

Stresses the importance of Christian community in addressing bioethical issues at the beginning of life. Presents perspectives of several Mennonite higher-education faculty.

555. Dyck, Cornelius J. and Dennis Martin, eds. *The Mennonite Encyclopedia. A Comprehensive Reference Work on the Anabaptist-Mennonite Movement, Volumes A-Z.* Scottdale, PA/Waterloo, Ontario: Herald Press, 1990.

Contains 1,300 entries on a wide range of topics related to Mennonite life including "Bible Colleges and Institutes," "Education," "Scholarship," "Seminaries," and "Theological Education by Extension." Provides profiles of Mennonite educators Noah Byers, Edmund G. Kaufman, John R. Mumaw, John L. Stauffer, and Sanford Calvin Yoder.

556. Flowers, Marshall Eugene, Jr. "Christian College Distinctives: A Study of the Institutional Satisfaction and

Morale at Christian College Coalition Institutions." Ph.D. dissertation. Claremont Graduate School, 1992.

Builds on faculty-morale-and-satisfaction study conducted by Rice and Austin. Probes organizational leadership and academic environment at four Christian College Coalition institutions including Eastern Mennonite University located in Harrisonburg, Virginia.

557. Gelfand, Lawrence E. "Foot Soldier in Academia: Jacob C. Meyer, Historian." *History Teacher* 25 (May 1992): 279-92.

Describes the life and career of Mennonite educator Jacob C. Meyer, professor of history at Western Reserve University. Cites Meyer's contribution to the Mennonite Church and Mennonite higher education.

558. Gundy, Jeff. "Beyond Conformity and Rebellion: Opposition, Community, and Mennonite Education." *Conrad Grebel Review* 8 (Winter 1990): 35-52.

Explores three movements in pedagogy identified as the "mainstream critique," the "oppositional pedagogy" approach, and the "Christian peace pedagogy" approach. Cites need for more clarity about what is most important in Mennonite educational curriculum and instruction.

559. Harrison, Carol. "A Decade Apart: Regionalization Revisited." *The Christian Leader*, 19 December 1989, pp. 14-18.

Reviews a ten-year-old decision to shift control of two Mennonite Brethren church colleges, Fresno Pacific College in California and Tabor College in Kansas, to district conference control. Asserts that district control helped to develop greater loyalty among constituent groups.

560. Haury, David A., ed. "A Bethel Sampler, 1887-1987." *Mennonite Life* 42 (March 1987): 1-47.

Chronicles the centennial of Bethel College (Newton, Kansas) as the oldest Mennonite College in North America. Offers the department histories including teacher education, music, fine arts, home economics, physical education, mathematics, and natural sciences. Culminates with a history of the Bethel Museum and an autobiographical sketch of Edmund George Kaufman whose presidency (1932-1952) helped shape the college.

561. Hawkley, Ken, ed. *Mennonite Higher Education: Experience and Vision*. Bluffton, OH: Bluffton College, 1992.

Contains eighteen chapters contributed by Mennonite educators. Explores historical background, contemporary environments, and future projections for Mennonite higher education. A symposium sponsored by the Council on Higher Education of the General Conference Mennonite Church, June 26-28, 1992.

562. Juhnke, James C. *Dialogue with a Heritage: Cornelius H. Wedel and the Beginnings of Bethel College*. North Newton, KS: Bethel College, 1987.

Highlights the influence of Cornelius H. Wedel, the first president of Bethel College. Also describes the various historical and theological forces that shaped the foundations of the college.

563.   Juhnke, James C. *Vision, Doctrine, War: Mennonite Identity and Organization in America, 1890-1930.* Scottdale, PA: Herald Press, 1989.

Traces denominational advances in colleges and hospitals in Chapter 6 and recounts the impact of modernist-fundamentalist controversy in the Mennonite Church in Chapter 9.

564.   Kauffman, J. Howard and Leo Driedger. *The Mennonite Mosaic.* Scottdale, PA: Herald Press, 1991.

Analyzes data from survey studies on North American Anabaptist groups. Contains an important chapter entitled "Emerging Institutions" in which Mennonite church schools and institutions of higher education are examined.

565.   Kauffman, Norman L., Judith N. Martin, and Henry D. Weaver. *Students Abroad: Strangers at Home.* Yarmouth, ME: Intercultural Press, 1992.

Assesses the relevance of study abroad to the academic experience of college students. Personal accounts of students from Goshen College and two universities illustrate student change through study abroad. Proposes that international education can serve as a prototype for what should happen in general education.

566.   Klassen, Roy Leon. "The Influence of Mennonite College Choral Curricula Upon Music Practices in American Mennonite Churches." Mus.D. dissertation. Arizona State University, 1990.

Ascertains perceptions of choral directors of six Mennonite colleges in the United States regarding college preparation of church musicians.

567. Kraybill, Donald B. "What Makes Mennonite Colleges Distinctive." *Gospel Herald*, 2 February 1993, pp. 1-4.

Proposes a margin of difference in Mennonite higher education, identifying distinctives in governance, mission, values, people, efficiency, connections, and commitment. Cautions that the seven distinctives can only be maintained through direct advocacy and support from the Mennonite constituency.

568. Miller, Susan Fisher. *Culture for Service: A History of Goshen College*. Goshen, IN: Goshen College, 1994.

Chronicles the history of Goshen College from 1894 to 1994. Follows a chronological sequence detailing the events that shaped a Mennonite liberal arts college nationally recognized for its enterprising leadership in service and international education.

569. Page, John Irwin. "A Study of Secularistic Trends in their Effect upon Seven Protestant Colleges of Kansas." Ph.D. dissertation. Kansas State University, 1989.

Explores trends toward secularization within seven Christian Colleges in Kansas. Includes Tabor College, a Mennonite Brethren college located in Hillsboro, Kansas.

570. Redekop, Calvin Wall and Samuel J. Steiner, eds. *Mennonite Identity: Historical and Contemporary Perspectives*. Lanham, MD: University Press of America, Inc., 1988.

Contains eighteen chapters examining the concept of identity among Mennonites. Chapter 8 includes a brief discussion of Mennonite higher education. Chapter 14 is titled "Philosophy and Mennonite Self-Understanding."

571. Schlabach, Theron F. *Peace, Faith, Nation: Mennonites and Amish in Nineteenth-Century America*. Scottdale, PA: Herald Press, 1988.

Chapter 11, titled "The Quickening at Century's End," provides background for new developments within the Mennonite Church in the late nineteenth century that fostered the development of church institutions including higher education.

572. Schrag, Dale R., ed. "Bethel College: Centennial." *Mennonite Life* 42 (September 1987): 1-19.

Devotes entire issue to Bethel College's centennial (1887-1987) celebration. Includes articles on the college's struggle for accreditation, campus architecture, and history of library and archives.

573. Seitz, Ruth Hoover. *The Way We Are*. Harrisonburg, VA: Eastern Mennonite College, 1992.

Depicts seventy-fifth anniversary (1917-1992) of Eastern Mennonite College and Seminary and Eastern Mennonite High School through photographs, captions, and brief essays.

574. Sheriff, John K. and Alain Epp Weaver, eds. *A Drink from the Stream: Essays by Bethel College Faculty and Staff*. North Newton, KS: Bethel College, 1991.

Presents essays by Bethel College faculty for purposes of modelling vision and scholarship to Bethel College students.

575. Showalter, Stuart Wesley. *The Role of Service-Learning in International Education: Proceedings of a Wingspread Conference, held April 26-28, 1989 at Racine, Wisconsin.* Goshen, IN: Goshen College, 1989.

Presents perspectives of several Goshen College faculty on the role of service-learning for higher education in international education. Cites the extensive experience gained in Goshen College's study-service term.

576. Sider, E. Morris, ed. "The Brethren in Christ Experience." *Brethren in Christ History and Life* 16 (December 1993): 279-395.

Explores what it means to be Brethren in Christ through the personal stories and critiques of educators and laypersons. Messiah College's role in shaping Christian experience is threaded throughout several narratives.

577. Stolzfus, Victor. *Church-Affiliated Higher Education.* Goshen, IN: Goshen College, 1992.

Presents exploratory case studies by a Mennonite college president of Presbyterian, Roman Catholic, and Wesleyan colleges. Contains appendix on Mennonite college governance.

578. Stuckey, Thomas L. "Cross-Sectional Analysis of Allegiance to Religious Beliefs Among Young Mennonite

Adults." Ph.D. dissertation. Bowling Green State University, 1991.

Investigates the changes in allegiance to Mennonite beliefs of young adults during the traditional college years.

579. Yoder, Elmer S. and Jewel Showalter. *We Beheld His Glory: Rosedale Bible Institute, The First Forty Years, 1952-1992*. Irwin, OH: Rosedale Bible Institute, 1992.

Chronicles the history of Rosedale Bible Institute located at Irwin, Ohio. Presents two parts: "An Historical Overview" and "Sketches from History."

580. Yoder, Nate. "Goshen College and the Modernism Question: Mennonites and Divergent Streams in American Protestantism." Paper presented at the Conference on Faith and History, 6 November 1992. Westmont College, Santa Barbara, CA.

Explores the historical context for modernist/fundamentalist theological debate regarding Goshen College in early twentieth century.

581. Zehr, Paul M. and Jim Egli. *Alternative Models of Mennonite Pastoral Formation*. Elkhart, IN: Institute of Mennonite Studies, Occasional Papers No. 15, 1992.

Identifies two alternative models of pastoral preparation followed by responses from critics. Presents helpful background on Mennonite philosophy of education.

CHAPTER 22
Independent Christian Colleges and Universities

William Vance Trollinger, Jr.

The category, independent Christian colleges and universities, is not a very large one. The reason for this is rather simple: as William Ringenberg has noted in the introduction to his helpful 1988 bibliography on such schools, "there are not many contemporary colleges and universities that are both continuing Christian in philosophical orientation and independent of denominational ties in governance."[1] While this may change in the future, given the weakening of denominational loyalties among American Protestants, the fact remains that there are not too many independent Christian colleges.

For purposes of this essay I will be looking at fourteen institutions.[2] I have divided these colleges into two sub-categories: evangelical institutions and fundamentalist institutions. As will be further discussed, the latter schools tolerate much less theological diversity, place much stricter behavioral regulations upon students and faculty, and are much more adamant about separating from both "the world" and from

Christians and Christian institutions that do not share their views.

The fact that evangelical and fundamentalist schools are quite different requires that I deal with each group separately. But I should note up-front that, in a number of ways, these schools are strikingly similar (more similar than some faculty and administrators at both sorts of colleges are willing to acknowledge). I will elaborate upon these similarities in the conclusion, but one point needs to be made up-front. Most independent Christian colleges are quite young, founded in the past 100 years or so (and in some cases, in the past few decades). Most were created, at least in part, in response to the well-documented "secularization of the academy."[3] The desire to provide a conservative Protestant alternative to secular higher education remains central to all of these schools, evangelical and fundamentalist alike.

Not all independent Christian colleges had their beginnings in the twentieth century, and for this fact we can thank the Methodists. The oldest independent Christian college, Taylor University, was founded by the North Indiana Conference of the Methodist Episcopal Church in 1847. Started as Fort Wayne Female College, the school soon admitted men. In 1890 it was renamed for Methodist missionary William Taylor (and soon thereafter relocated in Upland, Indiana). Also in 1890, and just a few hundred miles to the south, Methodist evangelist John Wesley Hughes founded Kentucky Holiness College, which would eventually become Asbury College, in honor of America's first Methodist bishop.[4]

Both Taylor and Asbury were among the very "few colleges representing the sizable holiness branch of Methodism,"[5] with its emphasis on the complete sanctification of the believer. As a result, frequent revivals and an intense pietism were a part of student life at Taylor and Asbury. Even as both schools gradually moved toward nondenominational status in the early twentieth century, they continued to be shaped by their holiness heritage. One result was that, when the fundamentalist-modernist battles broke out in the 1920s, these two schools were somewhat less involved than other independent Christian schools. This point should not be exaggerated: both Asbury and Taylor held to a conservative Protestant theology, and were not at all in sympathy with biblical criticism and theological modernism. But while they were certainly inclined to the fundamentalist side of the fight, they were generally less obsessed with pressing the case against the liberals. As William Ringenberg observes about Taylor, the school "spent much less time [in the early twentieth century] rationally defending its faith than it did emotionally experiencing it."[6]

This statement certainly does not apply to the school regarded by many as the preeminent conservative Protestant institution of higher education. Wheaton College began as Illinois Institute in 1852.[7] Established by Wesleyan Methodists, a small abolitionist group, the school struggled to stay afloat financially. In 1860, local Congregationalists rechartered the school as Wheaton College (for the town where it was located and the man who gave them land for the campus), placed it on sound financial footing, and established abolitionist Jonathan Blanchard as president.[8]

Wheaton blossomed under the leadership of Blanchard and his son Charles, who succeeded his father in 1882 and presided over the school until 1925. In terms of national prominence, Wheaton really came into its own in the 1920s. During that decade, fundamentalists, or militantly anti-modernist evangelicals, organized in an effort to scourge the major denominations of liberals and rid the public schools of evolutionists. For these fundamentalist crusaders, Wheaton came to be viewed as their college. One reason was because of Charles Blanchard's leadership role in the fundamentalist movement, as seen in his appointment as chair of the Committee on Colleges and Seminaries of the World's Christian Fundamentals Association (WCFA). Blanchard's school also had impeccable credentials as a theologically conservative institution, a point reinforced by the school's 1927 decision to make the WCFA creed, with its emphasis on Biblical inerrancy and premillennialism, the school's official doctrinal statement.[9] Finally, Wheaton's nondenominational status was attractive, in that it allowed ultra-conservatives from a great variety of denominations to attend. For all of these reasons, a virtual "Who's Who of Northern Fundamentalism",[10] including William Bell Riley and Lyman and Milton Stewart, actively supported and promoted Wheaton College as the fundamentalist college of choice.

Wheaton's preeminence did not foreclose the creation of other independent Christian colleges. The years of the fundamentalist crusade saw the founding of the following institutions: Southwestern Collegiate Institute (1919), in Siloam Springs, Arkansas, which would become John Brown University, and which was noteworthy for its distinctive emphasis on professional training; Bob Jones College (1926), which will be discussed below; and, Bryan College (1930), which was established in the town (Dayton, Tennessee) where the leader of the antievolutionist crusade fought his last and most famous fight, but which did not become the great fundamentalist university that some boosters had envisioned. Then, in 1940, Westmont College was founded in Los Angeles (eventually moving to Santa Barbara), with great hopes of becoming the "Wheaton of the West."[11]

But all of the aforementioned colleges notwithstanding, Taylor and Wheaton included, the most noteworthy conservative Protestant educational alternatives in pre-World War II America were the Bible schools. These institutions are the subject of a fine essay by Virginia Brereton elsewhere in this volume. But as a number of these Bible schools eventually evolved into independent Christian colleges, a few remarks are in order here.

The Bible School movement began in the 1880s, with the founding of New York Missionary Training Institute and, most important, Moody Bible Institute in Chicago. A host of such schools were created in the next few decades; relevant for our purposes are: Boston Missionary Training School (1889), which would eventually become Gordon College; in Los Angeles, Training School for Christian Workers, which later became Azusa Pacific University; Providence Bible Institute (1900), which would become Barrington College, before merging with Gordon College; in Minneapolis, Northwestern Bible and Missionary Training School (1902), later to add Northwestern College; and, the Bible Institute of Los Angeles (1908), which would become Biola University.[12]

These schools sought to inculcate laypersons in a conservative understanding of the Bible, while at the same time training them for work as evangelists, missionaries, and religious teachers. The schools listed above predate the fundamentalist crusade; however, as increasing numbers of conservative Protestants became alienated both from mainline denominations and their colleges and seminaries, they turned to these Bible schools for educational training and other services. In fact, Biola, Northwestern, and Gordon all served as centers of regional fundamentalist networks. It is no exaggeration to say that the Bible schools served as the educational wing of the fundamentalist movement.[13]

Most Bible schools began with few resources, minimal admissions requirements, and a short course of study. For example, the Bible Institute of Los Angeles began its existence in a "large suite of four rooms ... above a pool hall,"[14] while Boston Missionary School started "with no fixed curriculum, no formal entrance requirements, ... no buildings," and one instructor.[15] But these schools did not remain at this point. And it is not just that they got larger. As Virginia Brereton has established, over time the Bible schools began to move toward academic respectability: they began to "demand ... higher educational prerequisites of students," "acquire ... bigger and bigger libraries," and enter "larger number[s] of liberal arts subjects [into] the curriculum." Eventually, some former Bible schools were accredited as liberal arts colleges.[16]

The shift from Bible school to liberal arts college is precisely what happened with all four of the schools under consideration here. Gordon moved fastest to achieve academic respectability. By 1917, the school was awarding collegiate degrees; four years later, the school had adopted the name Gordon College of Theology and Missions, and was even beginning to offer some graduate courses. In the next few decades, Azusa, Biola, and Northwestern followed Gordon's march to academic respectability.[17]

It should be noted that the shift from Bible school to liberal arts college was not always painless. Some constituents were bound to see the increased emphasis on academics and professionalism as an abandonment of the school's mission. This viewpoint was particularly true at Northwestern. The liberal arts college was established there in 1944. When founder and president William Bell Riley died in 1947, Billy Graham became president, and immediately confirmed the worst fears of Bible school supporters by concentrating his energies on the college. The resultant infighting helped convince Graham to resign in 1952. By 1956 Northwestern split, with the Bible school supporters departing to create Pillsbury Bible Institute. Without Bible school or fundamentalist support, Northwestern College limped along, finally closing in 1966. But, in an incredible twist, a gift from the wife of a pizza mogul allowed the school to reopen in 1972. The reborn Northwestern was a liberal arts college, but it also required all students to have a second major in Bible. In this regard, Northwestern was following Biola's lead; in so doing, both institutions retained direct ties to their Bible school heritage.[18]

The advance toward academic respectability on the part of the former Bible schools reflects a larger trend among evangelical colleges (including independent evangelical colleges), particularly in the two decades after World War II. As Thomas Askew explains in a useful essay, in these years evangelical colleges strove mightily (and successfully) to secure accreditation, raise academic standards, improve the credentials and salaries of their faculty, increase enrollment, strengthen the financial base of the institution, and improve the physical plant. Some schools even engineered "upwardly mobile changes in location," from city to suburb: Gordon moved from Boston to Wenham, Biola moved from Los Angeles to La Mirada, and Northwestern moved from Minneapolis to Roseville.[19]

There would appear to be a number of reasons for this aggressive drive to move up the academic ladder in the 1950s and 1960s. Perhaps the simplest was a certain institutional imperative pressing these colleges to grow, to improve. Certainly this imperative was fueled by the fact that, as Askew notes, "in the postwar era, evangelical families and communities were experiencing upward social mobility, and their educational ambitions and expectations were rising with them."[20]

But there was more to it than social mobility. In the 1940s a number of leading Protestant conservatives came to the conclusion that fundamentalism had gone too far in its emphasis on denominational separatism, anti-intellectualism, and withdrawal from American culture. These evangelicals, or neoevangelicals, who in 1943 organized the National Association of Evangelicals, asserted that Christians needed to engage the culture, not simply resist it. But engagement was not enough; they also called on evangelical intellectuals to be about the task of shaping the life of the mind in the modern world. Of course this "shaping the mind" business is, well, a grandiose notion. But there is also no question that the emergence of this new evangelicalism, with its desire for intellectual engagement and achievement, played a crucial role in prodding many conservative Protestant colleges (including the independent colleges we have discussed so far) to strive for academic excellence.[21]

But for a number of neoevangelicals, including Carl Henry, editor of *Christianity Today*, these efforts were not sufficient. As they saw it, what was really needed was the creation of an evangelical university, with top-flight graduate programs. Throughout the 1950s and 1960s, a number of proposals were floated, including the idea of establishing such an institution on the campus of Gordon College. But the evangelical university remained a pipe dream.[22]

It is interesting to note, however, that the institution that may have come closest to fulfilling the evangelicals' vision appeared seemingly out of nowhere in the mid-1960s, and from (at least in the eyes of evangelicals in the Reformed tradition) the unlikeliest quarter. In 1965 the famous Pentecostal evangelist and healer, Oral Roberts, opened his nondenominational school in Tulsa. Roberts was not trying to create *the* evangelical university; his goal was slightly less expansive: to quote one historian, he sought to establish the "university of the entire charismatic movement." This goal is remarkable enough; even more remarkable is that, in striking contrast with all other independent Christian colleges, Oral Roberts University (ORU) began its existence with huge financial resources and a spanking-new campus. No years of classrooms in the church basement (or over a pool hall) for this school. With its array of futuristic buildings, including the massive Learning Resources Center (with its amazing audio-visual learning stations) and the 10,500-seat sports arena, ORU quickly became one of the leading tourist sites in Oklahoma.[23]

Despite the architecture and technology, in one sense Oral Roberts University was a throwback to a time when presidents dominated life at their institutions. From the school's inception, Oral Roberts viewed his university as a "semi-theocracy," with "God as the head of the school" and Roberts "'the appointed head by God.'"[24] Roberts ran the show, and his influence could be seen everywhere: in the 200-foot prayer tower in the middle of campus; in the requirement that all faculty and students be placed on an aerobics program (part of Roberts' concern with the "whole man"); and, most important, in the pervasive emphasis on "the charismatic working of the Holy Spirit." But the lack of a democratic governing structure did not seem to hinder ORU's growth. Within a decade of the first graduating class, 4,000 students were enrolled, and a number of graduate programs had been established.[25]

As evangelical colleges prospered and grew in the 1950s and 1960s, there also came an awareness that there might be much to be gained by working together with other evangelical schools, with whom they had much in common. This cooperative impulse seemed to be particularly strong among the independent Christian colleges, unencumbered as they were by denominational ties. When, in March of 1971, the presidents of ten evangelical institutions met to create the Christian College Consortium, four independent colleges were included: Gordon, Taylor, Westmont, and Wheaton.[26] (Asbury was added four years later.) At heart, the Consortium's mission was to improve and advance the cause of evangelical higher education in the United States. Toward that end, the Consortium schools developed a number of cooperative academic programs for students and faculty, and actively promoted "research and study among evangelical scholars on the integration of the Christian faith and academic learning,"[27] worked to attract curricular and faculty development grants, and continued to discuss the possibility of establishing an independent Christian university.[28]

Probably the most important achievement of the Christian College Consortium (CCC) was the creation, in 1976, of the Christian College Coalition (CCC). (One sign of a true evangelical academic insider is the ability to distinguish between the two CCCs.) The Consortium established this satellite organization for the specific purpose of providing Christian colleges with a unified voice in Washington, in order to protect the freedom and promote the interests of these schools. What is interesting is that the Coalition has become much more than just a lobbying organization. William Ringenberg's 1984 comments are even more true today: the Coalition is now "the primary interdenominational confederation of continuing Christian liberal arts colleges," in the process of "surpassing the parent organization in operation and significance."[29] The importance of Coalition affiliation had always been clear to the independent evangelical colleges, all 11 of which were early members of the Coalition (which had grown to 77 schools by 1993).[30]

As evinced by the Consortium and Coalition, as well as the numerous professional organizations of evangelical scholars (e.g., the Conference on Faith and History) and periodicals such as *Christian Scholar's Review*, it is clear that in the past two decades evangelical higher education has come of age in America. And the independent evangelical colleges, or many of them, have been on the leading wave of this development. This maturation is particularly clear in the development and expansion of graduate programs at places such as Azusa Pacific, Biola, and Wheaton. This "coming of age" is also clear in the increased visibility in the larger academic world of scholars from these institutions.

Despite these successes, a number of evangelical insiders have become increasingly critical of evangelical higher education. For example, a number of observers, including some folks teaching at evangelical colleges, have scathingly pointed out that almost all of these colleges are overwhelmingly white, Republican, and middle class, or, as Nicholas Wolterstoff has put it, "exclusive ethnic clubs of Euro-Americans."[31] Most particularly, there are very few African Americans either attending or teaching at these schools.

There is also the charge that evangelical colleges have accommodated too much to the prevailing culture. In his study of evangelical college students (including students at Gordon, Taylor, Westmont, and Wheaton), James Davison Hunter suggests that, when these students complete their four years, they have "less conviction" and "less confidence" in their Christian beliefs, and are "perhaps more vulnerable to ... worldly distractions." Douglas Frank continues a similar theme, suggesting that evangelical colleges, like evangelicalism in general, are in the process of selling their souls to "the demon of consumerism."[32]

That these critics are, for the most part, on the mark is a point worth noting. But it is also important to remember that such self-criticism is also a further sign of the "coming of age" of evangelical higher education.

We have concentrated our attention on evangelical institutions. But there is a second category of independent Christian colleges, i.e., the fundamentalist schools. A little historical background helps place these institutions within the context of the times in which they developed. When neoevangelicalism emerged out of the old fundamentalist movement in the 1940s and 1950s, there were many conservative Protestants who rejected what they saw as the evangelicals' sell-out to the larger culture. These Protestants, who proudly retained the label "fundamentalist," maintained both their militant antimodernism, as well as their insistence on separating, not only from "the world," but also from Christians who have not remained true to the faith. This separatism is a salient characteristic of fundamentalist colleges: not only have none of the schools examined below (as of yet) joined the Christian College Coalition, but their leaders often seem to expend more energy attacking evangelical colleges than criticizing more "secular" schools.[33]

All three independent fundamentalist colleges are in the Southeast, and were founded by successful evangelist-ministers. In 1926, fundamentalist evangelist Bob Jones established a college in Florida; after a stint in Tennessee, in 1947 he moved the school to Greenville, South Carolina, where it is today (and where it, as Bob Jones University [BJU], has been presided over by the second and now the third Bob Jones). One year before Jones left Tennessee, Baptist minister Lee Roberson established Tennessee Temple University in Chattanooga, as an extension of his Highland Park Baptist Church. Finally, and following a similar path to that of Roberson, radio/TV evangelist Jerry Falwell started Liberty University in 1971, also as an extension of his church (the Thomas Road Baptist Church of Lynchburg, Virginia).

These schools have been characterized by extremely authoritarian leadership. For the most part, there are no challenges to presidential rule; not only is there a certain amount of fear, but there is an understanding among employees that the man in charge is God's man, and hence deserves their allegiance. But when there are challenges to presidential authority, the response is swift and severe. Perhaps the most famous example occurred at BJU in the 1950s. A good number of faculty and staff had become frustrated with their very low salaries and the requirement that they must live on campus. Bob Jones Sr. and Jr. responded by building into the school by-laws a rule that no employee could complain about the institution; if such disloyalty occurred, that person was to be fired. When a good number of the faculty and staff resigned in protest, Jones preached a sermon on Judas; according to one of the departing administrators, Jones made it clear that "Judas was a much finer fellow, for he did have the grace to hang himself."[34]

In the same vein, these schools also have quite strict rules governing both belief and behavior. At Falwell's school, the student rules are known as "the Liberty Way," with requirements regarding dress, church attendance, and relations with the opposite sex (hand-holding only, as of the late 1980s). If anything, the regulations at BJU were even stricter, with prohibitions against off-campus dating "unless the couple is accompanied by a faculty member or a married couple."[35] And behavioral regulations do not just apply to students. At Tennessee Temple, at least in the 1970s, faculty members were required "to join the Highland Park Baptist Church, to fill out a weekly activity report verifying attendance at one week-night and two Sunday services ... and not to play cards, go to the movies, participate in mixed bathing, wear shorts, or [as regards men] grow a beard or wear long hair."[36]

For all of this -- the strict doctrinal and behavior requirements, the extremely authoritarian leadership, the pervasive emphasis on separation -- the reality is that these schools have thrived, both in numbers and programs. Bob Jones

University is a good example. Enrolling nearly 5,000 students in 1990, BJU has schools of Arts and Science, Religion, Fine Arts, Education, Business Administration, and Applied Studies. The school's success in the arts is nothing short of remarkable, particularly its film program (which actually won an award at the Cannes Film Festival) and its art museum (which has a superb collection, but, not surprisingly, no modern art). All at a place that, on separatist grounds, refuses to seek accreditation.[37]

Of course, whether these schools will maintain their separatist stance is open for debate. Some observers (including people at BJU) feel that Liberty University is showing signs of heading down the road toward the less militant, more inclusive evangelical schools.[38] But if these schools do, indeed, become more inclusive, one can rest assured that new, more separatistic institutions will rise up to take their place.

Independent evangelical and fundamentalist colleges are, indeed, quite different. There is no getting around the fact that the educational experience at, say, Gordon College is not at all the same as the educational experience at Bob Jones University.

Having pointed out the differences in the two types of colleges, it is interesting to note that prospective college students and their parents will often send applications to both sorts of schools. This practice was brought home to me when I taught a course here at Messiah (an evangelical, albeit not independent, liberal arts college) on fundamentalism and televangelism. During one of the class discussions, a couple of students alluded to the fact that the only other school they had applied to was Liberty University. Stunned, I asked for a show of hands of all those who had applied to Liberty or Bob Jones; approximately half of the students in that class of 35 answered in the affirmative.[39]

The fact that students apply apparently indiscriminately to both kinds of schools is not just an indication of naivete on the part of conservative Protestant families, nor is it simply a failure on the part of college public relations representatives to articulate clearly their particular school's vision. It is also an indication that evangelical and fundamentalist schools are not as different as individuals in both sorts of schools might assert. For one thing, the faith statements at both sorts of schools are often quite similar; while the statements at fundamentalist schools are typically longer and much more detailed, the fact is that, even at many of the evangelical schools, faculty are required to sign on to inerrancy and premillennialism statements. Moreover, both sorts of schools engage in a good amount of "boundary maintenance." While fundamentalist schools are much more concerned with strict, impermeable boundaries, and while a good number of faculty members at evangelical schools would not be allowed to teach at a fundamentalist school, the fact is that evangelical colleges can also be quite restrictive, and, on occasion, engage in a purge.[40]

Finally, and returning to a point made in the introduction, both sets of schools have sought, and still seek, to provide a conservative Protestant alternative to what they see as the pervasive secularization of state and even denominational colleges in the United States. Certainly this feeling is much stronger at fundamentalist colleges; certainly evangelical institutions are, generally speaking, more interested in dialogue with the rest of the academy. But there is no getting around the fact that both sorts of independent Christian colleges share a rather similar vision of themselves and their place in American education and American society.

Endnotes

1. William C. Ringenberg, "Independent Christian Colleges and Universities," in Thomas C. Hunt and James C. Carper, eds., *Religious Colleges and Universities in America: A Selected Bibliography*. New York: Garland Press, 1988, p. 208.

2. My list of schools includes: Asbury College, Azusa Pacific University, Biola University, Bob Jones University, Bryan College, Gordon College, John Brown University, Liberty

University, Northwestern College, Oral Roberts University, Taylor University, Tennessee Temple University, Westmont College, and Wheaton College. I readily concede that this list could easily be contested as being either too inclusive or too exclusive. Regarding the former, I can imagine that some may argue that schools such as Liberty and Tennessee Temple are so tied to a particular Baptist church that it does not make sense to call them independent. This point is well taken; however, these schools are not, strictly speaking, denominational schools, and I know of no other category in which these institutions can be properly located. Others may argue that I have left out schools whose denominational ties are so tenuous as to render them, in effect, independent. It may be true that I have omitted schools that could have been included, but determining where to draw the line between "denominational" and "independent" is a very difficult task. I suspect that, as denominational loyalties further weaken in America, this task will become even more difficult.

3. For the most complete treatment of the secularization of higher education, see: George Marsden, *The Soul of the American University: From Protestant Establishment to Established Nonbelief.* New York: Oxford University Press, 1993.

4. William C. Ringenberg, *Taylor University: The First 125 Years.* Grand Rapids, MI: Wm. B. Eerdmans, 1973, pp. 20-80; *1994-1995 Asbury College Bulletin*, p. 9.

5. William C. Ringenberg, *The Christian College: A History of Protestant Higher Education in America.* Grand Rapids, MI: Wm. B. Eerdmans, 1984, p. 175.

6. Ringenberg, *Taylor University*, pp. 70-71, 112-14; Ringenberg, *Christian College*, pp. 175-76.

7. This date comes from *InForm: Bulletin of Wheaton College, 1994-1995*, p. 5. But there seems to be some confusion in this regard. In his *Dictionary of American Christianity* entry on Wheaton, Paul Bechtel gives the school's founding date as 1848; but in his full-scale history of the school, Bechtel observes that "Illinois Institute began its first full year in 1854." *Wheaton College:*

A Heritage Remembered, 1860-1984. Wheaton, IL: Harold Shaw Publishers, 1984, p. 19.

8. Bechtel, *Wheaton College*, pp. 13-22.

9. Bechtel, *Wheaton College*, pp. 29-107; William Vance Trollinger, Jr., *God's Empire: William Bell Riley and Midwestern Fundamentalism*. Madison, WI: University of Wisconsin Press, 1990, p. 39; and Ringenberg, *Christian College*, pp. 173-74.

10. Thomas A. Askew, "The Liberal Arts College Encounters Intellectual Change: A Comparative Study of Education at Knox and Wheaton Colleges, 1837-1925." Ph.D. dissertation, Northwestern University, 1969, as quoted in Ringenberg, *Christian College*, p. 174.

11. *John Brown Catalog, 1993-1995*, p. 7; Ringenberg, *Christian College*, pp. 174, 194, 241; and *1993-1995 Westmont Catalog*, p. 3.

12. Virginia Lieson Brereton, *Training God's Army: The American Bible School, 1880-1940*. Bloomington, IN: Indiana University Press, 1990, pp. 71-77; S.A. Witmer, *The Bible College Story: Education with Dimension*. Manhasset, NY: Channel Press, Inc., 1962, pp. 72-74.

13. For an example of how this worked out in practice, see: William Vance Trollinger, Jr., "Riley's Empire: Northwestern Bible School and Fundamentalism in the Upper Midwest." *Church History* 57 (June 1988): 197-212.

14. Robert Williams and Marilyn Miller, *Chartered for His Glory: Biola University, 1908-1983*. Los Angeles: Associated Students of Biola University, 1983, p. 15.

15. Thomas A. and Jean M. Askew, *A Faithful Past, An Expectant Future: Celebrating a Century of Christian Higher Education*. Wenham, MA: Gordon College, 1988, p. 8.

16. Brereton, *Training God's Army*, pp. 78-86.

17. Askew and Askew, *A Faithful Past*, pp. 20-22.

18. Trollinger, *God's Empire*, pp. 151-56; Ringenberg, *Christian College*, p. 168.

19. Thomas A. Askew, "The Shaping of Evangelical Higher Education Since World War II," in Joel A. Carpenter and

Kenneth W. Shipps, eds., *Making Higher Education Christian: The History and Mission of Evangelical Colleges in America*. Grand Rapids, MI: Wm. B. Eerdmans, 1987, pp. 141-44, 151n10. As Askew notes, in those years other evangelical schools that moved to the suburbs included Malone, Calvin, and Bethel (MN).

20.   Askew, "Evangelical Higher Education," p. 141.

21.   For discussions of neo-evangelicalism and the life of the mind, see: George M. Marsden, *Reforming Fundamentalism: Fuller Seminary and the New Evangelicalism*. Grand Rapids, MI: Wm. B. Eerdmans, 1987; and Mark Noll, *Between Faith and Criticism: Evangelicals, Scholarship, and the Bible*. San Francisco: Harper and Row, 1987.

22.   Ringenberg, *Christian College*, p. 198.

23.   Ringenberg, *Christian College*, pp. 192-93.

24.   As quoted in David Edwin Harrell, Jr., *Oral Roberts: An American Life*. Bloomington, IN: Indiana University Press, 1983, p. 251.

25.   Harrell, *Oral Roberts*, pp. 219-52; Ringenberg, *Christian College*, p. 193.

26.   The other six original schools in the Consortium included Bethel College (MN), Eastern Mennonite, Greenville, Malone, Messiah, and Seattle Pacific. James Carl Hendrix, "The Christian College Consortium: 1971-1991." Ph.D. dissertation, Southern Illinois University, 1992, p. 50.

27.   Undated Christian College Consortium document, as quoted in Hendrix, "Christian College Consortium," p. 198.

28.   Hendrix, "Christian College Consortium," pp. 52-73, 120-28, 194-202.

29.   Ringenberg, *Christian College*, p. 207.

30.   Ringenberg, *Christian College*, pp. 204-07; Hendrix, "Christian College Consortium," pp. 120-23, 153-56, 262-63.

31.   Nicholas Wolterstorff, "Foreword," in D. John Lee, Alvaro L. Nieves, and Henry L. Allen, eds., *Ethnic-Minorities and Evangelical Christian Colleges*. Lanham, MD: University Press of America, 1991, p. ix. For further elaboration of these themes, see the essays in this volume.

32.   James Davison Hunter, *Evangelicalism: The Coming Generation*. Chicago: University of Chicago Press, 1987, p. 213; Douglass Frank, "Consumerism and the Christian College: A Call to Life in an Age of Death," in Carpenter and Shipps, eds., *Making Higher Education Christian*, p. 263.

33.   For further discussion of this antipathy toward evangelicalism on the part of fundamentalist college leaders, see: R. Wesley Hurd, "Liberty University: Fortress in the War for a Christian America." Ph.D. dissertation, University of Oregon, 1988, p. 170.

34.   Mark Taylor Dalhouse, "Bob Jones University and the Shaping of Twentieth Century Separatism." Ph.D. dissertation, Miami University, 1991, pp. 141-45; Hurd, "Liberty University," pp. 100-05; and Ringenberg, *Christian College*, pp. 182-83.

35.   Hurd, "Liberty University"; Dalhouse, "Bob Jones," pp. 254-56.

36.   Ringenberg, *Christian College*, p. 185.

37.   Dalhouse, "Bob Jones," pp. 2, 239-47.

38.   Hurd, "Liberty," pp. 257-63; Dalhouse, "Bob Jones," pp. 272-74.

39.   I am quite aware that the percentage was skewed upward because of the course topic. On the other hand, I would have been surprised if 25% of the students had applied both to Messiah and Liberty.

40.   For recent incidents at Gordon and Northwestern, see: "Catholics Need Not Apply," *Christian Century*, 9 October 1985, pp. 888-89; "Teacher Fired," *Christian Century*, 29 July - 5 August 1992, pp. 708-09; and William Thorkelson, "Christian Colleges Settle with Ousted Professors," 8 February 1993, p. 61.

Bibliographic Entries

582.   Askew, Thomas A., and Jean M. Askew. *A Faithful Past, An Expectant Future: Celebrating a Century of Christian Higher Education*. Wenham, MA: Gordon College, 1988.

Commemorates the 100-year anniversary of Gordon College's founding. Surveys the school's history, through text and photos, from its origins as a Bible institute to its current status as a liberal arts institution.

583. Carpenter, Joel A. and Kenneth A. Shipps, eds. *Making Higher Education Christian: The History and Mission of Evangelical Colleges in America*. Grand Rapids, MI : Wm. B. Eerdmans, 1987.

Contains numerous essays that deal primarily or in part with evangelical colleges. Includes: historical pieces; assessments of the academic goals and achievements of evangelical colleges; and (sometimes pointed) suggestions for improvement.

584. Dalhouse, Mark. "Bob Jones University and the Shaping of Twentieth-Century Separatism, 1926-1991." Ph.D. dissertation. Miami University, 1991.

Describes how Bob Jones University and its leaders, particularly the three generations of "Bobs Joneses," have exemplified, promoted, and led the separatist wing of American fundamentalism.

585. Flowers, Marshall E., Jr. "Christian College Distinctives: A Study of the Institutional Satisfaction and Morale at Christian College Coalition Institutions." Ph.D. dissertation. Claremont Graduate School, 1992.

Compares Christian Coalition colleges with other colleges in terms of faculty morale and satisfaction, with special focus on four schools (including Westmont College and Gordon College). Concludes that Coalition faculty are a happier lot.

586.   Hendrix, James C. "The Christian College Consortium, 1971-1991." Ph.D. dissertation. Southern Illinois University at Carbondale, 1992.

    Examines the establishment and development of the Christian College Consortium, with much attention to organizational structure and funding, and some attention to the Consortium's relationship to Christian Coalition colleges.

587.   Hunter, James Davison. *Evangelicalism: The Coming Generation.* Chicago: University of Chicago Press, 1987.

    Based upon an attitudinal survey of students and faculty at a number of evangelical schools, including some independent colleges. Asserts that young evangelicals have same lack of commitment to and confidence in traditional evangelical worldview.

588.   Hurd, Robert W. "Liberty University: Fortress in the War for a Christian America." Ph.D. dissertation. University of Oregon, 1988.

    Analyzes the development and growth of Liberty University, which the author sees as indicative of a fundamentalist renaissance in America, and symbolic of fundamentalists' (and Jerry Falwell's) desire for socio-cultural legitimacy.

589.   Kelley, Dean M. "The Supreme Court Redefines Tax Exemption." In *Church-State Relations: Tensions and Transitions.* Edited by Thomas Robbins and Roland Robertson. New Brunswick, NJ: Transaction, Inc., 1987.

    Explains and criticizes the 1983 Supreme Court ruling in *Bob Jones University vs. United States*, in which the Court asserted that racially discriminatory schools, including religious schools such as Bob Jones University, are not tax-exempt.

590. Kennedy, John W. "Is Liberty Losing Freedom by Playing Virginia's Tune?" *Christianity Today*, 19 July 1993, pp. 46-47.

Examines changes made by Liberty University to ensure that state aid would keep flowing into the institution.

591. Lansdale, David P. "Citadel Under Siege: The Contested Mission of a Christian Liberal Arts College." Ph.D. dissertation. Stanford University, 1990.

Examines the history of Wheaton College. Asserts that, since the 1960s, the school has lacked the institutional cohesion it enjoyed in its first century, in part because many faculty members are now seeking recognition from the larger academic community.

592. Lawton, Kim A. "Church-State Questions Vex Falwell's University." *Christianity Today*, 19 February 1990, pp. 36-37.

Describes legal battle over Liberty University's attempt to issue low-interest, tax-free bonds.

593. Lee, D. John, Alvaro L. Nieves, and Henry L. Allen. *Ethnic-Minorities and Evangelical Christian Colleges.* Lanham, MD: University Press of America, 1991.

Contains ten essays describing and decrying the ways in which Christian Coalition colleges, many of which are independent evangelical colleges, are alien and even hostile places for ethnic-minority students and professors.

594. Lowe, Stephen. "Forging an Agenda for Christian Higher Education in the 21st Century: An Old Testament Theology of Mission." Paper presented at the Southwestern Regional Meeting of the Evangelical Theological Society, Jackson, MS, March 3, 1990.

Calls on Christian college educators to turn to the Old Testament for a theology to undergird Christian higher education, and discusses how such a theology will promote the integration of faith and learning.

595. Maxwell, Joe. "Liberty U Weathers Debt Crisis; Falwell's 'Worst Year.'" *Christianity Today*, 10 February 1992, pp. 46-49.

Examines Liberty University's brush with bankruptcy, and Jerry Falwell's efforts to put the school on sound financial footing.

596. Ringenberg, William C. "Independent Christian Colleges and Universities." In *Religious Colleges and Universities in America: A Selected Bibliography*. Edited by Thomas C. Hunt and James C. Carper. New York: Garland Publishing, 1988.

Lists 45 articles, books, and dissertations that deal with independent Christian colleges. Includes philosophical and general works, as well as institutional histories and biographies of college leaders.

597. "Teacher Fired." *Christian Century*, 29 July-5 August 1992, pp. 708-09.

Discusses Northwestern College's firing of a Bible professor, in part because of his ordination as an Episcopal priest.

598. Thorkelson, Willmar. "Christian Colleges Settle with Ousted Professors." *Christianity Today*, 8 February 1993, p. 61.

Examines Northwestern College's settlement of suit charging school with religious discrimination in firing of Episcopal priest.

599. "Trinitarian Controversy." *Christian Century*, 9 October 1991, p. 903.

Reports on expulsion of three students from Liberty University because of their membership in the United Pentecostal Church.

600. Trollinger, William Vance, Jr. *God's Empire: William Bell Riley and Midwestern Fundamentalism*. Madison, WI: University of Wisconsin Press, 1990.

Explores Riley's theology and social thought, and examines the rise and regional influence of the Northwestern Bible School and Seminary. Concludes with a discussion of the creation of and controversy over the liberal arts college.

601. Trollinger, William Vance, Jr. "Riley's Empire: Northwestern Bible School and Fundamentalism in the Upper Midwest." *Church History* 57 (June 1988): 197-212.

Discusses the founding and growth of Northwestern Bible School and Seminary, with much attention paid to the role of Northwestern as the center of a regional fundamentalist empire. Concludes with the empire's demise.

602.   Winfrey, Marion Elizabeth. "A Historical Case Study Analysis of the Merger of Two Private Institutions of Higher Education." Ed.D. dissertation. Peabody College for Teachers of Vanderbilt University, 1989.

Analyzes the 1985 merger of Gordon College and Barrington College. Observes that while the merger succeeded, thanks in part to the efforts of the two school presidents, Barrington faculty and alumni did not find the merger process a positive experience.

CHAPTER 23
Church of the Nazarene Universities, Colleges, and Theological Seminaries

Harold E. Raser

Historical Overview

Higher education was a vital part of the foundations upon which the Church of the Nazarene was built, and has always been an important part of the denomination's story. In the United States today, the church operates two universities, six liberal arts colleges, a graduate theological seminary, and a Bible college. In addition, there are 26 undergraduate or graduate-level schools supported by the church in other parts of the world. The U.S. schools include the following institutions: Olivet Nazarene University, Kankakee, Illinois; Southern Nazarene University, Bethany, Oklahoma; Eastern Nazarene College, Quincy, Massachusetts; MidAmerica Nazarene College, Olathe, Kansas; Mount Vernon Nazarene College, Mount Vernon, Ohio;

Nazarene Bible College, Colorado Springs, Colorado; Nazarene Theological Seminary, Kansas City, Missouri; Northwest Nazarene College, Nampa, Idaho; Point Loma Nazarene College, San Diego, California; and Trevecca Nazarene College, Nashville, Tennessee. A combined total of just over 14,000 students was enrolled in these U.S. schools in the fall of 1994.

Early Nazarene history is a story of the union of several small independent churches and para-church organizations which were created to promote the cause of Christian holiness, a concept growing out of John Wesley's doctrine of Christian Perfection as shaped by the revivalism of nineteenth-century America. A popular cause in many American denominations prior to the Civil War, holiness (also referred to by terms such as "Christian perfection," "the higher Christian life," and "entire sanctification") lost ground in the late nineteenth century as American churches, and society in general, underwent wrenching material, social, and intellectual changes. In response, scores of independent interdenominational associations, bands, and societies formed to press the cause of holiness outside of the existing denominations. Such groups organized camp meetings for the promotion of holiness, published holiness papers, books, and tracts, ministered to the economically and socially marginal through downtown missions, orphanages, "rescue homes" for unwed mothers, and non-English speaking congregations, supported missionaries in various parts of the world, and sometimes founded schools. By the end of the nineteenth century several of these groups were well on their way to becoming full-fledged independent holiness churches or denominations.[1]

The present-day Church of the Nazarene was formed through the union of a half dozen or so of these holiness groups. These unions occurred periodically from the middle 1890s up to the early 1920s, the two most significant taking place in 1907 and 1908 (the latter date since designated as the official founding date of the church). Most of the groups participating in this "union movement" of holiness organizations had established colleges or schools to prepare young people for ministry and other forms of leadership in an environment supportive of the holiness movement's standards of doctrine and piety. As these groups merged to form the Church of the Nazarene, their schools together with all their interests (e.g., publishing, social welfare, missions) became a constituent part of the new denomination.[2]

These schools were a mixed lot. Some were primarily Bible schools that offered practical training for ministry and "Christian work." These schools usually limited their instruction to Bible content, public speaking/preaching, evangelistic methods, and sometimes music. Some of these schools also taught basic hygiene as well as nursing skills for those expecting to work in inner-city missions or serve abroad as missionaries. Several kinds of certificates or diplomas were awarded for completion of a prescribed course of study. The level of instruction in these Bible schools, or Bible Institutes, varied greatly.

While popular, the Bible school model was not the only one embraced by the holiness groups. Some schools intended from the outset to offer more than brief practical training for "Christian work"; they aimed to provide a broad liberal arts education in a Christian (more specifically "holiness") atmosphere. Some of these schools took the name "university" to underscore their intentions (e.g., Texas Holiness University, founded in 1899 at Peniel, Texas; Illinois Holiness University, founded in 1909 at Olivet, Illinois; and Nazarene University, founded in 1910 at Pasadena, California). While hardly true universities, these schools did offer a much broader curriculum than the Bible schools. Some also developed ambitious plans to develop full-fledged graduate schools for educating professionals in theology, medicine, and law -- plans that were never fully realized due to a variety of factors.

A few of the early holiness schools were little more than grammar schools or college preparatory "academies." The general trend, however, was for such schools either to add college-level work after a time, or eventually to become liberal arts colleges.[3]

By the time of the 1908 merger between the Pentecostal Church of the Nazarene (a group whose strength was along the

West Coast of the United States and in the Northeast) and the Holiness Church of Christ (a southern group), there were fourteen schools of various sorts being supported by members of these bodies. Since combined membership of the two groups was only slightly over 10,000, it was apparent that the denomination would not be able to officially support all of the schools. Thus, at the 1908 General Assembly that effected the union, a decision was made to designate three of the schools as "official" colleges of the Church of the Nazarene (known until 1919 as the Pentecostal Church of the Nazarene). The remaining schools were "endorsed," but not made official colleges of the church.

Three years later the Nazarene General Assembly designated six more schools as Nazarene colleges and created a General Board of Education to oversee the growing educational activity of the denomination. This new board was to monitor carefully the work of the schools, establish guidelines for certifying schools as "official" institutions of the church, and classify the schools into various groupings according to the level of instruction offered, the qualifications of their faculty, and the like. By 1915 three more schools had been designated as official institutions of the church (bringing the total to twelve) and brought under the supervision of the General Board of Education.

Twelve would be the high-water mark for the number of U.S. schools supported by the denomination. Beginning in 1915, there was a move both to improve the level of financial support for the schools and to improve the quality of the schools. The church also adopted more stringent guidelines for designating schools as "official" Nazarene institutions (chiefly that the members of their boards of trustees or regents be members of the Church of the Nazarene, and be elected in such a way as to be accountable to the denomination). The adoption of these guidelines resulted in the creation of several educational districts and the assigning of schools to these districts. Each district was to serve as the primary financial and student-recruiting base for the schools assigned to it. The church also adopted accrediting standards established by the United States Commissioner of Education as goals toward which all the schools should work.[4]

Eventually these efforts to improve the academic quality of the schools, strengthen their financial support, and bring them more closely under the direct control of the denomination brought about a reduction in the number of Nazarene institutions. Some schools were not amenable to Nazarene control. Some sank into debt and folded. Others merged as a way to survive. Also the conviction grew that the educational district plan would be most effective if each district supported only *one* college. This conviction resulted in placing additional pressure on some schools to merge.

By the early 1930s, the twelve schools of 1915 had been pared down to seven. One final merger in 1940 further reduced this number to six. These six remain the core of the current system of Nazarene colleges and universities. The six schools surviving in 1940 were: Eastern Nazarene College; Olivet Nazarene College (now Olivet Nazarene University); Pasadena College (now Point Loma Nazarene College); Trevecca College (now Trevecca Nazarene College); Northwest Nazarene College; and Bethany-Peniel College (now Southern Nazarene University).

Eastern Nazarene College

Eastern Nazarene College was founded in 1900 at Saratoga Springs, New York, as Pentecostal Collegiate Institute. Its sponsoring denomination was the Association of Pentecostal Churches of America, a group which merged with the western Church of the Nazarene in 1907 to form the Pentecostal Church of the Nazarene. It was one of the first three schools to be designated an "official" institution of the Church of the Nazarene. In 1902 the school relocated to North Scituate, Rhode Island, remaining there for fifteen years. In these earliest days the school was essentially a Bible college. By 1917, however, when the school relocated once again, this time to its present campus at Quincy, Massachusetts, it was rapidly becoming a four-year liberal arts college. Its liberal arts identity was quite firmly established by 1920.[5]

Olivet Nazarene University

Olivet Nazarene University grew from an elementary school founded by members of the Eastern Illinois Holiness Association at Georgetown, Illinois, in 1907. In 1908 the school relocated to the nearby village of Olivet and an academy was added. In 1909 the school added a college of liberal arts and became known as Illinois Holiness University. The Church of the Nazarene accepted sponsorship of the school in 1912, and in 1915 its name was changed to Olivet University. In 1923 the name was changed to Olivet College (a more accurate reflection of the nature of the school). In 1939 a fire destroyed much of the campus, prompting relocation to a new campus -- property formerly owned by St. Viator College, a defunct Roman Catholic school in Kankakee, Illinois. At the time of the move the name was changed to Olivet Nazarene College. In 1986 the school's name was changed once again, this time back to the earlier "university" designation to better reflect the breadth of academic programs and graduate studies offered by then.[6]

Point Loma Nazarene College

Pasadena College grew from Pacific Bible College, a school founded in 1902 at Los Angeles by the Church of the Nazarene, the western holiness body that contributed the Nazarene name to the present-day denomination. Pacific Bible College was one of the first three schools to be made an official institution of the church in 1908. In honor of a generous donor, the school was renamed Deets Pacific Bible College in 1909. In 1910 a new campus was purchased in Pasadena, California, and the school was named Nazarene University. Ambitious plans were drawn up for a liberal arts curriculum and extensive graduate work. In 1924 the school changed its name to Pasadena College, an indication that the early plans had only partially materialized. In 1973, frustrated in attempts to enlarge the Pasadena campus, the college purchased the former campus of California Western University on Point Loma in San Diego and moved there, at first taking the name Point Loma College, and then Point Loma Nazarene College.[7]

Trevecca Nazarene College

Trevecca College grew from the Pentecostal Literary and Bible Training School that was founded in 1901 at Nashville, Tennessee, as part of the Pentecostal Alliance, a holiness group active in Middle Tennessee. In 1910 the school was rechartered as Trevecca College for Christian Workers, and its curriculum reshaped into that of a four-year liberal arts college. In 1915 the parent body of the college became part of the Church of the Nazarene, and the college came under Nazarene control. During the period in which mergers of Nazarene schools were encouraged for financial and academic reasons, Trevecca absorbed two other holiness colleges. Even so, during the Great Depression the school fell into debt and lost its campus. Surviving precariously for several years in temporary quarters, by 1935 Trevecca had rebounded sufficiently to be able to purchase the nucleus of its present campus. Just prior to this purchase, in 1934, it was renamed Trevecca Nazarene College.[8]

Northwest Nazarene College

Northwest Nazarene College sprang from the Idaho Holiness School founded at Nampa, Idaho, in 1913. The school was the brainchild of Eugene Emerson, a holiness layman who dreamed of founding a Nazarene University in the Northwest like that in Pasadena, California. Renamed twice during 1916 -- first Northwest Holiness College, and then Northwest Nazarene College -- the school quickly developed like most similar holiness schools of the time: by about 1920 grammar school, academy, and Bible school instruction had given way to a four-year college liberal arts curriculum.[9]

Southern Nazarene University

Southern Nazarene University possessed the most tangled family tree of any of the Nazarene colleges. It was created through a series of mergers and could count at least five separate institutions as part of its lineage. The oldest school behind Southern Nazarene University was Texas Holiness University established near Greenville, Texas, in 1899. This school was one of the first three colleges officially adopted by the Church of the Nazarene. When the school spawned a small town called Peniel, the school became known as Peniel University, and then Peniel College. Other schools that eventually merged with Peniel under Nazarene auspices were: Arkansas Holiness College, founded at Vilonia, Arkansas, in 1900; Bresee College, established at Hutchinson, Kansas, in 1905; Beulah Heights College, started in 1906 at Oklahoma City and relocated in 1909 to Bethany, Oklahoma, under the name Oklahoma Holiness University; and Central Nazarene University, established at Hamlin, Texas, in 1910. The effort of the Nazarene General Board of Education in the early 1900s to strengthen the denomination's schools academically and financially set in motion a process of consolidation that eventually shaped Bethany-Peniel out of these many competing schools. In 1955 the resulting school was renamed Bethany Nazarene College, and in 1986 took the name Southern Nazarene University as it reorganized its academic departments and graduate degree programs into five distinct schools.[10]

All of these six schools that survived the winnowing process of the 1920s and 1930s had firmly established their identities as small liberal arts colleges. Some still had "academies" connected with them, and most still offered Bible college-type diplomas in Christian ministry alongside of regular undergraduate concentrations in religion or theology (and in a couple of cases Master's degrees in religion), but the primary mission of all the schools had clearly become liberal arts education.

One component of this liberal arts education was, of course, religion. One of the main motives behind the founding of all the schools had been to educate ministers for the holiness movement. For some, ministerial education had been at first their central, even exclusive purpose; for others, ministerial education had always been an important part of a larger mission. But, whatever the case, as all the schools absorbed by the Church of the Nazarene evolved into liberal arts colleges, ministerial education continued to be an important priority for them.

By the 1920s, however, some in the church were beginning to call for a central graduate theological seminary to educate ministers. Such a seminary, it was argued, could provide better theological education than the scattered colleges, and do it more economically. It was also recognized that a growing number of Nazarene ministerial students desired seminary-level education and were forced to seek it outside the denomination.

Interest in a graduate seminary grew throughout the late 1920s and the 1930s. In 1944 the Nazarene General Assembly authorized the establishment of Nazarene Theological Seminary, to be located at Kansas City, Missouri, the site of the international headquarters of the denomination. The seminary began operation in the fall of 1945. In 1971 it received full accreditation by the Association of Theological Schools in the United States and Canada.[11]

Until the late 1960s, the six colleges described above and Nazarene Theological Seminary constituted the system of higher education for the Church of the Nazarene in the United States. In the early 1960s, however, the church undertook a thorough review of its educational system. The church's concern reflected a general ferment in education in the U.S. at this time, including a marked upward trend in college and graduate school enrollment. The commission conducting the study presented a lengthy report to the 1964 General Assembly. Among other things, the report recommended that the church establish two new junior colleges. It also examined the possibility of founding a Bible college to provide ministerial training for persons unable to complete the regular college and seminary course of study -- largely adults with limited educational background, but stopped short of recommending that this be done.[12]

The report provoked lengthy and intense debate, but in the end the General Assembly voted to establish three new schools. MidAmerica Nazarene College began operation in 1967 at Olathe, Kansas, near Kansas City. Nazarene Bible College also opened in 1967 on a campus at Colorado Springs, Colorado. Mount Vernon Nazarene College opened its doors in the fall of 1968 at Mount Vernon, Ohio. MidAmerica and Mount Vernon, both originally created as junior colleges, were certified by the church as "senior colleges" in less than two years and authorized to offer four-year bachelor's degrees. Nazarene Bible College developed a variety of educational tracks, at least one of which prepared students to complete a bachelor's degree in religion with two additional years of study at MidAmerica. All three of the schools soon earned full accreditation from their respective accrediting associations.[13]

In recent years the Nazarene system of higher education in the United States appears to have achieved a solid footing. The system is neither rapidly expanding nor contracting. Severe financial problems, endemic in the early days, are more rare: most of the schools have been diligent in strengthening and broadening bases of financial support. Student recruitment in a highly competitive market has been vigorous. And overall, the quality of faculty and academic programs at the schools is higher than it has ever been.

Endnotes

1.　The most thorough overview of the American holiness movement is Melvin Easterday Dieter, *The Holiness Revival of the Nineteenth Century*. Metuchen, NJ and London: The

Scarecrow Press, 1980. A helpful analysis is also provided by Charles Edwin Jones, *Perfectionist Persuasion: The Holiness Movement and American Methodism, 1867-1936*. Metuchen, NJ: The Scarecrow Press, 1974. Brief, concise treatments of the movement are Robert S. Ingersol, "Holiness Churches and Associations" and Harold E. Raser, "Holiness Movement" in Daniel G. Reid, Robert D. Linder, Bruce L. Shelley, and Harry S. Stout, editors, *Dictionary of Christianity in America*. Downers Grove, IL: InterVarsity Press, 1990, pp. 541-47.

2.   For an overview of the denomination's development that includes attention to colleges, see Timothy L. Smith, *Called Unto Holiness, The Story of the Nazarenes: The Formative Years*. Kansas City, MO: Nazarene Publishing House, 1962, and Westlake T. Purkiser, *Called Unto Holiness, Volume 2: The Second Twenty-five Years, 1933-1958*. Kansas City, MO: Nazarene Publishing House, 1983.

3.   A helpful analysis of the variety of schools in the early holiness movement and the evolution of these schools over time is found in Oran Randall Spindle, "An Analysis of Higher Education in the Church of the Nazarene, 1945-1978." Ed.D. dissertation, Oklahoma State University, 1981, pp. 113-82.

4.   *Proceedings of the Fifth General Assembly of the Pentecostal Church of the Nazarene, 1919*. Kansas City, MO: Nazarene Publishing House, p. 84.

5.   James R. Cameron, *Eastern Nazarene College: The First Fifty Years, 1900-1950*. Kansas City, MO: Nazarene Publishing House, 1968.

6.   Carl S. McLain, *I Remember: My Fifty-seven Years at Olivet Nazarene College*. Kansas City, MO: Pedestal Press, 1983.

7.   Ronald B. Kirkemo, *For Zion's Sake: A History of Pasadena/Point Loma College*. San Diego, CA: Point Loma Press, 1992.

8.   Mildred Bangs Wynkoop, *The Trevecca Story*. Nashville, TN: Trevecca Press, 1976.

9. John E. Riley, *From Sagebrush to Ivy: The Story of Northwest Nazarene College, 1913 to 1988*. Nampa, ID: Northwest Nazarene College, 1988.

10. No single history of Southern Nazarene University has been written. The best overview is in Spindle, "An Analysis of Higher Education," pp. 117-20.

11. See Harold E. Raser, *More Preachers, And Better Preachers: The First Fifty Years of Nazarene Theological Seminary*. Kansas City, MO: Nazarene Publishing House, 1995.

12. Church of the Nazarene Education Commission, "A Study of the Educational Structure in the Church of the Nazarene: A Report From the Education Commission." Kansas City, MO, January, 1964.

13. Spindle, "An Analysis of Higher Education," pp. 189-92, and Donald S. Metz, *MidAmerica Nazarene College: The Pioneer Years, 1966-1991*. Kansas City, MO: Nazarene Publishing House, 1991.

Bibliographic Entries

603. Bond, Jim L. "A Strategy for Marketing Nazarene Higher Education in the 1990s." D.Min. thesis. Fuller Theological Seminary, 1993.

Advocates the marketing of Christian higher education through the utilization of concepts and strategies borrowed from the corporate/business world. Proposes that Nazarene schools study marketing concepts, develop intentional marketing strategies, reorder their organizational structures to facilitate effective marketing, and allocate sufficient funds to ensure success of marketing efforts. The author is president of Point Loma Nazarene College, San Diego, California.

604. Corlett, Lewis T. *Thank God and Take Courage: How the Holy Spirit Worked in My Life*. Edited and annotated by Frank G. Carver. San Diego, CA: Point Loma Press, 1992.

> Recounts in a very personal way the high points in the life of a Nazarene pioneer educator. The author/subject served as a teacher at two Nazarene colleges, as president of a third, and as the second president of Nazarene Theological Seminary.

605. Gresham, L. Paul. *Waves Against Gibraltar: A Memoir of Dr. A.M. Hills, 1848-1935*. Bethany, OK: Southern Nazarene University Press, 1992.

> Tells in popular style the life story of Dr. A.M. Hills, an early Nazarene educator/theologian. Hills served five schools connected with the Church of the Nazarene as a teacher and administrator during a formative period in Nazarene history.

606. Kirkemo, Ronald B. *For Zion's Sake: A History of Pasadena/Point Loma College*. San Diego, CA: Point Loma Press, 1992.

> Examines the history of Point Loma Nazarene College from its beginnings as Pacific Bible College in Los Angeles in 1902 to the present. Provides in-depth analysis of educational, theological, interpersonal, and larger cultural issues affecting the development of the school. The author teaches history and political science at Point Loma.

607. Metz, Donald S. *MidAmerica Nazarene College: The Pioneer Years, 1966-1991*. Kansas City, MO: Nazarene Publishing House, 1991.

Chronicles the first 25 years of one of the newest Nazarene colleges. The author, a member of the founding faculty and first Dean, presents a detailed account of the school's development and growth. Includes extensive appendices.

608. Raser, Harold E. *More Preachers, And Better Preachers: The First Fifty Years of Nazarene Theological Seminary.* Kansas City, MO: Nazarene Publishing House, 1995.

Tells the story of how the Church of the Nazarene's graduate theological seminary came into being, and how it has developed since its founding in 1945. The book, written by a professor of the history of Christianity at the seminary, was commissioned for the school's 50th anniversary.

609. Riley, John E. *From Sagebrush to Ivy: The Story of Northwest Nazarene College, 1913 to 1988.* Nampa, Idaho: Northwest Nazarene College, 1988.

Recounts the history of Northwest Nazarene College through its first 75 years of existence. Provides details of a typical transition from holiness grammar school to flourishing liberal arts college. The author served as president of the college from 1952 to 1973. Includes extensive appendices.

CHAPTER 24
Pentecostal Colleges and Seminaries: A Selective Overview

Edith L. Blumhofer

While it is true that American Pentecostals have often had misgivings about higher education, it is important to recognize that Pentecostals have generally valued certain kinds of training. The formats that early Pentecostals devised to provide ministerial training contributed to the gradual emergence of Pentecostal colleges and seminaries. Despite their regular debunking of "theological cemeteries" and their general dismay about the secular drift of American higher education, Pentecostals have always taken learning about the Bible seriously. They have been much more ambivalent about liberal arts education. Early in their history, many Pentecostals concluded that higher standards of denominational education had eroded the spirituality of the historic denominations; they responded with wariness to this challenge. Committed to "contending earnestly for the faith" by confronting people with their need of divine redemption yet determined not to replace fervent experience with intellectual rigor, early Pentecostals hoped to shelter their youth from the kinds of learning that seemed to challenge faith. They concluded that success in their evangelistic mission demanded institutions in which to equip ordinary men and women to propagate the Pentecostal message without challenging their own beliefs -- schools to indoctrinate rather than to hone critical skills. Over the years, the form and purpose of these institutions have modified significantly, reflecting changing class and economic realities as well as mainstreaming and institutionalization.

Historians quibble about precisely when the Pentecostal movement began, but most would concur that events at a non-traditional Bible school in Topeka, Kansas, on January 1, 1901, make an appropriate beginning to the story. That school, known as Bethel College (and later dubbed "The Parham School of Tongues"), was run by Charles Parham, an independent evangelist with Methodist roots. Parham modeled it after a school he had visited, The Holy Ghost and Us Bible School established by Frank W. Sandford near Lewiston, Maine. An early description of the format at The Holy Ghost and Us Bible School provides a glimpse of the way Bethel College proceeded:

> "Curriculum" there is none; it is the Bible.
> "Faculty" there is none; it is the Holy Ghost.
> "Length [of] course" there is none: students go
> when the Director sends them.[1]

Parham opened Bethel College on October 15, 1900, in a huge, rambling building on the eastern edge of Topeka, just beyond Washburn College. About 40 people responded to his invitation to study the Bible in "utter abandonment in obedience to the commandments of Jesus."[2] Parham advocated a combination of study and practice that superficially resembled that of the better-known Bible institutes of the day. Thus, at Bethel, students devoted mornings to study -- which usually involved discussing the Bible, chapter by chapter, listening to Charles Parham, and praying. Students devoted the afternoons to visitation and the usual practical forms of Christian service. Bethel College welcomed any who came, had no academic requirements, and exposed students to just one thing: Charles Parham's views on the English Bible. The school intended to equip students as evangelists and Christian workers by indoctrination, prayer, and practical experience. In this setting on January 1, 1901, Parham and his students tested the conclusion that is generally acknowledged as having formed the Pentecostal movement: an authentic baptism with the Holy Spirit would always be evidenced by speaking in tongues.[3]

The College of Bethel continued -- with a few interruptions for evangelistic forays into the surrounding countryside -- until late in the summer of 1901.[4] Over the next few years, Pentecostalism spread across the country. Its most dramatic public moment came in 1906 in Los Angeles, where meetings at a run-down mission on Azusa Street drew attention and seekers from around the world. By 1906, Parham and his workers in the Midwest had already established an enduring precedent: often when Pentecostal meetings won converts, evangelistic services would be followed by a short-term school, generally run by one of a handful of men recognized as gifted teachers. Such schools ran for four or six weeks and provided converts with intensive hours of daily training in the understanding and use of the English Bible. Pentecostalism was about religious experience, but Pentecostals argued heatedly about fine points of biblical interpretation. Thanks in part to short-term schools, they knew their bibles (King James Version) and could proof-text their beliefs.

The first generation of Pentecostal leaders included some who had been trained for ministry in traditional colleges and seminaries as well as those who had attended Bible schools like Moody Bible Institute or others run by various Holiness groups. The latter varied significantly in requirements. In some, students came and went as they felt inclined to various forms of ministry. Perhaps the best-known of the Holiness schools to become a Pentecostal institution was Holmes Bible and Missionary Institute (now Holmes College of the Bible) in Greenville, South Carolina. This school, first established in 1898 and related to the

Pentecostal Holiness Church (headquarters Oklahoma City), has the distinction of being the oldest continuing Pentecostal educational institution in the United States.[5]

The tradition of short-term schools following evangelistic campaigns was augmented by other methods of training workers. Sometimes those who were recognized as gifted teachers gathered groups of students who met daily for a year or more. From 1912 to 1914, David Wesley Myland ran such a school (he called it Gibeah) in Plainfield, Indiana. Myland had a solid record of writing, teaching, and preaching under the auspices of the Christian and Missionary Alliance before he embraced Pentecostalism. His seniority, experience, and reputation made it natural for him to teach aspiring Pentecostal ministers.[6]

Faith homes served similar educational roles, gathering aspiring workers for a year or more of communal living and study as well as supervised evangelistic and social outreaches. A cluster of faith homes in Zion City, Illinois, for example, was incorporated as the Zion Ministerial Training Homes.[7] Sometimes faith homes expanded to include Bible training schools separate from the homes, as in Rochester, New York, where several sisters operated the Elim Faith Home, and, in 1906, founded the Rochester Bible Training School which they brought into the Pentecostal movement when they embraced Pentecostal teaching in 1907.[8] Such schools were personality-driven and either changed significantly or ceased operation when the dominant leader left.

With the emergence of Pentecostal denominations (a term many Pentecostals resisted in favor of "fellowship" and "movement") came the need for systematic, ongoing ministerial training. While such training was not required, it served what was perceived as a growing need and seemed a likely way to guard against doctrinal innovation. Whereas the earliest Pentecostals had often thought formal education too time-consuming because of the imminence of Christ's second coming, the second generation perceived a need to move beyond short-term schools and to regularize institutions in which to indoctrinate students and pass on Pentecostal faith. By 1920, several Pentecostal denominations supported fledgling educational institutions. Their financial well-being was precarious, and their supporters had to counter those within the constituency who explicitly opposed regularized ministerial training, but a trend was clearly emerging. Over several decades, a handful of the ministerial training schools became Pentecostal Bible colleges.

With the formation of Pentecostal denominations, a number of early Pentecostal Bible schools (especially those associated with dominant individuals) closed or merged with denominational efforts. Some, like Beulah Heights Bible and Missionary Training School in Bergen, New Jersey, or Rochester Bible Training School in Rochester, New York, had trained an influential group of missionaries and future denominational leaders. Although they seldom had more than forty students in a given year, and although they valued spirituality and practice more than academic performance, they marked a transition from short-term schools to the permanent collegiate institutions with denominational support that would follow these independent efforts.

In the decade following World War I, small emerging Pentecostal denominations began forming educational institutions. The Church of God (Cleveland) established its first Bible institute (now Lee College) in 1918, seven years after a denominational committee had called for a school. In the same year, the Pentecostal Holiness Church established a school in Franklin Springs, Georgia (later named Emmanuel College). Holmes Theological Seminary in Greenville, South Carolina (established in 1898), though independent, also served the Pentecostal Holiness constituency. Unlike the above groups whose constituency was predominantly regional, the Assemblies of God had constituents scattered across much of the United States. It organized its churches into regional districts, several of which supported modest Bible institutes. The earliest promising school was probably Glad Tidings Bible Institute in San Francisco, a school established by Robert and Mary Craig, pastors of a large downtown church known as Glad Tidings Tabernacle. The first attempt by the Assemblies of God to create a nationally-supported educational institution came in 1920 with the opening of Midwest Bible School in Mt. Auburn, Nebraska. Lacking support, the school closed in nine months.

Late in the summer of 1922, the Assemblies of God tried again, this time in the headquarters city of Springfield, Missouri, where the denomination opened Central Bible Institute late in the summer of 1922. In 1925, the denomination's General Council mandated denominational representation on the boards of the growing number of regional, district-supported Bible institutes that also served their constituency. Meanwhile, in upstate New York, Ivan Q. Spencer reopened the Rochester Bible Training Institute, a school that had been closed by its founding leaders who objected strenuously to the centralizing and organizing trends that marked Pentecostalism in the 1920s. The reorganized school remained an independent Bible institute that resisted some of the trends toward standardized curriculum and embraced more radical charismatic teaching and behavior than most denominational Pentecostal schools tolerated.

During the 1920s, no Pentecostal enjoyed more visibility than nationally-acclaimed evangelist Aimee Semple McPherson. In 1918, McPherson had chosen Los Angeles as the hub of her expanding efforts. She dedicated Angelus Temple in January of 1923 and shortly thereafter opened a Bible institute to train pastors, evangelists, and missionaries. The institute moved to its own quarters in January of 1926 and came to be known as L.I.F.E. (Lighthouse of International Foursquare Evangelism).[9]

For the most part, students in such institutes obtained only the most rudimentary training. Some, unable to afford even the modest costs, failed to complete their two- and three-year programs. The persuasion that the schools should be open to all who expressed a call to ministry shaped admissions policies and occasioned the offering in some schools of one-year preparatory programs for those who had not completed a public school education.[10]

Pentecostal denominations were deeply divided about Bible institutes and "literary education." Denominational leaders in the Assemblies of God, for example, found it necessary to beg for cooperation and support for Bible institutes. The few Pentecostals who dreamed of denominationally supported liberal arts education found virtually no sympathy in either their constituency or their denominations. For the moment, Pentecostals were content with Bible institutes, many of which were dominated by strong faculty personalities. Libraries were small. Curricula emphasized Pentecostal doctrine and familiarity with the English Bible far more than critical thought or scholarly research. Few faculty members held advanced degrees. Some noticed that students did not necessarily intend to engage in ministry; some observers argued that because the movement lacked liberal arts schools, its Bible institutes were forced to serve all youth who wanted to receive their higher education within a Pentecostal context.

Even small Pentecostal denominations sacrificed to support their own schools. The Bible Standard Church established its institute in Eugene, Oregon, in 1925; Anglo Oneness Pentecostals (later the United Pentecostal Church) opened their first school in St. Paul, Minnesota, in 1937. This Oneness group quickly followed with nine more schools scattered across the country. Black Pentecostals threw their support behind a school opened in Goldsboro, North Carolina, in 1944.

The World War II era brought many changes. On the national scene, Pentecostals sought recognition as chaplains, and some Pentecostal schools adapted to meet government standards. In 1939, an Assemblies of God school, Southern California Bible College in Pasadena, became a four-year college with recognition by the state of California as a degree-granting institution. Other schools also became four-year colleges. The ongoing post-war need for chaplains fueled a small but growing debate over the feasibility of the creation of Pentecostal seminaries. During the

1940s, other changes occurred as well. Organizations of evangelicals devised accrediting standards for Bible schools that mandated components in the curricula of participating schools and brought standardization and streamlining to institutions that had not always valued uniformity and cooperation. Pentecostals sat on the founding board of the American Association of Bible Colleges in 1947, and Pentecostal schools were among the first to apply for accreditation. These steps necessitated better faculty salaries, higher standards of faculty preparation, library expansion, and curricular changes. Some schools resisted: LIFE Bible College, for example, was not accredited until 1980.

Cultural change and denominational institutionalization stimulated discussion of Pentecostal liberal arts education, something suggested by a few in the 1920s but only seriously considered after World War II. As more Bible institutes became Bible colleges, it seemed predictable that a few might press the possibilities of accreditation beyond the limited scope of the American Association of Bible Colleges and seek accreditation by the same regional accrediting associations that approved secular schools. Southern Bible College, since 1950 in Costa Mesa, for example, dropped its affiliation with the American Association of Bible Colleges in favor of accreditation by the Western Association of Schools and Colleges as a four-year liberal arts college.

The Assemblies of God, meanwhile, had established Evangel College in 1955 in Springfield, Missouri. The debate over a Pentecostal liberal arts college had been long and heated, but advocates prevailed, creating the first Pentecostal denominationally sponsored liberal arts college in the United States. Perhaps the best-known other Pentecostal denominationally sponsored liberal arts college is Lee College, sponsored by the Church of God (Cleveland) in Cleveland, Tennessee. Lee College has been a regionally accredited school since 1969.[11]

Meanwhile, as Pentecostal denominations increased the educational opportunities available to their youth, evangelist

Oral Roberts decided to create a Pentecostal university designed to serve both Pentecostals and adherents of the emerging charismatic renewal. He opened Oral Roberts University in 1964 on an ultra-modern campus in Tulsa, Oklahoma. Roberts' ability to raise money contributed to the rapid growth of the school, which, by the 1980s, had over 5,000 students. Roberts added professional schools, some of which by the 1980s drained the university's resources and the dwindling finances of the Oral Roberts Evangelistic Association. Although some of the professional schools floundered, the university continues to attract students from independent Pentecostal and charismatic backgrounds as well as from Pentecostal denominations.[12]

In 1978 Pat Robertson established another Pentecostal university (CBN University) near his home in Virginia Beach. CBN University offered graduate education in regionally accredited professional schools. His communications network assured wide publicity. The school quickly drew students from every state and many foreign countries, most of whom did not have classical Pentecostal roots.

The Assemblies of God began moving toward seminary education in the 1940s with the addition of a fifth year to the Central Bible Institute program, culminating in a B.Th. From 1949 until 1957, the school was known as Central Bible Institute and Seminary. Although the denomination authorized a seminary as early as 1961, not until 1973 did the Assemblies of God Graduate School (now Seminary) open in Springfield, Missouri.[13] Two years later, the Church of God (Cleveland) opened its school of Theology adjacent to its headquarters in Cleveland, Tennessee. Meanwhile, the Church of God in Christ in 1970 established a small seminary, Charles H. Mason Theological Seminary, within a six-school consortium of black seminaries in Atlanta, Georgia, known as the Interdenominational Theological Center. Oral Roberts University and CBN University operate graduate schools of theology within their universities. Several Pentecostal Bible Colleges (a few have recently dropped "Bible" from their names) offer limited M.A. programs. It is important to note as well that several thriving evangelical seminaries (e.g., Gordon-Conwell in South Hamilton, Massachusetts, and Fuller Seminary in Pasadena, California) include prominent Pentecostals in their faculties and attract a large number of students from Pentecostal denominations.[14]

Thus, higher education sponsored by Pentecostal denominations embraces a wide range of options. Bible institutes and non-accredited colleges still exist (as, for example, several operated by the Assemblies of God for Native Americans or the Apostolic Faith Bible College, Baxter Springs, Kansas); Pentecostal Bible colleges are scattered across the country, some offering accredited liberal arts programs in addition to more traditional Bible college majors; a handful of Pentecostal liberal arts colleges seeks to serve the movement's youth; a few denominational seminaries train ministers, missionaries, and chaplains. The tradition, however, does not require seminary education for its pastors. Nor does it require a college degree. Although Bible college education is encouraged, it is not necessary for all forms of ministry. Pentecostal educational institutions continue to struggle financially and cannot depend on consistent levels of support from the constituency or the denominational leadership. Side-by-side with older established schools are renewed independent efforts that reach back to older, pre-accreditation models that devalue critical thought and scholarly research: for example, Kenneth Hagin's highly successful Rhema Bible Institute in Tulsa, Oklahoma, or Gordon and Freda Lindsay's Christ for the Nations in Dallas, Texas.

Pentecostal and charismatic students have a variety of options within their tradition. These options offer varying degrees of academic emphasis and practical training.

Endnotes

1.   Quoted in Frank S. Murray, *The Sublimity of Faith: The Life and Work of Frank W. Sandford*. Amherst, NH: Kingdom Press, 1981, p. 162.

2.   Charles F. Parham, *A Voice Crying in the Wilderness*, 3d. ed. Baxter Springs, KS: privately published, n.d., p. 32.

3.   Edith L. Blumhofer, *Restoring the Faith*. Champaign, IL: University of Illinois Press, 1993, pp. 50-53.

4.   See, for example, "A Day and a Night: School of Tongues Holds Unique Observance," *Topeka Daily Capital*, 5 July 1901, p. 3.

5.   Nickels John Holmes, *Life Sketches and Sermons*. 1920.

6.   Edith L. Blumhofer, *Pentecost in My Soul: Explorations in the Meaning of Pentecostal Experience in the Early Assemblies of God*. Springfield, MO: Gospel Publishing House, 1989, p. 43.

7.   Gordon P. Gardiner, *Out of Zion*. Shippensburg, PA: Companion Press, 1990, pp. 307-22.

8.   Blumhofer, *Restoring the Faith*, pp. 78-79; Susan Duncan, *Trials and Triumphs of a Faith Life*. Rochester, NY: Elim Publishing House, 1910.

9.   Edith L. Blumhofer, *Aimee Semple McPherson: Everybody's Sister*. Grand Rapids, MI: Wm. B. Eerdmans, 1993, pp. 253-56.

10. Blumhofer, *Restoring the Faith*, p. 150.

11. Lewis F. Wilson, "Bible Institutes, Colleges and Universities," in Stanley M. Burgess and Gary B. McGee, eds. *Dictionary of Pentecostal and Charismatic Movements*. Grand Rapids, MI: Zondervan, 1988, pp. 57-65.

12. David E. Harrell, *Oral Roberts: An American Life*. Bloomington, IN: Indiana University Press, 1985, pp. 199-252.

13. Edith L. Blumhofer, *The Assemblies of God: A Chapter in the Story of American Pentecostalism*. Springfield, MO: Gospel Publishing House, 1989, pp. II, 126-28.

14. Cecil M. Robeck, "Seminaries and Graduate Schools," in Stanley M. Burgess and Gary B. McGee, eds., *Dictionary of Pentecostal and Charismatic Movements*. Grand Rapids, MI: Zondervan, 1988, pp. 773-76.

Bibliographic Entries

610. Burgess, Stanley M. and Gary B. McGee, eds. *Dictionary of Pentecostal and Charismatic Movements*. S. v. "Bible Institutes, Colleges, Universities," by Lewis F. Wilson. Grand Rapids, MI: Zondervan, 1988.

   Surveys the history of Pentecostal higher education with attention to its philosophy and historical expression. Includes a brief bibliography.

611. Burgess, Stanley M. and Gary B. McGee, eds. *Dictionary of Pentecostal and Charismatic Movements*. S. v. "Seminaries and Graduate Schools," by Cecil M. Robeck. Grand Rapids, MI: Zondervan, 1988.

   Surveys Pentecostal seminary education, noting some of the institutions that have failed as well as those that continue. Includes a brief bibliography that offers helpful orientation.

612. Corey, Barry. "Pentecostalism and the Collegiate Institution: A Study in the Decision to Found Evangel College (Missouri)." Ph.D. dissertation. Boston College, 1992.

   Uses field-based methodology, drawing on interviews and archival data to retrace the founding of Evangel College. Discerns patterns of decision making and locates them in the social movement occurring within the denomination. Making extensive use of primary sources and offering an excellent bibliography, this work probes a revealing episode in the emergence of Pentecostal higher education.

613. Numbers, Ronald L. "Creation, Evolution, and Holy Ghost Religion: Holiness and Pentecostal Responses to Darwinism." *Religion and American Culture* 2 (1992): 127-58.

Contains some revealing information on science departments at Pentecostal colleges, though its focus on educational philosophy and institutions is secondary to its main theme.

614. Owen, Michael G. "Preparing Students for the First Harvest: Five Early Ohio Bible Schools, 1905-35." *Assemblies of God Heritage* 9 (Winter 1989): 3-5, 16-19.

Traces the founding and fortunes of several small Pentecostal Bible schools, offering a glimpse into the ethos of Ohio Pentecostalism and its attitudes toward higher education. Popular in style, but nonetheless a worthwhile introduction.

EPILOGUE

James C. Carper
Thomas C. Hunt

The final years of the twentieth century will be difficult ones for American higher education. Essentially "flat" enrollments, declining resources, politicization of the curriculum, and a public that is skeptical of the cost-to-benefit ratio of postsecondary education are among the problems confronting both public and private institutions. Many students of higher education believe that, while these challenges are serious, a lack of vision is an even more critical problem. Simply put, many colleges and universities do not have a clearly articulated purpose -- thus lacking the "first tool" necessary to grappling successfully with the aforementioned crises.

The "vision problem" is particularly crucial for religious institutions. As can be seen from the previous chapters, these colleges and universities are a diverse lot. This is especially evident when one examines the history of this part of the American educational enterprise. Each institution is rooted in a unique religious soil that nurtures the purpose or direction of the institution.

Given the century-long process of secularization that has relegated religion to the periphery of American higher education, including many religious institutions, what does the future hold for these colleges and universities? Many will tenaciously maintain their faith commitments and offer a distinctive educational program, while those which long ago replanted their roots in the soil of secular academic excellence will continue to flourish. But what of those hundreds of institutions that are not characterized by either a strong religious orientation or a robust academic program or both? Has Solomon (Proverbs 29:18) predicted their future?

CONTRIBUTORS

Contributors are listed in order of their appearance in the book.

THOMAS C. HUNT received the Ph.D. from the University of Wisconsin. He is Professor of Foundations of Education at Virginia Tech. His major interest is history of American education with an emphasis on religion and schooling. He is the co-editor of *Religion and Morality in American Schooling* (1981), and co-edited, with James C. Carper, *Religious Schooling in America* (1984), *Religious Colleges and Universities in America: A Selected Bibliography* (1988), *Religious Seminaries in America: A Selected Bibliography* (1989), *Religious Schools in the United States K-12: A Source Book* (1993), (with Carper and Charles K. Kniker) *Religious Schools in America: A Selected Bibliography* (1986) and co-authored (with Mary A. Grant) *Catholic School Education in the United States: Development and Current Concerns* (1992). His articles have appeared in *Educational Forum, The Journal of Church and State, Momentum, The Catholic Historical Review, Paedogogica Historica, Journal of Presbyterian History, Religious Education, Methodist History, National Association of Episcopal Schools Journal*, and *High*

School Journal. He received the Thayer S. Warshaw Award in 1986 for his essay on "Religion and Public Schooling: A Tale of Tempest."

JAMES C. CARPER, (Ph.D. Kansas State University) is Associate Professor of Foundations of Education at the University of South Carolina, Columbia. He recently served as Director of the Education and Society Division, Office of Research (OERI), U.S. Department of Education; and is a past President of Associates for Research on Private Education. Professor Carper is co-editor with Thomas C. Hunt of *Religious Schooling in America,* and a three-volume series of selected bibliographies on *Religious Schools in America, Religious Colleges and Universities in America,* and *Religious Seminaries in America.* His articles have appeared in *Educational Forum, Mid-America, Journal of Church and State, Kansas History,* and *History of Education Quarterly.* His research interests include the history of American education and church/state conflicts in the educational arena.

RALPH D. MAWDSLEY is Professor and Chair, Department of Counseling, Administration, Supervision, and Adult Learning, Cleveland State University. Prior to accepting this position, he spent twelve years as Administrative Counsel and Vice President of Human Resources at Liberty University. His education experience includes twelve years as a teacher and administrator at a religious nonpublic school in Minneapolis, Minnesota, where he also served as Adjunct Professor at the University of Minnesota. In addition to his Ph.D. from the University of Minnesota, Dr. Mawdsley earned his J.D. from the University of Illinois. He has published widely on topics pertaining to all phases and all levels of education and currently has over 100 publications to his credit including eight books.

ROBERT L. MILLET is dean of Religious Education and professor of Ancient Scripture at Brigham Young University. He received his bachelor's and master's degrees from Brigham

Young University in psychology and his Ph.D. in Biblical Studies and 19th- and 20th-Century Religious Thought from Florida State University. He is the author or editor of many books and numerous articles on the doctrine and history of the LDS church.

WILLIAM C. KASHATUS is a member of Philadelphia Yearly Meeting of Friends and the Director of Religious Studies and Community Service at the William Penn Charter School. A graduate of Earlham College, Kashatus earned a doctorate in history of education at the University of Pennsylvania. He has published three books and over 100 articles on Quaker history.

RICHARD W. SOLBERG is a retired Lutheran pastor and educator, residing in Westlake Village, California. He is a graduate of St. Olaf College, Luther Seminary, and holds a Ph.D. in American history from the University of Chicago. He has taught at St. Olaf College, Augustana College (South Dakota), and California Lutheran University, El Colegio de Mexico, and served as Professor of History and Vice President for Academic Affairs at Thiel College in Pennsylvania. Until his retirement in 1982, Dr. Solberg was Director for Higher Education for the Lutheran Church in America. He is the author of *Lutheran Higher Education in North America* (1985); *How Church-Related Are Church-Related Colleges?* (1980); *God and Caesar in East Germany* (1961); *As Between Brothers* (1957), a history of world Lutheran relief efforts after World Wars I and II; *Miracle in Ethiopia* (1991), the story of a Lutheran-Catholic partnership for famine relief; and *Open Doors* (1992), the 50-year-anniversary history of the Lutheran Immigration and Refugee Service.

PETER P. DeBOER is Professor of Education at Calvin College in Grand Rapids, Michigan, with a Ph.D. in History of Education from the University of Chicago. He is the author of *Shifts in Curriculum Theory for Christian Education* (1983), *The Wisdom of Practice: Studies of Teaching in Christian Elementary and Middle Schools* (1989), *Origins of Teacher Education at Calvin College* (1991), co-author of *Annotated List of Chicago Tribune Editorials on Elementary and Secondary Education* (1992), co-author of *A Vision with a Task: Christian Schooling for Responsive Discipleship* (1993), and editor and co-author of *Educating Christian Teachers for Responsive Discipleship* (1993). He has published articles and book reviews in such journals as *History of Education Quarterly, American Journal of Education, Reformed Journal, Christian Scholar's Review,* as well as chapters in several books. A veteran teacher of some 42 years with experience at the elementary and high school levels, DeBoer has taught history and then professional education courses at Calvin College for 32 years.

ROBERT E. HOOPER (B.A. 1954, David Lipscomb College; M.A. 1955, Ph.D. 1965, George Peabody College of Vanderbilt University) is Professor of History and Elizabeth Gentry Brown Professor of Public Administration, David Lipscomb University. He has been a member of the faculty at Lipscomb since 1960, and served as Chair of the Department of History and Political Science from 1962 until 1992. His major publications include *Crying in the Wilderness: A Biography of David Lipscomb,* 1979; with Jim Turner, *Willard Collins: A People Person,* 1986; with David Enbgland, *A Century of Memories: A Centennial History,* 1992; *A Distinct People: A History of the Churches of Christ in the Twentieth Century,* 1993; articles in *Encyclopedia of Religion in the South,* 1984; and "Church of Christ Colleges and Universities" in Hunt and Carper, eds., *Religious Colleges and Universities in America: A Selected Bibliography,* 1988.

DANIEL R. GILBERT holds a B.A. from Middlebury College and an M.A. and Ph.D. from the University of Pennsylvania. He taught American History at Moravian College for many years and is now Professor of History Emeritus and College Archivist.

LOWELL H. ZUCK is United Church Professor Emeritus of Theology and History at Eden Theological Seminary, St. Louis, Missouri. He received his Ph.D. from Yale University. He is a member of the Historical Council of the United Church of Christ, and is director of the Eden Archives, St. Louis. His books include *Christianity and Revolution: 1520-1650* and *Socially Responsible Believers*. He is editing volume four of the Living Theological Heritage Series for Pilgrim Press (U.C.C. sources). His articles have appeared in *Church History, Bulletin of the Congregational Library, Historical Intelligencer, Zeitschrift fuer Religions-und Geistesgeschichte, Theology and Life, Church School Worker,* and *Pastoral Psychology*.

JOHN M. IMBLER, a graduate of Butler University in 1967, received his M.Div. and S.T.M. from Christian Theological Seminary in Indianapolis in 1971 and 1981 respectively. Ordained through the Christian Church (Disciples of Christ) in 1974, Dr. Imbler currently serves as Vice President for Administration and Director of Supervised Ministries and Director of Disciples Ministerial Formation at the Enid Campus of Phillips Graduate Seminary. He is also an Assistant Professor of Practical Theology at Phillips' Enid and Tulsa campuses.

DONALD S. ARMENTROUT is Professor of Church History and Historical Theology, Director of the Advanced Degrees Program, Associate Dean for Academic Affairs, and Charles Quintard Professor of Dogmatic Theology at the School of Theology, the University of the South, Sewanee, Tennessee. He received his B.A. degree from Roanoke College, Salem, Virginia, in 1961; his B.D. degree from the Lutheran Theological Seminary, Gettysburg, Pennsylvania, in 1964; and his Ph.D. degree from Vanderbilt University, Nashville, Tennessee, in 1970. He is an ordained pastor in the Evangelical Lutheran Church in America.

KENNETH M. SHAFFER, JR., is director of the Brethren Historical Library and Archives in Elgin, Illinois. He also serves as the book review editor of the journal *Brethren Life and Thought*. His most recent monograph is *Texts in Transit II*, which he co-authored with Graydon F. Snyder (1991). Mr. Shaffer received his

M.A. in Library Science from Northern Illinois University (1983), his M.Div. from Bethany Theological Seminary (1970), and his B.A. from Bridgewater College, Virginia (1967).

JOHN C. HOLMES earned a standard ministerial diploma at Mt. Vernon Bible College (Ohio), which is now L.I.F.E. Bible East in Christiansburg, Virginia. He earned an A.B. at Spring Arbor College (Michigan), M.A. in Ed. at the University of Akron (Ohio), and an Ed.D. at Pepperdine University at Los Angeles, California. He has served as a pastor, social worker, college instructor, and Christian schools superintendent. Currently Dr. Holmes and his family live in Westminster, Maryland, where he is involved in the pastoral team of a Foursquare Gospel Church which he founded. With the Association of Christian Schools International, Dr. Holmes is the Director of Government Affairs in Washington, D.C., and Coordinator of Postsecondary Member Schools. Dr. Holmes' doctoral research focused on Los Angeles County Christian school parents, and was completed in 1983. It was entitled "A Comparison Among Black, Hispanic and White Parental Expectations of the Evangelical Christian School." Dr. Holmes has published articles on church-state issues and religious private school concerns in such journals as the *Private School Monitor*. He is a regular contributor to the *ACSI Legal/Legislative Update, ASCI Today* and the *ASCI Daycare, Preschool, Kindergarten Newsletter* on federal legislation, regulation, and other issues.

GERALD P. FOGARTY, S.J., received his Ph.D. in history at Yale University and his theological education at Woodstock College and Union Theological Seminary in New York. Among his publications are *The Vatican and the American Hierarchy from 1870 to 1965* and *American Catholic Biblical Scholarship: A History from the Early Republic to Vatican II*. He taught at Woodstock College and at Fordham University before coming to the University of Virginia where he is professor of religious studies and history. He has also been a visiting professor at the Catholic University of America and will be Gasson Visiting Professor at Boston College in 1995-1996.

MARY A. GRANT was the Director of the Health Education Resource Center in the College of Pharmacy and Allied Health Professions, St. John's University, New York. She had been director of secondary library media centers in the New York and Philadelphia areas and served as library consultant to diocesan and private schools. Ms. Grant received her Master's Degree in Library Science and a P.D. in Educational Administration and Supervision from St. John's. She served as President of the National Catholic Library Association and was actively involved in CLA on both the national and local levels. Ms. Grant died suddenly on June 20, 1994.

ANNA M. DONNELLY is Associate Professor at St. John's University, New York, and coordinates the Humanities and Social Sciences library reference collections there. She holds graduate degrees in library science and American studies from Columbia University and New York University, and is a member of Project OPUS, a national research team that is developing a series of monographs on American religious history. She has chaired groups in the Reference and Adult Services Division of the American Library Association, has published papers on reference service, and regularly reviews reference sources and books on religion in America in professional journals.

JERRY M. SELF, Assistant Director of the Southern Baptist Education Commission, has pastored churches in Texas and Oklahoma and served as the ethics consultant for the Tennessee Baptist Convention. His writings include *Men and Women in John's Gospel* (Broadman Press, 1974); and *Is There Life After College* (The Sunday School Board of the Southern Baptist Convention, 1991). Self has the B.A. from Hardin-Simmons University and the Ph.D. from Southwestern Baptist Theological Seminary.

GEORGE R. KNIGHT has been Professor of Church History at Andrews University since 1985. Previously he was Professor of Educational Foundations at the same institution from 1976 to 1985. He has published and edited eighteen books. Among them are *Philosophy and Education: An Introduction in Christian Perspective* (1980, 1989); *Issues and Alternatives in Educational Philosophy* (1982, 1989); *Early Adventist Educators* (editor, 1983); *Myths in Adventism* (1985); *Angry Saints* (1989); *Anticipating the Advent: A Brief History of Seventh-day Adventists* (1993); and a history of Millerism entitled *Millennial Fever and the End of the World* (1993). He has served as editor of *Andrews University Seminary Studies*, research editor for *The Journal of Adventist Education*, and is currently serving as director of the Andrews University Press. His articles and essays in the fields of Church History and Educational Foundations have appeared in numerous periodicals.

HAROLD S. WECHSLER is an associate professor at the Margaret S. Warner Graduate School of Education and Human Development, University of Rochester. The author of *The Qualified Student: A History of Selective College Admission in America, 1870-1970*, and *Jewish Learning in American Universities: The First Century* (with Paul Ritterband), Wechsler is currently researching attempts to reduce campus prejudice between 1930 and 1960. He is a member of the Academic Council of the American Jewish Historical Society.

VIRGINIA LIESON BRERETON has written extensively in the areas of American religious education and the religious history of American women. Her books are *Training God's Army: the American Bible School, 1880-1940* and *From Sin to Salvation: Stories of Women's Conversions, 1800 to the Present.* She teaches at Tufts University.

L. GLENN TYNDALL is an ordained minister in the United Methodist Church and a member of the Virginia Annual

Conference. Since 1974, he has served as United Methodist Campus Minister, and Director of the Wesley Foundation, at Virginia Polytechnic Institute and State University in Blacksburg, Virginia. A native of Kinston, North Carolina, he received the Bachelor of Arts Degree in History from Duke University (1963) and the Master of Divinity from the Duke Divinity School (1966). In 1977 he received the Master of Arts Degree in Church History from Wake Forest University. He contributed a chapter on "United Methodist Schools" in *Religious Schools in America: A Selected Bibliography* by Thomas C. Hunt, James C. Carper, and Charles R. Kniker, in 1986. He also contributed a chapter on "United Methodist Seminaries" in *Religious Seminaries in America: A Selected Bibliography* by Thomas C. Hunt and James C. Carper in 1989.

JUDY H. MULLET is Assistant Professor of Education at Eastern Mennonite University, Harrisonburg, Virginia. She teaches educational psychology and special education courses at Eastern Mennonite University. She is President Elect for Membership for the Shenandoah Valley Virginia Chapter of Phi Delta Kappa. Mullet is currently a doctoral candidate in special education at Kent State University.

DONOVAN D. STEINER is Chair of the Education Department at Eastern Mennonite University, Harrisonburg, Virginia. He received his Ph.D. from Southern Illinois University in Education. In 1986 he was named as the first appointee to the Jesse T. Byler Endowed Chair at Eastern Mennonite University. He currently serves as an advisor on the executive board of the Virginia Association of Colleges for Teacher Education.

WILLIAM VANCE TROLLINGER, JR., is Associate Professor of History at Messiah College (Pennsylvania). Trollinger received his Ph.D. from the University of Wisconsin in 1984, and is author of *God's Empire: William Bell Riley and Midwestern Fundamentalism* (Wisconsin, 1990) and co-author of *Literacy in the United States:*

Readers and Reading Since 1880 (Yale, 1991). He is also co-director of the project, "Re-Forming the Center: Beyond the Two-Party System of American Protestantism."

HAROLD E. RASER is Professor of the History of Christianity at Nazarene Theological Seminary, Kansas City, Missouri. He is an ordained elder in the Church of the Nazarene. He is the author of *Phoebe Palmer, Her Life and Thought* (1987) and *More Preachers, And Better Preachers: The First Fifty Years of Nazarene Theological Seminary* (1995), as well as numerous articles and reviews that have appeared in reference works, scholarly journals, and denominational periodicals.

EDITH BLUMHOFER is Director of the Institute for the Study of American Evangelicals at Wheaton College. She received her B.A. and M.A. degrees in history from Hunter College of the City University of New York and her Ph.D. in American Religious History from Harvard University. Her recent books include *Restoring the Faith: The Assemblies of God, Pentecostalism and American Culture* (University of Illinois, 1993) and *Aimee Semple McPherson: Everybody's Sister* (Wm. B. Eerdmans, 1993).

AUTHOR INDEX

SUBJECT INDEX

Source Books on Education

PLAY IN PRACTICE
*A Systems Approach
to Making Good Play Happen*
edited by Karen VanderVen,
Paul Niemiec, and Roberta Schomburg

TEACHING SCIENCE TO CHILDREN
Second Edition
by Mary D. Iatridis with a contribution
by Miriam Maracek

KITS, GAMES AND MANIPULATIVES
FOR THE ELEMENTARY SCHOOL
CLASSROOM
A Source Book
by Andrea Hoffman and Ann Glannon

PARENTS AND SCHOOLS
A Source Book
by Angela Carrasquillo
and Clement B. G. London

PROJECT HEAD START
*Models and Strategies
for the Twenty-First Century*
by Valora Washington and Ura Jean
Oyemade Bailey

EARLY INTERVENTION
*Cross-Cultural Experiences
with a Mediational Approach*
edited by Pnina S. Klein

EDUCATING YOUNG ADOLESCENTS
Life in the Middle
edited by Michael J. Wavering

INSTRUMENTATION IN EDUCATION
An Anthology
by Lloyd Bishop and Paula E. Lester

TEACHING ENGLISH AS A SECOND
LANGUAGE
A Resource Guide
by Angela L. Carrasquillo

SECONDARY SCHOOLS
AND COOPERATIVE LEARNING
Theories, Models, and Strategies
edited by Jon E. Pederson
and Annette D. Digby

THE FOREIGN LANGUAGE CLASSROOM
Bridging Theory and Practice
edited by Margaret A. Haggstrom,
Leslie Z. Morgan,
and Joseph A. Wieczorek

READING AND LEARNING DISABILITIES
Research and Practice
by Joyce N. French, Nancy J. Ellsworth,
and Marie Z. Amoruso

MULTICULTURAL EDUCATION
A Source Book
by Patricia G. Ramsey, Edwina B. Vold,
and Leslie R. Williams

RELIGIOUS HIGHER EDUCATION
IN THE UNITED STATES
A Source Book
edited by Thomas C. Hunt
and James C. Carper